DISCIPLINARITY AT THE
FIN DE SIÈCLE

DISCIPLINARITY AT THE FIN DE SIÈCLE

EDITED BY

*Amanda Anderson and
Joseph Valente*

PRINCETON UNIVERSITY PRESS

PRINCETON AND OXFORD

Library of Congress Cataloging-in-Publication Data

Disciplinarity at the fin de siècle / edited by Amanda Anderson and Joseph Valente.

p.　cm.

Includes bibliographical references and index.

ISBN 0-691-08961-2 (acid-free paper) — ISBN 0-691-08962-0 (pbk. : acid-free paper)

1. Great Britain—Intellectual life—19th century.　2. English literature—19th
century—History and criticism—Theory, etc.　3. Universities and colleges—Great
Britain—Curricula.　4. Great Britain—History—Victoria, 1837–1901.　I. Anderson,
Amanda.　II. Valente, Joseph.

DA533 .D57 2002

306′.0941′09034—dc21　　　2001036268

British Library Cataloging-in-Publication Data is available

This book has been composed in Times Roman

Printed on acid-free paper. ∞

www.pup.princeton.edu

Printed in the United States of America

1　3　5　7　9　10　8　6　4　2

1　3　5　7　9　10　8　6　4　2
(Pbk.)

Contents

Acknowledgments

THE EDITORS especially wish to thank Michael Bérubé and Peter Garrett. Our greatest debt and thanks go to Carine M. Mardorossian, who provided invaluable assistance with all dimensions of this project. We also thank Mary Murrell and Fred Appel, our editors at Princeton University Press; Linda Truilo, our meticulous copy editor; and Theo Davis, who carefully read the proofs.

DISCIPLINARITY AT THE
FIN DE SIÈCLE

Discipline and Freedom

AMANDA ANDERSON AND JOSEPH VALENTE

IN THE CURRENT ERA, the basic organizational unit of intellectual life in the academy—the discipline—finds itself under reconstruction, in response to both internal and external pressures. Outside the academy, much humanities and social science scholarship is dismissed as overly specialized, arcane, and ideologically invested, and for that reason, socially and economically irrelevant. Inside the academy, the value and merit of disciplinary boundaries and methods have become a highly contested issue. A number of traditional disciplines with secure institutional homes have sought to stretch their boundaries, while a highly visible group of "post-disciplinary" programs and units—such as women's studies and cultural studies—have deliberately defined themselves against strict disciplinary affiliations, pursuing instead an eclectic combination of fields, methods, and theories.

These developments have occasioned tensions, debates, and disputes within and across the disciplines. Many critics of interdisciplinary innovation charge it with superficiality, lack of rigor, and abandonment of those carefully developed methodologies that have assured disciplinary integrity and success. Supporters of interdisciplinarity argue in return that their hybrid practices generate new forms of knowledge and answer to some of the most pointed charges against academic specialization and inaccessibility. At the institutional level, we can see the effects of this ongoing contest. Recognizing the claims of interdisciplinarity, many universities have inaugurated special humanities institutes, which typically bring together scholars from different disciplines working on similar issues or themes. Yet the overall budget structure of the university also shows deep intellectual, financial, and structural investments in traditional disciplinary boundaries, particularly in response to competition for "leading-department" status within colleges or throughout the university as a whole.

What has often been lacking in our current disciplinary debates is a longer perspective that would enable us to understand better their historical conditions and developments.[1] This collection proposes to help address this need by stepping back to consider the formation of disciplinary knowledge during the last third of the nineteenth century. The end of the Victorian era is especially important to the understanding of disciplinarity because this was the time which saw the emergence and professionalization of numerous disciplines or intellectual fields that might be broadly gathered under the rubric of the "human sciences": aesthetics, anthropology, sociology, psychoanalysis, sexology, and economics. We feel that such an undertaking is especially timely insofar as current celebrations of interdisciplinarity often harbor within them a deep—yet insufficiently examined—distrust of these traditional disciplines. Such traditional disciplines are seen at best as narrow and unimaginative, and at worst as complicit in larger forms of power and policing, as modes of *discipline* that participate in larger ideological agendas. For example, the editors of the highly influential collection *Cultural Studies* write, "It is problematic for cultural studies simply to adopt, uncritically, any of the formalized disciplinary practices of the academy, for those practices, as much as the distinctions they inscribe, carry with them a heritage of disciplinary investments and exclusions and a history of social effects that cultural studies would often be inclined to repudiate."[2]

The assumptions underlying such a statement, as well as the accompanying assumption of interdisciplinarity's inherent value or relative freedom from ideological complicity, merit close historical scrutiny. Indeed, the essays collected here stand as representative examples of a revisionist approach more attentive to the historical dimensions of disciplinarity. In part, they do so by providing more focused genealogies of specific disciplinary developments and interactions in a broad range of fields, including English, sociology, economics, psychology, and quantum physics. Such focused genealogies, both singly and jointly, thwart any precipitous claims that the story of disciplinary formation is one of consolidation, constraint, or ideological justification. Indeed, many of the essays present startling reversals of conventional wisdom. Viewed together, moreover, the arguments contained herein suggest a rather different story about the relationship between disciplinarity and the dialectic of constraint and freedom. Put most succinctly: if the tendency is now to associate interdisciplinarity with freedom, and disciplinarity with constraint, a closer look at the history of these disciplines shows that the dialectic of agency and determinism, currently distributed across the disciplinary/interdisciplinary divide, was at the heart of disciplinary formation itself.

The very term "human sciences" captures the inherent tension between a need for certain principles of causality so as to develop full-scale field models and a need to honor the voluntary and not fully predictable dimensions of human life and action. Indeed, the recurrent concern within the human sciences that scientific models of human action might obliterate or fail to register freedom and agency is testimony to the centrality of this problematic. The sixth book of John Stuart Mill's *System of Logic*, entitled *On the Logic of the Moral Sciences*, is one striking and early instance of this particular problematic, insofar as Mill acrobatically attempts to preserve a site of freedom in his proposed science of human character. In the *Logic*, Mill argued that we can understand human action as conforming to discoverable laws of causation if and only if we include the internal motives of individuals as one among the several forces conducing to make them act in the way that they choose. Mill's revision of the doctrine of Philosophical Necessity thus rests upon the sense that one can predict willed behavior: "We may be free, and yet another may have reason to be perfectly certain what use we shall make of our freedom."[3]

Mill's quixotic finessing of the problem of human laws did not issue in any full-fledged ethological science, as he had hoped, but the neologism selected by his German translator as the closest expression of "the moral sciences," *des Geisteswissenschaften*, certainly achieved prominence in the European cultural imaginary. And the dialectic of constraint and freedom certainly shaped the conceptualizing of those intellectual paradigms that did succeed and influence the understanding of human life and behavior in the modern era.

To take a central example, the political science of Marxism was both energized and divided throughout its powerful history by its simultaneous attachment to the revolutionary voluntarism of the *Communist Manifesto*, from which it drew its political force, and the historical determinism of *Capital*, upon which it based its scientific status. According to the latter, the triumph of socialism should proceed automatically from the iron laws of political economy, as advances in the means of production repeatedly fractured the existing relations of production. According to the former, the triumph of socialism required the strategic and deliberate expression of the collective consciousness of the proletariat. The theoretical debates over the so-called heresies of economism, technologism, and historicism, which dominated the first and second Internationals, and continued through the rise of the New Left, all emerged from this fundamental and finally irresolvable crux. So did related and still more urgent pragmatic debates on revolutionary methodology: to precipitate radical change was almost by definition to fall into the error of stealing a jump on the laws of history that would ensure the success of the socialist project; to abide the laws of historical development was to subject revolutionary activity and, by extension, the socialist project, to an endlessly self-perpetuating delay. Faced with this conundrum, Rosa Luxemburg fashioned a model of historical determinism with a strong logical resemblance to Mill's doctrine of Philosophical Necessity. By her account, the failures occasioned by precipitate revolutionary action form the groundwork, factor into the laws, of the dialectical triumph of socialism: that is, the necessity of history incorporates the waywardness of the collective will in working out its irresistible design.

That other monument of late-Victorian intellectual culture, psychoanalysis, was likewise theoretically grounded in a deterministic account of human agency that its own practical agenda looked, and claimed, to belie. The location of a pathogenic interplay of conflicting modes of desire (sexual vs. social, erotic vs. egotonic, eros vs. thanatos) proved crucial to the development of psychoanalysis as a hermeneutical discipline, but it threatened to compromise, not to say preclude, the possibility of the truly critical self-consciousness essential to the perfection of psychoanalysis as a therapeutic discipline. Freud's admonition that a patient's understanding of the nature and etiology of his or her symptoms does not entail nor even predict the patient's amelioration amounts to an implicit acknowledgment of this disciplinary rift upon which psychoanalysis was founded. To go beyond such symptomatic awareness (in both senses of the phrase), the patient must traverse his or her fundamental fantasy, a process that involves embracing the underlying conditions of human perceptual and behavioral tendencies, in order to reopen and to change—without controlling or even finally understanding—the patient's relationship to them. Just as Mill needed to find a measure of predictability in a nonetheless robust human freedom, so Freud needed to isolate an aleatory impulse in a nonetheless profound order of psychic necessity.

In each of these examples, the dialectic of freedom and constraint springs from and manifests conflicting epistemic and pragmatic stakes, divergent hermeneutic and therapeutic imperatives. On the one hand, the production of knowledge, including knowledge of the causes and consequences of social action, requires secure principles of determination, from which inferences and rules of evidence may be drawn. On the other hand, the initiation and performance of effective social actions, be it reformist or revolutionary, individual or corporate, requires a minimal degree of unconditioned agency, without which the changes wrought could not be directed to a designated end. This conflict is not only internal to but also, we suggest, constitutive of the formation of those orchestrated modes of discourse that we call intellectual or academic disciplines. Indeed, in this context, the term discipline captures the sense of a dual mandate, carrying the sense of a practical regimen into an economy of conceptual enterprise. If this is an accident of etymology, it is a happy one. For the abrasive slippage of the epistemic and the pragmatic affords a site for intertwining discourses to communicate with and distinguish themselves from one another simultaneously, bringing forth disciplinary boundaries from overlapping areas of interest and inquiry. It becomes evident, then, that disciplinarity was always interdisciplinary.

A CLEAR example of how the tension between scientific and humanistic models shapes and drives disciplinary development within the human sciences is provided by John Guillory's "Literary Study and the Modern System of the Disciplines," an essay that reconstructs the ways in which English emerged out of a contest between the study of language (philology) and the study of literature (belles lettres). In this case, philology's demise might be attributed to its overdeveloped scientism, which could not accommodate the forms of experience that characterize the human. Belles lettres, by contrast, was underdeveloped as a discipline insofar as there was too little determinism in its design—it did not begin to produce the kinds of laws and models that would enable regularized findings and reproducible methodologies. Two further conclusions might be drawn from Guillory's historical analysis. First, his uncovering of the contested nature of an emergent discipline confirms that disciplines are always constituted in relation to, and in a kind of dialogue with, other disciplines. And second, the current antidisciplinary impulse within cultural studies and other sectors of the academy might be seen, within the framework of this longer history, as simply replaying this earlier antiscientific impulse. For practitioners of cultural studies, the developed literary disciplines fail to acknowledge and account for forms of popular and everyday culture which exceed the formal categories and methodologies that are already in place. But consequently to call cultural studies an antidiscipline or even a multidiscipline is misleading insofar as disciplinarity was always defined against fields and methodologies that could not encompass its subject. Indeed, the specific precursor to cultural studies, literary studies, could be said to be antidisciplinary in its inception in precisely the way that cultural studies imagines itself to be right now.

The crucial point here is that claims to antidisciplinarity are always greatly exaggerated, insofar as intellectual developments require recognizable disciplinary methodologies to be minimally intelligible, and they typically involve both alliances and contests with preexisting fields. Arkady Plotnitsky's essay, "Disciplinarity and Radicality: Quantum Theory and Nonclassical Thought at the Fin de Siècle, and as Philosophy of the Future," provides a particularly dramatic example of the former point. Quantum physics, generally understood as a radical departure from previous forms of understanding, is by Plotnitsky's revisionist account actually deeply conservative in its preservation of fundamental principles of disciplinary practice: logical consistency, mathematics, explanation of data, unambiguous communication. Plotnitsky, in fact, argues that quantum physics is not only compatible with disciplinary principles but may also become necessary in order to maintain those principles. In this view, a certain disciplinary coherence characterizes both classical and quantum physics; disciplinarity is not the object against which radicality pits itself but remains a fairly constant structure accommodating the radical. This powerfully demystifying approach to the relation between radicality and disciplinarity might be extended, Plotnitsky provocatively suggests, to radical thought on a number of fronts, including philosophy and literary theory. In Plotnitsky's view, it would be possible to trace a historical codevelopment whereby radical thought in both the sciences and the humanities displayed a fundamental allegiance to conservation of method, even as it forwarded the most radical claims of modern and postmodern thought.

Adopting a comparative approach, Liah Greenfeld's "How Economics Became a Science: The Surprising Career of a Model Discipline" richly contextualizes the recurring tension between agency and determinism within the history of economics. Greenfeld situates her discussion of this politically influential science by tracing its French parentage in the seventeenth century, its complex German development in the eighteenth and nineteenth centuries, and its triumph as a coldly impersonal science in twentieth-century America. By placing the tradition of laissez-faire, and in particular the influential work of Adam Smith, within a more broadly European framework, Greenfeld brings to light a crucial modern tension between belief in universal laws and an insistence on the variability of national circumstances. Indeed, within Germany a dual emphasis on both of these dimensions of economic thought initially produced a bifurcation between *Staatswirtschaft*—the examination of historical, cultural, and institutional variability—and *Nationaloekonomie*—the formulation of universal laws that subtend all local variability. A delicate balancing act between these two approaches would eventually give way in Germany to a rejection of the universalistic approach in favor of the assertion of a human managerial will tuned to culturally defined needs and capacities. Interestingly, modern economic liberalism in England preserved a stress on individual liberty while simultaneously appealing to the larger determinism of the Invisible Hand, while German thinkers emphasized the historical uniqueness of individual culture, the fundamentally social nature of human beings, and the power of the state to guide and manage economic development. In each case, a rapprochement between agency and determinism is fundamental to the discipline's self-conception, although the two may be distributed differently.

For Greenfeld, it is a social motive above all—the desire for prestige on the part of its intellectual practitioners—that drove the triumph of scientistic, impersonal, and ahistorical forms of economics in early twentieth-century America. While Greenfeld acknowledges the progressive impulse toward ambitious social reform as a significant dimension of the history of American economics during the Gilded Age, it is ultimately the conservative classicists that prevailed, with their narrow focus on the establishment of economics as a legitimate and powerful science based on physics. As a consequence, contemporary economics is judged by Greenfeld to have cut itself off from material and human reality, even as its influence as a social science is unrivaled in the realm of policy-making. Greenfeld provocatively attributes the fate of economics to a more fundamental division between the social and natural sciences: in her view, the institutional history of the natural sciences is subordinate to their intellectual development as bodies of knowledge, while the forms of knowledge represented in the social sciences are fundamentally determined by the social roles and interests of their practitioners.

Henrika Kuklick's "Professional Status and the Moral Order" examines a range of professions and disciplines associated with the emergent social sciences during turn-of-the-century America. Like Greenfeld, Kuklick situates social science within its historical, political, and institutional frameworks, but she tells a very different kind of story. Bringing to light the self-understanding of early social scientists and other self-regulating professionals, Kuklick describes them as "self-conscious agents of history" pursuing a well-developed scheme of social reform that dovetailed with contemporary theories of social evolution. According to Kuklick, an evolutionary model was adapted by social scientists to promote a view of unconstrained human agency in the service of progressive political and moral ideals. In recovering this history, Kuklick aims to dislodge a prevalent assumption that early social science was unduly influenced by social determinism through the sway of the anthropological school of Franz Boas. She then contrasts the forces at work among early social reformers with the profound reconfiguration of the professions in our own era, particularly the erosion of power within the medical profession (though she sees similar attacks on professional authority in the university and within the field of social work). Diminishment of professional power and efficacy is attributed both to the decline of vocational ideals of disinterestedness and altruism, and to the loss of important protections for professionals against the demands of the market. In a way, Kuklick's explanation supports the more limited claims that Greenfeld makes about the dominance of classical economics, insofar as Kuklick attributes the loss of protections to a climate favoring free-market theories. By contrast, the earlier era, in Kuklick's view, was shaped by the intellectual and cultural framework of a progressive evolutionary theory that sought the self-conscious elaboration of communal, rational, and ethical ideals.

Despite an important divergence of approach with respect to the assumed motives of early social scientists, Kuklick's and Greenfeld's narratives share another similarity as well: both essays reconstruct key ways in which social science performed what we might call a contestatory emulation of scientific disciplines. This is reminiscent of the role that the conflict between science and letters played in Guillory's account of the rise of English as a discipline. In Greenfeld's account of economics, the key model science was physics, and any differences between human experience and natural laws were assiduously discounted. In Kuklick's broader account of the rise of professions, evolution provided the model, and was altered so as to accommodate the effectivity of human guidance, the power of human agency. In one case, the emulated discipline provides a limit to the explanatory power and human resonance of the model; in the other case, the emulated discipline allows for an expansive model of growth, development, and cooperation. In one case, the emergent discipline is constrained by its scientism; in the other, enabled. Viewed in tandem, these contrasting accounts reveal that disciplinarity, along with its constitutive forms of agency and determination, varies across the interactive but incommensurable political, cultural, and institutional histories in which they are embedded.

Ivan Strenski's contribution, "Durkheim, Disciplinarity, and the '*Sciences Religieuses*,'" provides a textured account of discipline formation in fin de siècle France. Again, the comparative approach is instructive, given the distinctiveness of government subsidy in French higher education, and given the particular stresses that cultures of belief place on the emergence of the science and sociology of religion. In tracing the powerful challenge that Durkheim and his followers waged against the Liberal Protestant bases of the Fifth Section of the École Pratique des Hautes Études—the institutional home of the "*sciences religieuses*"—Strenski reveals the effectiveness of those vibrant intellectual cultures that worked outside of and against official state patronage to promote new disciplinary paradigms. Strenski also shows the precise intellectual and political factors at play in this disciplinary agon. On the one hand, the Fifth Section served as a kind of haven for free thinkers and their ideological allies, those Liberal Protestants who promoted the idea of religious universalism and thereby aided in the fight against clericalism and Catholicism more generally. On the other hand, the crypto-theological commitments of the Fifth Section could not accommodate the firmly naturalist and societist approach of the Durkheimians, who fought hard to shift the terms of the debate. Both approaches were affected by political aims: the Liberal Protestants were funded by a state eager to understand and thereby control a deeply religious populace; the Durkheimians thought that the liberal view of religion ultimately was not adequate to the moral needs of a diverse Third Republic. The multilayered story told by Strenski exemplifies the competitive dimensions of disciplinary evolution, while bringing to the fore the particular political, cultural, and intellectual tensions that result when "science" aims to encompass religion.

AT this historical moment, of course, disciplinary studies, like its more famous relative, cultural studies, is dominated by the figure of Michel Foucault. His field-defining contributions have been to chart not only the rise of disciplines and the human sciences but also to elaborate the ways in which a distinctly modern form of subjectivity, marked by interiority and self-surveillance, arose out of new configurations of knowledge and power. In key respects, the present volume looks to a post-Foucauldian dispensation, keeping its distance from approaches that too easily assimilate bodies of knowledge to techniques of management—whether of the social body, the intellectual field, or the individual person. Nevertheless, the effort to show how disciplinary developments have affected both theories and practices of modern selfhood remains central to the project of rethinking the human sciences. This effort can also be adapted to the end of dislodging some of the comfortable pessimism of Foucauldian scholars, who do not sufficiently register the very struggle with questions of agency that has characterized the project of the human sciences since its inception. We spoke in broad terms at the outset about the dialectic of agency and determinism informing disciplinary development in the nineteenth and twentieth centuries, showing how that dialectic emerged at the conceptual and theoretical level in many disciplinary formations. Several of the essays in the volume vivify this issue by specifically exploring the relation between disciplinary developments and conceptions of selfhood.

In "Subjecting English and the Question of Representation," for example, Gauri Viswanathan suggestively reframes the "rise of English" in terms of the forms of subjectivity it assumed, promoted, and enabled. Viswanathan locates in early English-language pedagogy a Christian model of selfhood marked by inadequacy and in need of tutelage. Yet the function of English begins to shift in the nineteenth century in order to accommodate its heterogeneous readership, recasting the Christian model so as to promote a new civic and national identity, one whose capacity for improvement could be slated into a model of progress. For Viswanathan, what prompted this development was not so much a simple reaction on the part of a controlling institution, but rather the direct challenges and competing claims of a religiously plural society during the nineteenth century. The current scholarly emphasis on ethnicity has obscured this important disciplinary history and the fractured society that catalyzed it. Viswanathan also importantly claims that the new civic model of selfhood helped set the stage for more elaborate and far-reaching democratic claim-staking: as the forms of selfhood developed to accommodate plurality, they themselves enabled a further contest for expanded rights. Thus, a revisionist account of the rise of English enables us to trace the path whereby social groups emerged from their status as objects of moral pedagogy to become "subjects of their own history." Viswanathan's essay, besides insisting that we recognize the profound role played by religion in the contests for cultural and political legitimacy, also shows ways in which constructions of the self have both mediated and transformed disciplinary life.

In "Dying Twice: Victorian Theories of Déjà Vu," Athena Vrettos focuses on debates within the field of nineteenth-century psychology to explore an interdisciplinary fin-de-siècle topos distinctly concerned with the nature of selfhood and consciousness. In part attributing the appeal of déjà vu to the heightened awareness of temporality brought on by millennial thinking, Vrettos uncovers two basic attitudes toward this popular topic: on the one hand, a desire to protect the category of "normal" consciousness by pathologizing déjà vu experiences and, on the other, a belief that déjà vu was one experience among others that evidenced the permeable boundaries of consciousness. Analyzing the writings of four British psychologists, Vrettos uncovers responses that range from defended investments in rational control to the virtual embrace of layered consciousness. By reconstructing the competing explanatory models that emerged in order to account for déjà vu, Vrettos not only insists on a contested cultural field with differing attitudes toward the nature of human agency, but also brings to light both the interactions and contests among a range of intellectual and cultural fields, including literature, psychology, neurology, psychical research, and spiritual belief. The particular interdisciplinary formations that took shape here had in part to do with the nature of the topic: literary example was especially prominent not only because articulate examples of déjà vu could be found in fictional texts, but because the very act of rereading and quotation was formally continuous with the object under study. But the intellectual biography of déjà vu is also the result of specific contests for intellectual prominence within the larger European theater. Partly because of France's dominant role in producing ambitious theories of memory, British psychology attempted to carve out a niche for itself by focusing on topics associated with more mundane, everyday, psychological experiences.

Jeff Nunokawa's "Oscar Wilde, Erving Goffman, and the Social Body Beautiful" compares the models of agency and self-presentation that structure the British aestheticism of Oscar Wilde and the American sociology of Erving Goffman. His analysis draws out the ways in which Wilde's aestheticism aims to triumph over social regulation through an aggrandized form of theatrical agency, which he contrasts with Goffman's more modest notion of the agent's active involvement in social scripts. Because of its suggestive comparison of Wilde and Goffman, Nunokawa's essay allows us to understand aestheticism in protodisciplinary terms, as an intellectual and aesthetic project that sought to be at once theory and practice, that sought to understand everyday life in the way that sociology later would. Moreover, the forms of response to questions of social determination that Nunokawa locates in Wilde resonate profoundly with the contemporary project of queer theory, which shares with Wilde both a keen awareness of social laws and a compensatory, aestheticized voluntarism.

Not surprisingly, the dialectic of freedom and determinism that we have been tracing grows especially involved and self-conscious in those bodies of practical knowledge that interrogate the existing and optimal relations between the individual or corporate subject of civil society and the overarching power of the state. Lauren Goodlad's historical analysis of the career of "pastorship" in Britain from the New Poor Law of 1834 to the rise of the new mass politics after World War I, "Character and Pastorship in Two British 'Sociological' Traditions: Organized Charity, Fabian Socialism, and the Invention of New Liberalism," provides a textbook illustration of this tendency. In her meticulously detailed account, a British cast of sociology came to be born of the interanimating contest between a moral, voluntarist conception of human character, identified closely with the Charitable Organization Society (COS), and a rational, environmentalist conception of human character, identified with the Fabian Socialists. Each school not only gave a particular definition to its critical object—the people and behaviors to be studied —but also generated a corresponding method or strategy of treating this object, what Goodlad calls pastorship. If, as the COS contended, social phenomena ultimately result from the concerted volitional force of the individuals involved, then the best and only means of remedying problematic or dysfunctional phenomena is to minister to the character of those producing and suffering them. But if, as the Fabians contended, particular social ills are the rationally calculable effects of misshapen, far-reaching historical arrangements and economic conditions, then they could never be properly repaired except through similarly technical and wide-ranging adjustments in the conditions and arrangements themselves, adjustments of a scale and complexity requiring organized state action.

These battle lines, however, do not remain starkly drawn. The stubborn slippage of the epistemic and pragmatic registers of late-Victorian human science reasserts itself, bringing the two camps into full dialectical contradiction instead of static dichotomy. As a matter of logic, to postulate a fundamental moral freedom at the root of social causation is to incur a loss of predictability fatal to the project of social analysis. A play of truly autonomous world-making wills remains by definition impervious, in the final instance, to those contingencies or determinants from which the criteria for preferring one explanation or strategic projection over another must be elaborated. As a result, the COS needed to bolster its credentials of expertise by incorporating and then boasting of the scientific training of its field-workers and the rationality of its protocols, in a tacit concession to the superior epistemic purchase of the Fabian agenda. On the other side, the comprehensive determinism of the Fabians, like that of scientific Marxism, provided a strong theoretical basis for understanding the world but no basis at all for changing it in accordance with their will. The need to square their deterministic principles with their activist aims left the Fabians preaching the comparative virtue of aligning one's efforts with rather than against the momentum of historical progress. Taken in its worst light, this position is simply nugatory, since a fully deterministic universe admits neither obstruction nor facilitation in any case. Taken at its best, this position, as Goodlad sees it, opens up a space, however slender or rudimentary, for independent volitionality, in a tacit concession to the superior pragmatic potential of the COS agenda.

In Goodlad's account, the interpenetration of these antipodal viewpoints helped to bring forth a synthetic "third way," the New Liberalism of Winston

Churchill and David Lloyd George. In articulating the interdependence of self and state help, private and public responsibility, circumstantial determination and moral freedom, this new movement helped to sponsor the development of a mature sociological discipline. That is also to say, looking from the other end of the telescope, Goodlad isolates the contentious origin of British sociology, specifying how that discourse came to define itself over against its own warring constituents.

In the succeeding essay, "Victorian Continuities: Early British Sociology and the Welfare of the State," Simon Joyce illustrates that the effects of such contentious origins do not necessarily evaporate with the consolidation of a discipline in its own right, but rather have a tendency to linger or reappear in its subsequent deployments. Taking up the recent vogue among antistatist Anglo/American conservatives, he explores Victorian deliberations on fostering individual self-reliance. Joyce mounts a convincing, textually specific argument that Victorian social thought has been subject to highly selective and tendentious appropriation. Yet such appropriations are made possible in part by the profoundly ambivalent, even self-dissenting quality of Victorian thought itself. The central focus of Joyce's counter-revisionist study is the relationship between Gertrude Himmelfarb's immensely influential argument, *The De-Moralization of Society*, and one of her chief Victorian sources, the work of Charles Booth, most particularly *Life and Labour of the People in London* (1889). Himmelfarb wields the latter as a weapon to flay the contemporary welfare state and vindicate private industry and charity, but not without doing considerable violence, as Joyce sees it, to Booth's own social agenda. This violence, however, is one of reduction rather than traduction. Booth's writing condensed multiple and dissonant practices and beliefs that could readily coexist in the nascent discourse of sociology precisely because, as Joyce notes, it as yet "lacked a stable disciplinary base," being a "broad church of positivists, philanthropists, statisticians, social evolutionists, and anthropologists," rather than the monolithic institution suggested by Himmelfarb's genealogy. The dominant vision shared by these various thinkers, Joyce demonstrates, was a recognition of the very sort of state action that Himmelfarb conscripts Booth to condemn. But Joyce's argument goes still further in suggesting that a "stable disciplinary base," understood as a matrix for the kind of programmatic consistency that characterizes Himmelfarb's misreading of Booth's work, can exist only as a retrospective illusion which feeds upon the very interdiscursive flux that it denies or forgets.

The political right does not have a monopoly on this type of amnesia, as the final two essays in the volume denote. Both Christopher Lane and James Buzard take the largely left-identified, avowedly postdisciplinary formation of cultural studies to task for organizing itself around significant distortions or elisions of disciplinary history. Whereas Himmelfarb mistakes discursive equivocality for disciplinary uniformity so that she might embrace the latter as the sign and instrument of healthy social order, the experiments of cultural studies have, according to Lane and Buzard, mistaken their own relationship to such discursive equivocality in order to reject disciplinary coherence as both intellectually and politically coercive.

Christopher Lane's "The Arnoldian Ideal, or Culture Studies and the Problem of Nothingness" reassembles the extensive corpus of Matthew Arnold to illuminate the misrecognition involved in his ill repute as a "staunch traditionalist," an arbiter of canonicity, and the father of a mode of literary criticism that handed down cultural ideals for the purpose of enforcing social order and stability. Indispensable to this image of Arnold as, well, Himmelfarb, has been the omission or dismissal of a countervailing and still more pivotal strain in his work—what Lane calls "the problem of nothingness," the extradiscursive dimension that founds, stymies, and exceeds the possibility of cultural expression. To divine in Arnold's more prescriptive moments, as Lane does, a self-consciously inadequate response to this extradiscursive dimension, is to restore a proper ambivalence to his text, which is committed to both the necessity and the futility of cultural discipline. By this view, Arnold can be read as herald of the literary genealogy—from Pater to Wilde to cultural studies—that has so raged against him.

Cultural studies itself cannot discern this family resemblance, Lane insists, because of its own fundamental positivism, an embrace of multiciplicity—of identities, cultures, values, determinations—that neither engages, nor develops the tools to engage, the radical finitude which, as Derrida famously argues, underlies any such proliferation of differences. Staked as it is upon a latitudinarian politics of recognition and tolerance, cultural studies has great difficulty tolerating that which "resists discursive processing" or recognizing the embattled virtue of grappling, as Arnold does, with the "obstacles" to primary sense. In excluding whatever refuses to be confined to that most basic discursive discipline, the discipline of meaning, cultural studies bumps against its own limits or boundaries, which is to say, the limits on its disposition to transgress entrenched boundaries. Put another way, the economy of legible discourse—what Lacan terms the symbolic—forms a kind of disciplinary horizon that shelters cultural studies, in all of its interdisciplinary mobility, against the prospect of the irrecuperable, or what Lacan terms the Real.

In "Notes on the Defenestration of Culture," James Buzard adduces different and arguably more constraining limits on the vaunted transgressive power of cultural studies, of which the "chief principle," he writes, "seem[s] to be the avoidance of disciplinary self-definition." Reading the evolution of this "discipline that is not one" against the autocritique of the social anthropology that cultural studies claimed to supersede, Buzard finds the reputation for perpetual mobility and openness currently enjoyed by this new field to have originated in its bold but oversold reclamation of the concept of culture. The reclamation was bold inasmuch as the analytic paradigm of culture bequeathed by anthropology seemed discredited, beyond repair, "as an instrument of power/knowledge wielded at the behest of imperial governments"—the very sort of intellectually appropriative device that the rise of postcolonial theory might have been expected to rule out of court. The reclamation was to some degree bogus, however, insofar as it was primarily staked on extending the reach of "culture," understood by cultural studies as an honorific attribute, beyond the sphere of elite or respectable social achievements and to the habitus of the marginalized, the impoverished, the ignored, and the disdained. There is nothing, Buzard contends, particularly innovative in this latitudinarian gesture; the effort to promote recognition of subaltern cultural forms dates at least as far back as the Victorian era. Then it served, of all things, to delimit the nascent discipline of anthropology itself from the less systematized defenses of "civilization" associated with reputed traditionalists like Matthew Arnold. Given this history, Buzard infers that the elastic measure of culture adopted by cultural studies is less a solution to the difficulties recently confronting anthropology than a new spin upon them.

In the terms we have set forth, cultural studies has realigned the abrasive slippage of the epistemic and pragmatic imperatives without finally repairing it. In making sure that the predesignated groups to be studied could all lay claim, in Buzard's words, to a "culture of their own," social anthropologists incurred the objection that they had represented their "subject" peoples in a relatively uniform or monolithic manner suspiciously reminiscent of old-fashioned stereotyping. Through this left-handed patronage, the criticism runs, anthropology managed to reserve an individualizing unrestrictiveness to the cultures of the West, which did not suffer the assumption of coherence let alone homogeneity. Put another way, the pragmatic interests and motivations of Western anthropology were held to have corrupted its epistemic dimension: the evidence it produced and the conclusions it drew. Cultural studies, of course, would seem to have inoculated itself against these charges by making agency detection among the apparently disempowered the overriding priority of its enterprise. But even leaving aside the danger of overcompensation—and Buzard records some highly comical attempts to parse casual pleasures for political efficacy—such agency cannot be warranted except as a response to social conditions that tend to define the group in question on a culturally homogenizing if overdetermined basis: "race plus class plus gender plus sexual orientation etc." This methodology, what Diana Fuss and others have defended as a strictly "strategic" essentialism, does not avoid the pitfalls of stereotyping, but rather aims to generate enabling stereotypes, which is to say generalizing images conducive to certain kinds of political mobilization or consolation. No less than social anthropology, in other words, has cultural studies mortgaged its epistemic protocols to a pragmatic agenda, and the greater self-consciousness with which that liability has been engaged does not at all diminish its underlying disciplinary function (in both senses of the term). A field or "movement" committed to boundless inter- or transdisciplinarity finds its own more or less stable definition in the putatively emancipatory definitions that it imposes on the cultures it studies.

As Buzard and other contributors show, a disciplinary history of the present reveals that interdisciplinarity can only lay claim to the kinds of theoretical and practical "breaks" that it assigns itself by distorting or suppressing its relation to the past, which also means distorting or suppressing its own disciplinarity. What results is an inattention to the dialectic of agency and freedom that defines the science of the human. The essays in this volume help to reframe these issues. Combining critique and reconstruction, case study and theoretical meditation, these essays enact a more sustained inquiry into the nature and effects of disciplinary histories, one which can more fully comprehend the complex legacy of the human sciences.

NOTES

1. There are some notable exceptions. See, for example, Thomas Bender and Carl E. Schorske, eds., *American Academic Culture in Transformation* (Princeton: Princeton University Press, 1997); Charles Bernheimer, ed., *Comparative Literature in the Age of Multiculturalism* (Baltimore: Johns Hopkins University Press, 1995); Ellen Messer-Davidow, David R. Shumway, and David J. Sylvan, eds., *Knowledges: Historical and Critical Studies in Disciplinarity* (Charlottesville: University Press of Virginia, 1993).

2. Lawrence Grossberg, Cary Nelson, and Paula Treichler, eds., *Cultural Studies* (New York: Routledge, 1992), 2.

3. John Stuart Mill, *A System of Logic Ratiocinative and Inductive*, ed. J. M. Robson, vols. 7 and 8 of *Collected Works of John Stuart Mill* (Toronto: University of Toronto Press and Routledge and Kegan Paul, 1963–91), 8:836–37.

Part I

DISCIPLINARY FORMATIONS

CHAPTER 1

Literary Study and the Modern System of the Disciplines

JOHN GUILLORY

THE HISTORY of literary study in the Anglo-American university is marked by a striking discontinuity of which the consequences have been very great, if also poorly understood. When departments of English and modern foreign languages were created in the 1870s, the primary subject of study within these departments (as their names indicated) was not literature but *language*. By the 1940s, however, literature and its correlative discourse of "literary criticism" had thoroughly displaced language from its former position of disciplinary preeminence. It will not be my concern to chronicle that displacement, a story that has been ably recounted by Gerald Graff and others.[1] In this chapter, I look closely at two antecedent forms in which literature and language were studied in the late-nineteenth-century university: belles lettres and philology. I argue that the supersession of these earlier disciplinary forms was never complete; and I suggest at the close of this chapter that the residual effects of this failed transition trouble all subsequent versions of literary study.

BELLES LETTRES

Before examining the disciplinary forms of belles lettres and philology, it will be necessary to grasp synoptically the system of the disciplines in the centuries preceding the familiar modern troika of natural sciences, social sciences, and humanities. The early modern disciplinary system was dominated by the study of the classical languages and theology. This curriculum was very entrenched, and universities long resisted the introduction of more modern discourses of knowledge. During the seventeenth and eighteenth centuries, new discourses of knowledge were developed for the most part outside the university under the names of "moral philosophy" and "natural philosophy." With the exception of medicine, natural philosophy was pursued well into the nineteenth century outside the university, as the avocation of gentlemen who possessed private means for research, such as Robert

Boyle, or in the context of state-sponsored associations, such as the Royal Society. Moral philosophy was also often an amateur enterprise; but unlike natural philosophy, it found a niche in the eighteenth-century university system, where it branched into a number of discourses on ethics and society while maintaining a discreet distance from dogmatic theology. It was linked rather to the higher faculty of law or "jurisprudence," for which it provided a kind of propaedeutic, or theoretical foundation. Moral philosophy was a decidedly modern discourse in that its arguments were based, like those of the new science, on "experience." The problematization of this empirical foundation later specified the domain of philosophy in its later sense, as a discourse that reflects upon knowledge but is not necessarily scientific. As we shall see, the break-up of philosophy in the older sense enabled the modern humanities to emerge as nonempirical disciplines.

However modern in outlook, moral philosophy continued to be influenced by Greek and Latin texts on political and moral subjects. Yet the importation of classical thought into moral philosophy had little effect on the actual teaching of Greek and Latin texts in the university. Moral philosophy, as exemplified by the work of Locke or Shaftesbury, circulated in the print media of the eighteenth-century public sphere rather than in the university lecture halls. It was not until several decades into the eighteenth century that moral philosophy was assimilated into the university in lecture courses by new "professors of moral philosophy" such as Adam Smith. Still later, moral philosophy was institutionalized in American university curricula as a senior-level culminative course often taught by the university president (though the content of this course was usually a varied and quite indeterminate mix of modern subjects).[2] By contrast, study of the classics at the lower levels remained very conservative, rehearsing the rhetorical *paideia* of the ancients in an increasingly rigid fashion. The disconnection between moral philosophy and the classical curriculum explains why the first disciplinary form of vernacular literary study in the university emerged from moral philosophy and not from the classics. In fact, this disciplinary form—belles lettres—was proposed by its advocates as a supplement, and even eventually as an alternative, to the curriculum of classical languages and rhetoric. Belles lettres introduced vernacular literature into the university for the first time, as a distinctly modern subject.

In England, a decisive moment of innovation in the university curriculum might be located in 1748 with Adam Smith's course of public lectures on rhetoric at the University of Edinburgh, given at the instigation of Lord Kames. These lectures, followed in subsequent years by private seminars at Glasgow, were enormously influential, even though they remained unpublished until the present century. The substance of their argument was appropriated by Hugh Blair in his extremely popular *Lectures on Rhetoric and Belles Lettres* published in 1783, and running to dozens of editions over many decades. Blair was the first professor of "Belles Lettres," a name he appended to his official title as "Professor of Rhetoric" because it sounded more modern.[3] Smith and Blair may be said to have institutionalized belles lettres as a protodisciplinary form in the university; they have also been credited with the invention of "College English."[4] Today, bellelettrism signifies an egregiously "pretheoretical" discourse, devoted to mere effusions of appreciation and to groundless declarations of taste or judgment. Yet belles lettres emerged out of the discourse of moral philosophy, and it possessed all the theoretical sophistication of that discourse, by virtue of its very modern orientation to an empiricist epistemology.

Let us examine, then, the program of belles lettres as a candidate for disciplinary status. It consisted of two agendas. It was first of all a discourse of judgment or taste, designed to cultivate a faculty of discrimination, the ability to distinguish good writing ("fine letters") from bad. It thus held up examples of writing for inspection, pointing out "beauties" and "faults." In this respect, it was very close to a discourse that was already circulating in the sphere of periodical journalism, and which was called "criticism." The latter discourse was itself little more than a century old, but the important point to recognize here is that criticism was a discourse primarily of the new print media. Its practitioners were not usually associated with the universities. Criticism was addressed not to Greek and Latin works but rather to new works of vernacular literature, although the standards of judgment applied to these new works were supposed to be derived from the model of the ancients.

Throughout the eighteenth century, a close relation obtained between the practice of criticism and moral philosophy. Criticism provided moral philosophy with observations and examples drawn from literature that were useful for discoursing upon social life generally; hence it was possible for Shaftesbury, Hutcheson, Hume, Smith, and others to initiate philosophical reflection on the basis of problems in criticism, and even to elaborate ideas about the beautiful into philosophical systems that comprehended nothing less than "human understanding" or "human nature." These systemic theories, grounded in concepts such as Smith's "sympathy," and elaborated later in the century into philosophical notions of the "aesthetic," provided criticism in turn with sophisticated new terms for describing the process of judgment. This two-way exchange was enabled by the fact that both criticism and moral philosophy were dedicated to the end of refining conduct or of disseminating "polite" manners.[5]

Belles lettres, then, was first of all a translation of criticism into pedagogic form; it was an attempt to return criticism to the very "philosophy" that Joseph Addison's criticism famously brought "out of the schools." But as with any process of translation, criticism was also changed by its assimilation to the school. If criticism circulated mainly in the form of the periodical essay, belles lettres necessarily took the form in the university of a course of lectures. Such a course usually had no regular standing in the curriculum, but was rather grafted onto the existing discipline of rhetoric. Yet the introduction of a composite course known as "rhetoric and belles lettres" was more than simply a strategy for introducing the practice of criticism into the university; belles lettres was, in fact, made to function as a new *kind* of rhetoric. This was its crucial difference from criticism. Belles lettres was defined by a second agenda, then, of inculcating a practice of *writing*. In order to realize this aim, the critics themselves (chiefly Addison and Swift) were often cited as examples of fine writing or style, as models for rhetorical imitation.

By invoking the critics as model writers, Smith and his successors were able to develop new stylistic norms of clarity or "perspicuity" that were incompatible with the emphasis in the old rhetoric on ornament and "copious" elaboration.[6] In his authoritative history of eighteenth-century rhetoric, Wilbur Samuel Howell observes that Smith redirected the enterprise of rhetoric away from the traditional goal of persuasion and toward the goal of *communication*.[7] The purpose of communication was not to compel agreement by means of impassioned or devious language, but to convey ideas or sentiments accurately from one mind to another. Supported by a theory of "moral sentiments" in which calmer and more sociable affects were favored over the "passions" of antiquity, or the enthusiasms of theological debate, Smith's new rhetoric was a thorough displacement of the old.[8] The reorientation of language arts from persuasion to communication, which Smith did not invent but deliberately advanced, was nothing less than a shift in the ground of language, portending the most far-reaching transformation of Western discourses. If belles lettres was the sign of such an epochal shift, however, it initially occupied a surprisingly modest place in the curriculum. It was by no means the equal of the old rhetoric, or of classical studies, which continued to dominate the curriculum.

The use of vernacular literary models in the new rhetoric or belles lettres instituted at the university level a process of vernacularization already undertaken in many lower schools. Vernacular literacy was the primary means for enlarging the domain of "standard" English, which, in fact, had a very narrow social base before the eighteenth century. The aim of reducing the dialectal diversity of English to a standard was embraced by the schools, the state, literary culture, upwardly mobile class strata, and provincial speakers of English—for different reasons, perhaps, but with similar long-term effects. The goal of establishing a normative English was a powerful force driving the educational system toward the use of the vernacular, and toward the elevation of English literature to "classic" status. But the point we must emphasize here is that in the lower schools, the use of vernacular literature was linked to *grammar* rather than, as with belles lettres, to rhetoric. It is easy to see why this is so, given the social forces impelling the standardization of English. For the broad new educational constituency of middle- and lower-class students, as well as for colonized populations in the British empire, learning to speak and write English correctly (that is, normatively) was a condition for participation in the political and economic life of the nation. Correct English, as produced by a pedagogy utilizing the anthologies of "elegant extracts" that proliferated during the period, was to have an "improving" effect, mainly by purging one's language of impropriety, low diction, or dialect features. Belles lettres built on this foundation in correct speech by refining taste and manners at a higher level of education, where the practice of grammar could be supplemented by the cultivation of taste in reading and of style in writing.

Nevertheless, one has to acknowledge that there was no sharp break in the continuum of "improvement" from its base in correct language to its summit in the cultivation of "style," and thus no sharp break between the aims of vernacular education at the lower and upper levels. If we return to the university level, we can see that the new rhetoric was much closer to grammar in its aims than it was to the political oratory of the old rhetoric. However sophisticated the psychological notions that supported the stylistic norm of clarity in communication, the new rhetoricians claimed that clarity could be achieved most effectively by adhering to standards of grammar and usage. Hence Blair, and even more George Campbell, whose 1776 *The Philosophy of Rhetoric* was second only to Blair's in influence, devoted considerable discussion to issues of grammatical propriety. In its tendency to emphasize grammar, the new rhetoric pointed the way toward the increasing obsession of nineteenth-century rhetoric with correct usage, a concern that marked the emergence of composition at the end of the century, and has been successfully challenged only in recent decades.

The association of belles lettres with rhetoric thus ultimately failed to strengthen its curricular position. While the old rhetoric was a moribund discipline, without the political significance it had for classical society, or even for the humanists of the previous two centuries, the new rhetoric was increasingly narrow in focus, addressed to questions of correct usage and argumentation. Subordinate to moral philosophy, and only opportunistically related to the old rhetoric, belles lettres was condemned to the status of an underdeveloped discipline, always in danger of sinking to a merely effusive discourse of appreciation. In a similar fashion, the new rhetoric espoused by belles lettres displaced the old rhetoric but never successfully *replaced* it; that is, the new rhetoric never came to occupy the same position of centrality in the educational system as the old. As a consequence, the new rhetoric remained underdeveloped as well, always in danger of being reduced to the policing of usage by means of "composition" exercises, or to a form of "elocution" that was little more than the correction of pronunciation and grammar. In retrospect, it is not surprising that the aims of rhetoric were folded into the disciplinary form of belles lettres, and that the subdiscipline of composition, when it emerged in the later nineteenth century, drew its teachers from the staff of belles lettres. But we shall return to this important moment later.

As widespread and important as the establishment of linguistic norms and corresponding norms of taste in vernacular literature may have been in the lower schools and in the print domain, its expression as belles lettres remained a relatively minor development in the elite universities. Belles lettres and the new rhetoric, as Thomas Miller reminds us in *The Formation of College English*, originated in the provincial universities rather than at the center of the system, in Oxford or Cambridge. In the latter, where professors still lectured in Latin, vernacular education in any form continued to be resisted. Even in the universities of its origin, however, belles lettres was a marginal disciplinary formation. This point is of very great importance, because it suggests that there were compelling institutional constraints at the university level militating against the development of belles lettres as a discipline. Despite the growing success of its cognate pedagogies in the lower schools (but these were likewise, one must point out, not the elite "public" schools), belles lettres remained in some respects a marginal discipline throughout its history. In the eighteenth century, it never achieved the status of a regular curriculum; only later, in the nineteenth century, did this occur, and then in the peripheral institutions of higher education, the colleges and adult education schools for workers or women.

The failure of belles lettres to achieve full disciplinary status is all the more striking when it is contrasted with the success of "criticism" in the journalistic sphere. In such venues as the *Edinburgh Review* and the *Quarterly Review*, criticism became a capacious and indefinitely inclusive discourse, taking as its object not only poems or plays, but also social and political policies, and finally, society itself. Criticism in the print media became the venue for the emergence of the Victorian seers, the new critics of industrial civilization. From Carlyle to Arnold and beyond, the culture critics set themselves against modernity itself, and especially against science, the avatar of modernity. In this context, the relative weakness of belles lettres as a disciplinary form comes into focus. When we look at the evolution of the disciplines in the university of the later nineteenth century, we discover that discourses of knowledge were increasingly subject to norms of scientificity. If criticism found a place of great importance in the mass print media, its bellelettristic analogue in the university failed to maintain a link to the scientificity that alone would have assured its disciplinary status in the new constellation of disciplines. In this failure, belles lettres suffered a fate similar to that of moral philosophy. This point is of such great historical significance for the future of the disciplines as to require brief elaboration.

In the course of its history, moral philosophy generated a number of sub-discourses on various subjects. These discourses were at first underwritten by an empiricist epistemology, from which psychological propositions about "human nature" were deduced. Moral philosophy was at base a science of human nature. While the norm of scientificity, as I shall be able to demonstrate more fully in the next section, dominated all discipline formation in the nineteenth century, this norm did not remain stable. The same empiricist epistemology could no longer support equally the two pillars of natural and moral philosophy. While "natural philosophy" developed into more rigorous forms of "natural science," the fate of moral philosophy was more complex. In the nineteenth century, the normative scientific content of moral philosophy passed into the nascent discourses of "social science," by way of the transitional, protodisciplinary form of "political economy." Moral philosophy increasingly seemed more speculative than empirical. Discourse about the human world was confronted with the choice between adhering to the methodological protocols of natural science, according to the movement that came to be known pejoratively as "positivism," or asserting a fully incommensurable mode of knowledge, for which the establishment of an epistemological foundation then became problematic.

Husserl was later to describe this situation as nothing less than the "crisis of the European sciences," and to offer the phenomenology of the "life-world" as the long sought alternative to scientific empiricism. In Habermas's more recent sociological terms, Husserl's "crisis" represented a further complication in the ongoing differentiation of value-spheres, namely the predominance of the "cognitive-instrumental" over the "moral-pragmatic" and the "aesthetic-expressive" domains. When the burden of legitimating modernity passed over to the cognitive-instrumental domain, and particularly to science, both the moral and the aesthetic domains could be perceived as standing outside the field of rationality altogether, a position that complicated the development of moral and aesthetic discourses within the university.

The constitution of a hierarchy of rationalities—scientific, moral, aesthetic—determined the formation of disciplines in the late nineteenth century, and in particular the modern character of the humanities. The humanistic disciplines were able to maintain their status among the disciplines only to the extent that they continued to make empirical claims. Over the long term, such empirical claims were hard to sustain, and this fact condemned the humanities to their familiar insecurity in the modern constellation of disciplines.[9]

With this problem we are at the point of confronting a puzzling fact about the formation of the modern disciplines: the bipartite distinction of moral and natural philosophy somehow gave rise to the tripartite distinction of the humanities, social sciences, and natural sciences; or, to put this more complexly, a bipartite distinction subsisted into its tripartite successor, with the humanities now defined in opposition to all of the scientific disciplines. Discourse about the human world fell apart into two sets of disciplines, one of which was scientific, and the other humanistic. Hence social science and ethics, which both developed from within the body of moral philosophy, ended up on opposite sides of the distinction between the sciences and the humanities. In the course of this transition, the disciplinary form of belles lettres also lost its connection with the original empiricism of moral philosophy. Belles lettres was concerned with a kind of experience, which philosophy had come to call "aesthetic"; but this experience seemed no longer capable of being studied with sufficient empiricity to constitute science. Belles lettres declined into an intellectually weak discipline, which consisted on the one hand of a nebulous discourse of taste, and on the other of an increasingly arbitrary and rigid set of stylistic norms carried over from the new rhetoric of the eighteenth century. Already by the time of Matthew Arnold it could be held up to scorn, long before twentieth-century critics attempted to dismiss it altogether. However, the aims of belles lettres never disappeared completely from literary study; and it is still the case that literary education is widely identified with the task of imparting an appreciation of great works of literature, and subordinately of upholding English grammar. Belles letters remains an unsuccessfully repressed antecedent to literary study as we know it.

PHILOLOGY

Another question must be raised at this point about the historical reasons for the failure of belles lettres in the nineteenth-century university. We often hear that the historical mission of the university can be summed up in the concept of "culture." As the bellelettrists asserted the necessary connection between the refinement of taste and moral improvement, it would seem that belles lettres ought to have taken its proper place as the chief vehicle for the inculcation of culture in the university. The affinity between belles lettres and what Matthew Arnold called "culture" was attested by Arnold's antagonist, Frederic Harrison, who protested that talk of culture was "the silliest cant of the day" and "sits well on a possessor of *belles lettres*."[10] Belles lettres differed from the program of culture, however, in falling short of the socially transformative claims so often made by its German Idealist advocates, of "reconciling" the division of the head from the heart in modern civilization, or of establishing an extra-political basis for social harmony (as Arnold hoped). Nonetheless one would like to understand why the advocates of belles lettres in the nineteenth century failed, even after Arnold's push in this direction, to appropriate the concept of culture into the developing form of their discipline.

The answer to this question requires that we acknowledge a large divergence in the developmental trajectories of the German and Anglo-American universities. For figures such as Humboldt, Schiller, Schleiermacher, and Fichte, culture (the program of *Bildung*) was to be concretely realized in a new kind of university. The German Idealists had the authorization of the state to reconceive the university, for which Wilhelm von Humboldt provided a blueprint in his famous plan for the University of Berlin. As there was no analogous institutional project in England, Arnold transplanted culture, as it were, into the air. In fact, the Anglo-American university of the nineteenth century never adopted the rationale of culture or translated its program into curricular form.[11] Even in the German university, however, the idea of culture far exceeded the social possibilities of that institution, as Habermas remarked in an important essay on the reformers of the German university: "Taking the perspective of an idealist philosophy of reconciliation, they attributed to the university a power of totalization that necessarily overburdened this institution from the beginning."[12] The attempt at a top-down reformation of the national ethos was doomed to fail, whatever the merits of *Bildung*, because the reformers neither understood the limits of the university as an institution, nor could they predict its turn to other aims in the future.[13]

Habermas's comment on the Idealist origins of the German university reminds us that the project of culture was always linked to the development of the nation-state, and that culture, despite its invocation of universalist values, was to be realized in the form of *national* culture. The ideal of culture emerged in Prussia in part because the German principalities lagged behind other European nations in their consolidation as a nation-state. The university provided an opportunity to promote this goal, and so to establish a national culture in preference to the usual importation of French *civilité*. While the German *Kulturstaat* may have been eager to sponsor the university for this reason, nothing like such a project was called for in either England or the United States; in neither country was the university seen as the agent for producing national culture, or *Kultur*. In addition to its long-standing function of training the ministry, the Anglo-American university was primarily devoted to investing a ruling elite of the aristocracy or *haute bourgeoisie* with a distinct cultural capital.[14] The concept of culture as a national project did not successfully penetrate discourse about the university until much later—in fact, not until after the First World War, and not coincidentally just before the time in which literary criticism came to be reconceived as a university discipline.

If the concept of *Kultur* was only minimally significant for the development of the Anglo-American university, the German university did contribute a much more powerful ideal to its Anglo-American counterparts: *research*. In the German system, state sponsorship of an autonomous institu-

tion of scholarly research was justified because the ideal of culture was supposed to be realized through the teaching of the most distinguished scholars.
The ideal of culture was linked from the beginning with the production of
new knowledge, and not merely with cultivation of taste. In this respect, the
German university was more modern than its Anglo-American counterparts,
which by no means combined at this time the two functions of teaching and
producing new knowledge. In that sense, we should probably speak of "disciplines" as a modern institutional form, the union of teaching and research
functions in the university. Previously, university professors may not have
pursued scholarship at all; or if they did, their scholarship might have been
unrelated to their teaching in the university. Thomas Warton, for example, a
professor of poetry at Oxford in the eighteenth century and the author of the
first major history of poetry in England, lectured exclusively on Greek and
Latin literature. The unity of teaching and research in the German university,
on the other hand, implied that only teaching could translate new knowledge
into *Bildung*.

   Belief in the necessity of new knowledge and the cultural effects of teaching this knowledge sustained a powerful if temporary rapprochement
between what Dilthey later recognized as the distinct disciplinary forms of
Naturwissenschaften and *Geisteswissenschaften*. Knowledge of nature and
knowledge of humankind were enclosed within the overarching program of
culture, as defined by the discourse of philosophy. By the late nineteenth
century, however, as Habermas further noted in his essay, "the empirical
sciences that sprang from the womb of the philosophical faculty pursued a
methodological ideal of procedural rationality that doomed to failure any
effort to situate their contents encyclopedically within an all-encompassing
philosophical interpretation."[15] The ideal of scientific research thus overtook
and displaced the pedagogic aims of culture when the "empirical sciences"
came to represent that ideal exclusively. This displacement was all the more
striking, given that prior to the nineteenth century very little research in what
we would now call "natural science" was pursued in the university at all.
Conversely, the normative category of empirical science could encompass all
the forms of *Wissenschaft*. Hence, as we have already seen, the scholarly
discourses that developed into what we now call the "humanities" were just
as likely as the natural sciences to consider themselves "empirical"—but to
call these disciplines "humanities" is, of course, anachronistic, as our concept of "discipline" now presupposes the distinction between the humanities
and the sciences emergent in the nineteenth century. All of these disciplines,
let us recall, were still comprised within the faculty of "philosophy."

   One of the protohumanistic empirical sciences within this faculty, which
no longer exists as such, can in retrospect be identified as crucially mediating the distinction between *Naturwissenschaft* and *Geisteswissenschaft*.
This science was *philology*.[16] Inaugurated in the 1780s as the study of Indo-

European by Sir William Jones, and developed as a new science of language by Bopp, Rask, and the brothers Grimm, its significance as a scientific discourse was firmly established by Humboldt, who produced major works of comparative philology (as well as the famous plan for the University of Berlin). By giving nations a kind of cultural origin in language, philology effectively fused the philosophical concept of culture with that of the *ethnos*. It translated the Idealist program of culture into an empirical discourse, which grew rapidly in the first decades of the nineteenth century and endured for more than a hundred years.[17] Insofar as the philological method strongly affected research protocols in the other disciplines that we now call the "humanities"—classics, history, philosophy—it brought these disciplines into a close relation to the current standards of scientificity at the same time that it unified scholarly enterprises within a total view of the history of civilization or culture. One has only to invoke Hegel's philosophy of "universal history," in which the development of "spirit" is successively embodied in the *Volksgeist* of particular nations, to confirm the paradigmatic status of philology among the disciplines.

In his well-known account of the rise of philology, Hans Aarsleff notes its status as "the model humanistic discipline," which was also "factual, descriptive, classificatory, empirical, and comparative."[18] Further, its identity as an empirical discipline was never perceived as incompatible with its reliance on archival or textual evidence. On the contrary, philology and related historical discourses arguably advanced a more plausible claim to empirical standards of verification than earlier arguments in moral philosophy, which often seemed deductive or speculative by comparison.[19] Historical research did not necessarily require the kind of epistemological defense against empiricist or skeptical questioning that Kant sought to provide for morality or aesthetics. Throughout the nineteenth century, in fact, historical discourses made empirical claims complementary in kind and strength to those of natural science. Of course, historical discourses could maintain this claim to scientificity only insofar as they established *facts*. It was on the basis of determined facts that philology then sought to establish *laws* governing the regularity of linguistic change. In retrospect, one can see that this mode of argument deferred certain theoretical questions raised by the interpretation of textual evidence. These questions—denominated by the general field of the "hermeneutic"—first arose at the juncture between theology and historical discourse, and not necessarily in connection with philology. (It was much later still when the reading of "literary" texts could be considered a hermeneutic enterprise.[20]) In the meantime, philology developed an empirical mode of procedure, in which literary texts were considered to be only one kind of evidence (not necessarily the most reliable) for propositions concerning the history of language.

Remarkably, philology was able to defend its claim to scientificity through the end of the nineteenth century and beyond, and even to erect its theories alongside the powerful monument of Darwinian biology (as in the work of Max Müller). In *The Order of Things*, Michel Foucault presents this feat as an expression of the episteme: philology, biology, and economics rose to dominance as the "sciences of man" by developing techniques of historical interpretation, whose object might be the traces of Indo-European in modern languages, the fossil record, or the genealogy of the concept of "value," which Foucault sees as the object of "exegesis" through the whole of Marx's *Capital*.[21] Darwin's invocation of linguistic evolution as an analogue for natural selection, and Müller's echoing of the analogy in reverse, to some extent supports the argument that techniques of historical interpretation are what secures a discipline's status. But unlike philology, neither biology nor economics disappeared in the twentieth century. The decline of philology is a conspicuous and puzzling fact, given its former status as a science (Aarsleff calls philology "an aberration" in the history of language study).

This decline is all the more surprising because philology's esteem among the *Geisteswissenschaften* was instrumental in establishing the ideal of research in the university. The humanistic disciplines roused the university from its dogmatic slumber by calling upon it to take up the production of new knowledge, and, in Germany, by attracting state sponsorship for this task.[22] The humanists themselves undertook to bring the natural philosophers into the university. The association was at first to their advantage, but it also meant that humanistic scholarship had to sustain its identification with science at a time of rapid advances in the natural sciences and in technological applications that threw into relief the difference between the natural sciences and the humanistic disciplines.

The convergence of *Kultur* with an inclusive concept of *Wissenschaft* was very powerful in its effects, but ultimately unstable. In the later decades of the nineteenth century, philology began to move away from the biological analogy popularized by Müller, or the alternative Hegelian version of evolutionist philology espoused by August Schleicher.[23] This earlier version of philology, which was strongly linked to the program of *Kultur*, came to be regarded as dubious in the light of the "positivist" turn in nineteenth-century science, and the rise of more exclusive specifications of scientific method. A second phase of scientific philology, perhaps best represented by the German "neo-grammarians," attempted to set philology on solid scientific grounds by arguing that phonetic change could be described in terms of necessary laws; these laws no longer implied any overarching destiny of humankind, or a mission of *Bildung*. The link with *Bildung* was attenuated for philology, as for other disciplines. The task of "culture" could always be reclaimed by philosophy, but it came under increasing challenge from the "positivistic" disciplines.[24]

In England and the United States, the philologists who trained in the German universities of the late nineteenth century returned to their home institutions with a conception of their discipline more than ever prescribed by norms of scientificity, and much less concerned with culture. When universities and colleges began to organize disciplines into departments, beginning in the 1870s (Harvard created its language departments in 1872), it was the philologists who determined the direction and orientation of these departments. But the necessity of this development is not so obvious in retrospect, given the fact that teachers of rhetoric and belles lettres probably outnumbered the philologists. If the growing prestige of science enhanced the position of the philologists, this advantage was really the effect of a conjuncture, the coincidence of bureaucratic reorganization with a moment of heightened prestige for science.

The dominance of philology in the formation of the new departments confirmed the preeminence of language over literature as disciplinary object, at the same time that *both objects* continued to define different tasks of these departments. The division of language and literature into separate disciplines was no doubt prevented by the fact they were held together within the unity of the concept of *nationality*. It was the unity (or ambiguity) of "English" that permitted it ultimately to become the successor to Greek and Latin in the Anglo-American university.[25] For this reason the various attempts to separate language from literature bureaucratically proved unsatisfactory, even though the philologists often insisted on the absolute distinction between them, that is, on the difference between the science of philology and the nonscientific, bellelettristic study of literature.[26]

The continuity of these early departments with the discipline of literary study in its current form is belied by the exclusion of literature from the central place in the early disciplinary field. One need only return to the first volumes of the *Transactions of the Modern Language Association* to see how thoroughly the public self-presentation of the language departments, and the protocols of research in these departments, assumed the study of language in preference to literature.[27] As we have already established, belles lettres was underdeveloped as a discipline in the nineteenth century, as a consequence of having been cut off from its roots in the discourse—moral philosophy—that formerly endowed it with sophistication and even scientificity. This underdevelopment disadvantaged belles lettres and thus literature itself when the moment arrived for the organization of disciplines into departments. English departments continued to employ lecturers to teach literature or belles lettres (as well as rhetoric) to the undergraduates.[28] But literature was excluded from full disciplinarity by virtue of its internal exile, as the philologists came to dominate the teachers of literature within the structure of the department. This hierarchy was further institutionalized with the creation of graduate programs devoted increasingly to philological study. Departmental responsibilities and rewards were unequally distributed in relation to the two objects of study, language and literature.

Despite the confident affirmation of philologists such as Francis March that "English should be studied like Greek," it was obviously impractical for "English" at the *undergraduate* level to be organized entirely as the study of the English language.[29] The very coexistence of language and literature within the same departmental structure created soon enough the possibility for a fusion of the two disciplines of belles lettres and philology, for a *philological study of literature*, at least at the graduate level. In a discussion at the 1887 MLA convention, James Morgan Hart went so far as to suggest that future professors of literature "will make it their business to lay down for us laws for the critical study of literature which will do for us what the laws of Grimm and others have done for language."[30] The invocation of Grimm's law was no doubt reassuring for the neo-grammarians in the audience, who revered it as a precedent to their own scientific approach to language. Nonetheless one wonders how the philologists thought to subject literature to the rule of such laws. If "the critical study of literature" for the philologists had little to do with "criticism," as the bellelettrists conceived it, neither did this new subject remain strictly philological. It was another discourse altogether— *literary history*—that enabled the philologists to extend their research methods to literature, even though these methods conspicuously failed to eventuate in "laws." Literary history provided even those who were not trained in philology with topics for "research": discovering the sources and analogues for literary works, determining the development of forms and genres, establishing the canons of major authors, editing texts. But to what extent could these tasks claim the status of science, however empirical or even "positivist" they often were?[31] The extension of the philological method to literature entailed a certain risk to the very scientificity of that enterprise.

By the 1890s, the curricular structure of literary study in the university was organized according to the period concepts of literary history, the same period concepts that organize the discipline today.[32] By contrast, the discipline of "rhetoric and belles lettres" had been organized according to categories of *genre*, and with the aim of inculcating skills: speaking, reading, and writing.[33] The textbooks that anthologized literary works for "rhetoric and belles lettres" mixed older and recent works together, in no historical order, but with an emphasis on the use of recent literary works as models for imitation. Literary history abolished this anthological principle, along with its presentist bias, when it came to function as the matrix for both research and teaching. Its own anthological principle was, however, skewed heavily in favor of older work, and at the graduate level, in favor of the most remote literature in English, Anglo-Saxon. This peculiar skewing of literary history was determined, of course, by the necessity of fusing literary history with the research protocols of philology. Literary history had in fact never been a *discipline*. It descended from a mode of writing that was *antiquarian*, and that circulated in a kind of satellite relation to the university. It was scholarly without being institutionalized as the basis for a curriculum. Its empirical or "scientific" credentials were established for the scholars of the late nineteenth century by virtue of its status as a *historical-philological* discourse, and to do literary history was not necessarily to do "criticism."[34] Literary history was concerned with establishing facts, for example, whether and to what extent Chaucer's *Troilus* was influenced by Boccaccio's *Filostrato*. The proper understanding of older texts might depend upon these facts; but literary history did not usually advance beyond defending older texts against anachronistic understanding; it stopped short of fully interpretive hypotheses, and its judgments of quality were usually merely assumed. The antiquarian project was often sufficiently absorbing in its own right to defer questions of meaning and value indefinitely. At the undergraduate level, the convergence of philological method with literary history reinforced a tendency already present in undergraduate pedagogy to overemphasize memorization of historical facts.[35] This is not to say that literary history was merely trivial in its concerns or results, but that it was difficult to devise an engaging undergraduate pedagogy based on this discourse.

For this reason, the bellelettrists continued to practice a version of their established pedagogy, even within the new curricular matrix of literary history. Nor did the new disciplinary mode exclude "criticism," even among the philologists who taught undergraduates; but the place of judgment within such a quasi-scientific discipline was somewhat uncertain. The professors typically passed on received judgments about the great works of literature *along with* the facts of literary history, and as a consequence, value judgments were often reduced to a peculiar sort of fact. These judgments were not usually accompanied by an account of how they were determined, much less any inquiry into aesthetic questions generally. Supported by an examination system already oriented to the faculty of recall, this arrangement long prevailed in Anglo-American universities, at least until the inception of "practical criticism," which was conceived by reformers such as I. A. Richards as an attempt to reinvent a discourse of judgment neither positivist nor bellelettrist.

The decline of evaluative discourse, however, was not only an effect of the institutional hegemony of the philologists. It was overdetermined by the ongoing development of critical discourse outside the university. The problematization of evaluative criteria in post-Kantian or Romantic criticism had already to some extent undermined the basis for a *rational* discourse of evaluation, even as it inaugurated a very different, and perhaps more sophisticated, philosophical discourse of the aesthetic. It is my sense, however, that post-Kantian aesthetic discourse remained marginal to educational institutions, however essential it was to the development of nineteenth-century art forms. In the university, it was not philosophical aesthetics but belles lettres that was charged with the task of declaring the value of the "masterpieces." A great discrepancy emerged between philosophical aesthetics and the discourse of the bellelettrists, who were forced either to recycle older moral or generic criteria of judgment, or to convey the mysterious quality of the "aesthetic" by means of intellectually dubious performances of appreciation.[36]

Within the matrix of the literary historical curriculum, belles lettres continued to be represented, then, by a cadre of lecturers who saw their function as communicating an appreciation of literature, but who were as incapable of making their discourse scientific as they were perhaps disinclined. The cultivation of a refined or "humane" sensibility through the teaching of literature could be claimed as the special province of these lecturers (the "generalists," as Gerald Graff calls them), but this task was only weakly connected to the program of *Kultur* in its grand idealist form. In addition, this division of labor between appreciation and factual discourse divided literature itself from literary history. Literature was subjected to another sort of internal exclusion, one that the generalists were both to resist and to seize as an opportunity. Already discontent with their lot in the 1890s, they began to struggle with their philological colleagues over the aims and methods of literary pedagogy.[37] Graff has made this episode familiar to us as the recurrent conflict between the "scholars and the critics"; but the point I would wish to emphasize here is that the discourse of the "critics" (the bellelettrists) was too *undisciplined* to offer a serious intellectual challenge to the "scholars" (the philologists and literary historians). At the same time, the bellelettrists saw clearly that the extension of philological methods from language to literature often failed in the classroom to rise above a boring recitation of facts. This weakness of the scholars as teachers energized the bellelettrists, despite their marginal departmental status, and enabled them in the first decades of the new century to enlist the aid of literary critics in the journalistic sphere in a polemic against the scientized mode of literary study.[38]

The institutional shape of literary study at the turn of the century strikes us today as both familiar and very unlike what we do now. Literary history held together in an unstable departmental equilibrium the two discourses of philology and belles lettres. It papered over the tension between language and literature as distinct objects of study, while moderating some of the effects of relegating the former largely to graduate study, the latter largely to the undergraduate curriculum. At the same time, the residual "rhetoric" that inhered in bellelettristic pedagogy was rapidly being developed into the new subdisciplinary form we now know as "freshman composition." I cannot here take up the question of why composition broke off from the hybrid discipline of "rhetoric and belles lettres," except to note that composition took up language as object in a way altogether different from philology.[39] The distinction between language and literature that both divided and joined belles lettres and philology was thus repeated within belles lettres, as the occasion of a new distinction between the teaching of literature and the teaching of writing. But if it will not be possible here to pursue this further complication of our discipline's formation, it will at least be possible to underscore the fundamental incoherence at the origin of literary study as a discipline of the modern university.

A final question can be raised in contemplating the emergence of this highly unsatisfactory institutional arrangement in the 1890s, when four different disciplinary practices (philology, literary history, belles lettres, composition) came to cohabit under the roof of one department. This question concerns the demise of philology. We have seen that the formation of the modern disciplines was driven by the development of a principle of scientificity, and that the "humanistic" disciplines in the eighteenth and nineteenth centuries assimilated versions of this principle into their disciplinary practice. But this arrangement did not prevail over the long term. The strength of philology must have concealed a weakness, after all, since it did not survive as a discipline both humanistic and scientific. If belles lettres was underdeveloped as a discipline, philology was, I suggest, *overdeveloped*. Müller's claim that philology held "the highest place among the Physical Sciences"[40] already testifies to this overdevelopment, which was intimately related to the underdevelopment of belles lettres. In other words, we must see the claims of philology in retrospect as enabled in part by its capacity to distinguish itself from the nonscience of belles lettres. This disciplinary conflict entailed a highly symptomatic consequence: the mutual exclusion of language and literature as objects of study.[41]

This division was, of course, already confounded in the 1890s by the institutional development of English departments, which united the two faculties of language and literature. Literary study internalized the fault line between the sciences and the humanities; that line crossed the center of its discipline, and indeed it became in some irrevocable fashion constitutive of the discipline. In drawing so severe a distinction between the study of language and the study of literature, the philologists confirmed the positioning of literature already explicit in the public discourse of criticism, as represented, for example, by Matthew Arnold. Precisely because it resisted scientific treatment, literature could be positioned in opposition to science, to industrial civilization, to modernity itself. In the eighteenth century, by contrast, literature was a thoroughly modern category for organizing discourse, because all writing was perceived as a medium of communication, and a source of empirical knowledge. Writing reported experience, and even fiction was subject to a certain empiricist norm, in the form of fidelity to human experience or human nature. By the end of the nineteenth century, literature came to be identified with the nonliteral or figurative aspect of language, and with the fictional speech act. Literature became the repository of whatever in language was resistant to scientific rationality; on this basis it was given the further task of signifying a resistance to science itself, to modern civilization. Literature was opposed most of all to philology's attempt to reduce language to law. Foucault saw the importance of this development, which he noted cryptically in *The Order of Things*: "Literature is the contestation of philology (of which it is nevertheless the twin figure)."[42]

If the philologists overextended their claim to scientificity, the extremity of this claim became apparent when empirically based historical discourses came to be sorted out from the "natural" sciences at the turn of the century, and when a generalized epistemological crisis of the disciplines drove a wedge between different discourses of the human world. It was during the period between 1880 and 1920 that "human sciences" such as sociology were effectively distinguished from the natural sciences on the one hand, and from the "humanities" or "cultural" disciplines on the other. Philology was ultimately disadvantaged by this reorganization of the disciplines, because it straddled the new spectrum of the disciplines. It attempted first to claim language as its scientific object; and then, in the form of a positivistic literary history, it claimed literature as well, the object that seemed to resist science by its very nature.

The predicament of philology highlights in retrospect the adventitious relation of philology to literary study, a result of the conditions determining the formation of university language departments. Because these departments were defined initially by the connection between language and *nation*, each one became the site for studying both the *general* science of language and a *particular* national language and its literature. This situation accounts for the peculiar position of Anglo-Saxon in the history of the discipline. For the philologists, Anglo-Saxon could be held up as an origin both for the English language and for English literature, and in this way philology could associate its discipline with the general aims of national culture. But with the decline of Darwinian and Hegelian versions of philology, this rationale was much attenuated. Moreover, the "national literature" that circulated as such in literary culture outside the university had virtually no continuous relation to Anglo-Saxon literary works; its canon usually began with Chaucer. The philologists were in any case more interested in studying Anglo-Saxon as a language than in conveying an appreciation of its literature. The relation between language and literature was an unresolved conflict within the composite and incoherent discipline housed by the department of English. This conflict has remained with us, as the residue of this incoherence.

In the end, the failure of philology to establish the study of literature on scientific grounds weakened its claim to scientificity, and perhaps cleared the way for a new science of language—linguistics—which took up some of the methods of the neo-grammarians, but was no longer oriented chiefly toward the problem of linguistic change. The emergence of a new science of language did not prevent philologists from producing interesting works of literary scholarship, but it did prevent philology from maintaining its hold on language as its special or exclusive object. Even as linguistics emerged as a discipline in the first decades of the twentieth century, literature began to displace language as the primary object of the "language" departments.[43] After the First World War, the question of the relation between language and literature was reformulated by a transit through linguistics rather than philology. Anglo-American theorists such as Richards, and continental linguists such as Jakobson, raised the "contestation" between philology and literature to a new level of universality by positing a profound contradiction in language between a referential function and an antithetical "poetic" function. The problem of the relation of language to literature became the problem of "literary language."[44] Language was divided against itself, and literature became the name of its internal subversion.

The fate of philology may no doubt be read in the implications of the complex relation between language and literature as disciplinary objects, and for this reason we cannot say that philology declined only because its research program was exhausted (if indeed it *was* exhausted). The displacement of philology by linguistics is more mysterious, more involved with philology's adventitious and at the same time necessary relation to literature. Linguistics today has traveled very far indeed from its precursor discipline. As a "science of language," it is affiliated with psychology and neuro-physiology rather than literary study, with which it has almost no exchange. Looking back on this disciplinary history a century later we are compelled to acknowledge that literature has been made to play a kind of allegorical role in the development of the disciplines, as the name of the principle antithetical to the very scientificity governing discipline formation in the modern university. For this reason belles lettres was able to contend with philology, despite its institutional weakness. The decline of philology empowered the successor to belles lettres, literary criticism, to undertake an even bolder contestation of science; but criticism's repudiation of modern civilization was already deeply implicated in the category of literature itself.

NOTES

1. Gerald Graff, *Professing Literature: An Institutional History* (Chicago: University of Chicago Press, 1987); Michael Warner, "Professionalization and the Rewards of Literature," *Criticism* 26 (1985): 1–28; and William Riley Parker, "Where Do English Departments Come From?" *College English* 5 (1967): 339–51.

2. See Frederick Rudolph, *Curriculum: A History of the American Undergraduate Course of Study since 1636* (San Francisco: Jossey-Bass, 1977), 39. On the development of moral philosophy into the culminating senior course in the American university, he writes, "Developing into a kind of capstone course that was wonderfully reassuring in its insistence on the unity of knowledge and the benevolence of God,

moral philosophy by mid eighteenth century had achieved a dominance over logic, divinity and metaphysics in the course of study."

3. See Thomas Miller, *The Formation of College English: Rhetoric and Belles Lettres in the British Cultural Provinces* (Pittsburgh: University of Pittsburgh Press, 1997).

4. This claim is made by Franklin Court in his *Institutionalizing English Literature: The Culture and Politics of Literary Study, 1750–1900* (Stanford: Stanford University Press, 1992). Thomas Miller (*The Formation of College English*, 304) excludes Smith from the narrative of origins on the grounds that he was not a rhetorician. From the perspective of my argument, what is most important about this moment is not that Blair was a professor of rhetoric and belles lettres while Smith was a moral philosopher, but rather that belles lettres derived from moral philosophy and not from classics. In his informative study, Miller wants to claim simultaneously that rhetoricians inaugurated literary study and that literary study (in the form of belles lettres) displaced a politically engaged rhetoric with a depoliticized disciplinary form. The point of this account is, so to speak, epideictic, to praise rhetoric and to dispraise literary study. But the new rhetoricians of the eighteenth century cannot be credited with originating literary study and held up as the champions of politically engaged rhetoric at the same time. As Miller knows, the new rhetoric was very different from the old, and quite compatible with the aims of belles lettres.

5. On this continuity, Frederick Rudolph (*Curriculum*, 53) writes, "Beginning in the 1760s the idea of the 'man of letters' as a proper definition of the college graduate intruded into the curriculum the study of belles lettres—orations, history, poetry, literature. An emphasis on reason and observation, on rational moral behavior, replaced a reliance on divine law in the study of ethics."

6. See Adam Smith, *Lectures on Rhetoric and Belles Lettres*, ed. J. C. Bryce (Oxford: Oxford University Press, 1983; reprint, Indianapolis: Liberty Classics, 1985), 55: "In some of our former Lectures we have given a character of some of the best English Prose writers, and made comparisons betwixt their different manners. The Result of all which as well as the rules we have laid down is, that the perfection of stile consistes in Express<ing> in the most concise, proper and precise manner the thought of the author, and that in the manner which best conveyes the sentiment, passion or affection with which it affects or he pretends it does affect him and which he communicate[s] to his reader."

7. Wilbur Samuel Howell, *Eighteenth-Century British Logic and Rhetoric* (Princeton: Princeton University Press, 1971), 536–76.

8. While Hugh Blair is somewhat more latitudinarian than Smith in his tolerance for a diversity of prose style, the emphasis in Blair's work still falls heavily on the values of "perspicacity and precision." See Hugh Blair, *Lectures on Rhetoric and Belles Lettres* (1783; reprint, New York: Garland Publishers, 1970), where he writes, "The exact import of precision, may be drawn from the etymology of the word. It comes from '*praecidere*,' to cut off: it imports retrenching all superfluities, and pruning the expression, so as to exhibit neither more nor less than an exact copy of his idea who uses it" (69).

9. See Immanuel Wallerstein, et al., *Open the Social Sciences: Report of the Gulbenkian Commisson on the Restructuring of the Social Sciences* (Stanford: Stanford University Press, 1996), 6: "Sometimes called the arts, sometimes the human-

ities, sometimes letters or *belles-lettres*, sometimes philosophy, sometimes even just 'culture,' or in German *Geisteswissenschaften*, the alternative to 'science' has had a variable face and emphasis, a lack of internal cohesiveness."

10. Frederic Harrison, quoted in Matthew Arnold, *Culture and Anarchy*, ed. Samuel Lipman (New Haven: Yale University Press, 1994), 28.

11. Bill Readings argues in his *University in Ruins* (Cambridge: Harvard University Press, 1996) that the old university of "culture," which he understands to descend from Humboldt down to recent decades, has been replaced by the new university of "excellence," of which the normative principles derive from corporate managerialism. The Anglo-American university, however, did not assimilate the German concept of culture until after the First World War, and then only very partially, in the form of "general education" programs that have been confined for the most part to liberal arts colleges and some elite universities. Already in the first decades of the twentieth century, Thorstein Veblen complained that the imposition of corporate norms on the American university was pervasive. See his *Higher Learning in America: A Memorandum on the Conduct of Universities by Business Men* (New York: B.W. Huebsch, 1918).

12. Jürgen Habermas, *The New Conservatism: Cultural Criticism and the Historians' Debate*, ed. and trans. Shierry Weber Nicholsen (Cambridge: MIT Press, 1989), 108.

13. On the subject of *Bildung* and its fate, see the superlative study by Fritz Ringer, *Decline of the German Mandarins: The German Academic Community, 1890–1933* (Cambridge: Harvard University Press, 1969; reprint, Middletown, Conn.: Wesleyan University Press, 1990).

14. The exception here, and the principal context in which vernacular education was supremely important, was in preparation for England's foreign service. There it was a matter not of a national culture for England but of an imperial English culture for the colonies.

15. Habermas, *The New Conservatism*, 113.

16. Philology in the sense of the "study (or love) of language" is, of course, an old concept, appearing in both Greek and Latin texts, and importantly in medieval works (Capella's *The Marriage of Mercury and Philology*, for example). In the Renaissance, the new "philological" techniques developed by the humanists for the study of classical literature and the Bible responded to the fact of variation among surviving manuscript copies of texts. While these techniques were absorbed into the later discipline of philology, eighteenth-century philology was very different. It took the origins of modern languages as its chief subject and set out to make philology into a scientific discipline.

17. For a comment on the relation between language study and *ethnos* in the context of the recovery of Anglo-Saxon, see Hans Aarsleff, *The Study of Language in England, 1780–1860* (Minneapolis: University of Minnesota Press, 1967; reprint, 1983), 171.

18. Hans Aarsleff, *From Locke to Saussure: Essays on the Study of Language and Intellectual History* (Minneapolis: University of Minnesota Press, 1982), 32.

19. Aarsleff remarks the difference between the eighteenth-century debate about the "origin of language," which was a major topos for moral philosophy, and the very different sorts of arguments about the origins of European languages in philology.

20. Hermeneutics, as the formal practice of determining a text's meaning, was developed in its modern form by Friedrich Schleiermacher, who was interested primarily in biblical interpretation. For an interesting recent argument tracing the major questions of literary theory to hermeneutics, see Andrew Bowie, *From Romanticism to Critical Theory: The Philosophy of German Literary Theory* (London: Routledge, 1997). I would propose a different genealogy, however, in which the important question to raise is why hermeneutics had such a belated effect on academic literary study.

21. Michel Foucault, *The Order of Things: An Archaeology of the Human Sciences* (New York: Random House, 1970), 294–300.

22. Wallerstein, et al., *Open the Social Sciences*, 8.

23. For a brief account of August Schleicher's Hegelianism, see April M. S. McMahon, *Understanding Language Change* (Cambridge: Cambridge University Press, 1994), 319–21.

24. See Fritz Ringer, *Decline of the German Mandarins*, 296; also Fritz Ringer, *Fields of Knowledge: French Academic Culture in Comparative Perspective, 1890–1920* (Cambridge: Cambridge University Press, 1992), 196.

25. I touch here, however briefly, on the cause of the unequal relation between English and the modern foreign languages despite their presumed institutional equality. English has a cultural function for the Anglo-American university that the foreign languages cannot have, even though they also inherit the same task of integrating language and literature into a coherent modern discipline.

26. On the ambivalent relation of the philologists to the study of literature, see Kenneth Cmiel, *Democratic Eloquence: The Fight over Popular Speech in Nineteenth-Century America* (Berkeley: University of California Press, 1990), 179.

27. Perhaps the most telling document in the very first volume of the MLA transactions is the essay by H.C.G. Brandt, "How Far Should Our Teaching and Textbooks Have a Scientific Basis?" *Transactions of the Modern Language Association*, vol. 1 (1884), 57–63. Brandt's essay is a kind of manifesto for the new discipline. He complains that there are still "teachers of modern languages, who do not realize, that their department is a science." But among the philologists, Brandt writes, demonstrating this fact "will hardly be necessary. I need only recall here such names as ten Brink, Sweet, Skeat, Scherer, the father of the 'Jung grammatiker,' though Saturn-like he would now devour his own children, Sievers, Paul, Verner, Braune, Kluge, Grober, Tobler, Forster, Neumann. We recognize these men as the foremost among those who have developed within the last fifteen years the old humdrum empirical treatment of living languages into the scientific study of them of to-day" (58–59).

28. Kenneth Cmiel (*Democratic Eloquence*, 178) reminds us that the philologists did not introduce English Studies, which, as we have seen, existed in the form of rhetoric and belles lettres, but that they successfully territorialized the departmental form.

29. Francis March's comment is cited from his report on the program in English at Lafayette College, in William Morton Payne, ed., *English in American Universities* (Boston: D. C. Heath, 1895), 75. This volume brings together descriptions by professors at twenty universities or colleges of their undergraduate and graduate programs. The essays were commissioned originally for an issue of *The Dial*, and they constitute an invaluable snapshot of literary study as it existed in 1894. Lafayette College's program is slightly atypical for the degree of its emphasis on language,

which can be attributed to the influence of March. For the philologist March, literary study means "the study of the language as it is found in masterpieces of literature" (76). That the study of language required the reading of "masterpieces" was simply taken for granted. Another very useful view of the early state of the discipline is provided by the first volume of *Transactions of the Modern Language Association* (1884), which prints several essays on the teaching of language and literature. Typical of these essays is James Garnett's "English and Its Value as a Discipline" (68), in which he states, "The teaching of language is as strictly *scientific* as that of any of the natural sciences."

30. Quoted in Michael Warner, "Professionalization and the Rewards of Literature," 4. The quotation is drawn from the Proceedings of the 1887 MLA convention. Similar views were expressed by Francis March in his *Method of Philological Study of the English Language*, published in 1879, and by Theodore Hunt in *Studies in Literature and Style*, published in 1890. In "English in the College Curriculum," *Transactions of the Modern Language Association*, vol. 1 (1887), 127, Hunt recommends the application "of Professor March's Philological method to the study of Shakespeare."

31. See James Morgan Hart, in "The College Course in English Literature, and how it might be improved," *Transactions of the Modern Language Association*, vol. 1 (1884), 91. Here Hart typically stretches the claim for the scientific status of literary history when he asserts that the influence of Boccaccio's *Filostrato* on Chaucer's *Troilus* had recently been given a "mathematical demonstration." One can see in Hart's recommendation for research on such topics as "the evolution of blank verse" that the concept of "evolution" here is not a casual metaphor but a deliberate analogical extension from the domain of philology, which borrowed it from biology. Hart advocates such scientific modes of scholarship in strong preference to the vacuous pronouncements of literary merit common in bellelettristic writing. The philological treatment of literary history also privileged older literature and established Anglo-Saxon in the premier position it was to have for some time to come. The bias against recent or contemporary literature survived long into the twentieth century, until the teaching of modern literature became a battlecry of the New Criticism.

32. Hart ("The College Course in English Literature," 88) stresses "the importance of teaching literature by *periods*."

33. It should be recalled here that Hugh Blair's *Lectures on Rhetoric and Belles Lettres* was used as a textbook well into the nineteenth century. The very first "Professor of English Language and Literature" (so-called), the Rev. Thomas Dale, appointed at the new University of London in 1828, delivered several sets of lectures on Dramatic Poetry, Epic Poetry, Divinity, the History of Romantic Fiction, and finally, the History of English Literature. Until the late nineteenth century, genre, rather than literary history, was the more usual organizing principle for the study of English literature. For a discussion of Thomas Dale, see D. J. Palmer, *The Rise of English Studies* (London: Oxford University Press, 1965), 18–22.

34. The history of literary history has not been much discussed by scholars, despite its crucial significance in the formation of the discipline. The standard reference has long been René Wellek, *The Rise of English Literary History* (Chapel Hill: University of North Carolina Press, 1941). Our understanding of this subject has been updated and sophisticated with the publication of Jonathan Kramnick, *Making the*

English Canon: Print Capitalism and the Cultural Past, 1700–1770 (Cambridge: Cambridge University Press, 1998). Kramnick draws our attention to the largely forgotten debate between the public sphere critics and the literary historians of the eighteenth century over the judgment of vernacular literature. The modernist and even presentist bias of the critics was contested by mid-century literary historians such as Joseph Warton and Richard Hurd, who sought to establish scholarly standards for the reading of older works, and who in the process often came to value the vernacular "ancients" over the moderns. Kramnick thus backdates Graff's conflict between the scholars and the critics to the eighteenth century.

35. D. J. Palmer, *The Rise of English Studies*, 23.

36. It seems evident that for better or worse, post-Kantian aesthetics disabled the discourse of judgment based on criteria, redirecting it toward inquiry into the nature of aesthetic response. Criticism might now work backward from response to judgment, but without the old guarantees provided by criteria, which Kant summarily dismissed in the *Critique of Judgment*. This post-Kantian discourse was, to be sure, more sophisticated, but the loss of criteria also had the effect of rendering expressions of judgment in many contexts merely ineffable. The discursive poverty of evaluative discourse gave rise to dubious pedagogic techniques, such as those of Cornell University's Hiram Corson, for example, who famously advocated teaching literature exclusively by means of the "interpretive" recitation of passages from the masterpieces. See Hiram Corson's contribution to Payne, *English in American Universities*, 60–65. Professor Corson, it should be remarked, was also a noted philologist, and for that subject he surely practiced another style of teaching altogether. He exemplifies the split between philology and belles lettres by embodying it, which should remind us that this split is a disciplinary phenomenon and not only an effect of personal inclinations or conflicts.

37. In Britain, the opposition was led by John Churton Collins, who published perhaps the most famous of the diatribes against philology and for the teaching of literature, *The Study of English Literature: A Plea for Its Recognition and Reorganization in the Universities* (1891).

38. See Gerald Graff, "The Generalist Opposition," in *Professing Literature*, 81–97.

39. The contraction of rhetoric is evident in comments such as that of George E. Maclean of Stanford University, in Payne, *English in American Universities*, 159. "[T]he first duty of rhetoric," he claims, "[is] that of teaching students to speak and write the English language correctly."

40. Müller, quoted in Aarsleff, *From Locke to Saussure*, 35.

41. Hart ("The College Course in English Literature," 85) typically emphasizes the "two radically distinct matters, viz. language and literature."

42. Foucault, *The Order of Things*, 300. Cmiel (*Democratic Eloquence*, 165) also notes the narrowing specification of literature in the dictionaries of the nineteenth century, as literature ceases to denote "*all* learning" and comes to signify the imaginative genres. Cmiel also reminds us that at this point, oratory and history are excluded from the domain of literature.

43. The period during which philology successfully focused the profession on language exclusively was relatively brief, from perhaps 1870 to 1900. By 1904, the essays in *Transactions of the Modern Language Association* were almost all on liter-

ary historical subjects, that is, on literature. These essays were by and large still on older and more obscure texts; but several decades later, the preponderance of essays dealt with major works of literature from all periods.

44. We can appreciate the difference made by the reformulation of "literary language" as a linguistic question by contrasting what Jakobson means by literary language—a universal possibility of language use, the "poetic" function—with what Erich Auerbach means in his *Literary Language and its Public*—the *written* language of a particular culture, which is literary by virtue of being written, and not by virtue of being poetic.

CHAPTER 2

Disciplinarity and Radicality:
Quantum Theory and Nonclassical Thought
at the Fin de Siècle, and
as Philosophy of the Future

ARKADY PLOTNITSKY

> [T]he necessity of a final renunciation of the classical ideal
> of causality and a radical revision of our attitude towards
> the problem of physical reality . . . provides room for new
> physical laws, the coexistence of which might at first sight
> appear irreconcilable with the basic principles of science.
>
> *Niels Bohr*

"THE QUANTUM OF ACTION"

Quantum physics was inaugurated in 1900 by Max Planck's discovery that radiation, previously believed to be a continuous (wave-like) phenomenon in all circumstances, can, under certain conditions, have a quantum or discontinuous (particle-like) character. Planck made his discovery, widely seen as the single greatest discovery in twentieth-century physics, in the course of his attempt to formulate and then interpret the radiation law for the so-called black body (the usual model of the black body is a heated piece of metal with a cavity).[1] The limit where this discontinuity appears is defined by the specific frequency of the radiation of the body and a universal constant of a very small magnitude, h, now known as Planck's constant, which Planck himself termed "the quantum of action" and which turned out to be one of the most fundamental constants of all physics. The indivisible (energy) *quantum* (i.e., quantity) of radiation in each case is the product of h and the frequency ν, $E = h\nu$.

Eventually quantum phenomena proved to have a far more complex character, of which discontinuity is only an approximation. First of all, as became apparent around 1923, whether the phenomenon in question is radiation, such as light, wave-like according to the classical view, or what were classically seen as particles, such as electrons, all quantum objects may manifest their existence (if not themselves) in both wave-like and particle-like phenomena under different circumstances. Crucially, however, one can never observe both types of phenomena together. This duality signaled the epistemological complications that continued to multiply throughout the history of quantum physics.

The very use of the term "phenomena" requires qualification regarding the relationships between quantum objects and what is observable in experiments involving them, a controversial question to this day. Niels Bohr gave the term a rigorous sense as part of his interpretation of quantum mechanics, known as complementarity. (I shall explain the latter term presently.) He defined "phenomena" as referring to the macroscopic and, in terms of the physics of their description, classical (rather than quantum) experimental arrangements where such quantum effects as those associated with "waves" or "particles" manifest themselves, but only as *macroscopic* effects, rather than as properties of quantum objects themselves. These effects include those properties that we classically associate with "particles" or "waves," but only insofar as these properties pertain to certain parts of measuring instruments, as opposed to quantum objects themselves.[2] Classical physics, however, cannot account for the sum total of these effects, which necessitates a deployment of a very different mathematical formalism. This formalism was introduced around 1925 and has ever since been known as quantum mechanics. According to Bohr's interpretation of this formalism, it may not be possible to attribute the properties of particles and waves or any classical physical (or perhaps any) properties to quantum objects themselves. Nor, in Bohr's interpretation, are quantum objects described by this formalism, which instead refers to the effects of the interaction between these objects and measuring instruments upon the latter. These effects define phenomena in Bohr's sense. Quantum objects themselves must, thus, be seen as "entities" different from either particles or waves, while giving rise to one or the other type of phenomena (but never both types together) by virtue of their interaction with measuring instruments. Each type of phenomena (but never both together) appears (in either sense) as the effect of these interactions. Each phenomenon also appears in specific and always mutually exclusive circumstances, which can be rigorously defined and, whenever necessary, set up experimentally. In other words, the appearance of the particle-like or the wave-like phenomena uniquely depends on a particular type of experimental setup; and we can always arrange for such a setup and expect the appearance of the corresponding type of phenomena. We can, however, never combine both types of phenomena so as to ascertain, even in principle, all characteristic phenomenal properties in question, or construct any experimental setup that would enable us to do so (in the way it can always be done, at least in principle, in classical physics). We can observe either the wave-like effects or the particle-like effects of the interaction between quantum objects and measuring instruments, but never both simultaneously.

Thus, we can neither avoid phenomena of either type—either with wave-like effects or with particle-like effects—nor combine the phenomena of both types at any point. In some respects, the latter is true in classical physics as well. There, however, these two descriptions apply (directly) to the distinct and rigorously separable types of *objects*: particles are always particles, waves are always waves. A difference in the experimental setup would not change the nature of either type of object. By contrast, in quantum physics it is the difference in the experimental setup that defines the differ-ent—the wave-like or the particle-like—character of the observable phe-nomena for the same *type* of "objects," while the objects themselves are, ultimately, unobservable as such. While of the same type (electrons, photons, and so forth), two observed "objects" may not be the *same* as objects, and may not even be objects to begin with.[3] We can neither observe a proper fusion of phenomena of different types nor conceive of a single underlying quantum configuration that (even though unobservable and ultimately incon-ceivable) would itself possess both attributes as its coexisting aspects or effects. It follows that the concept of "underlying quantum configuration" or even such terms as "configuration" and "quantum" (or, it follows, attributing to this configuration any properties) is rigorously inapplicable in Bohr's interpretation. Thus, while always mutually exclusive, the two types of phe-nomena in question, those with "wave effects" and with "particle effects," are both necessary for a comprehensive overall quantum-theoretical descrip-tion. Bohr calls such phenomena complementary.

Far from being restricted to the wave-particle pair, complementary phe-nomena are common in, and are peculiar to, quantum physics. Indeed, they may be seen as defining it, especially in Bohr's interpretation, which he, accordingly, called "complementarity." Bohr realized that the mutual exclu-sivity of complementary phenomena is an advantage, since it allows one to avoid combining mutually exclusive attributes in the same phenomena. Arguably, the most significant complementary phenomena are those related to the measurement of physical variables, analogous or, in Bohr's view, sym-bolically analogous, to those of classical physics, such as position and momentum, or time and energy.

Such variables were seen by Bohr as symbolic for the following reason. Even though we sometimes (by convention) ascribe them to quantum objects, in actuality we can only measure the corresponding physical quan-tities (for example, either position or momentum, but never both together) pertaining to the classically described measuring arrangements. That is, we measure classical physical variables pertaining to certain parts of such arrangements, rather than to the quantum objects themselves. "Allegorical" may even be a better term here, especially if we follow Paul de Man's view of allegory. His formulation in "Pascal's Allegory of Persuasion" is particularly fitting: "[T]he difficulty of allegory is rather that this emphatic clarity of representation does not stand in the service of something that can be represented."[4] Indeed, this clarity may be said to stand in the service of that which cannot be represented by any means, allegorical or not. De Man's formulation is also fitting in that quantum mechanics is defined by its extraordinary clarity and lucidity that rivals that of the best classical theories. Quantum mechanics has nothing to do with vagueness or indeterminacy (except in the specific and precise sense of uncertainty relations, on which I shall comment presently), either in terms of its theoretical structure or in terms of its claims concerning the ultimate constituents of nature as such. Instead, it tells us—rigorously, clearly, lucidly—that it makes no claims of any kind in this latter respect and, in Bohr's interpretation, more radically that no such claims are possible. Quantum epistemology (again, at least in Bohr's version of it) ultimately may never allow us to speak of any properties of quantum objects and their behavior as such, but only of the effects of their interaction with the classically described measuring instruments. Accordingly, any physical description of quantum objects or their behavior based on conventional physical attributes can only be "allegorical" in the sense just defined. Classical physics can offer us only incomplete and partial—and specifically complementary—allegories of the quantum world, both in general conceptual terms and as specifically applied to the measuring instruments involved in a particular (and always unique) situation of quantum measurement. While, as I said, the relevant behavior of these instruments is described fully in classic terms, the (complementary) sum total of the effects of their interaction with quantum objects is rigorously unaccountable by means of classical physics. Indeed, nothing appears to be able to offer us more than, in this sense, partial and, specifically, complementary allegories of the quantum world, which cannot even be assumed to add up to a classical whole, even if an unrepresentable one. As a result of the circumstances just sketched, such (complementary) variables become subject to Heisenberg's uncertainty relations. Uncertainty relations express most immediately the strict quantitative limits absent in classical physics, on the simultaneous joint measurement of "position" or "coordinate" (q) and "momentum" (p), as expressed by the famous formula $\Delta q \Delta p \cong h$, where h is Planck's constant, and Δ designates the precision of measurement. (The same type of formula holds for time and energy.) In Bohr's interpretation, however, the uncertainty relations manifest the impossibility of not only simultaneous measurement but also the simultaneous determination or unambiguous definition of both such variables at any point.

Planck's discovery emerged from the investigation of the nature of energy, entropy, and chance (the concepts developed throughout the nineteenth century) at the level of the ultimate constituents of matter, which modern physics has defined as quantum ever since. The situation may have been imperfectly understood initially. Eventually, however, Planck's law and related developments, and our attempts to interpret them, radically transformed our understanding of physics and of the limits of our knowledge, scientific and philosophical, and its claims upon nature, technology, and mind. The transformation took a while, as did a more adequate interpretation of quantum phenomena themselves—more or less in the wake of quantum mechanics, introduced by Werner Heisenberg and Erwin Schrödinger in 1925–26.[5] It was not easy to develop an understanding of the strange and even mysterious character of the data in question. Nor was it easy to develop quantum theory itself—to work out a comprehensive mathematical formalism for it and to understand the nature of the physical and philosophical problems involved or (equally as difficult) of the solutions it offered. We are hardly finished with sorting these complexities out even now, in the year 2001, at least insofar as the debate concerning quantum physics continues. And no end appears to be in sight.[6] Thus, quantum physics and its radical implications frame two instances of the fin de siècle, that of the nineteenth and that of the twentieth century, or of the beginning of a new century. Indeed, along with radical theories in other fields and the debates they have continuously engendered, quantum physics and the debates concerning it (as those in other fields), gave the twentieth century the character of an incessant philosophical fin de siècle, and have taken us into the twenty-first century. They have made it the scene of what Nietzsche called a "philosophy of the future"—a philosophy that is always and forever yet to come.

"THE EPISTEMOLOGICAL LESSON OF QUANTUM MECHANICS"

The epigraph to this essay comes from Niels Bohr's reply, "Can Quantum-Mechanical Description of Physical Reality Be Considered Complete?" to Einstein, Podolsky, and Rosen's (EPR) famous article, by the same title, questioning the completeness of quantum mechanics as a physical theory.[7] These two propositions, which, respectively, open and close Bohr's argument, may be read together: "[T]he necessity of a final renunciation of the classical ideal of causality and a radical revision of our attitude towards the problem of physical reality . . . provides room for new physical laws, the coexistence of which might at first sight appear irreconcilable with the basic principles of science."

In accordance with the first statement, I shall designate as nonclassical or radical those theories, in any domain, that entail "the necessity of a final renunciation of the classical ideal of causality" and, in particular, "a radical revision of our attitude towards the problem of physical reality." Bohr argues for both in the case of quantum mechanics. At least, the latter can be interpreted consistently with the experimental data in question and the formalism of quantum mechanics, and this interpretation ensures the completeness of quantum mechanics as a physical theory within the proper limits of its application. I shall, accordingly, call classical those theories that are both causal and realist. Ultimately, a final renunciation of the classical ideal of reality may be at stake in Bohr's interpretation of quantum mechanics as well. Indeed, it is conceivable that no concept of reality that is, or even ever will be, available to us may be applicable to our description of the quantum world, assuming that the latter expression or such terms and concepts as "quantum" or "world" themselves could apply.[8]

My argument accords with the second proposition of my epigraph: the nonclassical or radical nature of certain theories or their interpretation in physics and elsewhere provides room for new laws, that is, rigorous propositions accounting for "regularities" in the behavior of objects or phenomena under investigation in these theories.[9] These laws may at first sight appear irreconcilable with the basic principles of science or other disciplines in question. In fact, however, such is not the case. On the contrary, such theories are not only compatible with the basic principles of the disciplines where they emerge, but in view of other aspects of those theories (such as the experimental data in question in quantum physics) they also become necessary at certain points in order to maintain these principles. Radicality becomes the condition of disciplinarity rather than, as it may appear at first sight and as it is often argued by the proponents of classical theories, being in conflict with it. Naturally, this circumstance may also entail a reconsideration of what constitutes the basic principles of science or other disciplines, including the functioning of classical theories—a reconsideration, that is, of what is decisive in enabling the practice of these disciplines.

First, I would like to explain further the terms just introduced. I call the theories in question nonclassical, rather than, say, postclassical for the following reason. It is true that their most radical forms may be argued to be relatively recent. In science, we find them in quantum physics or modern biology and genetics, and in certain areas of modern mathematics and mathematical logic. In the humanities, we encounter these theories beginning more or less with Nietzsche and then extending to, in particular, Heidegger, Bataille, Levinas, Blanchot, Lacan, Foucault, Deleuze, de Man, and Derrida. Certain key elements of such theories can, however, be traced in the earlier history of theoretical thinking in mathematics, science, and philosophy, beginning with some pre-Socratics. This tracing sometimes appears to allow for nonclassical interpretations of some among such earlier theories as a whole, rather than merely arguing that some of their elements can be used in nonclassical theories elsewhere. Such interpretations (whatever the degree of their viability) pose, first, the question of a more rigorous genealogy of nonclassical thought. Secondly, they also pose the question of whether such earlier theories are best read classically or nonclassically. Both are complex issues, which I shall not address here. At the same time, even as the tracing just indicated takes place, at its radical limits, nonclassical theoretical thinking is hardly more accepted by, or acceptable to, a large majority of the contemporary intellectual (including scientific) community than it has ever been.[10] It is this resistance that is primarily responsible for the continuing application of the characterization "radical" to nonclassical theories, by their proponents and critics alike. This resistance can be easily exemplified by recent debates, particularly those involving responses to the thought of the figures just mentioned.

A few further general qualifications and disclaimers are in order. My subject here is the implication of the state of affairs just described—the possibility, if not necessity, of a rigorous suspension of both causality and reality in interpreting the quantum-mechanical data and formalism, and their interrelationships—for the status of quantum mechanics as a physical theory. This is one of the central questions at stake in the Bohr-Einstein debate concerning "epistemological problems in atomic [that is, quantum] physics," to use the subtitle of Bohr's "Discussion with Einstein." Many key concepts and even specific formulations offered above are, however, of a general philosophical nature and, hence, are applicable to other fields of inquiry, in particular to the work of the representative nonclassical thinkers listed previously. An immediate example would be Bohr's extraordinary formulation to be discussed later: "In fact, in quantum physics, we are presented not with intricacies of this kind, but with the inability of the classical frame of concepts to comprise the peculiar feature of indivisibility, or 'individuality,' characterizing the elementary processes."[11] As will be seen, the intricacies in question concern the nature of probability in classical physics. Bohr's proposition, however, extends well beyond the question of causality (or even that of reality) and may be read as defining the essence of nonclassical thought in quantum mechanics and elsewhere. It may be useful to adjust the statement a bit to stress my point: "In these theories we are presented not with usual, if complex, intricacies of the classical kind, but with the inability of the classical frame of concepts to comprise the peculiar features characterizing the processes in question in nonclassical theories."

Accordingly, my argument, although it will deal primarily with quantum physics and Bohr, can be extrapolated to other areas and specifically to the work of the figures in the humanities whom I mentioned earlier. One can also consider the question of *interdisciplinarity* in this context—the question of how the introduction of nonclassical theories affects the relationships between different disciplines and the debates concerning these relationships, specifically at the fin de siècle, or over the course of the twentieth century, in its perpetual fin de siècle. Except by implication, this question cannot be addressed without extending this essay well beyond its intended scope.[12] An invocation of the currently fashionable and (in part by virtue of being fashionable) risky term "interdisciplinarity" may be misleading. I refer to the specific—nonclassical—epistemological configurations rigorously shared by different fields, where they may have different roles to play (for example, in physics versus certain areas of philosophy), rather than interactions between such fields themselves, be they more or less rigorous, or more or less loose. Such interactions and our views of them have sometimes been way too loose and superficial or, one might say, lacking in discipline (in either sense) in certain recent cases in the humanities, often in the name of interdisciplinarity. It may instead be appropriate and opportune to cite Bohr in introducing the second volume of his collected philosophical essays: "The following articles present the essential aspects of the situation in quantum physics and, at the same time, stress the points of similarity it exhibits to our position in other fields of knowledge beyond the scope of the mechanical nature. We are not dealing here with more or less vague analogies, but with an investigation of the conditions for the proper use of our conceptual means of expression. Such considerations not only aim at making us familiar with the novel situation in physical science, but might on the account of the comparatively simple character of atomic problems be helpful in clarifying the conditions for objective description in wider fields."[13] Bohr did, however, sometimes also speak more ambitiously (but not in print) of his "dream of great interconnections."

In part for the reasons just explained, no disciplinary knowledge of physics is required for understanding my argument, though I would stand by my claims concerning physics (and I think we must always try to be as accurate as possible in this respect). Indeed, to the degree that physics qua physics is involved, all my claims will be supported by arguments that are, in fact, Bohr's, if not quotations from Bohr. My main argument, moreover, concerns primarily Bohr's view of the relationships between disciplinarity and radicality (that is, nonclassical epistemology as, at a certain point, a necessary condition for maintaining the disciplinarity of physics). This argument would apply whether or not one agrees with his interpretation of quantum physics or his view of the basic principles of science. Although I argue that both are at the very least effective, for some they are epistemologically difficult to accept, as was the case for Einstein, who ultimately found quantum mechanics, and specifically Bohr's interpretation, consistent and effective but epistemologically unpalatable.

I am, it is true, also concerned with a certain philosophical generalization of Bohr's conceptuality. For the arguments similar to the one offered here concerning Bohr may, I would argue, be developed for thinkers in areas outside of mathematics or science. My claims, however, are also historically specific, whether they concern quantum physics or other fields. First of all, they are restricted to thinkers especially prominent in recent debates. Many of these figures are, in addition, often seen as responsible for the unproductive undermining of disciplinary stability and theoretical, scholarly, and intellectual norms and rigor. I would argue that this view is mistaken, or at least lacking in discrimination.

One could not deny differences among the work and attitudes of the thinkers themselves. In the work of some of them—specifically (in addition to Bohr) Heidegger, Levinas, Blanchot, de Man, and Derrida—radicality is, or at a certain point becomes, the condition of the continuity of disciplinarity and discipline (as both a field of study and a system of governing rules) in their fields. In these cases, one finds what may even be called, strange as it may sound in relation to these thinkers, an extreme disciplinary conservatism. I use this expression in the following sense. A departure from a given preceding (classical) configuration of thought is enacted, first, after exhausting the possibilities it offers for a new configuration, which may in fact arise in part from within the old one. Secondly, this departure is enacted under the extreme pressure of maintaining and perhaps conserving significant and even defining disciplinary aspects of the old configuration. In the case of new physics (relativity and quantum mechanics), Heisenberg, who was close to the events in question (in 1934), argued as follows: "Modern theories did not arise from revolutionary ideas which have been, so to speak, introduced in the exact sciences from without. On the contrary they have forced their way into research which was attempting consistently to carry out the programme of classical physics—they arise out of its very nature. It is for this reason that the beginning of modern [twentieth-century] physics cannot be compared with the great upheavals of previous periods like the achievements of Copernicus."[14]

The point concerning the time of Copernicus may require further qualification. However, it does suggest that there are other configurations, other views, and other effects of theoretical practice in whatever field one considers. Thus, one does find more manifestly or (it may be difficult to be certain) perhaps more manifest radical "moves," more pronounced and "speedier" departures from particular forms of disciplinarity. One can think, for example, of the cases of Nietzsche, Bataille, Deleuze, and Lacan as different from those of Bohr, Heisenberg, Heidegger, Levinas, Blanchot, de Man, and Derrida. In these cases, however, one might still argue for analogues, if not equivalents, of disciplinary conservatism, and indeed arguments to that effect. Thus, for Nietzsche and Deleuze, although in different ways, one's sense of the "discipline" (in either sense) and of theoretical rigor in fact requires an enactment of a much broader and deeper transformation, and indeed a redefinition, of a given disciplinary configuration or field. In the process, a given disciplinary history—such as that of philosophy, or, especially in Lacan's case, psychoanalysis—becomes refigured as well.[15] Bataille's is a still different and somewhat more complex case. His strong sense of philosophical or even, in a certain sense, scientific rigor is pronounced in spite and sometimes because of the strange shapes that his texts assume. There is, in the cases of all these figures, still a question as to the degree of manifestation, in their available texts, of the working through the preceding configuration before entering new theoretical territories. This type of question, however, would especially require extended treatments of each case just mentioned, which cannot be done within my limits here. A proper treatment of Lacan's case would, in addition, require a much more sustained engagement with psychoanalysis than is possible here.[16] In these cases, one also confronts more complex disciplinary and interdisciplinary configurations than in the case of mathematics or science, which are hardly free from these complexities either. The spectrum of disciplinary and interdisciplinary configurations in the cases in question is much broader, however, and, accordingly, one cannot avoid specificity and limitations in making the kind of argument I am making here. I would also argue, however, that the cases in question and, accordingly, the present argument concerning the relationships between disciplinarity and radicality, have a broader intellectual and political significance, especially in the context of recent debates. This matter will be considered later, although my argument concerning developments in the humanities will remain more provisional and will proceed primarily by analogy with my argument concerning Bohr, while keeping the differences in mind, in particular the specificity of mathematics and science.

This specificity remains crucial, first of all, in terms of the conceptual and historical, or, one might say, disciplinary rigor of the argument. It is also crucial, especially for the present analysis, for yet another reason. The case of mathematics and science, or, again, specific cases such as that of Bohr's work, may be disciplinarily (and interdisciplinarily) less complex than those of figures in the humanities, such as those previously mentioned. Or at least this type of complexity may be kept at bay somewhat more easily in the disciplinary practice of mathematics and science, rather than, say, in fully understanding Bohr's work. This specificity, however, also allows one to make a stronger, perhaps the strongest possible, overarching argument: in certain circumstances, extreme epistemological radicality is the condition of the continuation of disciplinarity and even arises as the outcome of extreme disciplinary conservatism. It is primarily in order to make the strongest possible case that the present analysis to some degree bypasses certain extrascientific complexities of Bohr's work and focuses on the relationships between the radical epistemology of quantum mechanics and the disciplinary specificity of physics there.[17]

Now, in physics the difference between classical and nonclassical theories may be defined (at least initially) without appealing to a priori ontological and epistemological claims upon the objects of investigation or the nature of the theory. Instead it may be defined in terms of physics itself (that is, in

terms of the constitution of the data in question and the structure of the
theories accounting for these data), as the difference between classical,
sometimes also called Newtonian, and quantum physics.[18] The first, however,
is indeed causal and realist, or at least it may be and commonly is interpreted
as such consistently with the data and mathematical formalism of classical
physics. The second is neither, at least in Bohr's interpretation. Nor, more
crucially, would this interpretation allow one to assume it as either causal or
realist. In other words, Bohr's interpretation of quantum mechanics does not
merely (in a positivist vein) renounce realism and causality in interpreting
quantum data, but instead rigorously *interprets* these data, as accounted for
by the formalism of quantum mechanics, as disallowing for both causality
and realism. The preceding formulations are asymmetrical. As I have indicated, there are arguments for classical-like interpretations of quantum
mechanics, and Bohmian mechanics is classical-like, causal, and realist,
although nonlocal. This question has always had much urgency in the debate
concerning quantum physics and, to a considerable degree, has defined this
debate. As I said, it is also, in principle, possible to interpret classical
physics in epistemologically nonclassical terms. This possibility is actually
more intriguing, although it has had rather less, if any, urgency. The classical
ideal has always dominated modern physics and largely motivated the search
for classical-like interpretations and versions of quantum theory as well.
These questions do not affect my main argument here, for which the possibility of a rigorous nonclassical interpretation of quantum mechanics, such
as that of Bohr, suffices. Beyond its immense philosophical significance,
however, this possibility is also crucial in terms of physics, since, as Einstein
was first to note, short of a nonclassical interpretation quantum mechanics
could be shown to be nonlocal, that is, to be in conflict with relativity.
Bohr's interpretation is also a response to this argument. I shall return to
these considerations in my discussion of the EPR argument.[19]

Classical physics, such as Newtonian mechanics, is or may be interpreted
as, ontologically, realist because it can be seen as fully describing all the
(independent) physical properties of its objects necessary to explain their
behavior. (At least, such is the case for idealized systems, when the properties in question are abstracted from other properties of the objects comprising a given system for the purposes of such a description.) It is or may be
interpreted as, ontologically, causal because the state of the systems it considers (these systems may, again, be idealized) at any given point is assumed
to determine its behavior at all other points. It is also, epistemologically,
deterministic insofar as our knowledge of the state of a classical system at
any point allows us to know, at least in principle and in ideal cases, its state
at any other point. Not all causal theories are deterministic in this sense.
Classical statistical physics and chaos theory (which is, in most of its forms,
classical and is sometimes a direct extension of Newtonian mechanics) are

causal or at least are assumed to be. They are, however, not deterministic even in ideal cases, in view of the great structural complexity of the systems they consider. This complexity blocks our ability to predict the behavior of such systems, either exactly or at all, even though we can write equations that describe them and assume their behavior to be causal. (Indeed the latter assumption is often necessary in these cases.) For similar reasons, it would be difficult to speak of Newtonian mechanics as truly deterministic (or even realist) in most actual cases, which need to be suitably idealized for Newtonian mechanics to do its job. In principle, however, as an idealization, it is a causal and deterministic theory, or can be interpreted as such, while classical statistical theory and chaos theory, are (while causal) not deterministic even as idealizations. In general, it does not follow that either causal or even deterministic theories are realist, since the actual behavior of a system may not be mapped by our description of it, even though we can make exact predictions concerning that behavior. Classical mechanics and chaos theory are, however, also realist insofar as such a mapping is assumed to take place, at least as a good approximation. By contrast, classical statistical physics, or at least the part of it that enables *statistical* predictions concerning the behavior of the systems it describes, is not realist insofar as its equations do not describe the behavior of its ultimate objects, such as molecules of a gas. It is, however, based on the realist assumption of an underlying nonstatistical multiplicity, whose individual members in principle conform to the strictly causal laws of Newtonian physics. The latter assumption becomes no longer possible in quantum mechanics in Bohr's interpretation.

We may expand the denomination "realist" to theories that are approximate in this sense, or further to theories that presuppose an independent reality that cannot be mapped or even approximated but that possess structure and attributes, or properties, in the usual sense. Indeed, realist theories may be described most generally by the presupposition that their objects in principle possess independently existing attributes (such as those conceived by analogy with classical physics) whether we can, in practice or in principle, ever describe or approximate them. Some, understandably, see this latter presupposition as a hallmark of realism.[20]

By contrast, Bohr's interpretation of quantum mechanics is irreducibly nonclassical. It is neither causal, nor deterministic, nor realist in any of the senses described above. The reasons for this are as follows. It is not only that the state of the system at a given point gives us no help in predicting its behavior or in allowing us to assume it to be causally determined, if unpredictable at later points (radical indeterminism and noncausality), but even this state itself cannot, at any point, be unambiguously defined on the model of classical physics (radical nonrealism). That is, the classical or classical-like concept of physical state cannot unambiguously apply.[21] This impossibility arises due to Heisenberg's uncertainty or indeterminacy relations, arguably the defining law of quantum physics, which, accordingly, have, in this interpretation, as much to do with the impossibility of realism as with the lack of causality.

It may be helpful to explain uncertainty relations in Bohr's interpretation, since there is so much confusion about them, especially in the humanities but sometimes even in specialized literature (in part because their meaning is interpretation dependent). In classical physics, the determination of the state of the system at any point—on the basis of our knowledge of it at a given point—is possible for the following reason. We always can, at least in principle, determine both locations and velocities or momenta (including their direction) for objects comprising this system at this point. The equations of classical physics allow us to do the rest. By contrast, in quantum mechanics (now in any interpretation), in view of uncertainty relations, we can measure with unlimited precision (that is, defined by the capacity of our instruments, rather than the nature of quantum physics), or indeed (at least in Bohr's interpretation) determine or unambiguously define either the position or the momentum of a quantum object. In Bohr's interpretation we need to speak, more accurately, of certain parts of a measuring instrument properly correlated with the object in question. We can never simultaneously determine both of these, as they are called, conjugate (the term retained from classical physics) variables. Instead such variables become rigorously complementary in Bohr's sense.

As follows from the above qualifications (concerning the necessity of always considering the measuring instruments correlated with the quantum objects), the situation is actually more complicated even in the case of a single variable. For we cannot, at least in Bohr's interpretation, unambiguously ascribe independent classical-like (or perhaps any) physical attributes to quantum objects. Accordingly, as Bohr argues, uncertainty relations "cannot . . . be interpreted in terms of attributes of objects referring to classical pictures."[22] Thus, uncertainty relations meaningfully apply to the data obtained in measurements resulting from the interactions between the quantum objects and the measuring instruments. They apply to the "indivisible" and always unique or, in Bohr's terms, (irreducibly) "individual" phenomena (using the latter term in the specific sense defined above). According to Bohr, "under [the] circumstances [of quantum mechanics] an essential element of ambiguity is [always] involved in ascribing conventional [and conceivably any] physical attributes to [quantum] objects."[23] This formulation ultimately applies even in the case of a single such attribute under all conditions, rather than only in the case of the joint attribution of complementary variables, more immediately forbidden by uncertainty relations.[24] This is arguably the most radical conception of nonrealism in quantum physics, which at the same time allows and, in Bohr's view, indeed enables one to maintain the rigorously scientific status of quantum theory. The main reason for this situation is, in Bohr's words (recurring throughout his writings), "the *impossibility of any sharp separation between the behavior of atomic [quantum] objects and the interaction with measuring instruments which serve to define the conditions under which the phenomena [i.e. what we actually observe] appear* [Bohr's emphasis]."[25]

From this perspective a more accurate explanation of the meaning of uncertainty relations is as follows. The *data* recorded in certain parts of our measuring instruments, as a result of their interactions with quantum objects, is of the same type as the data resulting from the measurement of classical objects in their interaction with measuring instruments. (In this sense, this macro-level data is "objective" or "realist.") In classical physics, however, we can, at least in principle, always measure both variables in question simultaneously, and indeed disregard or compensate for the interaction between the objects in question and measuring instruments. By contrast, in quantum mechanics we can only measure or, again, unambiguously define either one or the other *variable of that type*, but never both simultaneously. Hence, classical-like determinism is not possible even at this macro-level of measurement, while the *effects* of the interactions between quantum objects and measuring instruments upon the latter can be described in the realist manner. (Any single variable of either type by itself can always be predicted with the probability equal to unity, which, as will be seen, led Einstein to think, and to argue, that something is amiss in quantum theory, that it is perhaps incomplete. Not so, Bohr countered!) In Bohr's view, one can speak only of "variables of that type," rather than attributing them to the quantum object under investigation. Rigorously, such variables can be seen only as defining (in the classical manner) either the positional coordinates of the point registered in some part of the measuring instruments involved or, conversely, a change in momentum of another such part, under the impact of its interaction with the object under investigation. Hence, Bohr argues, in quantum mechanics the interactions between quantum objects and the measuring instruments can never be neglected or compensated for so as to allow us to attribute physical properties to quantum objects themselves in the way this can, at least in principle, be done in classical physics. As Bohr writes, "these circumstances find quantitative expression in Heisenberg's indeterminacy relations which specify the reciprocal latitude for the fixation, in quantum mechanics, of kinematical [position] and dynamical [momentum] variables required for the definition of the state of a system in classical mechanics." He adds a rather striking sentence: "[I]n this context, we are of course not concerned with a restriction as to the accuracy of measurement, but with a limitation of the well-defined application of space-time concepts and dynamical conservation laws, entailed by the necessary distinction between [classical] measuring instruments and atomic [quantum] objects."[26] In this interpretation, there is no presupposition that the quantum-mechanical formalism in any way describes the ("undisturbed") quantum process before the measurement interference takes place, or between instances of such interference. Accordingly, the formalism of quantum mechanics describes only these interactions and their impact on the measuring instruments, rather than the properties, even single properties (if one can still speak of properties here) or the behavior of quantum objects as such. In terms of the corresponding variables of the measuring instruments involved, both variables can never be simultaneously defined. By itself not even a single variable can ever be defined. Even in epistemologically less radical interpretations, the uncertainty relations prevent us, in practice and in principle, from determining or even defining the state of the system in the way we do in classical physics.

"THE TYPICAL QUANTUM EFFECTS"

Arguably the best-known manifestation of complementarity is that associated with the wave and the particle aspects of quantum phenomena. Once properly considered (that is, once we establish what we specifically observe as waves or particles, in what particular circumstances, and so forth), this aspect of quantum physics can be connected to the uncertainty relations, and both to the statistical character of quantum mechanics. These connections are described in most standard accounts of quantum physics, including Bohr's writings cited here. It may be useful to recall the key features of the double-slit experiment—the "archetypal" quantum-mechanical experiment.

The arrangement consists of a source; a diaphragm with a slit (A); at a sufficient distance from it a second diaphragm with two slits (B and C), widely separated; and finally, at a sufficient distance from the second diaphragm a screen (say, a silver bromide photographic plate). A sufficient number (for a full effect it must be very large, say, a million) of elementary particles, such as electrons or photons, are emitted from the source and allowed to pass through both diaphragms and leave their traces on the screen. (I am provisionally speaking for the moment in terms of quantum objects themselves.) A wave-like interference pattern will emerge on the screen, or more accurately, a pattern analogous to the traces that would be left by classical waves in a corresponding media, say, water waves on the sand. That is, the pattern will emerge unless we install particle-counters or make other arrangements that would allow us to check through which of the two slits the particles that hit the screen pass. This pattern is the actual manifestation and, according to Bohr's interpretation, the only possible manifestation of the "wave" character of the quantum world. The pattern would appear whether we deal with what would prior to the advent of quantum physics classically be seen as wave-like phenomena, such as light, or particle-like phenomena, such as electrons. In this interpretation, at least, one can speak of "wave propagation" or of any attributes of the classical-like phenomenon of wave-propagation (either associated with individual particles or with their behavior as a multiplicity) prior to the time when these registered marks appeared only by convention or symbolically, or, again, allegorically. (The same, however, is also true concerning the attributes of classical particle motion, in particular trajectories.) It is also worth keeping in mind that, in accordance with the overall scheme here presented, we see on the screen only classically manifested traces of quantum objects. The objects themselves are destroyed in the process of what Bohr called the "irreversible amplification" of all our encounters with quantum objects to the classical level.[27]

If, however, there are devices allowing us to check through which slit particles pass, the interference pattern inevitably disappears. Its appearance entails the lack of knowledge as to through which slit particles pass. Thus, ironically (such ironies are characteristic of quantum mechanics), the irreducible lack of knowledge, the impossibility of knowing, is associated with the appearance of a pattern and, hence, with a higher rather than lower degree of order, as would be the case in, say, classical statistical physics. (Chaos theory is something else again.) Indeed, this fact of the disappearance of the interference pattern—once we can (even if only in principle) know through which slit each particle passes—can be shown to be strictly correlative to uncertainty relations.

The behavior just described, sometimes also known as the quantum measurement paradox, is indeed remarkable. Other standard characterizations include strange, puzzling, mysterious, and incomprehensible. The reason for this reaction is that, if one speaks in terms of particles themselves (this appears to be the main source of trouble) in the interference picture, the behavior of each particle appears to be "influenced" by the location of the slits. Or, even more radically, the particle appears somehow to "know" whether both slits are or are not open, or whether counting devices are installed or not. The first possibility may appear to imply that each particle would spread into a volume larger than the slit separation or would somehow divide into two and then relocalize or reunite so as to produce a single effect, a point-like trace on the plate. (The distance between slits can be very large relative to the "size" of the particles, thousands of times as large.) This type of view is sometimes found in literature on the subject. However, whether or not one subscribes to the particular interpretation under discussion here, the standard view is more or less as follows. Although having both routes open always leads to the interference effect, once a sufficient number of particles accumulates, any given particle passing through the slits should be seen as an indivisible whole (or, in Bohr's interpretation, the corresponding effects upon the measuring devices are individualized accordingly). There is no evidence that would compel us to conclude otherwise. Placing a detector in the experiment would always confirm this—at the cost of losing the interference pattern, a circumstance that can, as I said, be shown to be equivalent to uncertainty relations. In the so-called delayed choice experiment, we can make alternative arrangements, revealing either the particle-like or the interference pattern, long after the event, while we can never observe any "spreading" or "division" of single particles.

The situation can also be given a statistical interpretation, equally manifesting this apparently inescapable strangeness of the quantum world. I shall follow Anthony J. Leggett's elegant exposition, describing a different but equivalent experiment, in which instead of slits we consider the initial state A, two intermediate states B and C, and then a final state E. (The latter is analogous to the state of a "particle" at the point of its interaction with the screen in the double-slit experiment.) First, we arrange to block the path via state C, but leave the path via state B open. (In this case, we do not attempt to install any additional devices to check directly whether the object has in fact passed through state B.) In a large number (say, again, a million) of trials, we record the number of particles reaching state E. Then we repeat the same number of runs of the experiment, this time blocking the path via B, and leaving the path via C open. Finally, we repeat the experiment again with the same number of runs, now with both paths open. In Leggett's words, "[T]he striking feature of the experimentally observed results is, of course, summarized in the statement that . . . the number reaching E via 'either B or C' appears to be unequal to the sum of the numbers reaching E 'via B' or 'via C.' "[28] The probabilities of the outcomes of individual experiments will be affected accordingly. (In Bohr's interpretation, quantum mechanics predicts these probabilities, and only these probabilities, rather than accounts for the motion of quantum objects themselves in the way classical mechanics does for classical objects.) The situation is equivalent to the emergence of the interference pattern when both slits are open in the double-slit experiment. In particular, in the absence of counters, or in any situation when the interference pattern is found, one cannot assign probabilities to the two alternative "histories" of a "particle" passing through either B or C on its way to the screen. If we do, the above probability sum law would not be obeyed and the conflict with the interference pattern will inevitably emerge, as Bohr stressed on many occasions.[29] One may also put it as follows: we must take into account the possibility of a particle passing through both states B and C (and through both slits in the double-slit experiment), when both are open to it, in calculating the probabilities of the outcomes of such experiments. We cannot, however, assume that either such an event or self-interference physically occurs for any single particle. Leggett concludes,

In the light of this result, it is difficult to avoid the conclusion that each micro-system [i.e., particle] in some sense samples *both* intermediate states B and C. (The only obvious alternative would be to postulate that the ensemble as a whole possesses properties in this respect that are not possessed by its individual members—a postulate which would seem to require a radical revision of assumptions we are accustomed to regard as basic.)

On the other hand, it is perfectly possible to set up a "measurement apparatus" to detect which of the intermediate states (B or C) any particular microsystem [particle] passed through. If we do so, then as we know we will always find a definite result, i.e., each particular microsystem is found to have passed *either* B *or* C; we never find both possibilities simultaneously represented. (Needless to say, under these [different] physical conditions we no longer see any interference between the two processes.) . . . (Clearly, we can read off the result of the measurement only when it has been amplified to a macroscopic [classical] level, e.g. in the form of a pointer position [of measuring instruments].)[30]

The first possibility corresponds to more familiar questions, such as "How do particles know that both slits are open or, conversely, that counters are installed, and modify their behavior accordingly?" The alternative proposed by Leggett would be as remarkable (or intriguing) as any "explanation" of the mysterious behavior of quantum objects. And it is always mysterious and, indeed, impossible, if one tries to think of such objects and their behavior as independent of their interaction with the measuring devices. In sum, any attempt to picture or conceive of this behavior (leading to the effects in question) in the way we do it in classical physics appears to lead to a logical contradiction; or be incompatible with one aspect of experimental evidence or the other; or entail (by classical or any conceivable criteria) strange or mysterious behavior; or require more or less difficult assumptions, as the one described by Leggett; or, as Einstein argued, imply nonlocality, forbidden by relativity. One finds the latter in David Bohm's and other interpretations based on hidden variables.

Bohr, by contrast, sees the situation as revealing the essential ambiguity in ascribing conventional (and perhaps any) physical attributes, such as wave-like or particle-like behavior, to quantum objects themselves or in referring to their independent behavior. As he writes, "To my mind, there is no other alternative than to admit that, in this field of experience, we are dealing with individual [interactive] phenomena and that our possibilities of handling the measuring instruments allow us only to make a choice between the different complementary types of phenomena we want to study."[31] At least, this interpretation allows one to avoid the difficulties and paradoxes just discussed.

In fact, eventually these individual (interactive) phenomena, rather than indivisible quantum objects, the ultimate atoms of nature, become Bohr's interpretation of the quantum "atomicity" (in the original Greek sense of being indivisible any further) of matter, discovered by Planck. By contrast, quantum "objects" themselves are not assigned and, it is argued, cannot be assigned atomicity any more than any other features, properties, and images—such as "wave-like." The phenomena in question are indivisible, first, in the sense that, in the situation of quantum measurement (or any interactions we may have with the quantum world), they are all that we can in principle have and the existence of which can be assigned a classical-like reality. This "invidivisibility" makes it impossible to isolate quantum objects rigorously. Bohr's phenomena are further indivisible in the sense of being unsubdividable. For any attempt at a subdivision of a phenomenon can only produce another indivisible phenomenon or a set of phenomena of the same nature; hence, such an attempt will always retain or reinstate complementarity (rather than allowing a reconstitution of it into a classical-like wholeness). Planck's or, now, Bohr's quantum postulate itself becomes a technological concept, the concept defined through the role of measuring instruments. As Bohr says, "the individuality of the typical quantum effects finds its proper expression in the circumstances that any attempt of subdividing the phenomena will demand a change in the experimental arrangements introducing new possibilities of interaction between [quantum] objects and measuring instruments."[32] Accordingly, in Bohr's interpretation, every event in question in quantum physics is individual in the sense of being unique, singular, unrepeatable, and, in itself, not predictable or, more generally, not comprehended by law, which in quantum mechanics applies only to collective regularities (such as the interference pattern in the double-slit experiment). Quantum atomicity (indivisibility) becomes quantum *individuality* in the ultimate sense of uniqueness of individual quantum events. Quantum "atomicity" appears at the level of the interaction between quantum (micro) objects and classical measuring (macro) instruments, rather than that of quantum objects themselves. From this perspective, the only "atoms" that can be rigorously described by quantum theory are "techno-atoms"—certain indivisible configurations of experimental technology. This circumstance prevents any possibility for quantum objects to appear independently, outside of, in this sense, techno-phenomenological enclosures of specific experiments. We only have access to certain effects of the interaction between quantum objects and measuring instruments upon such enclosures, of which the particular character is determined by these effects. In Bohr's interpretation, quantum mechanics describes such "closed phenomena" and only them, rather than the behavior of quantum objects themselves as the ultimate constituents of nature.[33]

At the (classical) level of phenomena, thus defined, all proper references to the data become "objective," that is, unambiguously defined and unambiguously reportable, and hence not subjective. One may even use the concept of reality (although not causality) in relation to this data, since one deals with the classical physics of measuring instruments. It also follows that "in complementary description all subjectivity is avoided by proper attention to the circumstances [of complementary measurement] required for the well-defined use of elementary concepts."[34]

"PROBABILITIES FOR THE OCCURRENCE OF THE INDIVIDUAL PROCESSES"

Due to complementarity (mutual exclusivity), "in this situation, there could be no question of attempting a causal analysis of [quantum] radiative phenomena [or any phenomena in question in quantum physics], but only, by a combined use of the contrasting [complementary] pictures, to estimate probabilities for the occurrence of the individual radiation processes." Bohr adds,

> However, it is most important to realize that the recourse to probability laws under such circumstances is essentially different in aim from the familiar application of statistical considerations as a practical means of accounting for the properties of mechanical systems of great structural complexity [as in classical statistical physics]. In fact, in quantum physics, we are presented not with intricacies of this kind, but with the inability of the classical frame of concepts to comprise the peculiar feature of indivisibility, or "individuality," characterizing the elementary processes.[35]

I cannot consider the history of the concepts of chance and probability in mathematics, science, and philosophy from the seventeenth century on, even though this and the earlier history of chance (from Democritus on) as well as the history of materiality (in particular atomism) are crucial here, as Bohr points out.[36] Instead, using this history as a background, I shall outline the *nonclassical* character of the quantum-mechanical concept of chance. Although not without its earlier predecessors, this character defines twentieth-century thinking about chance, whether mathematical-scientific (for example, not only in quantum physics but also in post-Darwinian biology and genetics) or philosophical (specifically in Nietzsche, Bataille, Blanchot, Lacan, Deleuze, de Man, and Derrida). It is worthwhile, however, to revisit the *classical* understanding of chance first.

Classically, chance or, more accurately, the appearance of chance is seen as arising from our insufficient (and perhaps, in practice, unavailable) knowledge of a total configuration of forces involved and, hence, of the lawful necessity that is always postulated behind a lawless chance event. If this configuration becomes available, or if it could be made available in principle (it may, again, not ever be available in practice), the chance character of the event would disappear. Chance would reveal itself to be a product of the play of forces that is, in principle, calculable by humans, or at least by God or Geist, as in, among others (but in an especially complex and interesting way), the thinkers Leibniz and Hegel. Most classical mathematical or scientific theories and the classical philosophical view of probability are based on this idea: in practice, we have only partially available, incomplete information about chance events, which are nonetheless determined by, in principle, a complete architecture of necessity behind them. This architecture itself may or may not be seen as ever accessible in full (or even partial) measure. The *presupposition* of its existence is, however, essential for and defines the classical view as causal and, on the definition given earlier, realist. On precisely this point classical reality and classical causality come together; or rather this point (the assumption of the ultimate underlying causal architecture of reality) brings them together.[37]

For example, if we cannot fully (rather than only in terms of probabilities) predict how the dice will fall, or fully explain why a particular outcome has occurred, it is because the sum total of all the factors responsible is, in practice, unavailable to us. These factors may extend from a particular movement of a human (or perhaps divine) hand to minute irregularities in the material makeup of the dice themselves. In principle, however, a throw of dice obeys the laws of classical, Newtonian physics (or else chaos theory, which would change the essence of the point in question). If we knew all such factors, we could predict and explain the outcome exactly by using these laws, which would describe both individual and collective behavior, and correlate them, in accordance with classical physical (or philosophical) laws.[38]

Subtle and complex as they may be, all scientific theories of chance and probability prior to quantum theory and many beyond it, such as chaos theory, and most philosophical theories of chance from the earliest to the latest are of the type just described. They are *classical* or, in the sense explained above, causal. Most of them are also, and, as was just pointed out, often interactively, realist. Combined, two of Alexander Pope's famous utterances, the closing of the Epistle 1 of *An Essay on Man* and his "Proposed Epitaph for Isaac Newton," encapsulate the classical view of chance and law, even though they are not without a few ironies. (Some of them can hardly be seen as unintended on Pope's part.) Pope writes,

> All Nature is but art, unknown to thee;
> All chance, direction, which thou canst not see;
> All discord, harmony not understood;
> All partial evil, universal good:
> And, spite of pride, in erring reason's spite,
> One truth is clear: Whatever IS, is RIGHT.
>
> (*An Essay on Man*, 289–94)

Nature and Nature's laws lay hid in night;
God said, let Newton be! and all was light.
("Proposed Epitaph for Isaac Newton, who died in 1727")

The *nonclassical* understanding of chance is fundamentally different, as should be clear from Bohr's formulation, cited above.[39] Nonclassically, chance, or (classical-like configurations are also allowed within nonclassical theories) nonclassical chance, is irreducible not only in practice (which may be the case classically as well) but also, and most fundamentally, in principle. There is no knowledge, in practice or in principle, that is or ever will be, or could in principle be, available to us and would allow us to eliminate chance and replace it with the picture of necessity behind it. Nor, however, can one postulate such a causal/lawful economy as unknowable (to any being, individual or collective, human or even divine) but existing, in and by itself, outside our engagement with it. This qualification (which, in Bohr's interpretation, entails and results from the suspension of realism at the ultimate level of description) is crucial. For, as I explained above, some forms of the classical understanding of chance allow for and are, indeed, defined by this type of realist assumption. By contrast, nonclassical chance, such as that which we encounter in quantum physics, is not only unexplainable in practice and in principle but is also irreducible in practice and in principle. It is irreducible to any necessity, knowable or unknowable. It is, in David Bohm's words, *irreducibly* lawless.[40]

Quantum theory requires, and depends on, the concept of the individual physical event. The individuality of such events is essential, in the strict sense of being irreducible. It is, in part, this concept that defines quantum mechanics as quantum, even though it has, Bohr argues, to be given a complex (and in particular nonrealist) architecture. This is what Bohr specifically achieves by configuring such events as indissociable from the irreducible interactions between quantum objects and measuring instruments. That is, even this individuality or/as uniqueness appears (in either sense) at the level of phenomena rather than of quantum objects themselves or, more accurately, as it may be called (in opposition to causality) the "efficacity" of individual (or any other) phenomenal effects. This efficacity itself may not tolerate the attribute of individuality, or for that matter chance, any more than any other attribute. While (and in part by virtue of) ultimately suspending the individual identity of quantum objects themselves, the individuality of each quantum phenomenon (in Bohr's sense) remains crucial. At the same time and by the same token, quantum mechanics offers us no laws that would enable us to predict with certainty the outcome of such individual events, or when some of them might occur. In contrast to classical statistical physics, the laws of quantum mechanics rigorously allow for the irreducible individuality, the irreducible "unlawfulness" or "lawlessness" of individual quantum events, even as, similarly (but not identically) to classical statistical physics, they provide a rigorous (statistical) account of the behavior of quantum collectivities. This is why Bohr says that "the recourse to probability laws under such circumstances is essentially different in aim from the familiar application of statistical considerations as practical means of accounting for the properties of mechanical systems of great structural complexity."

"An Essential Ambiguity"

It is, however, in confronting the question of reality that quantum mechanics reaches its most radical nonclassical limits (those of Bohr's interpretation) and becomes the site of the greatest epistemological debate in modern science. As we have seen, Heisenberg's uncertainty relations, arguably the defining quantitative manifestation of the nonclassical nature of quantum mechanics, may be even more about the lack of realism than causality and determinism in quantum physics.[41] The term "unknowability relations" has been suggested as reflecting the situation more accurately.[42] Quantum nonrealism, however, manifests itself across the spectrum of our encounters with the quantum world and the range of quantum theory.

In their famous article arguing for the incompleteness of quantum mechanics, to which Bohr's propositions cited in my epigraph reply, Einstein, Podolsky, and Rosen (EPR) propose the following, apparently rather natural and minimal, criterion of physical reality: "If, *without in any way disturbing a system* [emphasis added], we can predict with certainty the value of a [single] physical quantity [say, the momentum or the position of a "particle"], then there exists an [independent] element of physical reality corresponding to this physical quantity."[43] It may appear that this criterion applies to quantum mechanics as well. Recall that, in view of uncertainty relations, it is only a joint simultaneous determination of two variables involved in the quantum-mechanical physical description, such as "position" and "momentum," that is impossible in quantum mechanics. A determination or prediction of the value of a single variable is always possible, with any degree of precision. Some adjustment of the earlier argument is necessary. For, in contrast to the way the situation was described earlier, such a determination must now take place without "disturbing" the quantum system under investigation by measurement, that is, without first performing a measurement upon it, which is how quantum-mechanical predictions are made in more standard cases. More accurately, one should speak, as Bohr does, of not interfering with this system, since, as we have seen, there is no classical-like or otherwise specifiable (undisturbed) configuration that is disturbed in the process. This can indeed be done for *a single variable* in quantum mechanics in certain cases, such as that considered by EPR. (The fact that this can be done only for a single such variable remains crucial, as it indicates that uncertainty relations still apply in this case.) It is achieved by means of performing measurements on other systems (for example, as in the EPR argument, another particle) that have previously been in an interaction with the system (such as a particle) under investigation. (Here I am speaking conventionally of "particles" rather than, as would be more appropriate and as Bohr does, of "variables involved in the quantum-mechanical physical description.") Indeed, as Bohr argues in his commentaries on the EPR argument, in a certain sense, this is always the case in quantum-mechanical predictions. In any standard situation of quantum measurement, we can predict (in accordance with the uncertainty relations), say, the position of a particle after a preceding measurement took place (and on the basis of this measurement) and hence without interfering with the particle in question. In the EPR situation, which involves two particles, we have a slightly, but not fundamentally, more complicated case. Predictions (limited by uncertainty relations) concerning a given particle are possible on the basis of measurements performed on another particle that has previously been in an interaction with the first particle, but that, at the time of measurement, is in a region spatially separated from the latter. Hence, at the time of determination in question, there is no physical interaction either between the two particles or between any measuring apparatus and one of the two particles in question. This circumstance led some, beginning with Einstein, to conclude that there are some nonlocal connections involved. Einstein famously called them "spooky action at a distance." Bohr did not think that such connections are implied by the circumstances of measurement just described, in part because he saw them as correlative to the EPR criterion of reality, which he argued to be, in fact, inapplicable in quantum mechanics. "According to their criterion," Bohr wrote in his reply, "the authors therefore want to ascribe an element of reality to each of the quantities represented by such variables. Since, moreover, it is a well-known feature of the present formalism of quantum mechanics that it is never possible, in the description of the state of a [quantum-] mechanical system, to attach definite values to both of two canonically conjugate variables, they consequently deem this formalism to be incomplete, and express the belief that a more satisfactory theory can be developed."[44]

I shall not here present EPR's subtle argument and Bohr's equally subtle reply.[45] The key point is this. If one accepts the EPR criterion of reality as applicable in quantum physics, quantum mechanics can indeed be shown to be incomplete, or more accurately (this is, in fact or in effect, what EPR argue) either incomplete or nonlocal, that is, entailing an instantaneous action-at-a-distance, as just indicated.[46] The latter would be in conflict with relativity, which prohibits all such actions and which is an experimentally fully confirmed theory. Accordingly, perhaps the only effective counterargument would be to show that the EPR criterion is ultimately inapplicable in the situation in question in quantum mechanics. Epistemologically this would mean that quantum physics rigorously disallows even the minimal form of realism entailed by the EPR criterion. This is what Bohr argues. Or, again, at least he argues that one can interpret quantum mechanics accordingly, which is sufficient for my purposes here, since it makes a nonclassical view of quantum theory at least viable, even if not inevitable. It is a separate question whether other interpretations of quantum mechanics also allow one to handle these difficulties, which is beyond my scope here. At the very least, it may be argued that Bohr's was the first such interpretation. In any event, in Bohr's view, one cannot unambiguously ascribe, as EPR do in accordance with their criterion of reality, even a single physical attribute (or ultimately even identity) to a quantum object as such—that is, as considered independently of measurement and hence of our interaction with it by means of experimental technologies. As Bohr states at least three times in "Discussion with Einstein," in "the analysis of typical quantum effects," we are faced precisely with "the impossibility" of drawing "any sharp separation between an independent behavior of [quantum] objects and [their] interaction with the measuring instruments."[47] We cannot do so even though we can, in quantum mechanics, predict the outcome of such measurements on the basis of earlier measurements performed on the object in question or on the basis of contemporaneous measurements performed on other objects, which have previously been in interaction with the object in question, as indicated above. Hence, such measurements would not involve the object in question at the time of determination of the variables concerned, which is crucial to EPR.

It is worth keeping in mind the following circumstances of quantum measurements and the following aspects of Bohr's interpretation. Measuring instruments and the observable effects of their interaction with quantum objects are described classically (and thus also in the realist way), although the sum total of these effects cannot be accounted for by means of classical physics, and therefore requires quantum theory. The ultimate nature of this interaction is quantum, however, which makes it in practice uncontrollable (thus disabling the simultaneous exact measurement of both conjugate variables) and, in its quantum aspects, theoretically indescribable. In this latter respect, this interaction is no different from any quantum process, which, in Bohr's interpretation, is never theoretically describable as such; only its effects (upon measuring instruments) are, as Bohr says in the statement just cited. Bohr's customary caution and precision are especially crucial here: "quantum effects" are all that is available to us, never quantum causes. It is the irreducible interaction between quantum objects and measuring instruments that is responsible for the radical (Derrida would say "supplementary") epistemology of quantum effects without quantum causes, or any ultimate causes.[48] The interaction in question cannot be seen as the ultimate cause here, given that its ultimate nature is itself quantum.

Throughout his writing, Bohr stresses this interaction and its irreducible nature, which, he argues, define any phenomena that can be meaningfully considered in quantum physics. These are the circumstances that he has in mind when he says that "under these circumstances an essential element of ambiguity is involved in ascribing [any] conventional physical attributes [single or joint] to quantum objects [themselves]."[49] Given that this interaction is, in fact, irreducible, he is able to argue "a criterion like that proposed by [EPR] contains . . . an essential ambiguity when it is applied to the actual problems with which we are here concerned."[50] For, in view of this interaction, we cannot unambiguously ascribe, again as EPR do in accordance with their criterion, independent properties to quantum objects, ultimately even to a single such property, let alone both complementary ones, or again, at the limit, even independent identity to quantum objects.[51] Thus, "the apparent contradiction [found by EPR] in fact discloses only an essential inadequacy of the customary viewpoint of natural philosophy for a rational account of physical phenomena with which we are concerned in quantum mechanics."[52] Instead, the irreducibility of this interaction "entails the necessity of the final renunciation of the classical ideal of causality and a radical revision of our attitude towards the problem of physical reality," or, again, at least this interpretation of quantum mechanics allows one to effectively reply to the EPR argument.[53] This interpretation of quantum mechanics rigorously limits and redelimits (which is not to say abandons) both causality and reality in the sense of classical physics and of the classical philosophy of nature. Bohr's language here and throughout his works is the language of the disciplinarity of physics, and the language of concern with this disciplinarity.

The preceding summary is hardly adequate to do justice to, or fully to evaluate the merits of both sides of, the argument between Bohr and EPR, or the Bohr-Einstein debate more generally.[54] This is not the aim of, nor is it required for, my argument here, however, which concerns only Bohr's conclusions and the implications of these conclusions for his view of the basic principles of science. To cite these conclusions,

> [T]he argument of [EPR] does not justify their conclusion that quantum-mechanical description [of physical reality?] is essentially incomplete. On the contrary this description, as appears from the preceding discussion [i.e., in Bohr's interpretation], may be characterized as a rational utilization of all possibilities of unambiguous interpretation of measurements, compatible with the finite and uncontrollable interaction between the [quantum] objects and the measuring instruments in the field of quantum theory. In fact, it is only the mutual exclusion [in view of this interaction] of two experimental procedures, permitting the unambiguous definition of complementary physical quantities [such as position and

momentum], which provides room for new physical laws [i.e., the laws of quantum mechanics], the coexistence of which might at first sight appear irreconcilable with the basic principles of science [but is ultimately not]. It is just this entirely new situation as regards the description of physical phenomena, that the notion of *complementarity* [now in Bohr's extended sense] aims at characterizing.[55]

Bohr, intriguingly, omits "reality" here. This omission may have been deliberate, and is certainly telling. The completeness of quantum-mechanical physical description may no longer allow for reality in EPR's sense, that is, an independent physical reality, defined by postulating the existence, on the classical model, of physical properties of objects (or, again, conceivably, such classical-like objects themselves) as independent of their interaction with measuring instruments. Instead, in Bohr's interpretation, quantum-mechanical physical description refers to "phenomena" defined as the overall experimental arrangements within which quantum effects (such as marks left in our measuring devices) manifest themselves.[56] Thus, according to Bohr, the irreducible interaction between quantum objects and measuring instruments, while indeed incompatible with the classical ideals of causality and reality, is by no means incompatible with "the basic principles of science." This compatibility, however, is only possible if one properly interprets what is, in fact, available to an unambiguous account in the entirely "new situation" we encounter in the field of quantum theory, and what this theory actually unambiguously accounts for and how it goes about this accounting.[57] Bohr's interpretation, which rigorously follows this requirement, "may be characterized as a rational utilization of all possibilities of unambiguous interpretation of measurements, compatible with the finite and uncontrollable interaction between the [quantum] objects and the measuring instruments in the field of quantum theory." As such it also "provide[s] room for new physical laws [the laws of quantum physics], the coexistence of which might at first sight appear irreconcilable with the basic principles of science."

Bohr's argument is, thus, as follows: were it not for the irreducibility of "the finite and uncontrollable interaction between the [quantum] objects and the measuring instruments in the field of quantum theory,"

  a. EPR would be right: quantum theory would be incomplete, or else nonlocal (or at least short of an interpretation that ensures both completeness and locality); and
  b. there would be no room for the laws of quantum mechanics as physical laws (the same type of parenthesis as in statement "a" is required).

The laws of quantum mechanics may appear, in particular to EPR, to be "irreconcilable with the basic principles of science." Quantum mechanics, however, accounts for its data as well as any classical theory does for its data, which is what EPR tried, ultimately unsuccessfully, to question. It may, thus, depend on which principles one sees as basic to science, both in general and insofar as such principles can be applied in the case of quantum physics. Bohr argues as follows: if, rather than a conformity with a particular criterion of physical reality, such principles or criteria are the logical consistency of a given theory and its correspondence with the available experimental data, and if a theory can be seen as "exhausting the possibilities of observation," as, according to Bohr, quantum mechanics does within its proper limits and properly interpreted, then he cannot see how Einstein's argumentation could be directed toward demonstrating the inadequacy of quantum mechanics.[58]

"THE BASIC PRINCIPLES OF SCIENCE"

Accordingly, along with the reexamination of the classical ideals of causality and reality necessitated by quantum mechanics, a similar, and indeed parallel and interactive, reexamination of what constitutes the basic principles of science appears to be rigorously necessary. For, on the one hand, the EPR criterion of reality cannot unambiguously apply to the "entirely new situation as regards the description of physical phenomena" in question in quantum mechanics. On the other hand, quantum mechanics itself comprehensively accounts for these phenomena and, hence, is as rigorously scientific as any (classical) mathematical science in every respect (other than causality and reality). Clearly, one needs to (re)consider what the basic principles of science are. This is a crucial point: physics itself, not philosophy, requires this reconsideration, as Heisenberg observes in the passage cited earlier. Indeed, according to Heisenberg, "Bohr was primarily a philosopher, not a physicist, but he understood that natural philosophy in our day and age carries weight only if its every detail can be subjected to the inexorable test of experiment."[59] In the present case, this test may entail the irreducibly nonclassical character of natural philosophy once one considers nature at the quantum level, the level of its ultimate constituents. The basic principles of science must be weighed and, if necessary, adjusted accordingly.

Ironically, however, the basic principles of science (I shall spell them out presently), as seen by Bohr, are in accord with the defining aspects of the project and practice of classical physics, beginning with Galileo, to whom Bohr specifically refers in this context.[60] It is true that Einstein and many others would see certain other (philosophical) principles as equally basic. Accordingly, Bohr's argument concerning quantum mechanics also suggests that the basic principles of science qua science may, at a certain point, come into conflict with those metaphysical principles, however consistent the latter may be with classical physics.

What are the basic principles of science, according to Bohr's view? What would define the science and the discipline (both as a field of study and as a system of governing laws) of physics as, to use Galileo's locution, a (modern) "mathematical science of nature"? There are, as I can see it, more or less four such principles, which are described in the next paragraph. Further qualifications and nuances are necessary, partly in view of the massive recent reconsideration of the nature and the character of scientific knowledge. It may be shown that, in essence, these formulations are consistent with this reconsideration—at its best. The works involved are not without their own problems, sometimes as severe as those of the classical views in question in this reconsideration, with which, at their best, the principles in question can in turn be correlated. At the moment, however, I am more interested in arguably a stronger point, that of the compatibility of nonclassical epistemology even with the basic principles of science as seen from a traditional perspective, or at least with some of these principles, and possibly with the most crucial ones.

1. *The mathematical character of modern physics.* By this I mean the following; and I think, with both Galileo and Bohr, that this is what modern physics most fundamentally is: it is the usage of mathematics as a particular way of offering *convincing* arguments about certain aspects of and certain facts pertaining to the physical world, rather than necessarily mathematically representing the ultimate nature or structure of this world.[61] The latter, as we have seen, is rigorously impossible to do in quantum physics, at least in Bohr's interpretation. This point is crucially implicated in the Bohr-Einstein debate, and there appear to be significant differences in this respect between Galileo's and Newton's project and philosophy of science, or their philosophy of nature itself, as well. For Galileo a science of motion is a construction of convincing mathematical arguments about certain facts and aspects of nature. For Newton, it is a representation of nature, grounded in the classical realist claim that nature possesses a structure that can ultimately (at least by God) be represented mathematically. The latter view in fact defines the attitude, or one might say, ideology of most physicists including many of those who do quantum physics. Exceptions are few.[62]

2. *The principle of consistency.* While these physical theories (or the arguments and interpretations involved) may exceed their mathematical aspects—as may be the case especially in quantum physics—they must also offer logically consistent arguments. In his *The Interpretation of Quantum Mechanics*, Roland Omnès bases his whole interpretation of quantum mechanics around logical consistency.[63] There are important further nuances to this principle as well, which I must bypass here. In any event, these theories must be as logically consistent as anything can be.

3. *The principle of unambiguous communication.* These theories, in their mathematical and nonmathematical aspects alike, must allow, within the practical limits of the functioning of science, for the (sufficiently) unambiguous communication of both the experimental results and theoretical findings involved. This is what Bohr's interpretation of quantum mechanics also "provides room for," in part by virtue of exploring the possibilities of the unambiguous definition of all physical variables and aspects of physical description involved. (The concepts of "unambiguous definition" and "unambiguous communication" become especially crucial for Bohr in the wake of the EPR argument.)

4. *The principle of experimental rigor* (based, at least from Galileo on, on the concept of measurable quantities). These theories must correspond to and, within their limits, exhaust the experimental data they aim to account for, although this data is, of course, itself subject to interpretation. Certainly, in quantum physics, the question of how one interprets its data is as crucial as, and reciprocal with, that of how one interprets quantum theory. Much more is to be said on this point as well (even leaving aside the question of the social construction of theories and related arguments, which would affect the principles of consistency and unambiguous communication as well). The principle itself, however, remains crucial.

Physical laws would then be seen and defined as physical laws in accordance with these principles, which—this is my point—define *both* classical and quantum physics. In order, however, to maintain them rigorously in the case of quantum physics, one must, according to Bohr, accept the radical epistemology of quantum physics. If one does so, however, one must also abandon, at the level of the quantum world, certain other, primarily epistemological and ontological, principles, applicable, alongside the basic principles of science as just outlined, in classical physics. The epistemological radicality of quantum physics becomes, rigorously, the condition of its disciplinarity as physics, and indeed establishes the continuity with classical physics, which would otherwise be broken.[64]

According to this view, the break from classical physics occurs at the level of epistemology, not at that of the character and the practice of physics as a mathematical science or, since, as Heidegger argues, both define each other in science, as a mathematical-experimental science.[65] As I have stressed throughout, classical epistemology is not simply abandoned either. Along with classical science it continues to function within its proper limits and is often part of nonclassical theories as well, which often depend on it. Quantum epistemology itself is, of course, fundamentally and irreducibly reflected in both the specific character of the phenomena observed (unexplainable by means of classical physics) and the mathematical formalism that explains these phenomena. This is why Bohr often speaks of the *epistemological* lesson of quantum mechanics. He rigorously derives his radical epistemology from the mathematical-experimental structure of quantum theory.

The laws of quantum physics are the laws of nature only in the sense of corresponding to the "regularities" that nature allows to our interaction with it, specifically by means of experimental technology. The term is used by Bohr in speaking of "the new types of regularities," which we encounter as effects of the interaction between the ultimate quantum constituents of nature and our measuring technology, and which cannot be accounted for by classical physics.[66] Quantum mechanics, however, does not describe the nature or structure of these ultimate constituents themselves. There is nothing that quantum theory, or in view of its laws, conceivably any theory, can say about these constituents as such. As an epistemologically nonclassical theory, quantum mechanics may be said to represent the interaction between what is representable by classical means (which may indeed be seen as defining representability, accordingly always classical)—here measuring instruments, described by the laws of classical physics (which allows for a realist and causal interpretation)—and what is unrepresentable by any means, classical or nonclassical—here, "quantum objects." This unrepresentable is ultimately unrepresentable even as something that is absolutely unrepresentable, which is, epistemologically, merely a Kantian, things-in-themselves-like, form of classical representation. (The degree to which Kant himself subscribed to this "Kantian" view is a separate question.) The view just presented is generalizable to nonclassical theories elsewhere, and may indeed be seen as defining them.

Otherwise, however, quantum mechanics and Bohr's interpretation of it conform to all traditional principles defining the project and practice of the "mathematical sciences of nature" beginning with Galileo (whose title I cite here). Indeed, as I said, one might argue that, in contrast to Newton, Galileo sees the project of his mathematical sciences of nature, specifically his mathematical science of motion of material bodies, in epistemologically similar terms, as exploring certain regularities in nature and accounting for them by means of mathematical arguments. Of course, Galileo's physics is classical in other respects, in particular as regards causality. Quantum mechanics at the very least allows for, even if not necessitates (it may ultimately do this too), compatibility between "the basic principles of science" and nonclassical epistemology, and was the first theory to do so. One might argue (as Bohr does) that Einstein's relativity would pose some of these questions already and perhaps all of these questions, once all the chips or (we may never have all) more chips are in.

I would argue that the overall situation here described can be extrapolated to a number of figures mentioned earlier, specifically Nietzsche, Heidegger, Bataille, Levinas, Blanchot, Lacan, Deleuze, Derrida, and de Man. This, it may be added, also applies to the relationships between the thought of these thinkers and modern science in its nonclassical aspects. This is why there is a certain, perhaps fundamental, philosophical connection between nonclassical science and nonclassical philosophy. The list of figures in question is, as

I said, not random, and my argument may be more difficult in some of the cases just mentioned (and it will not be applicable at all in still other cases). As in Bohr's case, however, some of the most radical epistemological thinking involves the deepest concerns in regard to the basic principles of their disciplines. Obviously, in some of the cases just mentioned, the disciplinary determination itself—Philosophy? Criticism? Psychoanalysis?—or the determination of the stratifications within, and the interactions among, such fields is extremely difficult. Accordingly, some adjustment of the preceding argument will be necessary, to some degree in contrast with science and especially physics. There at least we have the discipline (in either sense) of mathematics, on the one hand, and of conformity to the experimental data, on the other, however complex these determinations become at certain points, or perhaps, in fact, always are. My argument, however, is that

    a. even in the case of science, nonclassical epistemology is not in conflict with its basic principles—it is or at certain points becomes the conditions of applicability of such principles; and

    b. one encounters what I called earlier the extreme disciplinary conservatism of the thinkers in question—a conservatism that runs contrary to common claims and some appearances, and that arises out of their extreme reluctance to bring a radical change in or shift to nonclassical accounts, which they finally do only at points and in regions where there is really no choice, in the sense that their discipline (in either sense) in fact requires it. Indeed, it appears that in such cases one needs to be both an extreme radical and an extreme conservative, along different lines, and sometimes even the same, or at least interactive and mutually depending, lines.[67]

That both of these facts are commonly overlooked largely accounts for the persistent misunderstanding of the thought of the figures in question, and for the misshapen nature of some of the recent debates in which they figure prominently.

"THE HIGHEST MUSICALITY IN THE SPHERE OF THOUGHT"

Einstein deeply understood this aspect—the simultaneously radical and conservative nature—of Bohr's thought, even though and perhaps because he never accepted his views or quantum mechanics as a way to describe nature. (He did, however, recognize its practical effectiveness.) In 1949, after a quarter of century of their debate, he spoke of some of Bohr's radical (in the present sense) physics as "the highest musicality in the sphere of thought."[68] A very good violin player and an admirer of Haydn, in particular, Einstein wanted and tried to give this music a more classical shape, and urged others to do so. Neither he nor others ever succeeded. Bohr, although, by contrast, a bad piano player, was in every sense a contemporary of Schönberg. Haydn, however, let alone Bach, Mozart, and Beethoven, may be much closer to Schönberg than Einstein thought. This is not merely, or even primarily, a statement about how to perform Haydn's music differently (although it is this, too). Instead this is a statement about Haydn as a classical composer, in either, or neither, sense of this strange, nonclassical word "classical."

NOTES

Epigraph is from Bohr's article, "Can Quantum-Mechanical Description of Physical Reality Be Considered Complete?" in *Quantum Theory and Measurement*, ed. John Archibald Wheeler and Wojciech Hubert Zurek (Princeton: Princeton University Press), 145–51.

1. I cannot here consider Planck's law and its history, or key events following Planck's discovery and leading to quantum mechanics and its interpretation. For arguably the best account of the early stages of this history, see Thomas S. Kuhn's *Black-Body Theory and the Quantum Discontinuity, 1894–1912* (New York: Oxford University Press, 1978). Bohr gives an excellent and conceptually crucial account in his "Discussion with Einstein on Epistemological Problems in Atomic Physics," *The Philosophical Writings of Niels Bohr* (hereafter *PWNB*), 3 vols. (Woodbridge, Conn.: Ox Bow Press, 1987), 2:32–36. Some of Werner Heisenberg's essays, in particular "Development of Concepts in the History of Quantum Mechanics" and "The Beginnings of Quantum Mechanics in Göttingen," both in *Encounters with Einstein* (Princeton: Princeton University Press, 1983), as well as his more technical works, are also exceptionally useful. See also introductory and historical material in volumes 5, 6, and 7 of *Niels Bohr: Collected Works*, 10 vols. (Amsterdam: Elsevier, 1972–96).

2. The latter concepts are not independent of other conventional idealized physical or mathematical attributes. In the case of particles, such attributes would include "position" and "momentum" (in their simultaneous application, no longer possible in quantum mechanics in view of uncertainty relations) or "trajectories of motion" in classical physics (classical-like trajectories are in turn, and indeed correlatively, prohibited in quantum mechanics in most interpretations). In the case of elementary particles of modern quantum physics, such attributes would also include their mathematically point-like (structureless) character, which is the standard and seemingly irreducible idealization in quantum physics. Short of string theories, it appears impossible to treat elementary particles otherwise, even though such "objects" are not seen as likely to exist in nature. Of course, from Newton on, the objects of classical physics, too, are often idealized as (massive) dimensionless material points, and more often the motion of classical objects as that of such points. There, however, this idealization is necessary because of practical complexities, rather than, as in quantum physics, because of the conceptual contradiction of the theoretical model itself. On the other hand, the "size" of the electron was also the problem for the classical electrodynamics (the theory of bodies moving in an electromagnetic field).

3. One can, in fact, consider this situation either in terms of Jacques Derrida's *différance* or in terms of Deleuze's matrix of "difference and repetition," or indeed by combining both—an intriguing, and as yet unexplored, combination in its own right.

4. Paul de Man, *Aesthetic Ideology* (Minneapolis: University of Minnesota Press, 1996), 51.

5. The formulations of both physicists were quickly proven to be mathematically equivalent. They do, however, entail subtle and significant differences in physics and epistemology—questions that remain largely unexplored in the historical and philosophical literature on the subject. The same point can be made concerning other versions of mathematical formalism of quantum mechanics, such as those of Paul Dirac, John von Neumann, and Richard Feynman. The work of other key figures, such as Wolfgang Pauli, Max Born, Pasqual Jordan, and, on the philosophical side, most especially Bohr, was equally crucial in the development of quantum mechanics.

6. Literature dealing with the subject is immense, matched by the number of interpretations of quantum mechanics itself. Already within the cluster of the standard or Copenhagen (or, as it is also called, orthodox) interpretations, to which Bohr's belongs, the range is formidable, even if one restricts oneself to such founding figures as Heisenberg, Born, Pauli, Dirac, von Neumann, and Wigner, in addition to Bohr. Bohr's interpretation itself underwent considerable evolution and refinement, and I here use primarily his later (after 1935) version of complementarity, specifically as explicated in "Discussion with Einstein" and related later works. The two main lines of thought within the Copenhagen cluster are defined by the argument whether or not the formalism of quantum mechanics describes the behavior of quantum objects themselves. The first line follows Dirac's and von Neumann's views; the second, pursued here, Bohr's. It may also be argued that Schrödinger's wave mechanics, too, is epistemologically more conducive to (which is not to say entails) the first view. Heisenberg's is more conducive to (and perhaps entails) the second. Feynman's version is still another story. Dirac's and von Neumann's versions are presented in their seminal works, P.A.M. Dirac, *The Principles of Quantum Mechanics* (Oxford: Clarendon, 1995) and John von Neumann, *Mathematical Foundations of Quantum Mechanics*, trans. Robert T. Beyer (Princeton: Princeton University Press, 1983), both of which are technical, however. The profusion of new interpretations during recent decades was in part motivated by the famous argument of Einstein, Podolsky, and Rosen (EPR), offered in 1935, concerning the incompleteness (or either incompleteness or nonlocality) of quantum theory, to which I shall later return. This profusion may, however, have been triggered by David Bohm's reformulation of the EPR argument in terms of spin and then his hidden-variables version of quantum theory (mathematically different from the standard version), introduced in 1952. This interest in new interpretations received a further impetus from John Bell's theorem (1966) and related findings, and then from Alan Aspect's experiments (around 1980) confirming these findings. Bell's theorem states, roughly, that any classical-like theory (similar to Bohm's) consistent with the statistical data in question in quantum mechanics is bound to involve an instantaneous action-at-a-distance and, hence, violate relativity theory. Bohm's theory does so explicitly, in contrast to the standard quantum mechanics, which does not. There are arguments stating that quantum mechanics does, in fact, involve an instantaneous action-at-a-distance, but these arguments remain at best inconclusive. These developments recentered the debate concerning

quantum mechanics around the question of nonlocality and the so-called quantum correlations, which correlations cannot be explained classically. *Philosophical Consequences of Quantum Theory: Reflections on Bell's Theorem*, ed. James T. Cushing and Ernan McMullin (South Bend, Ind.: Notre Dame University Press, 1989) offers a fairly comprehensive sample of the debates, although it requires some updating. David Mermin's essays on the subject of quantum mechanics in *Boojums All the Way Through* (Cambridge: Cambridge University Press, 1990) is one of the better nontechnical, although demanding, expositions of these subjects. By now, dealing only with nonrelativistic quantum mechanics, the list of interpretations of quantum mechanics includes, among others (and with many variations within each denomination) the many-worlds interpretation; the modal interpretation; the histories interpretation; the relational interpretation; and finally the hidden-variables versions. Among the most recent additions is Mermin's provocative proposal for what he calls "the Ithaca interpretation," which maintains that only statistical correlations between quantum events, not events (correlata) themselves, can be meaningfully considered by quantum theory. See David Mermin, "What Is Quantum Mechanics Trying to Tell Us?" *American Journal of Physics* 66, no. 9 (1998): 753–67, and references there. It may be argued, however, that Bohr's interpretation is at the very least as consistent and comprehensive as any available, albeit to some only unsatisfactorily so because of its radical epistemology. As I shall argue, however, his interpretation not only avoids a conflict with the disciplinarity of physics as science, but enables this disciplinarity. I have considered Bohr and quantum epistemology along the lines followed by this essay in further detail in my following works: *The Knowable and the Unknowable: Modern Science and Nonclassical Thought* (Ann Arbor: University of Michigan Press, 2001); "Reading Bohr," in *Proceedings of the NATO Advanced Research Workshop on "Decoherence and Its Implications for Quantum Computation,"* ed. Antonios Gonis and Patrice Turchy (Dordrecht: Kluwer, 2001); and in "Techno-Atoms: The Ultimate Constituents of Matter and the Technological Constitution of Phenomena in Quantum Physics," *Tekhnema: Journal of Philosophy and Technology* 5 (1999): 36–95; as well as in several earlier works: *Complementarity: Anti-Epistemology after Bohr and Derrida* (Durham: Duke University Press, 1994); "Complementarity, Idealization, and the Limits of Classical Conceptions of Reality," in *Mathematics, Science, and Postclassical Theory*, ed. Barbara H. Smith and Arkady Plotnitsky (Durham: Duke University Press, 1997); and "Landscapes of Sibylline Strangeness: Complementarity, Quantum Measurement, and Classical Physics," in *Metadebates*, ed. G. C. Cornelis, J. P. Van Bendegem, and D. Aerts (Dordrecht: Kluwer, 1998).

7. See Albert Einstein, Boris Podolsky, and Nathan Rosen, "Can Quantum-Mechanical Description of Physical Reality Be Considered Complete?" in *Quantum Theory and Measurement* (hereafter *QTM*), ed. John Archibald Wheeler and Wojciech Hubert Zurek (Princeton: Princeton University Press, 1983), 138–41. Bohr's essay by the same name appears in *QTM* on pages 145–51. (Due to a printing error, the order of pages is reversed in this edition: page 149 should precede page 148.) The exchange led Bohr to significant refinements of his previous version of complementarity, and, as I said, throughout this essay I refer to the post-EPR version.

8. The potential inapplicability of these terms and concepts appears to have prompted Bohr to say in a famous (reported) statement: "There is no quantum

world." The alleged statement appears in Aage Petersen, "The Philosophy of Niels Bohr," *Niels Bohr: A Centenary Volume*, ed. A. P. French and P. J. Kennedy (Cambridge: Harvard University Press, 1985), 305. One must exercise caution in considering such reported statements. It would be very difficult to conclude on the basis of Bohr's written works that he denies the existence of that to which the expression "the quantum world" refers. The statement may be read, especially given the context (the question of whether quantum mechanics actually represents the quantum world), by putting the emphasis on "quantum." Rather than indicating the nonexistence of "quantum" objects, it indicates the inapplicability to the latter of conventional "quantum" attributes—such as discontinuity (of radiation), invisibility (of quanta themselves), or any other physical attributes or, conceivably, any attributes at all; or even "objects," "constituents," and so forth; or of course individuality of quantum objects ("particles") or the wave-like character of quantum processes, once considered independently of observation. At the level of phenomena, certain individuality remains and the existence of the micro-level (that of the ultimate constituents of matter) efficacity of these phenomenal effects remain essential. Both have been at stake in quantum physics ever since Planck. In fact, Planck's law is incompatible with assigning identities to individual particles (or distinguishing them) within quantum-physical multiplicities, which is what makes Planck's and other statistical counting procedures of quantum physics differ from those of classical statistical physics. This statistical configuration is already phenomenologically inconceivable or, in Bohr's language, beyond pictorial visualization—an impossibility, as will be seen, that defines quantum physics for Bohr. This fact has far-reaching consequences in quantum physics, from Planck's law on. On the one hand, the identity in the sense of interchangeability of all particles of a given type (photon, electron, and so forth) is crucial; on the other, the identity also peculiarly manifests itself in the impossibility of assigning particle individual identity in certain situations, perhaps ultimately ever. In quantum field theories, such as quantum electrodynamics (QED), beyond the impossibility of distinguishing individual particles, one can no longer quite speak of the particles of the same type. An investigation of a particular type of quantum object (say, electrons) irreducibly involves other types of particles, conceivably all existing types of particles. This is the main reason why Heisenberg saw Dirac's discovery of anti-particles in 1928–32 (the process was somewhat prolonged), which entails this situation, as one of the greatest discoveries of modern physics, "perhaps the biggest of all the big changes in physics of our century" (*Encounters with Einstein*, 31). According to Heisenberg, quantum field theories push the complexities in question to their arguably most radical available limits, even beyond those of the standard quantum mechanics of Heisenberg and Schrödinger (31–35). The latter is a highly complex and little developed subject, which cannot be addressed here. The circumstances themselves in question, however, are not only consistent with but would reinforce the present argument.

9. I use Bohr's careful language when he points out that "the classical theories do not suffice in accounting for the new types of *regularities* [emphasis added] with which we are concerned in atomic physics" (*QTM*, 150). The classical theories are far from discountable in quantum physics (where they are necessary, for example, in the description of the behavior of the measuring instruments involved), let alone elsewhere.

10. This circumstance poses the question whether the *interpretations* of classical

theories pursued by such investigations are in fact radical or nonclassical, rather than classical readings of both classical and nonclassical theories in question. If (and when) this is the case, the paradox disappears. On the other hand, as has been pointed out (by, among others, Kant), there will always be "savants" who would find something pre-Socratic in anything, provided they are told what to look for. I am saying this not in order to dismiss all such rereadings of old texts via new theories, but to suggest that new theories always entail a precarious balance of (re)reading both the "old" and the "new," and new complexities in deciding which is which.

11. *PWNB*, 2:34.

12. I discuss these issues in *Complementarity* and in *The Knowable and the Unknowable*.

13. *PWNB*, 2:1–2.

14. Werner Heisenberg, *Philosophical Problems of Quantum Physics* (Woodbridge, Conn.: Ox Bow Press, 1979), 13

15. Compare, in particular, Gilles Deleuze and Félix Guattari's *What is Philosophy?* trans. Hugh Tomplinson and Graham Burchell (New York: Columbia University Press, 1993). The philosophical disciplinarity is defined and maintained in their analysis specifically as the invention of new "concepts" in their specific sense of the term. At the same time, however, this form of philosophical disciplinarity also gives uniqueness to each particular case—as posed by Descartes, Leibniz, Kant, Hegel, Nietzsche or, of course, Deleuze, or Deleuze and Guattari.

16. I am also not considering related but different questions of the creation of new disciplines, of paradigm change, and so forth (such as, "the Copernican revolution," for example). There is a large body of well-known literature on these subjects, most famously Kuhn's work and commentaries on it. I must also bypass such cases as those of Marx and Freud, or a number of others, including Foucault, who himself famously commented on the particular disciplinary status of Marx's and Freud's work and Marxism and psychoanalysis in "What Is an Author?" *Language, Counter-Memory, Practice*, ed. Donald F. Bouchard (Ithaca: Cornell University Press, 1977). I also refer readers to my previous commentaries on some of the subjects and figures here mentioned (especially Nietzsche, Bataille, and Derrida) in *Reconfigurations: Critical Theory and General Economy* (Gainesville: University Press of Florida, 1993), 63–112, 149–212; *In the Shadow of Hegel* (Gainesville: University Press of Florida, 1993), 84–95, 97–135, 264–86; *Complementarity*, 225–70; and, on Lacan, in *The Knowable and the Unknowable*.

17. I have considered the latter subject in *Complementarity* and *In the Shadow of Hegel*.

18. I am not saying "Newton's own project," which is subject to a complex interpretation, even though Newton appears to have subscribed to realism and causality.

19. I consider this question in detail in my work *The Knowable and the Unknowable*.

20. Thus Einstein's position belongs to that type of realism rather than to a more naive claim that physical theories should represent independent physical reality as such. The same may be said about the positions of other critics of quantum epistemology, such as Schrödinger, and of many classical figures, beginning with Newton or, more radically, Galileo. Indeed it would be difficult to find exceptions among major figures in the history of physics. Compare Schrödinger's account of the classi-

cal view in terms of *models* of (or approximating) physical reality in juxtaposition to the (nonclassical) view of quantum theory, born, he claims, "of distress," in his famous "cat paradox" paper (1935), "The Present Situation in Quantum Mechanics" (in *QTM*, 151–54). Bohr's argument, however, applies to such more complex views and takes them into account, rather than (as is sometimes claimed by Bohr's critics) only to more naive forms of realism. Indeed it is crucial that Bohr's interpretation also makes this form of realism and, arguably, all conceivable forms of realism inapplicable to his interpretation and possible to "the entirely new situation as regards the description of physical phenomena" that we encounter in the field of quantum theory in general (*QTM*, 148). Discussions of Schrödinger's "cat paradox" are found in many accounts of quantum physics. I have considered it in *Complementarity* (284–85, note 20).

21. There exists the quantum-theoretical concept of state defined via the formalism of quantum theory and specifically the so-called state-vector, the concept bound by the uncertainty relations. The concept of state is more significant within the Dirac/von Neumann paradigm, whereby the formalism of quantum theory is seen as describing the behavior of quantum objects themselves, than in Bohr's, which does not assign physical reality to the state-vector.

22. *PWNB*, 2:73.

23. Ibid., 2:40.

24. I have considered the details of this situation in "Techno-Atoms."

25. *PWNB*, 2:39–40.

26. Ibid., 3:5. Compare to ibid., 2:73.

27. Ibid., 3:3.

28. Anthony J. Leggett, "Experimental Approaches to the Quantum Measurement Paradox," *Foundations of Physics*, 18, no. 9 (1988): 939–52.

29. *QTM*, 146–47; *PWNB*, 2:46–47.

30. Leggett, "Experimental Approaches to the Quantum Measurement Paradox," 940–41.

31. *PWNB*, 2:51.

32. Ibid., 2:39–40.

33. Ibid., 2:73. On quantum "techno-atomicity," see my article "Techno-Atoms."

34. *PWNB*, 3:7.

35. Ibid., 2:34.

36. Ibid., 2:70.

37. The point was well realized by Schrödinger in his analysis of quantum mechanics in the "cat paradox" paper, "The Present Situation in Quantum Mechanics," cited above, which was largely inspired by the EPR argument. In particular, he observes, "If a classical state does not exist at any moment, it can hardly change causally" (154).

38. The situation is more complex in classical statistical physics as well (including in relation to thermodynamics). The classical view even of classical statistical physics (i.e., physics disregarding quantum effects) has been challenged more recently, in particular in the wake of quantum mechanics. I shall bypass these complexities here. If "classical" chance is ultimately only a manifestation, approximation, or perhaps misunderstanding of the ultimately nonclassical nature of the configurations in question in classical statistical physics, so be it. It suffices for the purposes of the present

argument that classical statistical physics appear to allow at least for a classical interpretation. For a relevant commentary see Lawrence Sklar, *Physics and Chance: Philosophical Issues in the Foundations of Statistical Mechanics* (Cambridge: Cambridge University Press, 1998), and references there.

39. *PWNB*, 2:34.

40. David Bohm, *Wholeness and the Implicate Order* (London: Routledge, 1995), 73.

41. Compare to Schrödinger's comment cited in note 20.

42. See Abraham Pais, *Inward Bound: Of Matter and Forces in the Physical World* (Oxford: Oxford University Press, 1986), 262.

43. *QTM*, 138.

44. *QTM*, 145.

45. I offer a detailed analysis of the situation in "Reading Bohr" and in *The Knowable and the Unknowable*.

46. I say "in effect," because "nonlocality" was not the main concern of the article itself, which focused primarily on the incompleteness of quantum mechanics. However, the alternative in question (of quantum mechanics being either incomplete or nonlocal) clearly emerges there, and was the main concern of Einstein at the time and even more so in his subsequent arguments on the subject. As I have indicated, the question of nonlocality is subtle and has been a major issue in recent debates concerning quantum mechanics. There are, as I said, no convincing (or at least widely accepted) arguments that quantum physics itself is nonlocal in the sense of its incompatibility with relativity. It may be argued, in view of Bell's theorem, that the data in question in (and accounted for by) quantum mechanics is incompatible with a theory that is both local and realist (in the same sense that classical physics is). This is a reasonably accepted argument among physicists and philosophers of quantum physics alike, including those who aim to argue for the more general nonlocality of quantum mechanics or the quantum world. In Bohr's interpretation, quantum mechanics is not a realist theory to begin with, and part of Bohr's argument is that this interpretation is fully compatible with relativity and, hence, local.

47. *PWNB*, 2:39–40, 52, 61.

48. Among Derrida's many discussions of "supplementarity," arguably the closest to the present context is that in *Speech and Phenomena*, trans. David Allison (Evanston: Northwestern University Press, 1973), 88–90.

49. *PWNB*, 2:40.

50. *QTM*, 146.

51. The nonlocality part of the EPR-type argument can be readjusted so as to refer only to the outcomes of measurements, rather than to quantum objects, which would lead to the considerations mentioned above. For an excellent discussion, see Mermin's essays on the subject in *Boojums All the Way Through*, 81–185. These considerations would not affect either Bohr's interpretation (including its local character) or the overall argument presented here.

52. *QTM*, 145–46.

53. I omit some intermediate propositions concerning the interactions between quantum objects and measuring instruments. They are important in explaining the reasons for Bohr's argument. However, they are fully consistent with the preceding analysis, presented more in terms of Bohr's later "Discussion with Einstein." While

not a substitute (rather a complement), this later work (1949) may be seen as further qualifying and refining Bohr's argument in his original reply (1935), and appears to be so seen by Bohr (*PWNB* 2:61).

54. The exchange reflects the most profound and subtle aspects of quantum mechanics itself and of Einstein's and Bohr's thought.

55. *QTM*, 148.

56. That, again, is not to say that "the quantum world" or, again, the corresponding (ultimate?) level of the constitution of matter, does not exist, but that the attribution of physical properties, including those of individual identity of particles, or conversely of wave-like substances, may not be possible at that level. Nor, however, would it follow (as some contend) that this suspension of the independently attributable particle identities, such as those of two "particles" in the EPR situation, in fact entails nonlocality. The two-quantum entities (for lack of a better word) involved would still be spatially separate, and, according to Bohr, there is in the EPR case certainly "no question of a mechanical [i.e., physical] disturbance of [one] system under investigation" by our interference with the other quantum system involved in the EPR thought experiment (*QTM*, 148). It is just that we cannot attribute independent physical properties, ultimately, even that of a "particle," to them. Once we assume that we can, as Einstein did, nonlocality indeed appears to follow. So his argument is not logically wrong. His assumption may well be wrong, or at least is not necessary.

57. The essential ambiguity of the EPR criteria, as applied in quantum mechanics, arises precisely from their failure to do so, however subtle and revealing of new aspects and "mysteries" of the quantum it may be. In particular, it is, again, the failure to see that "an essential element of ambiguity is in ascribing conventional physical attributes to [quantum] objects themselves," ultimately each complementary attribute taken by itself or, again, even to seeing such objects as particles (or as waves). This is the same ambiguity.

58. *PWNB*, 2:56–57. While the aforementioned qualifications, especially those concerning nonlocality, must be kept in mind, they would not affect the points made at the moment.

59. Werner Heisenberg, "Quantum Theory and Its Interpretation," in *Niels Bohr: His Life and Work as Seen by His Friends and Colleagues*, ed. Stephan S. Rozental (Amsterdam: North-Holland, 1967), 95.

60. *PWNB*, 3:1.

61. Obviously, an appeal to "convincing arguments" would indicate the complexities mentioned above. However, the core of the present argument concerning the disciplinarity of physics under the radical epistemological conditions in question would be maintained, indeed, I would argue, all the more so once these complexities are taken into account.

62. I refer to a forthcoming article by David Reed and Arkady Plotnitsky, "Discourse, Mathematics, Demonstration and Science in Galileo's *Discourses Concerning Two New Sciences*," *Configurations* (Spring 2001).

63. Roland Omnès, *The Interpretation of Quantum Mechanics* (Princeton: Princeton University Press, 1994). See also his *Understanding Quantum Mechanics* (Princeton: Princeton University Press, 1999).

64. It is true that one can technically practice quantum physics while subscribing to the classical philosophy of nature or of physics, including quantum theory.

65. See Heidegger's *What Is a Thing?* trans. W. B. Barton, Jr., and Vera Deutsch (South Bend, Ind.: Gateway, 1967), 93.

66. *QTM*, 150.

67. As Sylvan S. Schweber argues in his *QED and the Men Who Made It: Dyson, Feynman, Schwinger, and Tomonaga* (Princeton: Princeton University Press, 1994), in the case of quantum electrodynamics (QED), at a certain point in the history of quantum physics, it was the persistence in keeping the existing framework, with incremental modifications, rather than attempts at radically transforming it, that paid off. In the case of QED, it was, ironically, Dirac, its founder, who gave up on his creation and believed that yet another radical transformation, similar to that of the original quantum mechanics in relation to classical physics, would be necessary. Schweber speaks of the "extreme conservatism" of the figures mentioned in his title in this context and in this sense. From the present perspective, the extreme conservatism may apply even when a radical transformation is ultimately at stake. On the other hand, it cannot be seen as necessary in all conditions or at all points, even in science, although virtually all the founders of quantum mechanics appeared to conform to this view at the time of its emergence. We can never be certain what will ultimately pay off. In some respects the creation of modern QED was quite radical as well, particularly in employing rather unorthodox, and indeed mathematically strictly forbidden, techniques in the so-called renormalization procedure, the centerpiece of quantum field theory ever since. So the creators (it was mostly founded by Dirac and several others earlier) or perhaps "saviors" of modern QED, too, were both extreme conservatives and extreme radicals, just as were the founders of quantum mechanics earlier.

68. Albert Einstein, "Reply to Criticisms," *Albert Einstein: Philosopher-Scientist*, ed. Paul Arthur Schilpp (New York: Tudor, 1949), 45–47. It is true that Einstein here refers to Bohr's 1913 theory of the atom, which appeared at the time to hold some promise for a classical resolution, rather than to Bohr's and others' more radical view of the quantum. However, certain nonclassical features were in place in Bohr's work even then. Indeed, Einstein's statement refers precisely to Bohr's ability to do physics under these conditions of extremely uncertain foundations, of which Bohr was himself acutely aware at the time as well.

Part II

DISCIPLINES AND PROFESSIONALISM

CHAPTER 3

How Economics Became a Science:
A Surprising Career
of a Model Discipline

LIAH GREENFELD

THE SOCIAL SCIENCES—sociology, anthropology, political science, psychology, and economics—were the last of today's academic disciplines to acquire their current identity and to constitute themselves "sciences." Their institutionalization as such began late in the nineteenth century, with Germany leading the world in psychology,[1] and the United States, which closely followed Germany's lead in this area, pioneering the induction of the other disciplines into the status of science. In the United States, the establishment of the social sciences occurred simultaneously with, and was in an important way dependent on, the founding of the modern research universities, which replaced the denominational colleges as the pillars of the American system of higher education. The new universities were modeled on the German example, the first of them, Johns Hopkins, founded in 1876, being appropriately referred to as "Göttingen at Baltimore."

At this time the university, which originally—that is, in medieval Europe—was home only to law, medicine, theology, and, sometimes, philosophy, also emerged as the center of training in the natural sciences, first in the United States and then everywhere. In distinction to the social sciences, however, most of which did not exist as "disciplines" in the proper sense of the word—namely as areas of training disciples, and thus as continuous collective enterprises with practitioners engaged, among other things, in the training of the next generation of practitioners—before they were incorporated in the universities, natural sciences had long been professionalized and divided into specialized disciplines. In other words, a recognizable "social role" of the natural scientist,[2] in general, and recognizable social roles of physicists, chemists, biologists, specifically, already existed outside the university. Both the general social role of a social scientist and specialized social roles of sociologists, economists, and political scientists, however, came into being only with their establishment in the universities. Though the logic of their development and further specialization (the emergence of new disciplines) was little affected by their new institutional base, in the twentieth century, i.e., within the framework of the university, the natural sciences became increasingly specialized. In contrast, the social sciences, which broke into their several specialties at the moment of their establishment as research-university disciplines at the turn of the past century, retained their original frameworks during the course of it and, however narrow some of the specialists trained within them, produced no new specialties.

The social careers of the natural sciences, or their careers as specialized social roles, have, on the whole, followed their intellectual development as bodies of knowledge, rather than the other way around. The pattern of this development is captured by the term "progress": we say that scientific knowledge "advances" or "grows" in the sense that every new theory (tested and accepted by the scientific community) provides for more accurate understanding of the area in question; new theories do not simply replace, they supercede and add to the older ones. This progressive development is implied in the "scientific method," or—to use the classic Popperian formulation—the systematic practice of conjectures and refutations.[3] Conjectures in science, as in other spheres of human experience, are products of individual creativity or imagination: they are partly informed by the (necessarily incomplete) knowledge of reality one seeks to understand, but may be prompted by a myriad of unconnected stimuli. It is not in depending less on imagination that science differs from other intellectual endeavors, but only in that it methodically subjects products of scientists' imagination to the test of evidence. The nature of evidence varies across sciences, and the manner of data collection and analysis, therefore, varies too. What is appropriate in physics may not be appropriate in biology or sciences dealing with a reality different from both the provinces of physics and biology, as in the study of culture, for instance. The nature of empirical reality to which the scientific method is applied, however, while it affects the specific procedures followed in different sciences, does not at all affect the logic of the method in them and does not make any of them more or less "scientific" than the rest.

In its turn, the scientific method of conjectures and refutations is necessitated by the goal or orientation of the scientific activity as such, the central value around which the social institution of science is organized—the understanding of, in the sense of discovering regularities in, empirical reality—and thus by the social structure of science as an organized activity. The knowledge that is integrated into the cumulative scientific tradition is a function of the questions asked, the imagination of scientists trying to answer them, and the nature of evidence. The first two of these factors are open to external social influence and may reflect social demand, though more often they reflect only lacunae in the existing knowledge—the elements of empirical reality that the tradition in its present state leaves out or that are inconsistent with it. The nature of evidence (in distinction to its scope, which depends on the questions), however, is independent both of the state of scientific knowledge and the social environment; it serves as a constant corrective to the flights of scientific imagination, whatever the inspiration behind it. The dependence of science on evidence reinforces the inner logic of the scientific tradition that reflects its social structure. The accumulation or persistence of evidence inconsistent with existing theories—what Thomas Kuhn names "anomalies"[4]—leads to the creation of new theories capable of accounting for it. In rare cases of dramatic failure (on the part of the existing knowledge), it can lead to a paradigm shift—a radical reinterpretation of the nature of the problem (of the perspective and the needed approach)—and the establishment of a new tradition and scientific (sub)discipline.

The mechanism responsible for scientific development in general and for the emergence of new theories and specialties in science is psychological. It has to do with the dissatisfaction with the scientific tradition and its failure to do justice to its subject matter, and represents sensitivity to a species of inconsistency. Being directly related to the fundamental orientation of scientific activity, it is inherent in the social structure of science. External social factors play a greater role in the case of progress through specialization and paradigm shift than they do in "normal" scientific growth within existing social and intellectual frameworks,[5] stimulating unexpected conjectures and focusing attention on previously neglected areas of reality. Certain external social factors, such as demands and perceived opportunities for creation of new social positions and identities may, in fact, be necessary for the emergence of new social roles (thus disciplinary specialization) in science. Such external conditioning of new scientific disciplines is captured in the concept of "role-hybridization," developed by Joseph Ben-David.[6] But even in cases of disciplinary subdivision and the emergence of new social roles, social factors external to science come into play only after the general direction of research—the sort of questions to be asked—is already suggested by the scientific tradition, and are allowed to exert their influence only if this influence is consistent with evidence. An intellectual development alone, without external social factors contributing to role-hybridization, might not create a new field of study; the causes of its creation will, nonetheless and invariably, be found in the inner logic of this development. It is this autonomy of scientific tradition vis-à-vis its social environment that makes science radically different from other forms of knowledge. The source of this difference is the social structure of science—in the first place the fundamental goal or orientation of scientific activity, which dictates its method of conjectures and refutations, and thereby imposes on the institution a far greater degree of isolation than do the social structures of other intellectual pursuits and academic disciplines. Not only does this make the institution of science impervious to social demands, however much they may sway its individual members, and justify the claim of scientific knowledge to objectivity, but it also presupposes the unique, directed and cumulative, pattern of development reflected in the idea of "progress."

Interestingly, the careers of the social sciences have consistently deviated from this characteristic and necessary pattern. In them, intellectual development has followed upon the establishment of new roles, with disciplines emerging for reasons of social—rather than intellectual—interest. None demonstrates this better than economics—the model social science that, owing to the fame of its particularly rigorous methods, enjoys the highest prestige among its sister disciplines, and one that can reasonably lay claim to a tradition of its own at least as long as that of biology.

THE FRENCH PARENTAGE OF THE ECONOMIC TRADITION

It was in France that the concepts of an "economy," as a system of relations pertaining to the use and allocation of a polity's material resources, and of "economics," as a body of knowledge focused on such use and allocation, were born. The first represented an extension of the Greek term for "household" to all of France, which, in the light of the burgeoning absolutism of the early seventeenth century, when the concept was invented, could be—and was—perceived as a royal household. The second, which, obviously, drew on the increasingly common usage of the first, was the name of the teaching, chosen in the mid-eighteenth century by the first school, or group of intellectuals (it was too small to be called a movement), to dedicate itself to professing the subject. With the appearance of the term "economy," an "economic" tradition properly so called was born; and with "Économistes," economics as a discipline.

Two people were responsible for bringing the notion of "economy" as we know it into the world: Sully, the trusted minister of Henry IV, who entitled his treatise on royal administration *Oeconomies royales*; and a picturesque adventurer of the type popularized by the great Alexandre Dumas, Antoine de Montchrétien, who, in 1615, dedicated to the minor Louis XIII and the Queen Regent his *Traicté de l'Économie politique*. The emphasis in both texts was on administration, and both reflected the late-medieval conception of economic reality—based on the idea that the world was created with a certain, finite, amount of wealth (sufficient, under wise management, for the subsistence of humankind) that could not be increased—and which equated wealth with money, specifically coin. They also reflected the managerial spirit that was to become characteristic of absolutist (later, authoritarian) regimes, regarding the prince (later, the head of state) as the natural CEO of the domain/household entrusted to his care. Montchrétien added to this the *mercantilist* concern for *national* (both *avant le nom*) prestige, and insisted on self-sufficiency and competitiveness. It is, indeed, the precocious mercantilism and nationalism, signaled in the substitution of "political" for "royal," not the use of the word "economy," which make his title appear striking in the historical context.

The eighteenth-century "Économistes," despite the adoption of the maxim "*laissez faire*," had no quarrel with the managerial emphasis of the early absolutist bureaucrats. François Quesnay, the founding father of the discipline of economics (which he had to bring up as a single parent, for the rest of the group considered themselves his disciples and devoted their efforts to the interpretation and propagation of his ideas), expressly wrote his *Tableau Œconomique* for the edification of Louis XV and undoubtedly, like Sully and Montchrétien, saw economics as a science, or rather an art, of royal administration. At the same time, the school redefined the nature of wealth, posing agriculture, whose fruits directly satisfied humans' natural needs, as the only "productive" sector of the economy, for only it produced wealth that was "real." (The Économistes' other name, "Physiocrats," reflected this natural bias.) Manufacture, or industry, was defined as "sterile" activity; the school disregarded it. And in so far as the Économistes were violently opposed to commerce, whose only contribution to the public wealth was money, which was inedible and which nobody, in fact, needed, they were clearly antimercantilist and in this sided with their contemporary Adam Smith.

Smith was not an economist, but a moral philosopher, and never used the new-fangled French terms in his great treatise on economic matters, which he saw as a contribution to the ongoing philosophical debate. He acknowledged the Économistes as fellow travelers, but believed that he and they parted ways almost as soon as the two respective journeys began. In a short chapter in *The Wealth of Nations*, he referred to their "agricultural system" (or theory), commending its authors for what he saw as their disinterested concern for general welfare, but dismissed it as a plaything of a small sect of intellectuals that has "never been adopted by any nation [and] never has done, [nor was likely to] do any harm in any part of the world."[7] In the body of knowledge comprising modern economics, which now claims Smith, however innocent of such designs, as its founding father, Quesnay and his followers occupy a modest place, as do Sully and Montchrétien. Such neglect is, on the whole, justified. Altogether the French contribution to the emerging economic tradition and discipline was limited, as that of many a famous social scientist nowadays, to the invention of a few good titles and catchphrases, and in the history of economics, at least in the long run, the common notion to the effect that a good title is worth a good book finds no support whatsoever.

THE GERMAN FORMATION OF ECONOMICS
AS AN ACADEMIC DISCIPLINE

Having acquired its name in France, economics moved to Germany to become an academic discipline. Fortunately for the reader, Smith was not familiar with this development, for he would be able neither to discuss German economic thought with a similar economy of space, nor, probably, write his book at all, for all his time would have been spent on reading the German literature, which by the late eighteenth century could have filled libraries. German "economics" developed as a part of the "administrative sciences" or *Kameralwissenschaften* (so called from *Kammer*—the political cabinet of the prince). The economy was conceived of clearly, more so than in France, as a dimension of political reality and as a matter of policy. The idea that it was such a matter derived from two sources: one theoretical, or, rather, doctrinal, the other empirical. Already Erasmus, in the *Institute of a Christian Prince*, which he dedicated to a fellow Hollander, Charles Habsburg, who happened to be the German Emperor, included care and regulation of his subjects' material welfare among the responsibilities of an ideal prince, defined as a *pater familii* on a large scale. German Reformers offered the same paternalistic ideal to territorial princes, who were busy dismembering the Empire. The tone of their practical advice was mercantilist—and managerial—and economic life was placed firmly under princely control.[8]

The empirical factors that drew attention to economic questions came into play later and had to do with the growing fiscal needs of the territorial states, and in particular the military expenditure in Prussia, which in the late seventeenth and the eighteenth centuries was increasing dramatically. As in many other areas of German history and thought, which it was beginning to dominate, Prussia provided the most conspicuous example of emerging economic attitudes, and put them in bolder relief than other German principalities, but the approach was characteristic of all the lands and can be discussed as a general phenomenon.[9]

Economic vitality assumed importance as a means to traditional ends of dynastic government: glory and power, which "presuppose[d] an increasing population and flourishing manufactures."[10] Frederick the Great wrote in *Anti-Machiavel*, "The might of a state does not at all consist in the extent of its lands, nor in the possession of vast wastes or immense deserts, but in the wealth of its inhabitants and in their number. The interest of a prince is thus to populate a country, to make it flourish."[11]

The first works by German authors that addressed economic subjects essentially belabored this theme, providing rationalizations for the inclusion of the economy among the concerns of the ruler and functions of government. The way they went about it reinforced the original managerial aspect

of economic discourse and was to leave a profound imprint on the character
of German economic culture. Since the economy was a new field of interest
and the discussion of it broke new intellectual ground, the first thing to do, if
one wished to be systematic, was to define it, which they did by literally
translating *"oeconomia"* from Greek into German—*Haushaltung*, "keeping
house." In contrast to the first French economists, who adopted a translitera-
tion of the Greek word and used the original Aristotelian concept only as a
metaphor or a simile, the German authors thus carried the original meaning
of the Greek term over and actually identified (rather than compared for
heuristic purposes) the head of a state with the head of a family.

This conception gave rise to the so-called *Hausväterliteratur* (the *pater-
familii* literature), which flourished in the late seventeenth and early eighteenth centuries. Its "high point"—the primitive stage of German mercantilism or Cameralism—is considered to be the 1682 work by von Hohberg,
Georgica curiosa, which he opened with a declaration that *Wirtschaft* or
"Oeconomia is nothing else than a prudent carefulness to happily conduct a
Hauswirtschaft, to direct and to maintain." The German word was chosen
advisedly, the root, *Wirt*, denoting a private or public housekeeper, and the
original meaning of the derivative *Wirtschaft* being a "public house" or inn.[12]
Three things were necessary to run the *Wirtschaft* properly: God's blessing,
"without which nothing of use or good can be done"; and a *Hausvater* who
would (a) know his resources and (b) have good managerial skills, including
"people skills." Some works in this genre were general housekeeping manuals, including house plans, disquisitions on agriculture, and even medical
and culinary advice. But, on the whole, it represented a genre of political
theory, since the ideal *pater familii* to whom this literature was addressed
was the prince. "The ruler," wrote one author, "is in fact the same as a
Hausvater, and his subjects are, in respect of their having to be ruled, his
children."[13]

The subjects *had to be* ruled, but this was done for their own good, and
implied mutual responsibilities on the part of the ruler and the ruled. The
problem with the subjects was that they had various material needs, which
had to be satisfied if they were to be made useful for the prince, but lacked
sufficient acumen and integrity to satisfy these needs on their own. The
needs were determined by each one's social position, or *Stand*, though,
apparently, some people were unaware of this and desired what they did not
need. The state of satisfaction of socially appropriate (*ständmassig*) needs
was called "happiness." The furtherance of popular happiness was the
responsibility of the ruler by default, because it could not be left to the
devices of lesser persons. Happiness was a social, rather than an individual,
condition—the term denoted as much a good order as an experience of well-
being—and thus, given the unreliability of human nature in general, it
depended on regulation. To achieve happiness, people had to be managed—

and such management was government. It was only just that in return for the invaluable contribution the prince made to his subjects' happiness, they were expected to provide him with a sufficient tax base and, in general, the material means for the realization of his goals: the internal and external strength of the state.

In the first decades of the eighteenth century the *Hausväterliteratur*, whose authors were, by and large, administrators, was taken over by academics, and consequently replaced by a closely related genre, the focus of which was, however, on the need and means to train future administrators for the service in the prince's Kammer. This literature, which made "Cameral Sciences" an academic discipline, argued for the desirability of the state's having professors able to contribute to or teach it; it was implicitly self-promoting, which may explain the growing interest in the subject in academic circles, reflected in the increasing production of publications. In their attempt to persuade their audience—that is, territorial rulers—of the merits of their position, these Cameralists proposed several new definitions of economics which significantly added to its importance as an area of discourse. It was claimed that "the science of Oeconomie is essential to the Cammer, thus the teachings of Oeconomie is the genuine and proper founding principle upon which the whole state, from the highest to the lowest, rests,"[14] which, in effect, implied that economics was the foundation, rather than one aspect, of politics. The ideal Cameralist or state official, accordingly, was defined as "an experienced, good and prudent Oeconomus or householder."

The ideal-typical economic actor envisioned by German Cameralists was a theoretician, rather than a practical man of affairs. This was, among other things, related to the fact that, throughout this period (and all of the eighteenth century), the economy, which was discussed, remained very much an area of discourse, and not of activity. One author after another proposed a plan for a course of its study, defining it this way and that; its relation to better established areas of specialization was examined, and sometimes to ones that were as novel and unformed, as well as the profound question whether it represented a science or an art. It was eventually agreed that economics was a science,[15] that it was a *political* science with a focus slightly different from that of, for instance, *Polizei*, the nature of which, however, was unclear. As described by one of the exponents of economic science, Dithmar, "Police Science deals with Policey affairs, but what is understood by this is not agreed by all, in that some range under this only food, drink and human clothing, others, however, far extending it and opposing it to the judiciary." Another author suggested that the new discipline should focus in the first place on acquisition and production of goods, concerning itself also with administration.

In 1744 there already was a General Economic Dictionary, *Allgemeines*

Oeconomisches Lexicon, compiled by G. H. Zincke. It contained baffling entries of the sort:

> To pursue the business of subsistence [or nourishment, sustenance—*Nahrung-Geschäfte*] with property, or to use the same is called *wirtschaften* [to engage in economic activity?]. When however a property is prudently employed with application and labor, such that not only the necessities and comforts of physical life . . . but also wealth are adequate . . . then this is called *gut wirtschaften* [to engage in economic activity well?].

Or:

> *The art of householding or the art of keeping house*, oeconomy, oeconomic science, is a practical science, wherein the wisdom, prudence and art of nearly all learned sciences are applied to the end of the rightful concern for the business of subsistence or householding [*Nahrung-oder Wirtschafts Geschäfte*] so that one can recognize the true nature and condition of on the one hand in general the objects, purposes and specific conduct of such affairs, on the other the assistants, tools and advantages, partly the therein included affairs of subsistence.[16]

The consultation of the *General Lexicon* was certain to leave the reader thoroughly bewildered in regard to every particular point but one: the exceptional importance of the mysterious discipline of economics, the beneficiary as it was of the wisdom of all the learned sciences. And both, the bewilderment in regard to particulars and the realization of the significance of the matter under consideraton in general, could stimulate the desire for further study, and thus further the immediate goal pursued by the would-be economists penning these cumbersome works—the establishment of professorships in the new field they attempted to define.

Their efforts were crowned with success. Already in 1727, Friedrich Wilhelm I issued a decree to the effect that Simon Peter Gasser, who had impressed the king with his work in the administration, be appointed to a new chair in "Oeconomie, Policey and Cammeralsachen" at the University of Halle. Gasser assumed his newly established post and taught in the area of his expertise, namely on "buildings, cattle, fields, milling, duties and taxation, forestry and hunting." In the following years, more and more German universities created programs in Cameral studies, and increasing numbers of professors, from jurists and historians to specialists in veterinary medicine, crossed over into the new field and taught—among other things—what today we would call "business administration" and what they increasingly referred to as *Staatswirtschaft*, or "state economy." With the discipline thus officially recognized and accorded a definite position within the existing structure, it was time to pay closer attention to its contents, which was promptly done, with the Cameralist paradigm (if one may say so) firmly in place by the middle decades of the century.

This paradigm was chiefly the work of two men: Johann Heinrich Gottlob von Justi and Joseph von Sonnenfels. It is agreed that Justi was responsible for the introduction of the concept *Staatswirtschaft* into general academic discourse, when he made it the title of his authoritative statement of Cameralist principles. The book, which, together with Sonnenfels's later work, was to achieve canonical status, according to Tribe, first appeared in 1755 and ran to 1245 pages. In the preface to the second, "augmented" edition, which was published in 1758, after the first one sold out, Justi explained that he tried to keep the original text short, so that it could be used as a textbook. Sonnenfels's book, the 1765 *Principles of Police, Commercial and Financial Science*, was also conceived as a textbook, judged necessary for the reason of the lengthiness of Justi's respected opus, and therefore, exceeded the latter in the number of pages.

As could be expected, the treatment of a nonexisting body of doctrine at such length resulted in "a phenomenon of unwavering repetition,"[17] but did wonders for it: when Justi and Sonnenfels were done, the murky principles of Cameralism were clear as glass. Cameralism was identified with economics, which was a political science concerned with government or management of material resources. "We call the sciences dedicated to the government of a state the economic as well as Cameralistic sciences," wrote Justi in *Staatswirtschaft*,

> or [to preclude all confusion] the economic and Cameralistic sciences. Economics or *Haushaltungskunst* [the art of keeping house] has for its aim to teach how the means of private persons are to be preserved, increased and reasonably applied. What economics attempts to do in connection with the goods of private persons, the governmental sciences aim to do in the case of the total means of the state. Hence they properly bear the name of the economic sciences. We give them the name Cameralistic sciences, however, because the high Collegia which the sovereigns have established, to manage the preservation, expansion and use of the means of the commonweal, are usually called Cammern or Cammercollegia.[18]

"All the affairs of a state," he reiterated later,

> may be included under two main headings: they all aim either at maintaining and increasing the wealth of the state, or using and managing it wisely. Hence arise naturally the two main divisions of all the sciences devoted to the government of the state. In the first division we have to consider accordingly the business of maintaining and increasing the wealth and power of the state and the ways and means concerned with this. The principles and rules for this are contained in political science [*Staatskunst*], in the science of commercial policies, and in economy, or household management; for all these sciences have no other aim than to make clear the principles according to which the wealth of the state can either be maintained or increased.[19]

The wealth of the state was, at the same time, its strength, which, Justi declared—anticipating, as it happens, the argument recently proposed by Francis Fukuyama—"consists principally in common trust and love, which a wise ruler and happy subjects of a considerable state have for each other, so that the property of the state can be continually maintained and increased with united powers."[20] The trust and love on the part of the subjects, however, appeared to be a mere flourish of speech, for they were obliged to put their shoulders to the common effort and could not withhold their assistance, even if they mistrusted and disliked the ruler, because they—and their powers—were considered property of the state.[21] "*Guten Wirtschaft*," that is, "the proper use" of their powers and property, was a duty of the subjects, for otherwise, as Justi claimed, "they would be useless inhabitants, and incapable of paying their dues to the state."[22]

Of course, the "ultimate purpose" of the state, and of the subjects' obligation to render themselves economically useful, was the subjects' happiness. But Justi dispelled any hedonistic illusions one might harbor in its regard by ruling, "I understand here by happiness of the subjects the good order and condition of a state such that each is able, by his own efforts, to attain those moral and temporal goods which are necessary for a pleasant life according to his respective *Stand*." In fact, maintaining the various *Stände* in their "requisite relationship" was one of the primary duties of the state. Since wealth could be enjoyed only in peace, the prince had to see to that it prevailed and that the state was secure from external attack and at peace within its borders. Internal security—the focus of *Polizei*—referred precisely to keeping everyone, in every respect, in one's place; it involved the regulation of the moral and religious life of the subjects, as well as of their outward conduct, including fashion and diet. This definition of the purpose of the state economy as the maintenance of the established social order, with material demand held constant by the norms governing consumption in each class, presupposed a fundamentally static conception of the economic process. *Staatswirtschaft* was not supposed to be a growing economy.

On the whole, the German vision of economic reality was still conventionally and contentedly mercantilist, when in France Physiocracy had already replaced mercantilism as the dominant mode of economic thinking, and in Glasgow Adam Smith had already conceived *The Wealth of Nations*.[23] Nevertheless, the first German translation of the book appeared in Leipzig in 1776, the very year it was published in Britain. In March 1777, it was already reviewed. The reviewer, a professor of philosophy at Göttingen, J.G.H. Feder, considered Smith's work "a classic; very estimable both for its thorough, not too limited, often far-sighted political philosophy, and for the numerous, frequently discoursive historical notes." But he found problems with the "free trade" argument. "Too great competition" inside a country, he thought, was bound to produce shoddy goods and deceptions. As to international trade, the claim was "valid only at a certain stage of industry, wealth and enlightenment" and could not "be incorporated in the universal principles of state."[24] Thus the very first published assessment of Adam Smith's economic ideas in Germany sounded the note of historicism that, in the nineteenth century, would become characteristic of "scientific nationalism" in particular and of German economics in general. Skepticism in regard to individual freedom reflected the distrust of the (common) individual's intellectual and moral capacities, a distrust that underlay *Hausväterliteratur* and permeated German mercantilism, thus anticipating the later developments in economic thought, which were informed by the new, national sentiment and would reinforce this old attitude.

In 1792, a disciple of Feder, Georg Sartorius, taught Smith's doctrine in Göttingen as part of his curriculum in history. Four years later he published an exegetical *Handbook of State Economy*, based on his lecture notes, faithfully presenting Smith's arguments, but criticizing his ideas "on the unconditional application of the principle of free disposal of industry and capital, on the harmony of individual and social interests, on productive and unproductive labor, on taxes, and on certain other points," namely on virtually everything that was new in Smith's work, distinguishing it sharply from Cameralist/mercantilist orthodoxy.[25]

A colleague of Sartorius at the University of Königsberg, Christian Jakob Kraus, was upset by the publication of the *Handbook* and disputed the priority of the Göttingen historian in alerting the new generation to Smith's importance. Himself a professor of Practical Philosophy and Cameralia, Kraus was a man of extraordinary range of interests (besides state economy and practical philosophy, his courses at Königsberg included ones on Greek classics, history, mathematics, and Shakespeare) and of peculiar intellectual abilities, buttressed by an exceptional capacity for learning by rote. Intrigued by English literature, he undertook in 1776 to master the language, and, according to his biographer Voigt, accomplished this, starting from scratch, by memorizing Bailey's *Dictionary*. In 1777, his English was good enough to allow him to publish the translation of Young's *Political Arithmetic*, of which, however, he understood so little that, piqued, he then decided to turn to a systematic study of political economy. Apparently, understanding was Kraus's weak spot, perhaps because his intellect was overpowered by all the information he forced it to process (a problem that has become quite widespread in our own day and may be familiar). A later critic, a certain Kühn, wrote unamiably in 1902,

> Kraus . . . was not capable of expressing a single thought without immediate
> recourse to an authority . . . a scholar of reputation was not only incapable of
> intellectual production or even of outlining of ideas, but . . . had exceptional

difficulty in detecting something certain and correct in the range of opinions and counteropinions before him.[26]

But Kraus was a great teacher—at the time only Kant surpassed him in popularity at Königsberg[27]—and, more importantly, he had great students, who were to become Prussia's leaders during the period of its reforms. Already in 1795, one of them, von Schroetter, now a Minister of the Provincial Department of Old Prussia and New East Prussia, decided that Kraus should certify everyone entering the civil service in positions requiring expertise in economic matters.

Another former student and friend of Kraus, von Auerswald, published two posthumous collections of his notes, one on the subject of *Staatswirtschaft*, in five volumes, the other, a miscellany, in eight. The first four tomes of *Staatswirtschaft* had to do with Smith and represented, essentially, a compilation of paraphrases—and often verbatim quotations—from *The Wealth of Nations*. There was little rethinking and even less critical interpretation. Smith was allowed to speak to his German audience almost directly. The fact that he spoke through a teacher held by his students in reverence could only make Smith's arguments more compelling, especially since it is likely that Kraus would from time to time add his own voice to that of the great author, whose vicar he was, to emphasize the importance of the teaching. Kraus's opinion was that "the world has seen no more important book than that of Adam Smith; certainly since the times of the New Testament no writing has had more beneficial results than this will have, when it has become better known and has penetrated further into the minds of all who have to do with matters of state economy," a deeper study of which "for us Prussians of today is more necessary than ever." He thus both compared *The Wealth of Nations* to the word of God and stressed its patriotic significance. *Smithianismus*, a cult of Smith that existed among German state economists in the last years of the eighteenth century and first decades of the nineteenth, was a natural response to such encomiums.

Of course, *Smithianismus* had other sources as well. In his detailed study of the academic economic discourse in Germany during the century between 1750 and 1850, Tribe stresses the importance of the reinterpretation of the notion of Natural Law, and specifically of Kant's Critical Philosophy, in making Cameralists receptive to the liberal ideas of Adam Smith and preparing the ground for the transformation of the Cameralist *Staatswirtschaft* into the tellingly christened *Nationaloekonomie*.[28] There is no doubt that these intellectual developments, with their emphasis on the properties and capacities of the individual human being, the needs and reason, which were independent of one's social position, were of great moment. They reinforced, and to a certain extent reflected, a far more general phenomenon—the penetration into the wide sectors of the German public (if not yet the population in its entirety) of the idea of the nation. The idea of the nation transformed the image of social order that was, among other things, the foundation of the concept of *Staatswirtschaft*—it was no longer possible to conceive of the economy as a grand "house," passively awaiting the cares of the princely *pater familii*. The polity, the society, was no longer conceived of in terms of territory; it was a living, natural entity (which in its German interpretation would soon be reified and emerge as a collective individual), an animate, pulsating mass of natural energies, not somebody's inert possession. Economics, as an area of discourse, was reconceptualized as the study of these natural energies, and the concern with *Haushaltung*, with management and managers, necessarily receded into the background. It became possible to conceive of the drawbacks of excessive control and the advantages of letting nature regulate itself. This was the premise of Wilhelm von Humboldt's *Limits of State Action*. But it is important to realize that the individual was validated as the vessel for the self-expression and self-realization of the nation only: he (at the time, only one gender was believed to be politically, socially, or economically relevant) carried its energies in much the same way the vessels of an organism carry blood, and had no independent significance. The regulation of the economy by the state was harmful to the extent that it sapped these national energies by preventing their materialization; if it helped to tap them, it was all right.

Nevertheless, the emphatically individualist liberalism of *The Wealth of Nations* bore a certain, superficial, resemblance to the "new economics" that the nationalist reconceptualization of the social order inspired in Germany and, on the face of it, might have seemed closer to it than the old Cameralist thinking that it was replacing but perpetuating in spirit. The resemblance allowed a new generation of German "economists," who taught and published in the late 1790s and the early 1800s, to identify with Smith, while subscribing to ideas that were diametrically opposed to his. They recognized that Smith's criticism of the "mercantile system" applied to the Cameralist theory in the bosom of which they were brought up, but had no difficulty accepting the criticism, for they, too, rejected the idea of money as the foundation of national wealth (which was, they thought, what "mercantilism" chiefly meant) and were convinced of the superior importance of industry. In principle, they argued against the forcing of economic action by the state, for it was now a matter of consensus that, *ceteris paribus*, nature was best left to its own devices.[29] But it was perfectly acceptable for the state to try and make men realize what nature's way was.

There is no doubt that some of the appeal of Smith's theory, which was generally misunderstood, in Germany during these years can be attributed to the eye-opening, striking title of his book: *The Wealth of Nations*. In the context of nascent German nationalism (which was anti-French, and thus increased the appeal of all things British by default), this title, this focus on the nation, provided a ready framework for the reinterpretation of economic reality and the reorientation of economic discourse, necessitated by the adoption of national consciousness. It was only a peg, really, on which to hang a vision that was entirely independent of Smith's, but he provided the peg, and German "economists" seized on it. The redefinition of *Staatswirtschaft* as *Nationaloekonomie* allowed the emergent image of the economy to congeal within years or even months and put everything in its place.[30]

The new name made its appearance in 1805, when two authors, L. H. Jakob and F.J.H. von Soden, both reacting to Smith, used it independently in the titles of their books. Jakob was by far the more influential theorist of the two, his influence being felt clearly in the flood of books on national economy that appeared over the next decade, when, finally, economics became a *fashionable* subject in Germany.[31] He distinguished between the state and the nation, and between *Staatswirtschaft* and the *National-Oekonomie*. His focus was on "how is wealth formed in a nation?"—a question that was the province of the latter, new discipline. *Staatswirtschaft* was defined narrowly: according to Jakob, it dealt only with the management of state, or public, property, of which the rulers were the *Wirte*. It was thus properly divided into *Polizei* and finance. By contrast, "the expression *National-Oekonomie* or *National-Wirtschaft*," he wrote, "appears to me most appropriate to characterize a system of concepts in which the entire nature of popular wealth, its origin and [distribution], thus its Physik, should be analyzed." Elsewhere he noted, "*National-Oekonomie* or *National-Wirtschaftslehre* investigates the means through which the populace, under the protection of the government, achieves its end, namely the acquisition, increase and enjoyment of its property; the manner in which national wealth arises, is distributed, consumed and reproduced or maintained; and the influence which all circumstances and events in the state have upon this."[32] This brought the national economy back within the sphere of influence, if not the activity, of the state, and thus within the fold of the political sciences.

As a form of political economy, the "new economics" in Germany remained dubious of the universal validity of Smith's principles and, by and large, denied that they had such validity. Indeed, as Tribe writes, "*Nationaloekonomie* explicitly adopted [the] principle of variability of economic circumstance and need as a central tenet which marked it off from developments in France and Britain."[33] Certain authors, however, were willing to admit the existence of universal laws, though their operation in the case of every particular economy was mediated by variable historical circumstances. To examine these circumstances was the task of *Staatswirtschaft*, while the universal laws, first expounded in *The Wealth of Nations*, were, by association with Smith's work, referred to as *Nationaloekonomie*. This interpretation, which attempted to combine the idea of economics as a set of

natural, universal principles, independent of human volition, with its Cameralist opposite, stressing the defining role of the human (managerial) will,
soon bore the brunt of the attack on *Smithianismus*.

The trend came under attack precisely at the time when Prussian reformers attempted to make its ideas reality. It was spearheaded by the political philosopher of Romanticism Adam Müller and anticipated the theory
underpinning German economic nationalism of the later nineteenth century.
For a while economic thought developed (or, at any rate, existed) outside of
the academy and the title of an "economist" became free for all. In all other
respects, the new age was opposed to economic freedom. Perhaps,
England's specific situation justified this freedom. But, it was held, Germany was not England and could not be guided by such "Smithian" principles. The essence of Smith's theory, and of economic liberalism, was its
individualism, but German thinkers maintained that man was a social being,
and to present him as an independent actor was to alienate him from his
own nature. Concepts and phenomena that derived from the idea of the individual as an independent actor, such as private property, were alienating too,
and, in addition to estranging man from himself, alienated him from the
society of other men. Private property was dead property. As far as economic life was concerned, in other words, communism was the natural and
desirable condition.

The individualism of Adam Smith's "allegedly liberal" system, claimed
Müller, was "the most general manifestation of [the modern] anti-social
spirit, of [the] arrogant egoism, of [the] immoral enthusiasm for false reason
and false enlightenment."[34] It stripped all social relations of their warmth,
converting them into mere money relations. It increased alienation and
polarized society, relieving the upper classes of their traditional responsibilities and exacerbating the exploitation of the poor. It reduced the worker
"to a mere wage-laborer to be thrown on the dump-hill when no longer
useful to the big economic machine." Such principles could make a society
rich, but they could not make it wealthy, for the true wealth of nations was
"wealth that guarantees itself," reproducing its "organic" uniqueness. True
wealth had little in common with quantifiable notions of riches, prosperity,
or even material subsistence, and required different productive forces (and
notions of "productivity") from the ones stressed by Smith. To these real
productive forces belonged, first and foremost, "national moral capital,"
as well as the labor, including the mental and spiritual labor, of past
generations.

Some of Müller's pronouncements may remind the American reader of
the native apologists of slavery, in particular, the vehement George Fitzhugh
(incidentally, the first self-proclaimed "sociologist" this side of the Atlantic).
But they are even more reminiscent of Marx's castigation of economic freedom as an instrument of exploitation and alienation. In fact, Marx took up

most of Müller's economic ideas (the concepts of wealth, private property, communism as the natural, healthful, economic condition), used them, like Müller, as political weapons, and carried on Müller's project of infusing public discourse with economic concerns. Friedrich List could also see in Müller his precursor: he defined productivity in very similar ways and helped to articulate the concepts of "cultural," "social," and "human capital." It was the economic nationalism of Friedrich List, rather than the economic determinism of Marx, that carried the day in Germany. It was in the form of Listian economics, with its rejection of universally applicable principles, its suspicion of the natural proclivities of man, its trust in the guiding hand of the state (and the intellectual), and its respect for the historical uniqueness of each nation and its economy, that the discipline was reestablished in German universities of the modern era.

In the course of its German "formation," the discipline of economics followed the pattern characteristic of the development of speculative normative systems of thought, or, more precisely, ideologies. As such, it demonstrated an exceptionally high degree of permeability and dependence on external social influences. None of the innovations eventually incorporated in it, not even the introduction of Smith's theoretical principles, was necessitated or suggested by the internal logic of the economic tradition. In fact, the tradition developed no such logic, in the sense that there were no logical connections among its component parts, the *Hausväterliteratur, Staatswirtschaft,* and *Nationaloeconomie*; what was transmitted was no more than a disjointed series of theoretical positions, each one reflecting a particular social environment and, specifically, the social interests of its creators or propagandists, and united only by the latter's focus and institutional affiliation. This development, unlike that of science, was neither directed nor cumulative, but rather diffuse and sporadic; it was not development in the proper sense of self-sustained growth or evolution, but only in the metaphorical one of (externally induced) change. The German economic tradition could not claim to be universally valid, or objective, and did not aspire to such validity. Its character was openly subjective, and it derived its authority precisely from its commitment to (that is, its bias in favor of) particular political interests.

ECONOMICS MAKES A NAME FOR ITSELF IN AMERICA AND BECOMES A SCIENCE

The site of the next and last stage in the career of economics was the United States of America around the turn of the twentieth century. It was there that the dogmatic, normative academic discipline was officially reinterpreted as a science, in the sense that the word is used in the natural sciences, and rose to the authoritative position reserved in earlier times for religion. This momentous development was directly related to the rise of big business, though not in the sense that it "reflected" the new mode of production in a Marxian fashion, or "corresponded" in some mystical manner to the systemic needs of industrializing economy, but because big business provoked the group from which the first American economic "scientists" came. This group represented a sector of the traditional social elite of the American society: the "Progressives" who succeeded the "Mugwumps," almost entirely "native-born Protestants" and college graduates, many of whom "had considerably more than moderate means" and "had inherited their money." "The Progressive revolt," of which the early economics may be considered a part, wrote Richard Hofstadter,

> took place almost entirely during a period of sustained and general prosperity. . . . [Men] who might be designated broadly as the Mugwump type, were Progressives not because of economic deprivations but primarily because they were victims of an upheaval in status that took place in the United States during the closing decades of the nineteenth and the early years of the twentieth century. Progressivism, in short, was to a very considerable extent led by men who suffered from the events of their time not through a shrinkage in their means but through the changed pattern in the distribution of deference and power.[35]

The "status revolution" to which Hofstadter drew attention was a consequence of the emergence of the new class of super-rich, produced by big business, which of necessity upset the system of existing class relations and undermined the position of the traditional elite. Wealth has always been the basis of status in American society. Until very late in American history, merchants were the richest men in the nation. But only a few of them became millionaires: in 1831, Stephen Girard died leaving $6 million, while the estate of John Jacob Astor at the time of his death in 1848 was three times that amount. These fortunes were considered "immense."[36] The professions, especially law, offered the surest avenue of upward mobility. In his old age, Henry Adams recalled that "down to 1850, and even later, New England society was still directed by the professions [—] lawyers, physicians, professors, merchants."[37] It was not much different elsewhere, at least in the North. The liberal professions (money that was tied to education), it appears, had a higher status—in the eyes of the professionals themselves, at any rate—than merchants, despite the latter's superior wealth.

When Henry Adams returned from Europe at the end of the 1860s, the situation had already changed. According to Hofstadter,

> The newly rich, the grandiosely or corruptly rich, the masters of great corporations, were bypassing the men of the Mugwump type—the old gentry, the merchants of long standing, the small manufacturers, the established professional men, the civic leaders of an earlier era. In a score of cities and hundred of towns,

particularly in the East but also in the nation at large, the old-family, college-educated class that had deep ancestral roots in local communities and often owned family businesses, that had traditions of political leadership, belonged to the patriotic societies and the best clubs, staffed the governing boards of philanthropic and cultural institutions, and led the movements for civic betterment, were being overshadowed and edged aside in the making of basic political and economic decisions. In their personal careers, as in their community activities, they found themselves checked, hampered, and overridden by the agents of the new corporations, the corrupters of legislatures, the buyers of franchises, the allies of the political bosses. In this uneven struggle they found themselves limited by their own scruples, their regard for reputation, their social standing itself. To be sure, the America they knew did not lack opportunities, but it did seem to lack opportunities of the highest sort for men of the highest standards. In a strictly economic sense these men were not growing poorer as a class, but their wealth and power were being dwarfed by comparison with the new eminences of wealth and power. They were less important, and they knew it.[38]

The deprivation felt by the traditional elite was a relative deprivation (which is to say that they suffered not from a want of something, but from the knowledge that someone else had much more of what they had), yet it was relative deprivation of heroic proportions that corresponded to the vast distance which separated the old rich from the new. While in the 1850s and early 1860s, according to the 1885 *Report of the Committee [on Education and Labor] of the Senate upon the Relations between Labor and Capital*, "a man that had a farm worth $1500 or $2000 was considered 'A, No. 1,'" and the "richest man in town was worth some $4,000 or $5,000." A reporter who visited Andrew Carnegie in 1901, after the sale of Carnegie's company to J. P. Morgan's United States Steel Corporation for a quarter of a billion dollars, calculated that the *daily* income of the retired magnate amounted to $40,000.[39] No wonder that the old rich were coming to perceive poverty in an entirely different light, believed themselves destitute, and bitterly resented the so-called "plutocracy." "We are developing new types of destitutes," wrote an early-twentieth-century observer, Walter Weyl, "the automobileless, the yachtless, the Newport-cottageless. The subtlest of luxuries become necessities, and their loss is bitterly resented. The discontent of to-day reaches very high in the social scale."[40]

The traditional elite, perched on the highest rung of the social ladder, suffered from an uncommonly acute variety of common envy. Its condition was similar to that of a European nobility (most clearly, the *noblesse de race* and *d'épée* in France), threatened by the advance of the enterprising middle classes, and its reaction closely resembled that of the Duc de Saint-Simon to "vile bourgeoisie."[41] Like the French nobility, American notables sought solace in those aspects of their status that were inaccessible to the parvenus from below, however wealthy: the numbers of exclusive patriotic and genealogical societies, which played up the relative antiquity of the elite's American descent and the participation of their families in the formative episodes of the national history, apparently grew in direct proportion to big business and the fortunes of "robber barons."[42] But solace was not to be found there. Like the French nobility, American notables, therefore, also sought to diminish in their own eyes the great industrial capitalists. In the process, they constructed a sinister mythical image, which was at once terrifying and revolting. In utter disregard of the American ideal of equality, the old elite denied the merit of the big businessmen and was unsparing in the ridicule of their self-made character, their humble origins, and lack of cultivation.

What respectable men in America wrote about American businessmen sounded much like what German Romantic nationalists would write about the Jews, or Russian Slavophiles about the West. But the "crass materialism" of the "robber barons," their alleged lack of respect and understanding of high culture and religion, their presumed incapacity for friendship—all this was not enough to justify the elite's revulsion and savored too distinctly of sour grapes. The focus on personal deficiencies of the super-rich was counterproductive; as Walter Weyl noted, "[E]verywhere . . . we meet the millionaire's good and evil works, and we seem to resent the one as much as the other." The American people, in his opinion, were of necessity "looking beyond the titular offender in the search for a greater anonymous culprit."[43] They found it in the giant corporation, the organizational structure of big business, and the crime of which the latter, paradoxically but inevitably, was accused as "having ended our old time equality."[44] A grievance of the social elite was reinterpreted as a national affliction, a threat to the core American ideal; and a privileged group of people, intolerant of the workings of equality, appointed themselves its guardians on behalf of the community of those whom they considered their natural inferiors.

In the meantime, a revolution was under way in American higher education, which dramatically affected the situation of one particular group within the elite—the intellectuals. Up until the Gilded Age, which they so mercilessly derided, intellectuals occupied no clear place in American society. Their emergence as a social category, somewhere in the 1830s, was a result of a natural self-selection, made possible by the affluence of their families, which afforded them a life of leisurely observation and ratiocination. But while they lived that good life, they answered no expressed need in the community, fulfilled no manifest function, and formed no recognizable profession. From the very outset they had characteristic grievances, interests, and therefore an incipient ethos. But they did not constitute a community, and their sense of collective identity was "inchoate."[45] As intellectuals, they stood outside of existing organizational structures and had no structure of their own, which could perpetuate their traditions and give form to their style of life. In other words, they did not represent a status-honor group, or what in common parlance is called a class.[46]

Denominational colleges, which proliferated throughout the period, offered them no congenial home. The office of the college president was virtually monopolized by clergymen, and the office of the professor, who, in the words of Walter Metzger, had "something of the status of the nursemaid" to unruly adolescent boys,[47] with few exceptions, had little appeal to the scions of the best American families. The college was an essentially religious institution. According to reliable estimates, as many as one in three students in mid-century prepared for the ministry, which, in combination with equally or more clerical composition of the faculty (90 percent of college presidents and about 35 percent of the teaching staff were ministers between 1800 and 1860) lent the institution the look, if not the atmosphere, of a theological seminary.

The atmosphere of the college was rather more like that of an all-boys exclusive boarding high school, for the other two-thirds of the student body attended simply because respectable people did so, biding their time and expecting from this extended moratorium no advantages for the adult life that lay ahead. If they wished to enter such learned professions as law or medicine, the way to them lay outside the college through a system of apprenticeship, and their college education was largely irrelevant to their aspirations. If they desired intellectual excitement and wished to acquire a general education, as did Henry Adams, the college certainly was not the place to find it. The assumptions of American pedagogy were "dreary."[48] In 1854 Henry Adams wrote of Harvard, "[N]o one took Harvard College seriously. All went there because their friends went there, and the College was their ideal of social self-respect. . . . Four years of Harvard College, if successful, resulted in an autobiographical blank."[49] The students had to entertain themselves as best they could. According to Adams, this involved "substantial whiskey"; according to other sources, they made creative use of firecrackers.

Their wards' irrepressible joie de vivre and determined efforts to avoid dying of boredom were a source of intolerable nuisance for the college authorities, but in the end contributed greatly to the well-being of professors. The latter, as was already mentioned, were a humble, downtrodden lot. At the time, political correctness was not a major consideration, but, rather like today, college teachers were often hired not on the basis of subject-competence, but on the grounds of sectarian affiliation. In colleges that presented themselves as nonsectarian, neutrality was "presumed to lie in an equal division of the spoils" between sects, "in proportion to their respective strength in the community." In accordance with this early commitment to diversity, the University of Michigan, for instance, "for years pursued a policy of even-handed injustice, and named a minister of a different sect to each of its professorships."[50] Teachers whose chief qualification consisted in subscribing to an orthodoxy could not be expected to shine with the light of genius or even of acquired learning, and did not. As a result, they did not carry much authority. The trustees, who were even more orthodox and at least as competent in most subjects of instruction as the professors, had little respect for them and treated them as low-level employees. In Princeton, we are told, they criticized the grammatical construction of sentences in the faculty "minutes." "It is doubtful," wrote Metzger, "that the most intrusive board of trustees today would ever display toward its faculty so marked an attitude of contempt."[51]

The lowliness of the professorial office was felt all the more sharply because of the status differential between the faculty and the trustees: the latter were pillars of the community, who enjoyed above-average wealth and prestige—the former, as a rule, lacked social lustre altogether, for little but necessity would attract one to a career of college teaching until late in the nineteenth century. They were "hopelessly outclassed." Thanks to the student indomitability, however, the professors had to be, little by little, granted more respect by college authorities, for it was not to be expected that, abject as they were, they would be obeyed by the rambunctious progeny of the social elite. Thus "the college teacher was elevated from the position of a powerless subaltern to the status of an executive officer in the realm of discipline and instruction," the crucial factor in this being "the prosaic and commonplace, but disquieting and relentless, problems of the lack of student discipline."[52]

Another persistent problem that plagued antebellum colleges—the constant budget deficit—also profited the professors. To ease their distress, the colleges had to appeal to the generosity of the alumni, who were equal, if not superior, to the trustees in status. The presence of a powerful secular group disturbed the college hierarchy, weakened the position of the clerical boards, and by default added to the authority of the professoriate. With the change in their position came a change in the methods, and eventually subjects, of teaching.

While student discipline and financial difficulties pushed the colleges toward reforms that beneficially affected the status of the professors, other factors pulled them in the same direction. The most important of these factors was the emergence of German universities as the model for American academics. The pilgrimage of American intellectuals (not college professors) to Germany began in earnest after 1850, though some pioneers, such as Bankroft, made the journey decades earlier. Unlike in the United States, the universities in Germany did represent the center of intellectual life, and professors, especially in the humanities, who were intellectuals by definition, enjoyed great prestige.[53] Altogether, some nine thousand Americans were educated in Germany in the nineteenth century (200 before, the rest after 1850), most of them in Göttingen and Berlin, the two greatest universities, where the social superiority of the German professor was most pronounced. They were duly impressed and, in the words of a historian, "reacted enviously." Longfellow, who attended Göttingen in 1829, compared the shining example of the Teutonic world of letters to the sectarian parochialism of the college at home. The German university collected together "professors in whom the spirit moved—who were *well enough known* [emphasis added] to attract students to themselves," and "what has heretofore been the idea of an University with us?" The answer was simple and depressing: "Two or three large brick buildings—with a chapel, and a President to pray in it!" The German professor was a scholar—a priest at the altar of knowledge, an expert, and, more than that, a creator, a perfect man with an authority to advise rulers and lead who "appeared to be the very embodiment of learning in its most exalted form"; his American counterpart was "a nondescript, a jack of all trades, equally ready to teach surveying and Latin eloquence, and thankful if his quarter's salary is not docked to whitewash the college fence."[54] The pilgrims returned with their aspirations inflated, bitterly resentful of the orphan existence to which the American society condemned its best and brightest, and convinced that the university was the rightful home of the intellectual and "professor" his proper title. Having seen their "ideal of a university not only realized, but extended and glorified" in Germany, they determined to transplant it to the native shores—to "do something" for the nation, as they put it.[55]

Fortunately, this was the age of big business and "robber barons" who were philanthropically inclined, and they provided the money for the realization of the intellectuals' ambition. Magnificent new institutions, conceived as research universities came into being: Johns Hopkins—the Göttingen at Baltimore, blessed at birth with $3.5 million by a local capitalist who played the fairy godmother; Stanford—launched with $24 million its founder made in his railroad business; the University of Chicago—revived and swept into greatness with Rockefeller's gift of $34 million. Modeled specifically on the German faculty of philosophy—the leading and most prestigious faculty in German universities for most of the nineteenth century, and exclusively devoted to the disinterested pursuit of knowledge and cultivation of intellectual superiority (and the intellectually superior)—the American research university developed differently. The graduate school—the preserve of the professor (professor accomplished and professor in the making), rather than the student—was only one of the many divisions, the rest of which catered primarily to the needs of groups other than the professors. There was the undergraduate college, the chief function of which was still to educate adolescents and mold them into men, and the professional schools, which trained doctors, lawyers, engineers, and—yes—business managers. Nevertheless, the university provided a definite social position for intellectuals, which they previously lacked, a structural foundation that would support their collective ethos, a self-perpetuating organizational framework, within which they could realize their social interests, maintain their status, and from within which they boldly faced the rest of society. It allowed them to perceive themselves as a community, "an order of learning" (defined as "academic order"), of which it became the center, making possible formal careers and granting degrees—the closest this society came to the titles of nobility. It gave them a "sense of strength," a "new dignity," "a new conception of the self, of its powers, privileges and obligations."[56] In short, it made American intellectuals into a class.

An unrelated revolution in thought endowed this class with prestige which was at least equal in value to the millions supplied by the "robber barons." This revolution was launched by the publication of Darwin's *Origin of Species* in 1859, and accompanied by a shift in attitudes that propelled science to the apex of the scale of social values. The acceptance of Darwinism in the United States was "remarkably rapid."[57] The colleges at first resisted it. In 1880, nine eastern college presidents, including those of Yale and Princeton (but not including President Eliot of Harvard, who was among the first to defect to the revolutionary evolutionary camp) were asked whether they encouraged the teaching of Darwinian evolution on their campuses. Unanimously, they rejected the idea as preposterous. But these were no longer the dark ages, and German-educated professors—many of them in new rich universities, founded and funded by "robber barons," and some in reforming ones, such as Harvard—were no longer lowly nursemaids to unruly upper-class adolescents, but upper-class adults, more than any other group in society conscious and jealous of their superior status. They countered with an "imperious claim to gnostic superiority." Scientists, they said—and they used the term in the German manner, as a synonym for "intellectuals," "scholars," and "professors"—knew best; they represented human intellect in all its power, and human intellect was "the sole *discoverer* of truth"; they were the only ones who had the mastery of scientific method, and this method was "the sole *organon* of its discovery." "No other method of inquiry now commands respect," asserted President Eliot. This was true. The Darwinian revolution, which dealt a lethal blow to the image of empirical, especially human, reality sponsored by the Christian religion, elevated science to a position of unquestionable authority previously reserved for religious and civic leaders of the nation. "The two decades between 1880 and 1900 were decades for praise for science," writes Edward Shils. "Great businessmen and leading state politicians as well as a few major national politicians and important publicists and, in a vague way, much of the electorate, joined in the appreciation of this kind of knowledge and the university as its proper organ."[58]

The science so elevated was, specifically, natural science, but humanistic scholarship and, in particular, the favorite pastime of secular intellectuals—social philosophy (and criticism)—upheld its cause against clerical detractors, professed devotion to its truth, and believed that, in exchange for such interested service, they could pretend to its proud status. The identification of science and university in the public opinion encouraged such pretensions. Besides, in a time of frightening economic growth and social upheaval that such growth implied, a thought that change was implicit in the natural process and occurred for the better brought comfort, and people were ready to see society as an extension of Darwinian evolution. They were not about to quibble over such minor matters as the record and credentials of those who told them what they wanted to hear. Herbert Spencer was wildly popular. Edward L. Youmans, the editor of the *Popular Science Monthly*, who propagandized his Darwinian sociology in America, did not distinguish between (actual) natural and (projected) social sciences. The authority of the natural sciences, which reflected their world-shaking accomplishment, was complacently and eagerly generalized to include the latter, though the social sciences had nothing to show for themselves. In the America of "robber barons," there was a palpable desire that social sciences should exist—a social demand for social sciences. American intellectuals capitalized on it.

The first area of social philosophy and criticism to declare itself a science in America was that of political economy. Before the Gilded Age, which inaugurated the age of the universities, the American social elite, and in particular the intellectuals, showed little interest in economic questions. Political economy preoccupied lesser mortals: college presidents and an occasional professor; recent immigrants (who had an ax to grind with the mother country); and practicing businessmen, whose hands (and minds) were anyhow already dirty. This led Charles Dunbar, an intellectual, a professor at the reformed Harvard of President Eliot, to declare in 1876 that there was no political economy in the United States. "The United States," he said, "have, thus far, done nothing towards developing the theory of political economy."[59]

However, Dunbar's conclusion was not warranted by the evidence. It is true, college presidents who taught Smithian economics as a division of the required course on moral philosophy, which it was their privilege and responsibility to deliver, added nothing to the English classics, before whose majesty, to paraphrase Henry Adams, they knelt in self-abasement. Protestant clergymen, they attempted to bring errant Britons back into the fold of Christian religion and thus equated the invisible hand with the hand of the rational, benevolent, Christian God. They saw no difference between the principles of political economy and those of morality, claiming that "almost every question in the one [could] be argued on grounds belonging to the other" and believed that free trade, which they revered "as something *holy*," was, literally, "the will of God."[60]

This was not so with exponents—mostly men of affairs—of the protec-
tionist "American System" (also called the "national school"), "which dominated the practical policy of the country" well into this century.[61] Preached
vigorously by Henry Carey, it enjoyed wide acclaim around the economically alert world, regarded with interest in Britain and France, and taken
very seriously in Germany and Japan, where it was taught in business
schools. Dunbar dismissed Carey's importance. "It cannot be said," he
admitted, "that Mr. Carey has not engaged attention outside of his own country, for his works have been translated and circulated in nearly every important language of Europe," and Mr. Mill himself on several occasions paid
"him the distinguished tribute of singling him out in an especial manner
from a throng of opponents." Nevertheless, Dunbar was unwilling to forget
that "to lead a school is not necessarily making a contribution to the science"
and was confident that "not much of Mr. Carey's work will be found
wrought into the political economy of the future."[62] As it happened, he was
in a position to see that the prophesy was fulfilled.

While people of Mr. Carey's ilk tried to uncover the springs of American
economic life,[63] upper-class intellectuals reacted to it with uncomprehending
amusement and sometimes a sourer sentiment. But with the coming of big
business, they began paying attention to the newly important sphere of social
activity, which came to loom so uncomfortably large in their heretofore comfortable world. Obviously, they did not like what they saw. Their economic
thought, therefore, took the form of mournful philosophizing and ethical
preaching. They regarded the prodigious economic growth of their time, as
Walter Weyl so well said, as "positively immoral." When "robber barons"
build for them great universities, within which they were allowed to believe
that social criticism was science (endowed with the authority of religion,
thanks to Darwin), these intellectuals, in the words of Richard Hofstadter,
"had become disposed . . . to agitate themselves [visibly] about things that
had previously left them unconcerned" or, rather, reserved, and took their
place at the head of the so-called "main stream of liberal dissent."[64]

It was, clearly, not "the avidity of intellectual desire," the "irrepressible
desire to understand" an aspect of empirical reality, that Edward Shils, projecting his own ideals onto the members of the world of learning in general,
believed to have inspired American social sciences, that motivated the founders of the native discipline of economics. The motive behind the emergence
of economics was revealed by one of its first professors, Simon N. Patten,
who taught at the University of Pennsylvania. In an 1893 essay in the *Yale
Review*, entitled "The Scope of Political Economy," he wrote,

The boundary lines between the various social sciences have not been fixed by
any systematic study of their relations nor by any logical order or sequence.
They have their place in history because of the practical interest which *social*

reformers have had in them as means of securing progress [emphasis added], or at least as a means of maintaining the existing social order against retrogression or decay. Each succeeding social science has had the same aim—*to give new sanctions to the progressive forces of society* [emphasis added]. Each science, however, has succeeded in conquering but a section of the general field of social science, and this section it holds against its newer rivals. *Religion, morality, natural law, politics, and economics have arisen to answer the one supreme question: What is the binding authority to which appeal can be made and for which men will have respect* [emphasis added]? For a time, the potent force that held men and nations in peaceful relations was religion. When its authority began to decline, an appeal was made to moral principles, in the hope that they would increase the respect for law, and thus advance the interests of social progress. When this hope failed, resort was had to natural law, to politics, and finally to economics: and from *each of these sciences* [emphasis added] laws and practical rules were secured that have helped to resist the forces that tended to dissolve society, and in many cases have been real causes of social progress.[65]

The interest behind economics was practical, it was an interest in the binding authority and respect that would allow social reformers (presumably, people who discerned the optimal direction of society development—what Jacobin philosophers referred to as an elite of intelligence and virtue) to orient society in that optimal direction and resist the forces of evil that tended to dissolve it. Economics, thus, was a functional equivalent of religion, morality, a certain kind of political philosophy, and politics, all of which were, by fiat of poetic license, created "sciences," thereby justifying the identification of economics as a science as well. What distinguished this younger sister from its venerable siblings was its rationality. "Economics," defined Patten,

> is the science of positive utilities—the realm where no other motives are recognized except those resulting from changes in the amount of our measurable pleasures and pains. If all our actions depended upon judgments reached by reasoning from premise to conclusion, there would be no social science but economics. . . . All social science would be purely utilitarian—a mere calculus of pleasure and pain—and at the same time economic.[66]

Such rationality made economics the most scientific of the "social sciences." It was also the broadest, for, while not all judgments were reached by reasoning from premise to conclusion, they were all ultimately reducible to such reasoning. Patten lamented "confining" or "reducing" economics to a theory of the production of goods, the increase of material wealth. Combined with "the popular belief that the pursuit of wealth was the source of moral and political degeneration," this narrow definition could only deprive the discipline of its legitimate subject—"the general welfare of the community."[67]

This American conception, formulated about a year before the twentieth century in one of the leading modern universities, was quite similar to the one found in the German *Hausväterliteratur* of the late 1600s.

American intellectuals of the Gilded Age, however, were not advisors to territorial princes, and their project was a good deal more self-centered than that of their unlikely predecessors. They wanted to have political influence, of course, but the main reason behind their hankering for the authority of science was the desire to protect, maintain, and improve their status, always unsatisfactory and now threatened by the Juggernaut of big business. Social reform was the most ambitious, but, as it happened, not the best strategy through which to achieve this goal, though it was adopted by several very influential early economists besides Patten, among them Richard Ely, the founder and long-time first secretary of the American Economic Association. In view of the intellectuals' objectives, it was essential that their "science" be accepted as an academic discipline. Yet, there were weighty objections to the definition of a new academic discipline in this manner. On the one hand, the German idea of "pure" scholarship spurned partisanship (even though it approved of nationalism)—and would-be economists were almost without an exception "Germany-returned." On the other hand, pronounced policy-orientation undermined and offended the already established professors of political economy or its variously titled equivalents in the reformed elite universities (such as Dunbar, Taussig, Laughlin at Harvard, Sumner at Yale, and so on), who believed—with the fervor and certainty one associates with religious belief—in the truths of the classical, laissez-faire, school. According to Francis A. Walker, the second president of MIT and the first president of the American Economic Association, with these illustrious personages, whose allegiance had to be secured at all costs, laissez faire "was not made the test of economic orthodoxy, merely. It was used to decide whether a man were an economist at all."[68]

For a while, the disparate contingents of the little troop followed separate paths. In April 1882, J. L. Laughlin, at the time an instructor at Harvard, wrote to Edward Atkinson,

> The matter of the "American Society of Political Economy" (?) has been simmering in my mind, and I have now thought it worth proposing some plan. As you say, "bores" must be excluded. So, it seems best to approach a few of the leading economics first. . . . It ought to be made a dignified body, for it can be authoritative and useful in many ways. It could encourage economic studies by offering prizes, as in France, for work which deserves it well, and propose many subjects affecting our own country for which it offers honorable rewards.

The motley group of ten "leading economists" he proposed consisted of two businessmen, Edward Atkinson (the addressee) and David A. Wells; two university presidents, Francis Walker of MIT and Andrew D. White of Cornell; Carl Schurz, a statesman and publicist; and five professors, of whom four actually taught political economy: Simon Newcomb (Professor of Mathematics in the U.S. Navy), Charles Dunbar (Professor of Political Economy at Harvard), William Graham Sumner (Professor of Political and Social Science at Yale), Arthur Latham Perry (Professor of Political Economy and History at Williams College), and Laughlin himself.

The Political Economy Club (as the organization was named), modeled on its British namesake, was formed at the end of 1883, with an inaugural meeting at the home of Horace White of the *New York Evening Post*. The mathematician Newcomb was elected president. "Your reign is undisputed," commented Laughlin. "We are only too glad to have a double star at the head of our constellation." The topics of discussion at the club's meetings, however, were disputed. Horace White and David Wells (two men of affairs) proposed the question, "What ought to be the policy of the Democratic Party with regard to the tariff?" This was "far better," they thought, "than an academic discussion" on something else. Laughlin retorted in a letter to Newcomb:

> The one who regards a discussion of principles as "academic" will not further the progress of our science. And as economists we ought to meet this tendency at once, gently but firmly. . . . I think it would be very undignified for a Club of professed economists to talk at their dinner of the policy of the Democratic party.

White countered Laughlin's objection with the claim that "the English and the French societies of economists take up questions relating to party politics, and I don't see why we may not." He was seconded by Atkinson, who did not like "the 'Socialists of the Chair' [i.e., *Kathedersozialisten*—the German "academic socialists"] or the 'Economists of the Closet,'" and wished "to make the Political Economy Club a little more of a force" than a faculty club, which it promised to become. Evidently, businessmen and professors among the "professed economists" did not see eye to eye.[69]

There was dissention among the professors as well. Younger members, such as Richard Ely, were impatient with the timidity of the "conservative" academic position. In 1884 Ely proposed an alternative organization for "economists who repudiate *laissez faire* as a scientific doctrine," and in September 1885 the American Economic Association was "officially inaugurated . . . following discussions among a miscellaneous group of scholars, ministers and social reformers who were attending the second meeting of the American Historical Association." The Historical Association, in the person of its founder and secretary Henry Baxter Adams—Ely's senior colleague in the history department of Johns Hopkins University—gave its blessing, and a section of recently baptized historians enthusiastically converted and professed themselves economists. "The idea of an economic association," writes

Coats, "was undoubtedly German in origin," being inspired by *Verein für Sozialpolitik*, but "Ely's call met with a warm response not only from the young scholars who had been impressed by the reigning German school of historical economics but also from leading historians, prominent past, present, and future university presidents like Gilman, Andrew White, C. K. Adams, W. W. Folwell, and Francis A. Walker (who was also a distinguished representative of the older generation of economists), such outstanding liberal ministers as Lyman Abbott and Washington Gladden, and officers of the American Social Science Association."[70] Ely's economic ideas were derived largely from German sources: he considered economics, or, rather, political economy, to be an essentially ethical teaching, whose purpose was the promotion of the highest welfare of all citizens; defined economic freedom as "merely relative"; favored restrictions, insofar as they were "in the interest of the whole people, not of a few privileged individuals or classes"; and believed that it was the duty of the state (which he consistently capitalized) to regulate economic institutions and manage "natural monopolies, such as gas, electric light, water supply, street-car lines, steam railways, etc." In a modern democracy, where the state was "not something apart from us and outside us, but we ourselves," it was rightfully the chief economic actor, the beneficence of whose intervention was revealed with particular clarity by the example of Germany (presumably a model democratic society). "Governmental action is one of the most powerful factors promoting civilization," Ely wrote in the 1889 *Introduction to Political Economy*, "and in a country like Germany we observe a high civilization, every part of which is largely the result of governmental activity."[71] Remarkably, while true to the theoretical principles of *Nationaloekonomie*, his rendition of it entirely lacked its sentiment: he wished to change his society, rather than make it great among others.

According to Newcomb, Ely's association was "intended to be a sort of church, requiring for admission to its full communion a renunciation of ancient errors, and an adhesion to the supposed new creed." As the main tenet of this creed appeared to be the faith in direct state action as the means of righting all wrongs, the "conservative" classicists, ensconced in the best universities, considered the association a travesty and scornfully ignored repeated invitations to join it. Their eyes were focused on "prestige and influence," and they insisted that "the economists as a body . . . strongly disapprove[d] the attempt to 'popularize' economics by giving too much weight to the conclusions of uninstructed public sentiment," to which, they believed, Ely's definition of economics as social advocacy was tantamount.

Within years, this has indeed become the position of the economists as a body. After all, what the great majority of them wanted was "scientific status and prestige," and "they sought to attain [it] by dissociating themselves from the past, and by establishing economics as an independent scholarly discipline, free from theological, ethical, historical and sociological connotations and, above all, free from the taint of missionary zeal and political partisanship." In 1892 the American Economic Association, following a heated discussion in which Ely's program was "effectively repudiated," elected Charles Dunbar as president. Ely left Johns Hopkins and moved to the University of Wisconsin, where he became a Professor of Economics and Director of the School of Economics, Political Science, and History. (This was not a sign of a precocious interest in the interdisciplinary approach, but of the persistent uncertainty as to what economics, political science, or even history was.) In 1894–95, Ely supported his friend John R. Commons, also an "economist," in founding ("on ideas similar to those prevailing when the AEA was started") the American Political Science Association. Other one-time economists in the meantime were redefining their commitment to social reform as "sociology."[72]

The ideological stringency of the American Economic Association was briefly replaced by broad tolerance of competing agenda and, as there was a need for a new common ground to replace the old ceded to softer social sciences, for a while a belief prevailed that "political economy [was] swinging back to a renewed attention to practical or business affairs." This tolerance went so far indeed that certain members entertained the idea to elect a businessman as president in 1899. Of course, this misguided attempt at fraternization with the enemy was instantly brought to a stop, there being a wide agreement that "we should remain a scientific body." As J. B. Clark explained, "At the bottom even the philistines will have more respect for such a body than they would for one that should put a man of affairs at its head. I may be wrong, but I dread any yielding to the view that economic wisdom resides outside of the schools and inside of the counting house."[73] (This was similar to asserting that biological or physical truth was to be found not in nature, but in the universities.)

Unclear as to what their discipline was, early American economists never doubted that business education it was not. They must have taken pride in the uselessness of their "economic wisdom" for practical men whether in counting houses or industrial plants; that it was, indeed, useless is attested by the constant and, until the twentieth century, largely unsuccessful attempts of the business community to establish business schools alongside the proliferating departments of economics. The University of Chicago (no doubt encouraged by its benefactor) established one earlier than most. But President Harper reported in 1903 that its progress was intentionally kept slow, "the desire of the authorities being not to lay too great emphasis upon work of this character, in contrast with the longer-established college work, in the early years of the University." Columbia, for its part, successfully resisted a formation of a business school until much later and managed to block even the establishment of a course in commercial history, geography, law, and accounting, which the New York State Chamber of Commerce offered to finance. When the business school was finally established in 1916, Professor Seligman of the Department of Economics revealed what was the reason behind the University's dawdling: "[The] Department of Economics and others realized the real obligation was graduate work and research rather than professional teaching." Economists were preoccupied with bringing up more economists, to carry on their values and represent their interests; they had no wish to abet the sinister forces which it was the responsibility of all social sciences to resist. Indeed, this was the position of academics in general. "We must educate away from the controlling forces of society," declared members of the National Educational Association in 1898; "those forces are not ideal, and it is the business of education to strive for the ideal."[74]

In the Gilded Age, the "professed economists" who were professors of economics were among the most idealistic of the nation's teachers. Material reality interested them very little and they knew very little about it. Their concerns were strictly spiritual or in the Durkheimean sense "moral"—they were preoccupied with their position on the scale of social honor. Their academic subjects, the agenda that drew them to economics in the first place, reflected their fear of losing status to the successful entrepreneurs and irritation at the enormous gains in prestige the latter seemed to owe to their business ability. Their first and natural impulse was, therefore, to diminish these upstarts—and it was long before this impulse died away. But social criticism, as such, could not accomplish their objective, which was to assert their superiority and improve their status in American society, with which they were never happy. Their best chance lay in becoming scientists. Scientists were indeed elevated in this nation to the position of high priests and diviners of ultimate meanings, which in European societies, such as Germany and France, belonged to secular intellectuals in general. But this eminently attractive identity came with a heavy price tag.

The idea of science among American intellectuals who professed themselves economists could not reflect the nature of their social subject matter, of which they were ignorant; nor could it reflect a deep understanding of the activity of natural scientists, of which they were ignorant as well. They were left, therefore, with the model that natural scientists constructed for the benefit of the lay audience, and this was a very demanding model. Knowledge becomes science, said the astronomer and mathematician Chauncey Wright, "when it ceases to be associated with our fears, our respects, our aspirations—our emotional nature; when it ceases to prompt questions as to what relates to our personal destiny, our ambition, our moral worth; when it ceases to have man, his personal and social nature, as its central and controlling objects."[75] The poor professors, who were desperately interested in questions relating to their personal destiny and ambition, thus were pushed into the cold embrace of the classical—laissez-faire—theory, for it was the only approach that could be fitted into this Procrustean bed. It was impersonal, ahistorical, and long since separated from the social context in which it had its roots. It was so abstract that the man of whom it ostensibly treated became as remote as a distant star and assumed the respectable qualities of a mathematical equation. It reduced the immense complexity of social reality to a few relatively simple rules, and it presented these rules, which it called "economic laws," as unchanging and universal.

The dynamics of intellectual development normally responsible for the emergence of new scientific disciplines were absent, and nothing but external social interests (most salient among them, status considerations) stood behind the choice of this paradigm. Smithian principles informed American academic economics before it was elevated to the dignity of science, but these were seen as moral principles, integral to a general ethical/religious doctrine. An element of a creed, they were self-evident and never subjected to a systematic test by evidence. The Germany-returned intellectuals, who reinvented economics as a science (in the broad sense of German *Wissenshaft*) within the new research universities modeled on the German example, challenged this Smithian view. Their challenge, however, was motivated not by the inconsistency of this theory with empirical reality, but by its inconsistency with the Listian economics then reigning in Germany. Several other paradigms were tried on for size, including the (somewhat watered down) *Nationaloekonomie*. But the spectacular rise in status of science in the English sense of the word (with its emphasis on experimental, empirical investigation) made advocacy of social engineering and the regulation that it implied counterproductive in regard to the central social interest that moved new American economists, and it was rejected explicitly on these grounds. This central social interest—the interest in status—before long pushed the economists back into the embrace of the "classical" paradigm as the only one that lent itself to articulation in the formal manner represented particularly by physics. This story of origins explains why economics in the course of the twentieth century did not advance cumulatively, but developed in a pattern of revolutions around and variations on a central theme, characterized by frequent revivals and then temporary interments of a limited number of approaches (mercantilism/Keynsianism vs. classical, demand vs. supply, etc.) and characteristic, perhaps, of scholasticism or an art form, but not of any of the known sciences. There has been no progress in economics in the sense in which it is clearly evident in physics, biology, and their numerous proliferating subdisciplines.

And so, if we apply to this case the sensible maxim that defines a duck as something that walks and quacks like a duck, we must conclude that economics is not a science. Rather, in keeping with the animal kingdom, economics is a wolf in sheep's clothing. It parades under a false identity. It wields an enormous authority in our society, claimed by right of its assumed scientific name, but its authority is that of a soothsayer, for it has no more knowledge of the complex empirical reality considered to be the area of its expertise, than does the lay audience hungry for its wisdom (in fact, certain sectors of this audience, though they may not trust in themselves, have immeasurably more of such knowledge). In plainest terms, it is a fraud.

I hasten to add that the above is in no way intended to cast aspersions on the integrity of individual members of the American economic profession. The deception they collectively practice is in the first place a self-deception. The only transgression they can be accused of is not understanding, and never reflecting on, what makes an intellectual discipline a science, and there can be no doubt that they sincerely believe in the scientific nature of their pursuits, for they take pride, and thus are truly invested, in their professional identity. Moreover, committed as it was at birth (though by mistake) to the formal rigors of physics, economics has developed into a formidable tradition in its own right, irresistibly impelled along the path of increasing formalization, ever more "theoretical, mathematical, and quantitative." As other esoteric traditions, it necessarily encouraged the cultivation of very special skills and gave rise early to stringent standards of excellence.[76] The practice of economics today, unquestionably, requires great intelligence, so much so that few among the uninitiated can understand what economists do. A distinguished member of the group, George Stigler, wrote recently that the profession was producing "a literature that no person could possibly read—the limits imposed by sanity are stricter than those imposed by time. Indeed, it is a literature that perhaps is read by a number of economists only moderately larger than the number of writers. The best memories can recall only a tiny fraction of this literature, and if the literature were irrevocably destroyed, most of it would utterly perish from human knowledge."[77]

Paradoxically, the more exclusive economists become as a group, the more specialized their skills, and the more formalized and abstract their theories, the surer their hold becomes on their chosen identity, for society at large concurs with them in their idea of science as formal, quantitative, and inherently incomprehensible to the public. The surer their identity, the greater their authority as a science. And the greater their authority as a science, the more highly credentialed economists exchange mathematical modeling for social preaching (whether along the lines of *Staatswirtschaft* or free enterprise) and parlay their technical proficiency into positions of generalized opinion leaders.[78] The role of the economist as a guru has never been so influential, and while economics makes it possible only because of its identification as a science, no other science enjoys similar influence.

Does the crowd not perceive the nakedness of the king? Are even little boys too wise to let the terrible truth slip their tongue? The new millennium dawns under the sign of the discipline of economics. It is not the sign of the all-mighty dollar, mind you, but that of the All-knowing Authoritative Academic.

If, under the circumstances, one needs consolation, it may be found in the thought that this, too, shall pass.

NOTES

1. Joseph Ben-David and Randall Collins, "Social Factors in the Origins of a New Science," in *Scientific Growth: Essays on the Social Organization of Science*, ed. Gad Freudenthal (Los Angeles: University of California Press, 1991), 51–52, 54.

2. Joseph Ben-David, *The Scientist's Role in Society: A Comparative Study* (Chicago: University of Chicago Press, 1971), 16–17.

3. Karl R. Popper, *Objective Knowledge: An Evolutionary Approach* (New York: Clarendon, 1979), 81.

4. Thomas S. Kuhn, *The Structure of Scientific Revolutions*, 2nd ed. (Chicago: University of Chicago Press, 1970), 52–65.

5. Ibid., 10.

6. Joseph Ben-David, "Roles and Innovations in Medicine," in *Scientific Growth*, 45.

7. Adam Smith, *An Inquiry into the Nature and Causes of the Wealth of Nations* (Indianapolis: Liberty Classics, 1981), 663.

8. J. W. Horrocks, *A Short History of Mercantilism* (London: Methuen, 1925), 138–40.

9. Much literature on German economic history, and an overwhelming majority of general studies, concentrate on Prussia. In the context of discussing agrarian development of the eighteenth century, John H. Clapham, for example, writes, "As Prussia after 1815 was the sole state representative of almost all Germany, with lands stretching from the servile Slavonic east to the free Dutch west, the Prussian development deserves the closest study. It illustrates every point of importance" (*The Economic Development of France and Germany, 1815–1914* [Cambridge: Cambridge University Press, 1936], 42). Keith Tribe, in turn, points out that "the history of the German economy in the eighteenth century is dominated by Prussia—whose territories and institutions extended across northern and eastern Germany. . . . Cameralism first developed in Prussian universities." (*Governing Economy: The Reformation of German Economic Discourse, 1750–1840* [Cambridge: Cambridge University Press, 1988], 8).

10. G. Schmoller, "Friedrich Wilhelm I und das politische Testament von 1722," quoted in Tribe, *Governing Economy*, 9.

11. Friedrich II, quoted in Tribe, *Governing Economy*, 19. Also see discussion in Hajo Holborn, "Welfare and Power," in *A History of Modern Germany, 1648–1840* (New York: Alfred Knopf, 1964), 240–42.

12. See Tribe, *Governing Economy*, 24, 51.

13. Ibid., 19.

14. Ibid., 35.

15. *Wissenschaft,* which corresponds to the modern English notion of "scholarship."

16. Tribe's translation of the passages from Zincke's Lexicon that appear in *Governing Economy* (54, 51) are slightly modified, highlighting the nature of the German terms in parentheses.

17. Tribe, *Governing Economy,* 60.

18. J.H.G. von Justi, *Die Staatswirtschaft oder systematische Adhandlung aller oekonomischen und Cameralwissenschaften, die zur Regierung eines Landes erfordert werden,* vol 1 (Leipzig, 1958), 32. The English translation appears in *The Introduction of Adam Smith's Doctrines into Germany,* ed. and trans. C. W. Hasek (New York: Columbia University Press, 1925), 36.

19. Justi, *Die Staatswirtschaft,* 59–60; Hasek, ed. and trans., *The Introduction of Adam Smith,* 37.

20. Justi, *Die Staatswirtschaft,* 45; quoted in Tribe, *Governing Economy,* 68.

21. See Justi, *Die Staatswirtschaft,* 48, Hasek, ed. and trans., *The Introduction of Adam Smith,* 38. First edition (Justi, 5) quoted in Tribe, *Govering Economy,* 73.

22. Justi's Vienna lecture notes, quoted in Tribe, *Governing Economy,* 62.

23. *The Theory of the Moral Sentiments,* in which Smith announced his plan for *The Wealth of Nations,* it will be remembered, appeared in 1759.

24. J.G.H. Feder, in *Göttingische gelehrte Anzeigen,* 10 March 1777 and 5 April 1777; also quoted in Hasek, ed. and trans., *The Introduction of Adam Smith,* 63–64.

25. Hasek, ed. and trans., *The Introduction of Adam Smith,* 79.

26. E. Kühn, quoted in Tribe, *Governing Economy,* 147.

27. According to W. Roscher, who finds inexplicable the meagerness of Kraus's published output. See Hasek, ed. and trans., *The Introduction of Adam Smith,* 87.

28. Tribe, *Governing Economy,* 149–58.

29. This idea was backed by the additional authority of the Physiocrats, who also enjoyed a brief vogue in Germany in the 1770s and the 1780s, though the Germans' final judgment on their contribution was quite similar to what Smith thought: it was irrelevant. A German professor in 1786 put it rather unkindly: Physiocracy, he said, was like "a girl as beauteous as an angel, but unfortunately a virgin" (quoted in Tribe, *Governing Economy,* 130).

30. Tribe, who does not at all focus on nationalism and the place of *Nationaloekonomie* in its development, notes nevertheless, "[At first] the name for this 'new economics' had a strategic value and was itself the object of controversy" (ibid., 171).

31. "At no time before had so many books on economics appeared in so short a time," writes Hasek of this period (*The Introduction of Adam Smith,* 94).

32. Jakob, *Grundsaetze,* vii, 4 (quoted in Tribe, *Governing Economy,* 170).

33. Tribe, *Governing Economy,* 167.

34. Goetz A. Briefs, "The Economic Philosophy of Romanticism," *Journal of the History of Ideas* 2, no. 3 (1941): 287–95; Hans. S. Reiss, *The Political Thought of German Romantics* (Oxford: Basil Blackwell, 1995), 142–50.

35. Richard Hofstadter, *The Age of Reform: From Bryan to F.D.R.* (New York: Vintage, 1955), 144, 134–35.

36. See James Oliver Robertson, *America's Business* (New York: Hill and Wang, 1985), 87–89.

37. Henry Adams, *The Education of Henry Adams: An Autobiography* (1907; New York: Modern Library, 1996), 32.

38. Hofstadter, *The Age of Reform*, 137.

39. Edward Chase Kirkland, *Dream and Thought in the Business Community, 1860–1900* (Chicago: Elephant Paperbacks, 1990), 6.

40. Walter E. Weyl, *The New Democracy: An Essay on Certain Political and Economic Tendencies in the United States* (New York: MacMillan, 1913), 244–46.

41. See Liah Greenfeld, *Nationalism: Five Roads to Modernity* (Cambridge: Harvard University Press, 1992), 139–40.

42. "Of 105 patriotic orders founded between 1783 and 1900, 34 originated before 1870 and 71 between 1870 and 1900," writes Hofstadter (*The Age of Reform*, 138, note 8). He continues, "The increase of patriotic and genealogical societies during the status revolution suggests that many old-family Americans, who were losing status in the present, may have found satisfying compensation in turning to family glories of the past. Of course, a large proportion of these orders were founded during the nationalistic outbursts of the nineties; but those too may have had their subtle psychological relation to status changes. Note the disdain of men like Theodore Roosevelt for the lack of patriotism and aggressive nationalism among men of great wealth" (ibid.).

43. Weyl, *The New Democracy*, 245–46.

44. Ibid., 247. Weyl continued, "In actual fact we always had less equality than we now like to believe. . . . Americans have never worshiped a rigid equality of wealth. They have always been willing to condone inequality which was measurable, which could be overcome in a lifetime, which represented, or might represent, superior attainments of the wealthier. But present inequalities differ so widely in degree from our old inequalities as to differ in kind. The rich are so rich that they can hardly help growing richer. A multimillionaire may be dissipated, lazy, imbecile, spendthrift, and yet automatically he gains more in a month than the average man earns in a lifetime" (ibid., 247–48). The latter was a theoretical possibility, however. As far as we know, neither Rockefeller, nor Carnegie, nor any number of other eminent capitalists, was an imbecile or an idler. They were resented all the same, and since it was awkward to resent them for their virtues, they were attributed imaginary vices.

45. I borrow the adjective from Edward Shils, who writes, "Until the formation of the Johns Hopkins University, the learned world in the United States was rather inchoate. It had no center, it had no hierarchy" ("The Order of Learning in the United States from 1865–1920: The Ascendancy of the Universities," *Minerva* 16, no. 2 [1978]: 187).

46. What Shils calls "an order of learning" was not yet an order in this sense.

47. Walter P. Metzger, *Academic Freedom in the Age of the University* (New York: Columbia University Press, 1961), 31.

48. Ibid., 5.

49. Henry Adams, *The Education of*, 54–55.

50. Metzger, *Academic Freedom*, 26–27.

51. Ibid., 30.

52. Ibid., 32.

53. This was chiefly the result of their role as architects of German nationalism, which allowed them to position themselves advantageously within the German culture and national consciousness. See Greenfeld, *Nationalism*, chapter on Germany.

54. Shils, "Order of Learning," 174.

55. Henry Wadsworth Longfellow, "Higher Education in America" (Andrew Dickson White, 1871). Quoted in Metzger, *Academic Freedom*, 100–101. Only Shils's own idealism and dedication to learning could lead him to believe that this determination reflected in the first place "the avidity of intellectual desire," "the all-decisive fact of the love of learning," and the "irrepressible desire to understand," to which noble sentiments the wish "to confer legitimacy on and elevate the status of the new academic professions and to increase their public influence" (which he admits) was but secondary ("Order of Learning," 162, 167, 168, 174). As in any social movement, which inevitably unites people on the basis of the lowest common denominator, behind it was an avidity of a very different kind.

56. Shils, "Order of Learning," 174, 176.

57. See Metzger, *Academic Freedom*, 46–48.

58. Shils, "Order of Learning," 168, 194.

59. Charles F. Dunbar, "Economic Science in America, 1776–1876," *North American Review* 122 (January, 1876): 140.

60. See Frances Wayland, preface to *The Elements of Political Economy* (1837); John McVickar, *First Lesson in Political Economy* (1825), 34, 23. Both are quoted in J. F. Normano, *The Spirit of American Economics: A Study in the History of Economic Ideas in the United States Prior to the Great Depression* (London: Dennis Dobson, 1943), 62. (Wayland was the president of Brown University; his book was the most popular textbook on the subject before the Civil War. Reverend McVickar was the first professor of Political Economy at Columbia College and, apparently, the first to teach it in the country.)

61. Normano, *The Spirit of American Economics*, 81.

62. Dunbar, "Economic Science," 137–38.

63. See Paul K. Conkin, *Prophets of Prosperity: American's First Political Economists* (Bloomington: Indiana University Press, 1980), 171–280.

64. Hofstadter, *The Age of Reform*, 149.

65. Simon N. Patten, "The Scope of Political Economy," *The Yale Review* (November, 1893): 264–87.

66. Ibid., 274–75.

67. Ibid., 267–69.

68. Quoted in A. W. Bob Coats, "The First Two Decades of the American Economic Association," in *The Sociology and Professionalization of Economics: British and American Economic Essays*, vol. 2 (London: Routledge, 1993), 207.

69. Quotations from this discussion are found in A. W. Bob Coats, "The Political Economy Club: A Neglected Episode in American Economic Thought," in *The Sociology and Professionalization of Economics*, 225–38.

70. Coats, "The American Economic Association," 205–6.

71. Richard T. Ely, *An Introduction to Political Economy* (New York: Hunt & Eaton, 1894), 72, 85–90.

72. Coats, "The American Economic Association," 205–14. Also see Albion W. Small, "Relations of Sociology to Economics," *The Journal of Political Economy* (March, 1895): 169–84.

73. Quoted in Coats, "The American Economic Association," 216.

74. Stanford Wharton, other sources, quoted in Kirkland, *Dream and Thought*, 66, 86, 93–94, 96–101.

75. Chauncey Wright, quoted in Metzger, *Academic Freedom*, 80.

76. This both attracted to economics, and created a niche for, people with special abilities and inclinations (for instance, those who were good at math, though, perhaps, not passionate enough about it to devote their lives to pure mathematics, or those who enjoyed formal, abstract reasoning for the sake of it) whose social interests were significantly different from those of the founders of this academic profession.

77. George Stigler, *The Economist as Preacher* (1984), 223; quoted in Coats, "Learned Journals in Economics," 197.

78. This professional authority—a reflection of the formality, abstractness, and esoteric nature of the discipline—was communicated by association to such of its members who were not at all, or less, formal, abstract, and esoteric, but engaged, for instance in descriptive studies or policy recommendations. It was well established by World War I and from then on allowed the coexistence of theoretical, practical, and descriptive orientations in economics. Theoretical work has been regarded most highly. But, normally, most influential policy advisors have also been the most prominent theorists, and had first to establish themselves as such.

CHAPTER 4

Professional Status and the Moral Order

HENRIKA KUKLICK

THE REORGANIZATION of work in the United States during the period roughly bounded by the Civil and the First World Wars has been the subject of a voluminous scholarly literature. This scholarship has focused on both industrial labor and the range of occupations that is the topic of this paper—the well-remunerated and highly regarded pursuits we customarily term "professions." These include, but are not limited to, the traditional learned professions of physician, lawyer, and clergyman; and a range of occupations that were dramatically reconfigured at the end of the nineteenth century—such as that of the engineer, whose training ground shifted from the shop floor to the classroom—and that of the university professor, whose area of specialization might not have been recognized as such at the beginning of the century, and who was (if employed at an elite institution) now expected to produce original scholarship.[1] Certainly, the work of traditional learned professionals was and has remained distinct from that of others in one respect: traditional professionals manage life crises—matters that are for them, in contradistinction to their clients, quotidian occurrences, and for which they have developed routine procedures—performing duties analogous to those also required of persons whose jobs are far less prestigious, such as, say, policemen and undertakers.[2] But this paper treats only those occupations that in the late nineteenth century as well as in our day have been accorded professional status *both* because they have enjoyed high social standing *and* because their practice has been organized in a distinct form—defining characteristics that suggest that physicians, say, have more in common with engineers and college professors than with policemen.

Studies of professions have emphasized two structural features that have been the basis of professionals' claims to authority since the end of the nineteenth century. One, they were organized as *communities* of practitioners, each putatively possessing its own exclusive domain of esoteric expertise, the fundamentals of which were conveyed in formal training programs established in universities—the overall avowed purpose of which had moved away from moral education toward inculcation of specialized knowledge. Two, they were granted powers of self-regulation, frequently sanctioned by state licensing laws, which permitted professional groups to expel individuals whose occupational performance was substandard. Professionals justified their occupational structure with the claim that its form guaranteed their social function: that the high standard of practice instilled in professionals during their rigorous training was enforced throughout their careers by self-regulatory mechanisms that ensured that all practitioners would render services of high quality to all clients—regardless of clients' personal characteristics (including their ability to pay for experts' ministrations). Thus, the professionals' ideology explained away an apparent paradox: insulation from social pressures guaranteed a high level of social responsibility rather than its absence.[3]

Scholars have, however, paid scant attention to the phenomenon I will emphasize: how the self-conscious professionalizers of a century ago understood the purpose of their efforts. To recent scholars in particular, my subject has seemed practically irrelevant. Professionals' avowed motives, which once seemed altogether admirable, now seem suspect, as having been merely self-serving rationalizations. Current conventional scholarly wisdom has supplanted that of a generation (or two) ago, which represented professionalization as but one manifestation of an increasingly meritocratic social order, to which professionals' newly rationalized skills were essential, and in which professionals' increased material and status rewards constituted just recompense for their contributions to collective well-being.[4] Recent scholars have stressed that differences of class, race, and gender have both selectively shaped individual professionals' career trajectories and constituted limiting constraints on clients' access to expert services. And they have debunked professionals' claims that their specialized knowledge has entitled them to jurisdiction over specific substantive spheres, arguing that the barriers professionals have erected to protect their actions from public scrutiny have served as much to conceal the extent of their ignorance as to effect the advertised benefits of a system of peer review of occupational performance. Moreover, current scholarship reflects wider opinion—as, indeed, did the scholarly analyses of a century ago—a point to which I will return.

I am not suggesting that recent critiques have no merit. Moreover, the rhetoric of professionalization of the late nineteenth and early twentieth centuries can easily be construed as almost shameless. For example, the liberal economist Richard T. Ely argued that because expertise of the sort he possessed could be used to effect positive social change, it was "the most convincing proof of the divinity of Christ."[5] And Ely spoke for many other members of the new class of self-styled experts to which he belonged—including persons whose politics were far more conservative than his—when he identified this class as "a natural aristocracy"; they were the legitimate elite of a social organism composed of interdependent individuals who differed in "power, capacity, [and] requirements," entitled to provide societal leadership not least because they "live[d] for the fulfillment of special service."[6] And a congeries of reformers—including (but hardly limited to) college presidents, heads of federal government agencies, anthropologists, engineers, lawyers, physicians, psychologists, and social workers—were virtually unanimous in their judgment that a new, meritocratic order required that possessors of valuable skills be rewarded with money and status in appropriate measure.[7]

Specialists' fitness to play leadership roles in society, many sorts of educators claimed, derived as much from their training as from their inherent qualities, for educational discipline developed character as well as skills, molding persons who would repudiate selfish partisanship and act on behalf of society as a whole.[8] Indeed, professionals often represented themselves as uniquely qualified to undertake such action, and their pleas for freedom to regulate the performance of their occupational tasks without interference from nonspecialists betrayed near contempt for the general public. Consider, for example, the chemist Ira Remsen's argument that the masses were incapable of determining their own needs and inordinately impressed by scientific displays that "any clever trickster" could mount; it was more likely that scientists would produce findings beneficial for humankind (ultimately, if not immediately) if they were relieved of the obligation to win public approval, free to pursue pure science without regard for its possible practical applications.[9] Likewise, Edmund James asserted in his 1910 presidential address to the American Economics Association that the lot of the entire population would improve if trained experts were granted the power to manage the nation's resources efficiently.[10]

Recent scholarship has successfully demonstrated clear disparities between professionals' claims and the realities of social life, disparities that have persisted from the nineteenth century to the present. Consider that in the late nineteenth century parental social status was the most important factor in recruitment to and distribution of students within the stratified university system. And established distinctions of wealth and power determined both clients' access to experts' services and the hierarchy of prestige within professions, so that, for example, among lawyers a group of (still-existing) elite firms emerged to provide the tactical guidance that facilitated a wave of large-scale business consolidations.[11]

Nevertheless, the rhetorical formulae of professional ideology were understood quite differently a century ago than they are in our day, and their authors would likely see only a superficial resemblance between the changes they envisioned and their actual legacy. Professionalizers advanced the interests of the educated class, certainly, but they also promoted a general scheme for social reform from which they themselves did not intend to benefit alone. Representative of the population of self-conscious professionalizers were the contributors to the social scientific discussion of this era, many of them not social scientists by trade, to whose ideas I now turn.

SELF-CONSCIOUS AGENTS OF HISTORY

If we understand early social scientists as a group to be representative of a larger population, we take them on their own valuation, for they did not describe their ideas as esoteric wisdom. Anthropologists, economists, political scientists, psychologists, and sociologists claimed no more for their theories than that they were refined versions of then-contemporary common sense. Indeed, they recognized what we now see when we read their writings—that the different disciplines were barely distinguishable—observing that the branches of social science had yet to become mature, specialized enterprises.[12] Nevertheless, they did not forecast that when the various human sciences became clearly differentiated, their practitioners would inevitably cease to be concerned with mundane issues.

That is, the social scientists of a century ago understood themselves in historical terms, as agents of specific evolutionary trends. As E.R.A. Seligman put it in his chronicle of the development of economic thought, social scientists' ideas were shaped by social circumstances, and "must be regarded primarily as the outgrowth of the particular conditions of time, place, and nationality under which the doctrines were evolved." And it is notable that of all of the contributions to the collection in which Seligman's historical essay appeared, his was the only one that occasioned no rebuttal, for economists in this period regarded his position as unexceptionable, though they differed on many issues.[13] In general, then, social scientists' vision of their place in history meant that they agreed that their schemes would be embraced—and would endure—only if, like other successful innovations, they had adaptive value for social life.[14] Each individual act might seem to its agent to be the product of "its origin and its goal," William James observed, and yet each act was but "one link in the vast chain of processes of which history is made. . . . You think that *you* are acting and you are only obeying someone's push. You think that you are doing *this*, but you are doing something of which you do not dream" [italics his].[15]

Conspicuous among the ideas of late-nineteenth-century social thinkers was the lament for lost virtues of the simpler society of the past, a recurrent motif of cultural criticism in the United States (and elsewhere). That is, economic factors were responsible for the proliferation of visible symptoms of pathological disorder—such as polluted air, substandard housing, and unsettled social conditions—which were the consequences of rapid industrialization and urbanization, the dysfunctional dynamic of which was itself exacerbated by considerable immigration. The social environment was unhealthy because wealth was increasingly concentrated in the hands of the few, the poor were growing increasingly numerous and resentful, and workers were becoming alienated as their division of labor became ever more elaborated. In particular, workers obliged to perform highly specialized tasks lost comprehension not only of the value of their labors to their specific enterprises but also of the contributions that their work made to the successful operation of society as a whole, becoming both disinclined to do their jobs properly and consumed by hostile passions. Indeed, the nation's social ills were coming to a crisis, posing a problem "really of life and death," as the New York pediatrician Henry Dwight Chapin observed to the American Social Science Organization, suggesting that outright class warfare was imminent.[16] Certainly, some dismissed the notion of a lost golden age as sentimental fiction.[17] But few agreed with William Graham Sumner that painful social conflicts were necessary to evolution.[18] Industrial strife was evidence of regression to "barbarism and not [of] civilization," as Richard Ely put it, invoking the specter of degeneration that many then saw looming large over supposedly advanced societies.[19]

Nevertheless, even the most gloomy of social scientific forecasts were customarily qualified with prophesies of the problem-solving potential of the social sciences: scientific reasoning, applied to social problems, could cure the ills for which it was in some measure responsible. That is, the social sciences represented the liberal alternative to the conservative critique of modernization exemplified by the writing of Henry Adams and his kind, in which technological change was also understood as a source of societal fragmentation.[20] Social scientists spoke for a significant group of Americans, usually termed "Progressives," whose numbers and influence had been growing since the 1870s, and whose efforts were animated by their search for what Olivier Zunz has recently characterized as "a 'via media' between *laissez faire* and the dangers of socialism," both of which "were inadequate for an industrializing nation"—the former "not capable of responding to the challenges of a new political economy," the latter "too drastic a departure from American traditions of individualism and entrepreneurship."[21] As is well-known, many early social scientists were children of clergymen or were themselves former clergymen (or both), persons who understood social inquiry as a moral calling that ought not to be limited to scholarship alone but that should entail practical action, such as service in settlement houses and participation in local politics. And their theories rationalized their view of history, as well as their understanding of their own place in it.

Over time, they believed, the social sciences would grow more rigorous, and as they did, their potential utility would also grow.[22] And as the social sciences' applicability to practical matters grew, their practitioners would incur unavoidable moral obligations to undertake work in service to society. Their task, according to sociologist Lester Ward, was "to help on a certain evolution by averting an otherwise equally certain revolution."[23] Because progressive change occurred in different sectors of society at different rates, the task of social scientists was to eradicate so-called survivals of earlier stages of evolution—institutions and attitudes that cultural developments had rendered obsolete. Political scientists, for example, should specify constitutional changes that would make the formal political order suitable for general social needs.[24] Psychologists should define that "reflective consciousness of self" required for adjustment to contemporary life.[25] Sociologists should determine "in what ways and to what extent social phenomena may, with a knowledge of their laws, be modified and directed toward social ideals," so as to *"accelerate social evolution"* [italics his].[26] Economists should establish the proper role of the state in the regulation of economic affairs, since the conditions that once permitted free market competition no longer obtained—a proposition that even the most fervent proponents of laissez faire accepted to a limited degree.[27]

Evidently, the evolutionist scheme that underlay reformers' recommendations bore little resemblance to the creed of the archetypal "Social Darwinist."[28] Social scientific opinion was not unanimous, certainly, and individuals quibbled over details in the historical pattern they saw unfolding. Nevertheless, one may fairly judge that there was widespread agreement that with evolution humans became, in the words of philosopher James Tufts, liberated from "the body of original instinctive impulses which comprise the natural self," acquiring instead "a voluntary self in which socialized desires and affections are dominant."[29] Once humans had gained control over their physical environment, satisfying "the demand of the body for nourishment and protection," as sociologist Franklin Giddings observed, they could attend to "the demand of body and mind for exhilarating activity; for the pleasures of sight and sound, of imagination and of sentiment, and for the deeper satisfactions of understanding and faith."[30] In sum, the view that evolution permitted human action to proceed practically unconstrained by natural limits—environmental factors or base biological impulses—was promoted by many social thinkers. We therefore must reject what has become conventional historical wisdom: that many varieties of human scientists were persuaded to embrace social determinism through the singular efforts of one of their factions—the anthropological school of Franz Boas, whose ideas gained wide currency not least because they had popular, as well as esoteric, appeal.[31]

Certainly, some social scientists suggested that questions about the role of conscious choice in human progress defied solution and should be tabled, at least for the moment, if not forever—a view that anticipated the behaviorist model that would prevail in psychology after World War I. But most, regardless of their primary disciplinary interest, accepted John Dewey's psychological model of learning as a recursive process, in which adaptive behavioral modification followed recognition of error.[32] According to psychologist C. H. Judd,

The importance of consciousness in the evolutionary process is that it solves the age-long opposition of individual and environment in a new way, giving to both a unique recognition and to the individual a supremacy over external conditions which none of his other functions ever permitted. Contrast consciousness with the nutritive function. Through digestion much material is taken into the organism and is used to build up animal tissue, but there is no reflex influence in the outer world. The environment is not made, through the process of digestion, more digestible for the future. When, however, we discover through consciousness how to use the world for the ends of individual life, the environment itself can be modified so that it will from that time on be different in its relation to the evolved individual.[33]

Moreover, it seemed that rational calculations became increasingly important in human conduct as evolution progressed. Indeed, the development of the social sciences was itself compelling evidence of humans' growing powers of self-management. "Human society" was, as Edmund James said, "for the first time in its history . . . reflecting upon its own constitution, the ends and purposes of its own existence."[34] And for many (if not all) social scientists, it followed that when humans progressed to the higher stages of evolution they became not only rational but also altruistic, ethical beings—a judgment often explained with Lamarckian biological reasoning.[35] Spiritually animated humans were predisposed to cooperative action. Arguably, cooperative behavior was a defining human trait: even primordial humans were fundamentally social animals. Perhaps interpersonal competition had had positive value during the human species' earliest days, ensuring the "survival of the fittest," but the exigencies of existence in unimproved nature must also have encouraged humans to band together to overcome their common problems. And as evolution proceeded, cooperation became the predominant mode of human interaction, effected by the development of formal social institutions that fostered both rational and moral behavior.

Indeed, rational and ethical judgments were coterminous because both were products of collective efforts; they derived from "the workings of the social whole . . . in the complex interactions and interrelations which constitute the whole," as John Dewey argued in his 1900 presidential address to the American Psychological Association.[36] Not least because Dewey had a genius for seizing the liberal political middle ground of his day, as Alan Ryan has recently observed, it is worth quoting at length from this address, which exemplified the brief for professionalism advanced by social reformers of his time. Optimal practice of any skill, Dewey asserted, depended on

an *organic* connection . . . between the theorist and the practical worker—through the medium of the linking science. The decisive matter is the extent to which the ideas of the theorist actually project themselves . . . into the consciousness of the practitioner. It is the participation by the practical man in the theory, through the agency of the linking science, that determines at once the effectiveness of the work done, and the moral freedom and personal development of the one engaged in it. It is because the physician no longer follows rules, which, however rational in themselves, are yet arbitrary to him (because grounded in principles that he does not understand) that his work is becoming liberal, attaining the dignity of a profession, instead of remaining a mixture of empiricism and quackery. It is because, alas, engineering makes only a formal and not a real connection between physics and practical workingmen in the mills, that our industrial problem is an ethical problem of the most serious kind. The question of the amount of wages the laborer receives, the purchasing power of his wage, of the hours and condition of his labor, are, after all, secondary. The problem primarily roots in the fact that the mediating science does not connect with consciousness, but merely with his outward actions. He does not appreciate the significance and bearing of what he does; and he does not perform his work because of sharing in a larger scientific and social consciousness. If he did, he would be free. . . he would have entered into the ethical kingdom.[37]

Thus, persons developed their spiritual potential by equating their individual and group identities and by recognizing that because group achievements were the emergent products of social interaction, they were far more significant accomplishments than the sum of contributions of individuals qua individuals could be.

Because human capacity to recognize ethical/rational truths depended on the organization of collectivist groups of all sorts—from political units to scientific research communities—human improvement could be deliberately fostered. And work groups were the paramount vehicles for realization of human cooperative potential. Since individual alienation and social disintegration were products of the fragmentation of labor, these disorders could be cured if work were reorganized to foster individuals' identification with their occupational groups, Workers would then become conscious of their responsibilities to society. To quote sociologist Albion Small,

[L]ife will be raised to its highest power when it ceases to be a struggle for dominance among interests, and becomes a cooperative enterprise between men committed to team work between their interests. . . . Security of occupation, influence upon and income from occupation, not as determined by the rules of obsolescent interest-politics, but as indicated by performance of function within the occupation—these are achievements to be realized in high degree in the course of the next two or three generations. . . . [M]en of the forward look will more and more . . . concentrate their labors upon the aim to realize life as a community of reciprocated functions.[38]

Furthermore, the workplace was the site in which it was most obvious that individualism was pathological, for the person who labored in individualistic fashion—with neither the support to be gained from consultation with colleagues nor a sense of collective purpose—was prone to all manner of ailments, from depression to a dramatically shortened lifespan.[39]

Professional groups exemplified the socially grounded morality and rationality characteristic of advanced society, demonstrating that the fullest expression of humans' capacity to behave rationally was action designed to improve collective welfare. That is, professional organization was defensible primarily as a means to moral reform, for the elevated technical standard at which professionals could be expected to perform their duties was inextricable from the ethical obligations they accepted.[40] But I must emphasize that the proponents of professional organization understood their occupational groups as only one type of the corporate bodies through which social integration could be effected.

Indeed, the most telling evidence of professionalizers' expectations was their attitude toward ordinary laborers, and especially to workers' efforts to organize unions. That is, many reformers believed that workers were no different from high-status professionals: they, too, could become integrated members of society at large by becoming well-adjusted members of occupational groups.[41] Unions were moral communities, assuming responsibility for the well-being of their members by developing social welfare schemes, as well as "set[ting] their powers against drunkenness and immorality . . . [and] encourag[ing] thrift and education."[42] Such efforts, as well as unions' manifest objective—improvement of laborers' employment conditions through collective bargaining—raised workers' standards of living and thus militated against both strikes and those irrational, purposeless acts of violence directed against management that individuals might commit out of frustration. According to political scientist Jeremiah Jenks, the organization of labor enabled disputes to be settled by peaceful means that would "render full justice to laborers without oppressing employers or checking the productivity of either."[43]

Just as—if not more—important, workers acquired "increased scope of self-direction," according to economist John Commons, when they won freedom from management coercion through union organization; and, he continued, "useful labor thus becomes a motive in itself, and the industrial institution, like other institutions, is established on its own clarified, persuasive basis, the love of work."[44] In sum, by encouraging cooperation rather than conflict, joining persons in common purposes so that they subordinated their individual objectives to collective goals, unions were agents of evolutionary progress, bringing the "human . . . into greater prominence over the selfish animal nature," as the long-time leader of the American Federation of Labor, Samuel Gompers, told his audience at a meeting of the American Social Science Association.[45]

That opposition to unions was socially counterproductive was evident from the results of employers' systematic efforts to discourage union organization. A company town such as Pullman, Richard T. Ely noted, was intended to be a community that would provide a functional alternative to union solidarity, but it was a failure as such. Its residents were provided material comforts of high quality, but because they were deprived of opportunities to regulate their own lives, they did not develop genuine community spirit.[46] And scientific management, the repertoire of industrial techniques given formal articulation in 1911 in F. W. Taylor's *Principles of Scientific Management*, might have succeeded in destroying laborers' social cohesion, setting worker against worker and thus eradicating the tendency to collusion against management, of which unionization was just one expression. But because Taylorism turned workers into alienated laborers, it did not serve the interests of workers, employers, or society as a whole.[47]

Moreover, however prominent a place the creation of socially cohesive work groups occupied in human scientists' schemes for social reform, work units were not the only objects of reformers' attentions. Social scientists believed that many groups based on nontraditional affinities (that is, not grounded in such loyalties as ethnic and religious ties) could perform functions analogous to those of occupational groups. See, for example, the arguments of those who wished to restore to the American city a measure of the autonomy that it had lost since the Civil War, so that its leaders could become more responsive to local needs: the reconstructed urban environment would then give rise to "a solidarity which contains a measure of altruism," permitting restoration of the "ideas of justice between man and man which once prevailed," according to Edgar J. Levey.[48] Indeed, residential neighborhoods within the city could be seen as the loci for creation of social solidarity—which was itself equivalent to occupational solidarity in the scheme promoted by Melusina Fay (Mrs. Charles S.) Peirce, who called for socialization of childcare and housework within neighborhoods, arguing that this reform would elevate women's customary role and thus advance social evolution.[49] Or for the rapidly escalating numbers of young people who pursued higher education, the physical places they inhabited as students—classrooms, laboratories, and athletic fields—could be deliberately transformed into sites for inculcation of the idealized mode of cooperative behavior. In these sites, what mattered was less the formal object of student attentions than the transformative experience of collective, purposive action, which students would subsequently reenact in leading socially constructive occupational lives.[50] And in residential facilities in which behavioral deviants were confined—such as hospitals for "inebriates" (as alcoholics were then termed)—therapeutic regimens were devised to join patients in groups that performed productive labor, so that individuals would learn to realize norms of social responsibility that they could apply to their conduct in the outside world upon their release.[51]

Of course, the professionalizers' model of individual self-realization effected through identification with occupational and other social groups could
not be preserved intact once the evolutionary scheme that underpinned it was
discredited.[52] Certainly, the model survived in modified form as a post–
World War I elaboration of Progressive ideology, and, indeed, in the theories
of mass society promulgated during and after World War II. These schemes
resembled their antecedent insofar as they suggested measures to prevent the
United States from becoming a mass society—an aggregate of isolated individuals. Nevertheless, post–World War I theories differed dramatically in
their vision of ideal social order, for in them the virtue of strong social
groups was *not* that they engendered feelings of loyalty that naturally
extended to the entire social organism but that they *contained* members'
sentiments of social solidarity within the boundaries of delimited populations. That is, because professional and other groups gave meaning to individual lives, members of these groups supposedly became immune to the
lure of mass movements promoted by trade unions, radical political parties
and the like, as well as resistant to the extension of state authority.[53] It is
beyond the scope of this paper to account for the decline of the evolutionist
model of social integration, but before I move on to a discussion of current
developments I want to point out that late-nineteenth- and early-twentieth-
century American liberal reformers were not unlike their fellows elsewhere;
Émile Durkheim's model of social integration much resembled the American
one, for example, as did that of the reforming intelligentsia in Britain—
which included figures such as Thomas Huxley, Karl Pearson, and Sidney
and Beatrice Webb.[54]

An End to Professional Authority?

It is significant that the onset of scholarly skepticism about the merits of
professionalism in the 1960s coincided with clients' protests against professional authority. Initially vulnerable to attack were the relatively powerless
groups among professionals—university faculties and social workers—
though one must also note that professors and social welfare providers participated in (and even led) the campaigns of students and recipients of social
services, and that (ironically) their stated objectives much resembled those of
nineteenth-century professional reformers.[55] Indeed, it would be easy to document the further erosion of professional power with examples drawn from
the recent histories of social work and university teaching, and perhaps especially easy to do so with illustrations of the currently parlous state of the
academy—the growing percentage of part-time workers among instructors,
leading to the practical elimination of tenure in many institutions; the lack of

occupational solidarity denoted by the so-called culture wars; and even the intellectual strategies embraced by many disciplines.

Nevertheless, similar changes may be observed in the experiences of other, higher-status professional groups. Their recent histories also provide impressive illustrations of loss of powers of self-regulation on the community level, as well as of the decline of autonomy in individual occupational practice. For example, lawyers and dentists (along with other sorts of health care providers) now advertise their services through subway posters, highway billboards, and the print and broadcast media. Advertising was once judged unethical, because a disregard for pecuniary concerns was believed a defining characteristic of professional occupations. But lawyers' and dentists' commercial strategies signal more than a deconstruction of yesteryear's genteel fiction: whether they have reluctantly allowed clients to determine the course of action in various proceedings or treatments, marketed routine services at competitive rates, or been compelled by insurance companies to accept set fees for given procedures, lawyers and dentists are now often pieceworkers, rather than experts who are compensated for their *advice*—which might be, in some cases, to take no action. And those who continue to sell advice, such as lawyers (particularly those who work in those firms that constitute the elite of the profession, which are growing increasingly large and bureaucratized), may be paid for their time rather than for performing variously priced tasks, but they have to record their labors for clients on time sheets marked with grids dividing lawyers' work days into units as short as six minutes—and they have to meet production quotas of billable hours.[56]

Moreover, just as the most compelling evidence that the professional creed of a century ago was not merely the self-serving ideology of a would-be elite is provided by its inclusion of appeals to enlarge the self-regulatory powers of the laboring classes, the most compelling evidence of the decline of professional authority in our day is provided by the embattled state of the medical profession. That is, in all of the classic accounts of the growth of professional power, it is the population of physicians who have—appropriately—served as exemplars of a community that has acquired monopolistic control of an occupational sphere by virtue of possession of both an exclusive body of expertise and extremely effective mechanisms of self-regulation. But today, as Rosemary Stevens suggests, in the medical profession there is movement "toward a system of specialties defined by the job market rather than by the professional system of specialist qualifications."[57]

We are all aware that constraints on physicians' judgments have been imposed by the institutions in which they work, by insurance companies, and by patients treating medical care as a consumer good; that physicians are suffering loss of income (though they are hardly impoverished); and that the diminished status of their profession has been reflected in declining rates of application to medical schools. Medicine today is far removed from the ideal-typical model of the self-regulating, independent profession: more than half of American doctors are now salaried employees; in particular, the vast majority of recent medical graduates occupy salaried positions in Health Maintenance Organizations, clinics, or hospitals; and virtually all doctors now have at least one contract with a managed care company. Thus, physicians have lost much of their erstwhile freedom to set their own performance standards. They routinely face directives that limit their office time with patients, restrict their therapeutic options, and set the fees they may charge for medical procedures at levels lower than those they once received. Not least of the reasons for recent changes in medical practice is that many hospitals and HMOs have been acquired by profit-seeking companies concerned to trim the costs of health care (though cost-cutting measures imposed on nonprofit and for-profit medical operations alike have not yielded expected savings).[58]

The choices patients make in treating medicine as a consumer good have a range of consequences. Some of these enlarge, rather than reduce, physicians' discretionary powers. For example, Preferred Provider Organizations (PPOs), which do not restrict physicians' actions to the extent that HMOs do, are proving more popular than HMOs.[59] But patients have grown increasingly distrustful of their physicians, not least because of revelations that in the recent past medical mistakes have been made with shocking frequency.[60] And patients now have access to information permitting them to become active participants in the management of their own care, as well as enlarged powers to seek legal redress for unsuccessful therapy: data about hospitals' death rates for specific procedures and about individual doctors' professional mishaps are now in the public domain; the Food and Drug Administration now permits direct advertising of ethical drugs; and health-care providers, no different from the vendors of any other services, are now legally liable if their treatments do not yield advertised benefits.[61] Because medical innovations are regularly reported in the mass media (often with inadequate attention paid to physicians' reservations about their merits), patients are demanding—and receiving—treatments that seem to them preferable to previous therapies.[62] Consumer power is most evident among sufferers from the most intractable ailments—as, arguably, was also the case in the past.[63] Members of AIDS advocacy groups, for example, have blurred the line between medical specialists and disease victims; not only are they able to make informed judgments about treatment options but they have also become sufficiently familiar with work on the scientific research frontier to affect the very process by which new therapies are developed, lobbying successfully for premature closure of clinical trials and release of drugs of uncertain efficacy.[64]

Indeed, what may be irrational patient-consumer choices have significantly altered the market for physicians' services. Doctors have been obliged to recognize that they compete for patients with providers of alternative therapies. According to a recent survey, more visits are now made to alternative medical providers than to primary care physicians, and the percentage of Americans who treat their ailments with some sort of alternative care is rising. Hence, physicians can no longer afford to ignore unorthodox medicine. They have recently mounted studies that evaluate procedures such as acupuncture, herbal remedies, and magnet therapy, and are now offering their patients such services as instruction in meditation as an aid to stress reduction, as well as providing medical students with courses in what they prefer to call "complementary medicine."[65]

Certainly, it would be wrong—or, at least premature—to write medicine's obituary as a powerful profession, unable to exert considerable control over its working conditions. The combined efforts of health-care experts and various federal-program administrators have been directed toward reducing the population of physicians practicing in the United States—a tactic that proved extremely effective at the beginning of the twentieth century, when physicians' status rose as their numbers diminished, following the closure of those medical schools deemed substandard in the 1910 report produced by Abraham Flexner under the auspices of the Carnegie Foundation for the Advancement of Teaching.[66] Autonomy in medical decision making is being reasserted through collective action—including unionization, once anathema to the American Medical Association and now promoted by it (in guarded form, and in competition with opportunities for organization offered under the auspices of established trade unions). Hospital managers' efforts to reorganize their institutions' structures to make them more efficient have been hampered by physicians, since, in the words of one *New York Times* reporter, "hospitals are one of the few businesses in America in which employees call the shots." And the bills of patients' rights passed by a number of states' legislatures have been framed as much to enhance physicians' autonomy as to serve patients' interests—though these are arguably entirely compatible ends.[67]

More significant as emblems of deprofessionalization are the signs that physicians are themselves willingly compromising collective craft standards. Consider the untrammeled capitalism that has prevailed in the practice of medically assisted reproduction (which involves not only physicians but also renumerated providers of a range of services, such as laypersons who recruit egg donors and women who bear implanted embryos to which they have no biological relation)."[68] Because the specialty of assisted reproduction has not been regulated in the United States as it has been elsewhere, this country has become a mecca for infertile couples from all over the world. Although recommendations to curb risky procedures have been made by the medical elite, American specialists in assisted reproduction have made treatment choices that violate medical values in order to keep their clinics commercially profitable—decisions encouraged not least because the Centers for Disease Control publish an annual consumer guide to fertility clinic success rates.[69] In order to insure relatively high rates of impregnation and live births, physicians here have been prepared to induce multiple pregnancies in numbers that are prohibited elsewhere, though they know that they are thus heightening the probability that mothers and infants will suffer various medical complications. And they have also been prepared to offer such services as custom mixing embryos for fees in excess of $16,000. Fertility doctors have recognized that their practices are ethically problematic, but have rejected regulation as a solution to their dilemmas, hoping that future technological developments will eliminate the need to make difficult choices.[70]

The practice of medically assisted reproduction represents a sensational illustration of abdication of ethical responsibility, but it is hardly an isolated instance. Consider that many physicians participating in clinical trials of experimental drugs have apparently violated the expected scientific standards thereof, seduced by the large financial bounties per patient paid by pharmaceutical companies eager to market drugs that may prove hugely profitable.[71] Consider that the *New England Journal of Medicine* and the *Journal of the American Medical Association*, the journals purveying supposedly authenticated knowledge to doctors, now publish studies of questionable methodological quality that are designed to gain attention in the mass media and thus increase the journals' appeal to and circulation among lay readers—so that doctors confronted with patients who are familiar with the journals' contents will feel obliged to take out subscriptions.[72] Consider the willingness of plastic surgeons to serve as fashion slaves.[73] And consider that the American Medical Association has lost power to effect collective standards as its membership has declined (the vast majority of physicians belonged to it in the 1960s; only a minority do now). For example, the AMA has failed to discourage entrepreneurial doctors from taking out patents on medical techniques—acts unknown two decades ago and rare in the 1980s—several of which are now granted each week, despite the AMA's judgment that insistence on proprietary rights to use specific techniques violates the code of medicine as an "altruistic calling" in which knowledge is "community property."[74]

Evidently, physicians still invoke the professional ideal of social service articulated a century ago, though today the gap between the ideal and the real is manifestly considerable.[75] And today wide currency is given to a scientific mantra that revives a theme popular a century ago: the human species will soon benefit from recent, exponential growth in the fund of scientific knowledge, and will soon have the resources that will enable it to control its own evolution.[76] And today, when, as was the case a century ago, the gap between rich and poor is widening (globally as well as locally), there are frequent echoes of the social criticisms of a century ago, laments for a lost (substantially fictitious) golden age. Nevertheless, marked changes have occurred in American professional lives during this century, perhaps especially during recent decades, and these changes represent the disappearance of self-regulation effected through corporate organization.

What situation is denoted by such developments? I certainly do not want to argue that erstwhile professional community solidarity necessarily conduced to altruism and disinterestedness, but I also do not want to argue that the professional moral ideal has had no practical impact. Once, the organization of occupational communities was understood as a means to counter the corruption of professional standards that might be induced by the pressures of the marketplace (though such organization was also a means to control the marketplace as such, to impose practitioners' conditions on clients' purchase of services, and thus to protect incomes). Now, the prevailing ideology seems to be that regulation of professional behavior is best left to the free play of market forces (notwithstanding the nostalgic yearnings of those who would have it otherwise). Certainly, there now exist many persons motivated to "live for the fulfillment of special service," but they arguably have rather restricted access to both the means and the opportunities to do so.

Of course, professional groups have been accustomed to representing themselves as moral communities because their *internal* economies were unregulated: no matter whether the commodities being exchanged were criteria to authenticate ancient Greek sculptures or evidence to prove string theory, free trade in the market of ideas was supposed to guarantee that the best of them would prevail. But nonprofessionals used to have no standing in this marketplace. Now they do, not least because many professionals understand themselves as mere technicians, having abandoned the belief that their occupations are moral callings, which require that they both treat clients holistically and consider the social implications of professional decisions.[77] Consider, for example, the rhetoric scientists now frequently use to disclaim responsibility for the potential applications of their work: science has its own momentum, and the only limitations that should be imposed on technical applications of scientific findings are the sum products of individuals' market choices; scientists need not be troubled by ethical concerns because laymen will naturally act in their own best interests.[78]

That many practitioners of the knowledge-based occupations that have been accorded the status of professions are now prepared to sell their skills in an unfettered marketplace testifies to a questionable faith that humans are thoroughly rational beings—beings who are capable of calculation and action in the service of their own interests, and whose selfish decisions will in the aggregate effect collective good. I must observe that this faith in the existence of Adam Smith's benign "Invisible Hand" is manifestly counterfactual, that we see everyday, everywhere, considerable evidence that individual choices are often at least foolish, if not outright destructive, for both the persons who make them and society as a whole. In sum, social critics of the late nineteenth and early twentieth centuries were right in at least one respect: corporatism did serve as protection against market forces. We are now all participating in an experiment testing the pessimistic predictions that their theory also implied.

NOTES

1. Not least of the reasons that students of the history of this period have found professions of extraordinary interest is that during this time the number of occupations claiming professional status grew enormously. Note, for example, that 245 national professional associations were founded between 1870 and 1900. See Olivier Zunz, *Why the American Century?* (Chicago: University of Chicago Press, 1998), 9.

2. Although categorizing occupations according to the emotional qualities of their practitioners' interaction with clients represents a provocative insight that can inspire interesting research, pursuit of this line of reasoning lies outside the scope of this paper. See Everett C. Hughes, *Men and Their Work* (Glencoe, Ill.: Free Press, 1958).

3. The literature from which these generalizations derive is enormous. See, for example, Andrew Abbott, *The System of Professions* (Chicago: University of Chicago Press, 1988); Randall Collins, *The Credential Society* (New York: Academic Press, 1979); Eliot Freidson, *Professional Powers* (Chicago: University of Chicago Press, 1986); Samuel Haber, *The Quest for Authority and Honor in the American Professions, 1750–1900* (Chicago: University of Chicago Press, 1991); Magali Sarfatti Larson, *The Rise of Professionalism* (Berkeley: University of California Press, 1977); Elliot A. Krause, *Death of the Guilds* (New Haven: Yale University Press, 1996); Paul Starr, *The Social Transformation of American Medicine* (New York: Basic Books, 1982).

Much scholarly attention has been focused on the professoriate in particular, and especially on social scientists and the formation of their disciplines from the end of the nineteenth century. Most useful are Peter Novick's *That Noble Dream* (New York: Cambridge University Press, 1988); and Frank Striker, "American Professors in the Progressive Era: Incomes, Aspirations, and Professionalism," *Journal of Interdisciplinary History* 29 (1988): 231–57.

4. See, for illustrations of now suspect views, Kingsley Davis and Wilbert E. Moore, "Some Principles of Stratification," *American Sociological Review* 10 (1945): 242–49 (hereafter cited as *ASR*); William J. Goode, "Community Within a Community: The Professions," *ASR* 22 (1957): 194–200; and Talcott Parsons, "The Professions and Social Structure," *Social Forces* 17 (1939): 457–67. For one effort to document the gradual development of American society into a meritocracy, see Peter Dobkin Hall, *The Organization of American Culture, 1700–1900* (New York: New York University Press, 1982).

5. Richard T. Ely, quoted in Zunz, *Why the American Century?* 28.

6. Richard T. Ely, "Fundamental Beliefs in My Social Philosophy," *The Forum* 18 (1894): 183. For a more secular—and more politically conservative—statement of

equivalent import, see Hugo Münsterberg, 1914, quoted in Matthew Hale, Jr., *Human Science and Social Order* (Philadelphia: Temple University Press, 1980), 125.

7. See Jane Addams, "The Chicago Settlements and Social Unrest," *Charities and the Commons* 20 (1908): 164 (later *The Survey*, hereafter cited as *C&C*); Edward Cummings, "A Collectivist Philosophy of Trade Unionism," *Quarterly Journal of Economics* 13 (1898): 158–59 (hereafter cited as *QJE*); P. Maxwell Foshay, "The Organization of the Medical Profession," *The Forum* 32 (1901): 491–92; George M. Gould, "Is Medicine a Science?" *The Forum* 8 (1889): 419–27; G. Stanley Hall, "Universities and the Training of Professors," *The Forum* 17 (1894a): 297–300; David Starr Jordan, "The Need of Educated Men," *Popular Science Monthly* 46 (1894): 167 (hereafter cited as *PSM*); Richard MacLaurin, "Some Tests of Academic Efficiency," *PSM* 76 (1910): 491–92; S. M. MacVane, "The Economists and the Public," *QJE* 9 (1894): 132–34; W. J. McGee, "The Science of Humanity," *American Anthropologist* 10 (1897): 246 (hereafter cited as *AA*); A. Marston, "Original Investigations by Engineering Schools: A Duty to the Public and to the Profession," *Science*, n.s., 12 (1900): 397–400; Adolf Meyer, review of *Psychotherapy* by H. Münsterberg, *Science*, n.s., 30 (1909): 153; Editorial, "Science and Party Government," *PSM* 20 (1882): 696–98; J. W. Powell, "The Administration of the Scientific Work of the General Government," *Science*, n.s., 5 (1885): 51–55; H. S. Pritchett, "The Relation of Educated Men to the State," *Science*, n.s., 12 (1900): 666; Unsigned editorial, "The Administration of Scientific Work," *Science*, n.s., 12 (1900): 737–39; R. H. Thurston, "The College-Man As Leader in the World's Work," *PSM* 60 (1902): 357; Maximillian Toch, "The Influence of Chemistry on Civilization," *Science*, n.s., 30 (1909): 698; Francis A. Walker, "Democracy and Wealth," *The Forum* 10 (1890): 245; Robert A. Woods, "Social Work: A New Profession," *C&C* 15 (1906): 471.

8. See, for example, Clarence Ashley, "The Training of the Lawyer and Its Relation to General Education," *Journal of Social Science* 37 (1899): 299 (hereafter cited as *JSS*); Josiah Parsons Cooke, "Scientific Culture," *PSM* 25 (1884): 578; C. F. Dunbar, "The Academic Study of Political Economy," *QJE* 5 (1890): 398; A. Lawrence Lowell, "Inaugural Address of the President of Harvard University," *Science*, n.s., 30 (1909): 500.

9. Ira Remsen, "The Science *versus* the Art of Chemistry," *PSM* 10 (1877): 694. There is some irony in the fact that one product of Remsen's work was his discovery, along with Constantine Fahlberg, of saccharin in 1879. On this, as well as his scientific ideology, see Owen Hannaway, "The German Model of Chemical Education in America: Ira Remsen at Johns Hopkins (1876–1913)," *Ambix* 23 (1976): 145–64.

10. Edmund J. James, "The Economic Significance of a Comprehensive System of National Education," *Papers and Discussions of the American Economics Association* 1 (1911): 21–23.

11. See, for example, Colin Burke, *American Collegiate Populations* (New York: New York University Press, 1982); Robert W. Gordon, "Legal Thought and Legal Practice in the Age of American Enterprise, 1870–1920," in *Professions and Professional Ideologies in America*, ed. Gerald Geison (Chapel Hill: University of North Carolina Press, 1983), 70–110.

12. See, for example, James Rowland Angell, "The Province of Functional Psychology," *Psychological Review*, n.s., 14 (1907): 62 (hereafter cited as *PR*); W. J. McGee, "The Trend of Human Progress" *AA* n.s. 1 (1899): 407–408; Bernard Moses,

"Certain Tendencies in Political Economy," *QJE* 11 (1897): 387; Albion Small, "The Era of Sociology," *American Journal of Sociology* 1 (1895): 6 (hereafter cited as *AJS*); Monroe Smith, "The Domain of Political Science," *Political Science Quarterly* 1 (1886): 2 (hereafter cited as *PSQ*); Thorstein Veblen, "The Preconceptions of Economic Science," *QJE* 13 (1899): 125.

13. E.R.A. Seligman, "The Continuity of Economic Thought," in *Science Economic Discussion*, by H. C. Adams, R. T. Ely, A. T. Hadley, E. J. James, Simon Newcomb, Simon Patten, E.R.A. Seligman, R. M. Smith, F. W. Taussig (New York: Science Company, 1886), 12.

14. See, for example, James Rowland Angell, "The Influence of Darwin on Psychology," *PR*, n.s., 16 (1909): 162–63; Franklin Giddings, "Imperialism," *PSQ* 13 (1898): 585–86; William Graham Sumner, "Purposes and Consequences," in *Earth-Hunger and Other Essays* (1913; reprint, New Brunswick, N.J.: Transaction, 1980), 67; Lester Ward, "Static and Dynamic Sociology," *PSQ* 10 (1895a): 209.

15. William James, "The Experience of Activity," *PR*, n.s., 12 (1905): 9–10.

16. Henry Dwight Chapin, "Social and Physiological Inequality," *PSM* 30 (1887): 757. See also John Bates Clark, "The Limits of Competition," *PSQ* 2 (1887): 52; John R. Commons, "Is Class Conflict in America Growing and Is It Inevitable?" *AJS* 13 (1908): 756–66; Robert M. Hoxie, "Scientific Management and Social Welfare," *The Survey* 35 (1916): esp. 678–79; Edmund J. James, "The Place of the Political and Social Sciences in Modern Education," *Annals of the American Academy of Political and Social Sciences* 10 (1897): 368–72 (hereafter cited as *Annals*); A. A. Tenney, "Some Recent Advances in Sociology," *PSQ* 25 (1910): 518; Woodrow Wilson, "The Study of Administration," *PSQ* 2 (1887): 197–222.

17. See, for example, Simon Patten, "The Relation of Sociology to Psychology," *Annals* 8 (1896): 452; William Graham Sumner, "The Absurd Effort to Make the World Over," *The Forum* 17 (1894): 96–98.

18. William Graham Sumner, "Do We Want Industrial Peace?" *The Forum* 8 (1889): 415.

19. Ely, "Fundamental Beliefs," 174. See also, G. Stanley Hall, "The New Psychology as a Basis of Education," *The Forum* 17 (1894): 715; Edgar L. Hewett, "Ethnic Factors in Education," *AA*, n.s., 7 (1905): 8; Grace Peckham, "The Nervousness of Americans," *JSS* 22 (1887): 37; John Wesley Powell, "Sociology, or the Science of Institutions," *AA*, n.s., 1 (1899): 742; John Tyler, "The Pathology of Education in Its Biological Aspect," *JSS* 43 (1905): 152–62; Thorstein Veblen, "The Instinct of Workmanship and the Irksomeness of Labor," *AJS* 4 (1898): 195–96. And see Charles Rosenberg, *No Other Gods* (Baltimore: Johns Hopkins University Press, 1976), 99–108.

20. See, for example, Merritt Roe Smith, "Technological Determinism in American Culture," in *Does Technology Drive History?* ed. Merritt Roe Smith and Leo Marx (Cambridge: MIT Press, 1996), esp. 26–28.

21. Zunz, *Why the American Century?* xiii–xiv.

22. I reject the argument made by Mary Furner and others who have followed her—that late-nineteenth-century social scientists had to renounce social activism of any sort as a necessary condition of the professionalization of their disciplines. See her *Advocacy and Objectivity* (Lexington: University of Kentucky Press, 1975).

23. Lester F. Ward, "The Utilitarian Character of Dynamic Sociology," *AA* 5 (1892): 103.

24. See Leo Rowe, "The Problems of Political Science," *Annals* 10 (1897): 165–85.

25. James Mark Baldwin, "Sketch of the History of Psychology," *PR*, n.s., 12 (1905): 144. Note that "adjustment" became the watchword of psychiatrists in this era, denoting the goal of (somehow) conditioning individuals to behave in fashions appropriate to their social circumstances; see Jack D. Pressman, *Last Resort* (New York: Cambridge University Press, 1998).

26. Lester F. Ward, "The Purpose of Sociology," *AJS* 2 (1897): 455, 457.

27. See Irving Fisher, "Why Has the Doctrine of *Laissez Faire* Been Abandoned?" *Science*, n.s., 25 (1907): 18–27; and see Clarence F. Dunbar, "The Reaction in Political Economy," *QJE* 1 (1886): 19–23; Arthur T. Hadley, "Economic Laws and Methods," in *Science Economic Discussion*, by H. C. Adams et al., 96.

28. See Robert Bannister, *Social Darwinism: Science and Myth in Anglo-American Social Thought* (Philadelphia: Temple University Press, 1979).

29. Tufts in John Dewey and James H. Tufts, *Ethics* (New York: Henry Holt, 1908), 397.

30. Franklin Giddings, "The Economic Significance of Culture," *PSQ* 18 (1903): 451.

31. See, for example, James Mark Baldwin, "The Genesis of Social Interests," *The Monist* 7 (1897): esp. 352–53; Daniel G. Brinton, "The Factors of Heredity and Environment in Man," *AA* 11 (1898): 276; John Bates Clark, "The Basis of War-Time Collectivism," *American Economic Review* 7 (1917): 788 (hereafter cited as *AER*); Charles H. Cooley, "The Processes of Social Change," *PSQ* 12 (1897): 68–69; Frank Fetter, "Social Progress and Race Degeneration," *The Forum* 28 (1899): 228; Lee Frankel, quoted in "Summer Session of the New York School of Philanthropy," *C&C* 20 (1908): 391; Franklin Giddings, "Social Self-Control," *PSQ* 24 (1909): esp. 474–78; William Torrey Harris, "The Definition of Social Science and the Classification of Types Belonging to Its Several Provinces," *JSS* 22 (1887): 4; McGee, "Science of Humanity," esp. 432–44; Simon Newcomb (writing under the pen name of "Aristides"), "The Elements Which Make Up the Most Useful Citizens of the United States," *AA* 7 (1894): 350; Simon Patten, "A New Statement of the Law of Population," *PSQ* 10 (1895): 50; Powell, "Sociology, or the Science of Institutions," 745; W. G. Ripley, "Geography as a Sociological Subject," *PSQ* 10 (1895): 649–50; Edward A. Ross, "The Genesis of Ethical Elements," *AJS* 5 (1900): esp. 763–68; James E. Russell, "The Advanced Professional Training of Teachers," *JSS* 39 (1900): 79–80; E.R.A. Seligman, "Social Elements in the Theory of Value," *QJE* 15 (1901): 347: Walter Sheldon, "The Evolution of Conscience as a Phase of Sociology," *AJS* 8 (1902): 370; Albion Small, "The Evolution of a Social Standard," *AJS* 20 (1914): 14–17; Veblen, "The Instinct of Workmanship," 195; Lester F. Ward, "Relation of Sociology to Anthropology," *AA* 8 (1895): 248; Frederick Adams Woods, "Laws of Diminishing Environmental Influence," *PSM* 76 (1910): 313–16.

For one of the many analyses reporting Boas's influence in inspiring social determinism (in this case, disapprovingly), see Carl Degler, *In Search of Human Nature* (New York: Oxford University Press, 1991). There is no question that Boas himself participated in the dissemination of the characterization of his social scientific influence that scholars such as Degler have reiterated. See, for example, a cover story featuring Boas, "Environmentalist," *Time*, 11 May 1936, 37–44.

32. John Dewey, "The Reflex Arc Concept in Psychology," *PR*, n.s., 3 (1896): 357–70. For one critique of Dewey's functionalist position, see Edward L. Thorndike, "The Evolution of Human Intellect," *PSM* 60 (1901): 60. For the clarion call to behaviorism, see John B. Watson, "Psychology as the Behaviorist Views It," *PR*, n.s., 20 (1913): 158–77.

33. C. H. Judd, "Evolution and Consciousness," *PR*, n.s., 17 (1910): 84.

34. Edmund J. James, "The Place of the Political and Social Sciences in Modern Education," *Annals* 10 (1897): 365.

35. On Lamarckism in the social thought of this period, see George W. Stocking, Jr., *Race, Culture and Evolution* (New York: Free Press, 1968), 234–69. See also James Mark Baldwin's argument that "*[A]ll truth is confirmed hypothesis*," and "all *reason is truth woven into mental structure*" [italics his], in his article "The Influence of Darwin on Theory of Knowledge and Philosophy," *PR* 16 (1909): 209. See also Angell, "Influence of Darwin on Psychology," 156; Brinton, "Factors of Heredity," 275; Carlos Closson, "Social Selection," *Journal of Political Economy* 4 (1896): 454 (hereafter cited as *JPE*); Ward, "The Purpose of Sociology," quoted in Bannister, *Social Darwinism*, 128. And note that even the conservative William Graham Sumner believed that humans became more cooperative beings with the progress of evolution; see Bannister, *Social Darwinism*, 105–109.

36. John Dewey, "Psychology and Social Practice," *Science*, n.s., 11 (1900): 332.

37. Ibid., 324–25. And see Alan Ryan, *John Dewey and the High Tide of American Liberalism* (New York: W. W. Norton, 1995).

38. Albion Small, "The Evolution of a Social Standard," *AJS* 20 (1914): 16–17.

39. See, for example, G. Stanley Hall, "Recent Observations in Pathological Psychology," *JSS* 43 (1905): 140–41.

40. See, for example, Baldwin, "Influence of Darwin on Theory of Knowledge and Philosophy," 210–12; Arthur Bentley, "The Units of Investigation in the Social Sciences," *Annals* 5 (1895): 933; C. B. Davenport, "The American Society of Naturalists: Cooperation in Science," *Science*, n.s., 25 (1907): 361–6; W. F. Hillebrand, "The Present and Future of the American Chemical Society," *Science*, n.s., 25 (1907): 81–95; William B. Hornblower, "Has the Profession of the Law Been Commercialized?" *The Forum* 18 (1895): esp. 680–82; McGee, "The Science of Humanity," 246; H. Hewell Martin, "The Study and Teaching of Biology," *PSM* 10 (1876): 300; Charles S. Peirce, quoted in Thomas L. Haskell, "Professionalism *versus* Capitalism: R. H. Tawney, Émile Durkheim, and C. S. Peirce on the Disinterestedness of Professional Communities," in *The Authority of Experts*, ed. Thomas L. Haskell (Bloomington: Indiana University Press, 1984), 205; Sidney Sherwood, "The Philosophical Basis of Economics," *Annals* 10 (1897): 208. And for further analysis along these lines, see Haskell, "Professionalism *versus* Capitalism," esp. 203–14; David Hollinger, "The Defense of Democracy and Robert K. Merton's Formulation of the Scientific Ethos," in *Current Perspectives in the History of the Social Sciences*, ed. Robert Alun Jones and Henrika Kuklick (Greenwich, Conn.: JAI Press, 1983), esp. 9–12.

41. See Hugo Münsterberg, *Psychology and Industrial Efficiency* (Boston: Houghton Mifflin, 1913), 305.

42. Harry Robinson, "Organized Labor and Organized Capital," *JPE* 7 (1899): 345.

43. Jeremiah Jenks, "Trade-Unions and Wages," *JSS* 28 (1891): 57.

44. John R. Commons, "A Sociological View of Sovereignty," *AJS* 5 (1900): 825.

45. Samuel Gompers, "Trade-Unions: Their Achievements and Methods," *JSS* 28 (1891): 41. See also Jane Addams, "Trade Unions and Public Duty," *AJS* 4 (1899): esp. 454–60; Edward Bemis, "The Benefit Features of American Trades Unions," *PSQ* 2 (1887): 274–90; George Gunton, "Social Influence of Labor Organizations," *JSS* 28 (1891): 101–107; Arthur T. Hadley, "Economic Laws and Methods," in H. C. Adams et al., *Science Economic Discussion*, 92–97; Royal Meeker, "The Promise of American Life," *PSQ* 25 (1910): 696–97; W. A. Purrington, "How Far Can Legislation Aid in Maintaining a Proper Standard of Medical Education?" *JSS* 25 (1888): 34; Victor Yarros, "Social Science and What Labor Wants," *AJS* 10 (1913): 308–22.

46. Richard T. Ely, "Pullman: A Social Study," in *The Land of Contrasts*, ed. Neil Harris (1885; reprint, New York: George Braziller, 1970), 118–32.

47. See, for example, Frank Carleton, "Scientific Management and the Wage Earner," *JPE* 20 (1912): 834–45; John R. Commons, "Organized Labor's Attitude Toward Industrial Efficiency," *AER* 1 (1911): 468–69; Hoxie, "Scientific Management and Social Welfare," 673–80, 685–86.

48. Edgar J. Levey, "Municipal Socialism," *PSQ* 24 (1908): 41–42. See also Frank Goodnow, "Municipal Home Rule," *PSQ* 10 (1895): 1–21; William Ivins, "Municipal Government," *PSQ* 2 (1887): 291–312.

49. See Dolores Hayden, *Redesigning the American Dream* (New York: W. W. Norton, 1984), esp. 28–29, 72–74, 87, 95, 129.

50. Between 1870 and 1900, American institutions of higher education expanded at a phenomenal rate: in 1870 there were about 52,300 undergraduate and less than 50 graduate students, whereas the numbers of these had grown by 1900 to approximately 237,000 and 6,000, respectively. See Zunz, *Why the American Century?* 9. On efforts to reform colleges and universities to fulfill late nineteenth-century behavioral ideals, see Larry Owens, "Pure and Sound Government: Laboratories, Gymnasia, and Playing Fields in Nineteenth-Century America," *Isis* 76 (1985): 182–94; Hannaway, "The German Model of Chemical Education in America."

51. See Sarah W. Tracy, *From Vice to Disease: A Social and Cultural History of Alcoholism in the United States, 1870–1920*, forthcoming.

52. Different disciplines turned against evolutionary arguments in different ways. Psychologists, for example, argued that the task of differentiating living organisms by calculating the relative importance of consciousness in their adaptive processes was impracticable, and anthropologists decided that moral standards were functionally equivalent in all societies. See Watson, "Psychology as the Behaviorist Views It"; A. L. Kroeber, "The Morals of Civilized People," *AA*, n.s., 12 (1910): 437–47.

53. See, for example, Ellis W. Hawley, "Herbert Hoover, The Commerce Secretariat, and the Vision of an Associative State, 1921–28," *Journal of American History* 61 (1974): 116–40; Daniel Bell, "America as a Mass Society: A Critique," in *The End of Ideology* (essay 1955; reprinted New York: Collier Books, 1961), 21–38; Eliot Freidson, "Communications Research and the Concept of the Mass," *ASR* 18 (1953): 313–17; Talcott Parsons, "Some Sociological Aspects of the Fascist Movement," *Social Forces* 21 (1942): 138–47; Richard P. Gillespie, *Manufacturing Knowledge* (New York: Cambridge University Press, 1991).

54. On Durkheim's social theory, see, for example, John Allcock, "Editorial Introduction to the English Translation," in *Pragmatism and Sociology*, by Émile Durkheim (Cambridge: Cambridge University Press, 1983), xxiii–xli; and see Anson Rabinbach's description of the French Third Republic ideology of "Solidarism," which had obvious affinities to Durkheimianism, in his *Human Motor* (New York: Basic Books, 1990), 206–208. On British analogues to this theory, see, for example, Henrika Kuklick, *The Savage Within: The Social History of British Anthropology* (New York: Cambridge University Press, 1991), esp. 27–74. See also Haskell, "Professionalism *versus* Capitalism."

55. There are obvious parallels between the goals of 1960s activists and those of Progressive reformers: social workers urged empowerment of clients so that they might become managers of their own lives, and professors promoted students' freedom to pursue meaningful educational careers and to repudiate morally illegitimate authority. Whatever the relationship between 1960s activism and the developments of subsequent decades, however, both social work and university teaching have suffered deprofessionalization. For social workers, life experience similar to that of clients has become as vital a credential in work with disadvantaged persons as formal training. See, for example, Marie R. Haug and Marvin B. Sussman, "Professional Autonomy and the Revolt of the Client," *Social Problems* 17 (1969): 153–61. In universities, some changes made during the 1960s in response to students' demands have been reversed—but these do not indicate professors' increasing power to negotiate the terms of their employment. Reimposition of distribution requirements may be advertised as a restoration of academic standards abandoned in the 1960s, but it has evident economic value for administrators: to reduce student options in course selection is to minimize uncertainty in staffing needs, facilitating cost containment by allowing colleges to operate with fewer faculty members. And provision of a range of services designed to curb the rowdy behavior long found on college campuses and improve the general quality of student life may mean restoration of college authorities' determination to act *in loco parentis*. Yet, it is also a response to consumer demand—students' and parents' insistence on better living conditions—as well as a preemptive measure, designed to make the residential student experience so attractive that its providers do not suffer from competition from institutions that, by various means, manage to offer higher education at low cost; on this point, see Ethan Bronner, "In a Revolution of Rules, Campuses Go Full Circle," *New York Times*, 1 March 1999, p. A1.

56. See, for example, Julie Stoiber, "Law firm offers its services through pre-paid, tailored plans," *Philadelphia Inquirer*, 24 July 1995, p. E1; Nina Bernstein, "Battles Over Lawyer Advertising Divide the Bar," *New York Times*, 19 July 1997, p. 1; Laura Mansnerus, "Law Firm Goes Mass Market With 1–800 Subway Ads," *New York Times*, 15 November 2000, p. B1. I am also indebted to Wendy Lea Brown, Esq., for information about current law firms' practices.

57. Rosemary Stevens, "Introduction to the Updated Edition," in *American Medicine and the Public Interest* (1971; updated, Berkeley: University of California Press, 1998), xxvi.

58. See, for example, "Doctors' Median Income Slipped Again in '97," *New York Times*, "National," 16 May 1999, p. 28; Milt Freudenheim, "Insurers Tighten Rules and Reduce Fees for Doctors," *New York Times*, international edition, 28 June 1998,

p. 1; Diana Jean Schemo, "Medical School Applications Drop Sharply; Minorities' Rise Slightly," *New York Times*, 27 October 2000. One should note that managed care has not proven as economical as was anticipated, for various reasons, though HMO's rights to give physicians financial incentives to limit health-care costs have survived legal challenges; see Michael M. Weinstein, "In Denial. Managed Care's Other Problem: It's Not What You Think," *New York Times*, 28 February 1999, "Week in Review," p. 1; Linda Greenhouse, "HMOs Win Crucial Ruling On Liability for Doctors' Acts," *New York Times*, 13 June 2000, p. A1.

59. Recent calculations indicate that the percentage of employees covered by HMOs has been declining, and that PPOs have at least 40 percent more members than the former. PPOs appeal to patients largely because they do not insist that primary providers mediate contact with specialists and do allow use of physicians outside the network (at more cost to the patients); see Milt Freudenheim, "Loosely Managed Care Is in Demand," *New York Times*, 29 September 1998, C1. It is perhaps in response to market demand that HMOs are relaxing their supervision of physicians' decision making, though it is also the case that their data indicate that close supervision is uneconomical because physicians' requests for sanction of procedures are generally approved—and HMOs have other means of monitoring physicians' actions; see Stacey Burling, "HMO change won't cure troubles with industry," *Philadelphia Inquirer*, 14 November 1999, p. D1.

60. A recent study of veterans' hospitals uncovered a frightening inventory of medical mistakes, including (but not limited to) prescription and/or administration of the wrong drugs, surgery on the wrong body part or the wrong patient, and the use of malfunctioning devices. Of course, responsibility for these mistakes lies not only with physicians but also with dispensing pharmacists, overworked nurses, pharmaceutical companies (for using identical packaging for drugs with antithetical properties, for example, or for publishing reference manuals that recommend prescription of their products in doses that are quite possibly excessive), and medical device manufacturers (for producing badly designed machines). In response to this report, hospitalized patients have been warned that they should take steps to prevent medical errors (such as painting their bodies before surgery to indicate which of their body parts requires attention), and measures are being effected to require reporting of medical errors by all health-care providers. See, for example, Todd S. Purdum, "California to Set Level of Staffing for Nursing Care," *New York Times*, 12 October 1999, p. A1; Denise Grady, "Too Much of a Good Thing? Doctor Challenges Drug Manual," *New York Times*, 12 October 1999, p. F1; Robert Pear, "A Clinton Order Seeks to Reduce Medical Errors," *New York Times*, 7 December 1999, p. A1; Abigail Zuger, "The Healing Arts, Cast in Shades of Gray," *New York Times*, 14 December 1999, p. F7; Robert Pear, "Report Details Medical Errors in V. A. Hospitals," *New York Times*, international edition, 19 December 1999, p. 1; Peter T. Kilborn, "All-Out Attack to Cut Mistakes in U.S. Hospitals," *New York Times*, international edition, 26 December 1999, p. 1; Jennifer Steinhauer, "A Cautionary Tale About Policing Doctors," *New York Times*, 21 November 2000, p. A1.

61. See, for example, "How to launch your own search for good care," *Philadelphia Inquirer*, 29 March 1998, p. A16; Ellen Ruppel Shell, "The Hippocratic Wars," *New York Times Magazine*, 28 June 1998, pp. 34–38. Arguably, the recent ruling of New York State's Court of Appeals that health-care providers may be sued

for false advertising has set a precedent that will make physicians far more vulnerable to legal action, since such cases will be easier for consumers to win than malpractice suits; see Randy Kennedy, "Court Says Consumer Laws Apply to Medical Advertising," *New York Times*, 5 May 1999, p. B4. And see Jennifer Steinhauer, "Albany Bill Would Help Patients Learn Doctors' Discipline Records," *New York Times*, 27 December 1999, p. B1.

62. Consider, for example, the consumer-driven growth of the practice of fibroid embolization, an alternative to hysterectomy or myomectomy that requires only local anesthesia for catheterization through a small incision in the thigh to inject material that reduces the blood supply to and thereby shrinks fibroids—benign gynecological tumors that among 20 to 40 percent of women over 35 are found to have grown to sufficient size to pose such problems as heavy menstrual bleeding, severe pain, and infertility. See Susan Gilbert, "A Less Invasive Alternative for Fibroids," *New York Times*, 6 April 1999, p. F7.

63. See, for example, Jack Pressman's observation that in the 1940s physicians, under pressure from patients' families, agreed to perform lobotomies on mental patients whom they did not consider likely to benefit from them. Physicians acceded to families' demands not only because families "paid the bills" but also because the patients suffered from psychiatric disorders that defied cure by less heroic measures (Pressman, *Last Resort*, 305). One must note that everyday medical practice has long presented evidence of patients' consumer power—such as doctors' willingness to yield (inappropriately) to patients' requests for prescriptions for antibiotics to treat viral diseases.

64. Steven Epstein, "Activism, Drug Regulation, and the Politics of Therapeutic Evaluation in the AIDS Era: A Case Study of ddC and the 'Surrogate Markers' Debate," *Social Studies of Science* 27 (1997): 691–726.

65. One measure of the rising popularity of alternative therapies is the finding that in 1997 more than two-fifths of Americans treated their ailments with alternative care of some sort—up from about a third in 1990. On these issues, see, for example, Jane E. Brody, "Acupuncture: An Expensive Placebo or a Legitimate Alternative?" *New York Times*, 18 November 1997, p. F9; Lawrence K. Altman, "Study on Using Magnets to Treat Pain Surprises Skeptics," *New York Times*, 9 December 1997, p. F3; a special issue of the *Journal of the American Medical Association* (11 November 1998) entirely devoted to alternative medicine; Dan Gottlieb, "In meditation class, an attempt to deal with stress," *Philadelphia Inquirer*, 21 August 2000, p. C1.

66. Whatever *causal* mechanisms may be at work, the *correlation* between the decline of physicians' status and the growth of their numbers seems straightforward: the proportion of doctors in the general population has grown, from 151 for every 100,000 people in 1970 to nearly 300 in 1990. But because the immediate outcome of measures designed to cut the national supply of physicians would be a reduction of hospital staffs to a level whereby they could no longer function effectively, hospitals have become sites for resistance to these measures; see "Many Hospitals Quit Plan to Train Fewer Doctors," *New York Times*, 1 April 1999, p. A1.

67. I quote Jennifer Steinhauer, "Hospital Mergers Stumbling As Marriages of Convenience," *New York Times*, 14 March 2001, p. A1. As of June 1999, about 40,000 of the nation's doctors belonged to unions, up from about 25,000 in 1996, and the American Medical Association has determined to organize two categories of phy-

sicians—salaried employees and medical residents (federal labor law now prohibits unionization of the self-employed)—competing with unions that have sought to organize physicians, such as the American Federation of Teachers and the American Federation of State, County and Municipal Employees. Proclaiming that its purpose is to fight restrictions that compromise patient care, the AMA has insisted that its unionized physicians will not strike. Patients' bills of rights denote the effectiveness of physicians' legislative lobbying campaigns as much as (if not more than) enhanced patient power; many restrict patients' rights to bring legal actions for malpractice, and many restore some elements of the free market in medical services by, say, forbidding managed care plans to restrict patients' access to specific medical specialists. On these issues, see Elisabeth Rosenthal, "Competition and Cutbacks Hurt Foreign Doctors in U.S.," *New York Times*, 7 November 1995, p. A1; Peter T. Kilborn, "Doctors Organize to Fight Corporate Intrusion," *New York Times*, 1 July 1997, p. A12; Peter Kilborn, "Bills Regulating Managed Care Benefit Doctors," *New York Times*, 16 February 1998, A1; Steven Greenhouse, "AMA's Delegates Vote to Unionize," *New York Times*, 24 June 1999, p. A1; Carey Goldberg, "Referendums From States Are Seeking to Overhaul the Health Care System in the U.S.," *New York Times*, 12 June 2000, p. A22.

68. For example, surrogate mothers—whether they carry embryos to which they have no biological relation or that are created from their own eggs and sperm harvested from donors or the intended father—are paid on average $15,000 for a first surrogacy and $20,000 for a second. See Elinor Burkett, "Meet the Baby Broker," *Glamour*, January 1999, p. 156. And in the recent past, women who endure the medical interventions that prepare them to become egg donors have routinely received fees as high as $5000 per procedure, though fees as high as $50,000 have been offered in advertisements directed to outstanding college students and have been solicited on the Web site of a former Playboy photographer, who offered to procure eggs from former models. Market prices for human eggs may vary from region to region. Rebecca Mead, "Eggs for Sale," *New Yorker*, 9 August 1999, 56–65; Marie McCullough, "Life for sale: Market for a woman's eggs is heating up," *Philadelphia Inquirer*, 8 March 1998, p. A1; Unsigned news story, "Report Suggests Limits on Pay for Egg Donors," *New York Times*, 5 August 2000, p. A9.

69. For examples, see the following: the recommendation by the Center for the Study of Human Reproduction that hormonally induced ovulation induction, which carries with it the high risk of multiple births, should cease, and that in vitro feritilization become the infertility treatment of choice; and the recommendation by the American Society of Reproductive Medicine that payment for human eggs should be limited to compensation for inconvenience, time, and medical demands of donating eggs at infertility clinics. See Marie McCullough, "Study urges end to a fertility method with multiple-birth risk," *Philadelphia Inquirer*, 6 July 2000, p. A3; Unsigned news story, "Report Suggests Limits on Pay for Egg Donors," *New York Times*, 5 August 2000, p. A9.

70. American physicians have routinely implanted four or five embryos in a woman's uterus; elsewhere, doctors are permitted to implant two or three. For discussions of various issues in the practice of assisted reproduction, see Gina Kolata, "Clinics Selling Embryos Made For 'Adoption,'" *New York Times*, 23 November 1997, p. 1; Gina Kolata, "Infertile Foreigners See Opportunity in U. S.," *New York Times*, 4 January 1998, p. 1; Gina Kolata, "Harrowing Choices Accompany Advance-

152 CHAPTER 4

ments in Fertility," *New York Times*, 10 March 1998, p. F3; Unsigned news story, "Fertility Clinics' Boom in Babies," *New York Times*, 9 February 1999, p. F8.

71. A recent study indicated that physicians could receive payments as high as $4,410 for each patient that they enrolled in a clinical trial; see Kurt Eichenwald and Gina Kolata, "Drug Trials Hide Coflicts for Doctors," *New York Times*, international edition, 16 May 1999, p. 1.

72. Articles intended to appeal to lay audiences include those claiming spectacular benefits from simple life-style changes—say, walking a few hours a day or eating fish once a week; see Shell, "The Hippocratic Wars." There is also evidence that medical journals' contents have been tainted by commercial considerations, and that medical public relations firms and drug companies have paid doctors to sign their names to ghost-written articles or to write commissioned pieces. See Lawrence K. Altman, "Some Authors in Medical Journals May Get Paid by 'Spin Doctors.' Professor Says he was offered $2,500 to write an editorial," *New York Times*, 4 October 1994, p. C3.

73. See, for example, an account of plastic surgeons willing to tailor liposuction procedures to suit the dimensions of specific dresses women wished to wear; Monique P. Yazigi, "Last Minute Fittings at the Plastic Surgeon," *New York Times*, "Sunday Styles," 19 December 1999, p. 1.

74. Sabra Chartrand, "Why Is This Surgeon Suing? Doctors Split Over Patenting of Their Techniques," *New York Times*, 8 June 1995, p. D1—quoted on D5 is Dr. John Glasson, chairman of the AMA's Council on Judicial and Ethical Affairs. Patented techniques include specific methods to diagnose Alzheimer's disease, to treat an aneurysm, and to make a type of surgical incision that eliminates the need for stitches. And see Kurt Eichenwald and Gina Kolata, "When Physicians Double as Entrepreneurs," *New York Times*, 30 November 1999, p. A1. Note that 75 percent of physicians belonged to the AMA in the 1960s, while by June 1999 membership had dropped to 34 percent.

75. Of course, as many scholars argue, there has always been a gap between the ideal and the real in medical practice; see, for example, Rosemary Stevens, "Old, New and Déjà Vu," unpublished paper, University of Pennsylvania, November 1998. There is obvious merit in their argument, not least because one would be hard pressed to identify *any* area of social life in which behavior fully satisfies normative expectations. Nevertheless, contemporary physicians seem obviously less vehement in their rhetorical claims to altruistic motives and awareness of social obligations than were their predecessors.

76. Gina Kolata, "Scientists Brace for Changes in Path of Human Evolution," *New York Times*, 21 March 1998, p. A1.

77. That many physicians understand their role in purely technical terms is evidenced by their widespread (if not entirely dominant) view that they need not attend to the emotional needs of their patients. See, for example, Susan Gilbert, "Forget About Bedside Manners, Some Doctors Have No Manners," *New York Times*, 23 December 1997, p. F7. For one analysis of contemporary lawyers that points to a similar development, see Robert Gordon, quoted in David Margolick, "Like Sex Acts, Lawyer's Job Is a Matter of Definition," *New York Times*, 26 September 1998, p. B7.

78. For a particularly egregious version of this argument, see Lee M. Silver, *Remaking Eden* (New York: Avon Books, 1997). See also George Johnson, "Ethical Fears Aside, Science Plunges On," *New York Times*, 7 December 1997, "Week in Review."

CHAPTER 5

Durkheim, Disciplinarity, and the
"Sciences Religieuses"

IVAN STRENSKI

WHAT IS FRENCH "DISCIPLINE"?

"Disciplines" are one of the ways in which we regulate intellectual interests in the realm of knowledge. In France, such regulation occurs largely through the power of the state to legitimate and recognize those species of knowledge we call the "disciplines." Thus, when the French noun, "discipline" refers to something other than military order or punishment, it refers to a regime of rules governing an interest and craft, typically of scholarship and teaching within institutions of learning, most of which are reliant on state legitimation.[1]

But like other interests, these disciplined interests and crafts have a social and cultural character as well as an intellectual one. Here, I acknowledge debts to what Pierre Bourdieu and, lately, Fritz Ringer have written about "intellectual fields."[2] In Ringer's view, a "discipline" resides in what he calls an "academic culture"—"an intellectual field or subfield, a network of inter-related and explicit beliefs about the academic practices of teaching, learning, and research, and about the social significance of these practices."[3] In this paper, I want to show how the intricate relations among the intellectual, cultural, and political aspects of what was known in France from the mid-nineteenth century as the *"science religieuse"* played their parts in the life of a discipline. This is mainly to tell the story of the liberal Protestant intellectual and ideological bases of the Fifth Section of the École Pratique des Hautes Études and the way this Protestant study of religion was contested in fin de siècle France by no less a notable figure than Émile Durkheim and his team of collaborators in the Durkheimian group.

A brief survey of the involvement of political structures in the legitimation of knowledge illustrates a pattern repeated into the present day in France. The recognition of history as a particular species of intellectual interest and craft goes back to 1554, where we find mention of a royal "historiographe" charged with chronicling the doings of the monarch.[4] In the time of Louis XIV, the Crown in effect recognized certain disciplines by sponsoring various archives, libraries, and specialized research academies where activities recognizable by today's successors in the "disciplines" were carried on. The ancien régime continued this trend and founded institutions designed to promote certain practical disciplines, such as the applied arts of engineering and mining by founding the École des Ponts et Chaussées (1775) and the École des Mines (1778). Following this lead, the Revolution created the famed École Polytechnique (1794). In 1795, the École Normale Supérieure was founded to train a cadre of *instituteurs* charged with carrying the ideals of the Enlightenment into the classroom.[5] Closely linked with the disciplines of philosophy and the sciences, the École Normale Supérieure stood for a kind of *culture générale* that was felt to embody France's unique intellectual genius as informed by the Revolution's vision of a transformed humanity. The nineteenth century saw the creation as well of a series of specific, craft-exclusive schools for training specificalists of various sorts, for instance, the École Supérieure de Télégraphie, (workers in telecommunications), the École de Chartres (archivists), and the Écoles Française de Rome and Athènes (archeologists). It was thus within these institutions and their attendant cultures that certain disciplined intellectual interests and crafts were nurtured.

In the humanities and social sciences in France during the late nineteenth and early twentieth centuries, the professionalization of scholarship changed much of the academic landscape. The rate of such legitimation and recognition, and along with it, the rapidity with which "disciplines" appeared, quickened with the foundation of the École Pratique des Hautes Études and its division into "Sections" in 1868. Because of its massive power to subsidize activities within it, the nation-state in effect played a role as exclusive guarantor of the legitimacy of disciplines. Thus, if no chair of "The History of the Study of Religions," say, were to exist in the Fifth Section of the École Pratique, then one would not be able in France to speak of this history as a "discipline"—even though it may exist in other countries. The original four "sections" and, thus, four disciplines so legitimated in the École Pratique were mathematics (I), chemistry and physics (II), natural history and physiology (III), and history and philology (IV). In 1886, the Fifth Section (*sciences religieuses*) came into being. Disciplines thus formed within and around a variety of institutions of higher learning, archives, libraries, research academies, professional associations, and even, as we will see, under different circumstances, around publishing ventures such as academic journals.

DISCIPLINES AS CULTURAL WORK

But while state action can *recognize* an intellectual activity as a discipline, it is also possible to say that the disciplines did not necessarily *originate* from state action. In France, private institutions, such as the many *écoles libres* and amateur *sociétés savantes* flourished in France from the nineteenth century onward.[6] Witness to the vitality of the life of the disciplines in France were the many *écoles libres* that sprang up in the late nineteenth and early twentieth centuries. In the absence of official recognition of the economic and political studies, École Libre des Sciences Politiques was founded. It, in turn, gave birth to the Collège Libre des Sciences Sociales in the absence of official sanction for a school of social sciences in the École Pratique des Hautes Études. After a while, the Collège gained some governmental subsidy and became a consortium of independent institutions, the École des Hautes Études Sociales in 1901.[7] It was precisely within this milieu of independent intellectual activity that the Durkheimians got their new sociology started, even though individually they had been well ensconced within the official world of the state apparatus of public higher education long before sociology was recognized as a discipline. Indeed, as we will see, the example of the Durkheimians shows how a new discipline and a vibrant intellectual culture can be formed outside the patronage of the state—here around a periodical, Durkheim's *L'Année sociologique.*

The Durkheimian *équipe* manifested all the requirements for being the social basis of a "discipline" in the sense that I am borrowing from Ringer and Bourdieu. Thus, in terms of its cultural identity, the support staff of *L'Année sociologique* referred to themselves self-consciously as a kind of social grouping dedicated to advancing Durkheim's attempts to sociologize certain dominant disciplines such as philosophy and history. The *équipe* even captured something of this spirit of joint membership in a distinctive academic culture in referring to themselves in the late 1890s as a Durkheimian "team." The etymology and the then current use of the term *"équipe"* suggests focused labor as on a ship's crew, where indeed our words "ship," "skiff," "skipper," and such reflect the original root meaning of *équipe.* In Durkheim's day, *équipe* also echoed with the ideas of a competitive sports team, such as the *"Équipe Casino"* or *"Équipe GAN"* in the Tour de France. Pushing this analogy a little further, Durkheim's "team" of editors, reviewers, and contributors did indeed function like a competitive sports team, sharing a culture of common beliefs about approaches to the study of society, which set them apart from others. In its time, the zeal and swagger of the *équipe* in mounting vigorous partisan attacks on other clusters of scholars won them a good deal of ill will. In their private correspondence, Durkheim's closest confederates, Henri Hubert and Marcel Mauss, were not above making scathing remarks about their opposites in the camps of competing academic cultures. In a tone of determined, if cloaked, opposition, apparently, to the pious Christians in the Fifth Section, Hubert wrote Mauss in 1898 that he relished the mischief that their "polemics" would spread among their religious colleagues:

We shouldn't miss a chance to make trouble for these good, but badly informed, souls. Let's stress the direction of our work, let's be clear about our aims so that they are pointed, sharp like razors, and so that they are treacherous. Let's go! I love a fight! That's what excites us![8]

TAKING THE FIFTH: POSITIVISM AND PROTESTANTISM

Perhaps sensing this contempt for their old-fashioned ways, many elements of the French intellectual and academic scene suspected the Durkheimians of gross ambition—the notorious "Durkheimian imperialism." They were correct. Indeed, the Durkheimians had targeted the *science religieuse* of the Fifth Section of the École Pratique for attack and conquest—a campaign not only aimed at a discipline but also at a way of life, an academic culture, and more. What was at stake, both intellectually and culturally, were the Durkheimian attempts to replace the dominant Liberal Protestant culture of the *science religieuse* that had prevailed in the Fifth Section from its foundation.

From the beginning, the leadership of the Fifth Section in the person of Albert Réville (1826–1906)—a figure renowned for his "documentary interests"—articulated the norms of this common culture.[9] This "discipline" of what Réville understood to be a "scientific" study of religion—the *science religieuse*—was charged, in Réville's words, "to study the facts, the testimonies, the texts, in order to extract from them their meaning and value, and to apply to them the fruitful methods of modern critical study, and never to allow theological passion to invade the serene temple of erudition."[10] In this way, the Fifth was thus identified with and effectively dominated by "old school" *érudites*—"historicist" historians and philologists devoted to the careful study of religious texts and traditions. They reproduced faithfully the spirit of the critical historicist culture epitomized by the leading historical periodical in France from the middle nineteenth century, the *Revue historique*, in their own academic journal, *Revue de l'histoire des religions*.

But, like cultures of the ethnic sort, the academic culture of the Fifth Section was defined by opposition to the culture of religious belief and practice of others—chiefly the dominant religious culture of French Roman Catholicism. In many ways, the promotion of history as a "scientific" discipline—and hence the *science religieuse*—was the work of free thinkers and their ideological allies, French Liberal Protestants. "Science" for them provided a source of independent authority over against the claims of Catholic tradition. Among the religious communities of France, it was the Protestants then who mattered most in the field of the academic study of religion.

Before the First World War, French Protestants numbered only about 600,000 inhabitants, or 12 percent of the entire population of France.[11] Of these, only a fragment could be called theological conservatives or evangelicals. The rest are what have come to be known as Liberal Protestants or "Extreme" Liberal Protestants. Evangelicals and liberals differed primarily in their attitudes toward Enlightenment rationalism. Thus, the more evangelical wing of the Protestant community tried to resist a total slide into rationalism by launching periodic religious revivals or evangelical awakenings ("*réveils*"). The *réveils* sought to reignite practical religious experiential life, and to assert a degree of doctrinal conformity in a movement perennially championing freedom of conscience and thought.[12] Against the vaguely pantheistic deism of the liberals, the evangelicals, then, reaffirmed the christology of the Athanasian creed (Jesus is "true God from true God, begotten not made, of the same substance as the Father"),[13] the sinfulness of humankind, the "vicarious atonement and salvation by faith in the sacrifice of Christ," the divine inspiration of the Bible, and, for unrepentant sinners, eternal damnation.[14]

By contrast with the Catholics, the Liberal Protestants practically merged with Enlightenment Deism and religious humanism. In Liberal Protestant theology, "one finds Locke, Condillac, Montesquieu, Rousseau, Voltaire, more easily than Calvin."[15] Deistic rationalism in this context (apparently largely Rousseau's)[16] consisted in a belief in a supreme, but nonintrusive, god, creator of the world according to the natural laws we discover in the sciences, and whom we could know by reason alone, unaided by revelation. Humanity was portrayed as having been given in equal proportions a pure and unsullied primordial monotheistic revelation. But thanks to the Fall and those ever-conniving priests, humanity's grip on this religion weakened and it fell into savagery of broad dimensions: magic, political injustice or sheer ignorance, polygamy, bloody (sometimes human) sacrifice, "superstition," ritualism, fetishism, animism and so on. The mission of Christ was to destroy these degenerate forms of historical religion that had arisen since the Fall, then to restore the primordial natural religion with a new and unprecedented "revelation." In its turn, the Reformation saw itself returning to the essence of Christ's mission, by destroying those "pagan" elements that it felt had reentered Christianity through Catholicism.

Because of its generous scope and application, this particular kind of Deistic rationalism entailed universal humanism. People had no need of special divine revelation or institutional structures because all humans were innately and in essence "naturally" religious by virtue of their common humanity. Every human being shared a common primordial religion, even evident today beneath the many differences of the religions of the world. Albert Réville, for example, tells us quite explicitly that "the principle of humanity guides religion along higher paths . . . [and that the] truer a religion is, the more absolute the homage it will render to the principle of humanity."[17] Thus another legacy of the Enlightenment was its universality, its affection for the ideal of humanity.

Despite the evangelical *réveils* of the nineteenth century, the greater part
of French Protestantism (later to become the core of the Liberal movement)
held fast to the Enlightenment rationalist religious norms.[18] Samuel Vincent
(1787–1837), the great forebear of French Liberal Protestantism, for example, took Christ to be merely an excellent guide of human conduct, not a
transcendental spiritual being. In this way, despite periodic surges in evangelical popularity, the liberal traditions of Deistic rationalism held firm in
France right through to the end of the nineteenth century. On the occasion
when the evangelicals tried to enforce discipline at the 1872 Synod, they
produced a formal split between "liberal extremists" and conservatives,[19]
ensuing in a series of spectacular defections of several leading liberal clergymen. Prominent among the rebels were a group of personal comrades, Tim-
othée Colani,[20] Edmond Schérer,[21] Félix Pécaut,[22] and Albert Réville.[23] They
all shared beliefs reminiscent of the old Deistic rationalism inherited from
the days of the Revolution: resistance to supernaturalism, such as the belief
in miracles, and thus an openness to science. As dissenters they cherished
the freedom of individual conscience, religious tolerance, and freedom of
thought. From their ranks many anticlerical leaders were drawn, since they
arose from a tradition that originated in organized resistance to Catholic
ecclesiastical authority. Commentators of the day characterized extreme
Liberal Protestantism merely as "a form of free thought touched with
Christianity."[24]

Significantly for our story of the character of academic disciplines in the
study of religion, as a result of his rebellion against the evangelicals, Albert
Réville sought institutional refuge in the École Pratique des Hautes Études,
Fifth (religious sciences) Section. There, under the patronage of the French
state, he felt he could continue the trajectory of his Liberal Protestant intellectual interests free of ecclesiastical interference. As an institution, the Liberal Protestant-dominated Fifth Section contrasted with institutions like the
seminary, and officially ruled out "theology" and other practical or pastoral
disciplines from its curriculum. This self-definition-by-contrast reached such
heights that at one point it was argued that a formal requirement for election
to the Section be atheism! No believers need apply! A key feature of the
common culture of the Fifth Section was then the "positivism" (borrowing
again from Ringer) typical of much of the humanities in France in the late
nineteenth and early twentieth centuries.[25]

Now, even though we can first speak of a large overarching discipline of
the positivist "*science religieuse*"—in the singular—the Fifth Section was
officially named as such in the plural "*sciences religieuses*." This indicated
no more than the division of the subject matter into a number of specialized
positive sciences, subdisciplines, or *enseignement*. The diversity of subdisciplines within the Fifth Section reflected as well the existence of several
positive sciences and their subcultures within them. Thus, members of the

Section brought with them something of the academic cultures from which they had been drawn, chiefly philosophy, history, theology, philology and so on, but also the many more narrowly delineated *sciences religieuses* such as the study of Rabbinic and Talmudic Judaism, the religions of Rome and Greece, esotericism in the West, religions of India—which, officially at any rate, were taught according to canons of "scientific" history. The study of the texts of the sacred languages, such as Hebrew or Sanskrit, would constitute additional subdisciplines, taught according to the regulations laid down by the philological disciplines.[26]

Despite their common positivist culture and avowed commitment to disinterested inquiry, the members of the Fifth Section tended as well to affiliate and identify with partisan political tendencies and groups. Liberal Protestants such as Albert Réville, Jean Réville (1854–1908), and Maurice Vernes were just as loyal to the program of Gambetta's republican anticlericalism and their own traditions of unitarian latter-day Deism as to any ideals of disinterested "scientific" scholarship. For them, no conflict existed between their loyalty to science, on the one side, and to the anticlerical republicanism of the Radical Party, on the other. They were actually one struggle fought at two levels.

For their part, the Durkheimians identified themselves with many of these same causes as the Liberal Protestants, but without embracing the theological commitments often tacitly made by the Liberal Protestants. More than anything else, they identified with their master and made membership in the *équipe* a principal source of academic culture affiliation and disciplinarity. For instance, in being "Maître de Conférence" Hubert taught numerous courses—*conférences*—on topics concerning the "history" of primitive religions of Europe, such as courses on the survival of Germanic religion in ancient Gaul. He also employed his archeological expertise in courses on the study of prehistoric burial structures, and brought to bear the Durkheimian interest in myth and ritual in the lectures he gave, for example, on religious seasonal festivals of the ancient Germans. Thus, Hubert's approach to religious materials was shaped both by Durkheim's new discipline as well as by what he had learned during his previous intellectual formation as a "scientific" historian and archeologist.

Now, while the Durkheimians shared much of the critical positivist ethos of the Fifth Section, they differed enough so that in time they were seen (correctly) by the Liberal Protestant majority as a threatening foreign culture. The Durkheimians, in effect, challenged both the positivism of Liberal Protestant scientific historical practice and the theological agendas prevalent among the Liberal Protestant membership of the Fifth Section. First, the Durkheimians felt that the positivist erudition of the Protestant historians and philologists was insufficient to produce explanations. These historians were satisfied to chronicle events, but not to offer explanations for them. And, since the positivists took the basic categories of inquiry as a given, they could not and would not raise fundamental questions about their categorial status.[27] Notions like "sacrifice," "magic," or even "religion" circulated in the Liberal Protestant study of religion, but without being subjected to fundamental questioning. The Durkheimians made it a part of their program to take responsibility for the concepts invoked in the study of religion. Thus, in their early work, they published efforts seeking to lay down *how* notions like "sacrifice," "magic," "taboo," "mana," and such *ought to be* used. What should the responsible student of religion *permit to be counted* as an instance of "sacrifice"? Is sacrifice a kind of gift? What is the relation of sacrifice to the sacred? Is expiation necessarily contained in the idea of sacrifice? Should sacrifice be restricted to theistic contexts, or can we speak of sacrifice as independent of or even prior to the existence of gods? These questions, for example, would form the intellectual backbone of Hubert and Mauss's little book, *Sacrifice: Its Nature and Functions* (1899). Second, the Durkheimians also went to war against the crypto-theologizing of the Liberal Protestant philosophers, theologians, and psychologists because "these good, but badly informed, souls," in Hubert's (fighting) words, begged all the very same important questions about the nature of religion that the Durkheimians had determined to shape to their own needs. Whereas others had been content, at worst, to live and let live—notably the Jewish members of the Section, in the face of what must have been an often unbearable sense of Christian theological triumphalism—the Durkheimians often attacked the views of their Protestant colleagues.[28] Marcel Mauss felt that the work of one of his colleagues in the Fifth Section and perhaps the leading Protestant philosopher of the day, Auguste Sabatier, was "a matter less of analyzing facts than of demonstrating the superiority of the Christian religion."[29] The "discipline" of Durkheimian sociology was articulated in part in relation to the prevailing positions held by the Protestants of the Fifth Section. It is to this opposition that I now turn.

CHRISTIAN APOLOGETICS EMERGES INSIDE THE FIFTH SECTION

While the Fifth Section can be taken as being unified around its positivism, and divided into various sorts of positive sciences of religion, at least two subcultures and thus subdisciplines should be distinguished within the Fifth Section. Both of these subcultures stood for ways of unifying the theoretical basis for the work of the Section, but were ultimately in deep contradiction with the positivism of the Fifth, even if at the time they were felt to be consistent with its positivist scientific ethos. This contradiction arises mainly from the understandably unthinking assumption of the Liberal Protestants in the Fifth Section that their pale religious views could give no offense—even to liberal Catholics, Jews, and freethinkers. On the other hand, intransigent Roman Catholics could be ignored because they could never win election to the Fifth Section anyhow.

This first subculture consisted of Liberal Protestants who increasingly turned toward the pursuit of positive theological agendas, all the while without abandoning the positivist historical writing which was typical of the Section from the days of its founding. This permitted the likes of Albert Réville to speak of a discipline at once scientific, but also with the unmistakably imperious air of theology. Thus, the Liberal Protestant founders spoke of *"the* science of religion" in the exclusive singular. In this, Albert Réville merely reflected the ultimate origins of this odd combination of scientific and theological programs pioneered by Friedrich Max Müller and his Dutch fellow-traveler (very influential among the Liberal Protestants of the Fifth Section), Cornelis P. Tiele. Max Müller's "science of religion" was committed to an *apologetic theological* program—a faith-guaranteeing search for evidence of a universal natural human religion—and at the same time, a search undertaken by the strictly "scientific" procedures of historical and philological scholarship of the day. When speaking in an historical idiom to historians, he would talk of uncovering empirical evidence pointing to the existence of a stage in human history dominated by a universal primal or natural religion—virtually identical in content to the beliefs of the French Liberal Protestants. In putting his views to psychological or philosophically minded thinkers, Max Müller would couch his arguments in terms of evidence of an innate religious mental faculty, a neo-Kantian religious a priori, if you will. One of its standard-bearers, Jean Réville, spoke accordingly of the "permanent needs and aspirations of religion in the human soul" echoing his father's similar sentiments concerning the religious a priori.[30]

Such theologizing apologetics stirred little controversy at the time of the foundation of the Section for a number of reasons. First, as a variant form of the natural religion of Enlightenment Deism, it conformed to a major stream of secular religious thinking still alive and well among the unchurched elites of the Third Republic. With roots reaching as deep as the sixteenth-century thought of Jean Bodin and carried forward into the modern age by many of the *philosophes*, the idea of a natural religion seemed (except for notable exceptions such as David Hume) self-evident. Such a natural religion was felt to supply the basis for morality, and thus for social stability—both desirable even in revolutionary periods. And finally, it was harmless, since unlike, say, Catholicism, it had little institutional basis and no clergy to conspire against the polity. How could the bourgeois humanism of the Third Republic find anything sinister in the "Fatherhood of God and the brotherhood of man"—a belief that was said to sum up the content of this tepid common faith?[31]

But by the end of the century, the beginnings of a second, more particularist, Christian subculture formed primarily around Jean Réville, son of the Section's founder, Albert Réville. Reminiscent of some of our own post-modernist thinkers in religious studies, Jean Réville sought openly to bring theology—and even an explicitly Christian theology—into the Fifth Section as part of a then current revolt against positivism, all the while still giving lip service to science. In his day, for example, Jean Réville could declare "the greatest fidelity to the rigorous method of scientific history."[32] Yet, in virtually the same breath he also swore to go even further out on the anti-positivist and apologetic limb of history writing in a series of pronounce-ments he made about the future of the history of religions.[33] Says Jean Réville: "Religious universalism, and I should add . . . Christian universal-ism—this is what the science of religion teaches modern society."[34] His break with the old pale Deism as well as the historicism and positivism dominant in the Fifth Section was part of a general dissatisfaction with the religious liberalism and historicism that we know came to a head in the fin de siècle. While leaders of this movement against historical positivism, such as Henri Berr, founder of the new journal *Revue de synthèse historique*, sought a more self-consciously comparative, theoretical, and interdisciplin-ary sort of history, theologically inclined members of the Fifth Section like Jean Réville saw the rolling back of positivism as an invitation to Christian theologizing in the university.[35]

It was against these moves by the newly emboldened theologians, as well as against the old positivism, that we might also speak of the beginnings of yet a third subculture, consisting of the Durkheimians and their sympa-thizers. Durkheimian efforts in the study of religion, along with their attacks on the *science religieuse* were just another part of their wholesale quarrels with established disciplines like philosophy, psychology, history, anthro-posociology, and ethnography in the interests of establishing his brand of sociology in France.[36] Against historian Charles Seignebos, a historian of great influence in the Fifth Section, for example, Durkheim argued for a new look at the powerful claims of the discipline of history against his own upstart sociology. Durkheim argued that history was in effect a branch of sociology and not another "discipline" over or against sociology. How can they be opposed so exclusively when, in Durkheim's view, sociology must always be historical?[37] For Durkheim, sociology differed from the old-style erudite history practiced by most members of the Fifth Section only in being both comparative and explanatory. So, sociology did the work of history even better than history did itself.

Against the Liberal Protestant apologetic programs then launched in the Fifth Section, the Durkheimians wished to establish a firmly naturalist and societist foundation for the study of religion. Religion was not the special a priori extra-social something beloved of the theologians and historians of Liberal Protestant persuasion. Religion was rather an eminently social and human thing, and one that demanded study with all the tools of positive science and scholarship. While the essentially unitarian and even innocuous religion of Liberal Protestantism underlying the *science religieuse* might have served in earlier times to ground the values of the Third Republic, that was no longer the case. For a host of reasons, notably the crisis of French nationalism at the fin de siècle, the Durkheimians felt that the individualistic and new sectarian notion of religion embodied in the Liberal Protestant culture of the school, as expressed in the conception of the *science religieuse* prevailing there, would not equip France to face the dangers that lay ahead. With its Christian theological presumptions, becoming more and more explicit in the pronouncements of influential figures like Jean Réville, the liberal religion articulated by the Liberal Protestants was not general enough to provide a moral center for the diverse Third Republic. Durkheim spent much of his adult life trying to articulate just what such a common moral system suitable for the Third Republic might be, and in doing so developed his well-known social notion of the nature of religion and the discipline of sociology fit for studying it and society at large.

POLITICS, *Sciences Religieuses*, AND FUNCTIONALISM

What may surprise those unfamiliar with the ins and outs of the religious history of France is that the French should have pioneered disciplines devoted to the study of religion at all. Yet, the list of practitioners and institutionalized forms already mentioned gives the lie to this assumption. To their number we can also add Ernest Renan, Albert Réville, Georges Sorel, James Darmesteter, Jean Réville, Salomon Reinach, Sylvain Lévi, and others. On the institutional side, the foundation at the École Pratique des Hautes Études of the Fifth (Religious Sciences) Section itself, together with a chair at the Collège de France and a world-class academic journal (the *Revue de l'histoire des religions*), bear witness to the continued official national sponsorship of the study of religion since the middle of the nineteenth century. Today, this venerable institution houses some forty-eight established chairs within its halls. It is odder yet to think of a nation renowned for its anticlericalism—at least among the modernizing elite of the republican regimes well known for their anticlerical and dechristianizing zeal—to have chosen the leadership of the Fifth Section from a small subdiscipline within it, which went by the name of *"science religieuse."* Yet, that is what this elite did. I have already suggested that the reasons for this are political. Let me conclude by filling out this story. It is, like all political stories, a tale of control, regulation, and disciplining.

The need to control religion has a long history in France. Louis XIV's fear of national disorder caused him to seek control over religion. He felt that religious unity would function to promote the political unity the nation needed.[38] A century or so later, Voltaire felt that it was in the interests of the state to maintain religion—but only in the interests of maintaining good order in the realm.[39] Napoléon, too, assumed the same view of religion's political utility—even if that national religion was to be a traditional religion like Catholicism. His reasoning was complex. First, he, like the fathers of the French Revolution, felt that religion functioned better than any conceivable substitute for maintaining social order, thus for smoothing the way for trouble-free implementation of his own political goals. Furthermore, given the Catholic nature of France, it was simply more politic to sponsor it as the de facto religion of the realm than to seek to found a new religion. At any rate, obedience to the Emperor was the real "essence of religious obligation of the French subject and citizen."[40] This conviction, repeated in so many different ideological contexts, may help us understand why religion's *function* in society was defended so readily by later, even anticlerical-tending, figures from Renan to Durkheim. French social thought simply generalized from French political experience.

Behind the interests of the state, then, in disciplining and sponsoring the *study* of religion was their perennial political concern for order. Control over *knowledge* of religion would inform ability to control religion in the interests of the state. With social functionality in mind, it is then a short step to begin understanding how a nation with such strong anticlerical traditions among its elites might be among the leaders in sponsoring the discipline of the study of religion. It was only prudent that since religion did function in manifestly important ways in French society that those charged with obligation to the nation should well understand it. This spirit still prevails in today's France. It is no accident that France, with its large Muslim population, its former colonies in the Muslim world, and its economic entanglements there today, should lead the world, if not Europe, in Islamic studies—much as the former Soviet Union had done and today's Russia still does to a large extent. In 1906, Jean Réville spoke with remarkable frankness in launching a spirited functionalist defense of the *science religieuse* as a way of getting intellectual purchase on the then troublesome intransigent Catholic opponents of the Third Republic. The *science religieuse*, said Jean Réville, would notably serve the cause of liberal "tolerance" by "describing the rise and fall of all the various credos and dogmas that had been declared absolute and immutable."[41]

RELIGION AND POWER IN FRANCE

Given its particular traditions of state involvement in matters of education, it is therefore natural to think that in France, in order to speak about the academic culture or regime of an officially sanctioned discipline like the *science religieuse*, we need also to talk about political cultures or regimes at the same time. This point is cardinal because the kind of religion, in effect, officially established in the Fifth Section was Liberal Protestantism. Behind the discipline of *science religieuse* lies the uneasy history of the relation of religion—Roman Catholicism—and politics in France. From the time of Charlemagne, the religious and political forces of France have danced their little dance around each other. Religious forces have both shaped and been shaped by political ones; every political regime in French history has had in some way to contend with religion.

It is useful to distinguish three levels at which politics has had to contend with religion. First, every regime in French history has had to take into account in one way or another the reality that the mass of its population consists of Catholics of varying degrees of faithfulness. This population supplies the social base of the persistently Catholic culture of the nation. It constitutes that vast population steeped in Catholic tradition, custom, and values, learned in churches, schools, and at the mother's breast. Even in periods of supposedly fierce dechristianization, such as the Revolution, recent studies have shown how much of the values and motivation of the Revolution itself, the quest for social justice prominent among them, were norms inculcated by the traditions of Catholicism.[42] Every regime, and in particular those, like the Third Republic, perceived as antagonistic to Catholicism, needed to find ways of allaying fears of repression or at least disguising them well enough to avoid out and out resistance to the state. A study of the decades-long struggle of the Third Republic to wrest control of education from the Catholic religious orders would reveal how protracted an effort this was.[43]

Second, at least since the reign of Louis XIV, the relation of "religion"—the organized church—to the state has been highly ambiguous. Even in periods where the political regimes have been regarded as dominated by "religion," the relation between religion and regime has more often than not been a constant tug of war in which throne and altar have alternately sought to pull the other under its domain of influence.[44] This is so no matter whether we consider "religion" to refer to the official ecclesiastical hierarchy or to one of the many religious orders or movements (those of the Jesuits, Oratorians, Assumptionists, or Jansenists) or lay organizations (such as the Compagnie du Saint Sacrément) influential throughout French history.

At the risk of great, if not gross, generalization, I believe one can declare the state the eventual winner in this protracted struggle. Thus, for example, no matter how pious and popular the Jansenists may have been, nor how much the Bourbons took upon themselves the role of defenders of Catholicism against the Reformation, that did not stop Louis XIV from allying Catholic France with the Protestant powers against the Catholic Hapsburgs.[45] Nor did Jansenist religious popularity do much to save Port Royal from suppression. Neither can we say that the fate of the even more redoubtable Jesuit order differed. While, from their position close to the Bourbon throne, the Jesuits seemed to have been responsible for the demise of the Jansenists, royal suspicion of them by Louis XV effected their expulsion from France.[46] Similarly, no matter how much of a show of reconciliation Napoléon made with the Vatican, nor no matter how much his regime subsidized the salaries of the French clergy, in the end, these were calculating if not cynical attempts to bind religious forces to state policy in the compromising embrace of cooptation. This regular and successful employment of state power, whether by outright suppression or compromise, thus established a pattern of subordination of religion to politics in France that prevailed at least into the time when the discipline of *science religieuse* was established in France in the middle nineteenth century.

This then brings me to the third sense in which politics and religion are related—the very institutional foundation of the discipline of *science religieuse* at the École Pratique des Hautes Études, Fifth Section, in 1886. Despite the great mass of French Catholic faithful in the population and the power, however compromised, of the church, in France the academic culture, and thus the *disciplinary* character of the *science religieuse* was profoundly Protestant. Not only was the Fifth Section led by Liberal Protestants—a small minority in an already small (12 percent) portion of the national population—it continued to be led and staffed chiefly by Liberal Protestants into the early decades of the twentieth century when the Durkheimians made their appearance. Worse yet for the Catholics, the establishment of the study of religion in France was made at the expense of the Catholic faculties of the Sorbonne. With the creation of the École Pratique des Hautes Études, Fifth Section, the Catholic faculties of theology were reconstituted outside the Sorbonne as the Institute Catholique.

Ostensibly, the official—and I think partly disingenuous—reason for banishing the Catholic faculties, while the Protestant Faculty of Theology stayed in place, was that the Catholics were charged with no longer performing their contracted (Napoléonic) roles of training clergy for practical ministry in parishes throughout France.[47] They had instead constituted themselves as an agency for the production of knowledge about religion, but from a particularly Catholic perspective. Why this should matter to the government can, I believe, only be explained by the government's interest in controlling the production of knowledge about religion in the face of intransigent Roman Catholic dominance over the French church. It was thus not in the broad political interests of the Third Republic to foster this intransigent type of "Catholic" knowledge about religion, so to speak. Instead, the Third Republic seems to have decided it needed to seize authority over the most prestigious knowledge about religion, as it has always done, for "*raisons d'état.*" In the wake of the First Vatican Council's assertion of papal authority and with it the reinvigoration of the intransigent and ultramontane parties in

France, all hopes of liberal Catholic dominance of the French church were by 1886 dead. Finding alliance with intransigent Roman Catholics impossible—not to mention unwelcome from the intransigents who clung to the restoration of monarchy throughout the century—the Third Republic acted in a perfectly expedient political way. They deprived the Catholics of hegemony over knowledge about religion and transferred it to a tiny faction of an already tiny portion of France's religious communities—the extreme Liberal Protestants. The Third Republic was already regarded popularly as the "revenge of the Reformation," so the foundation of the Fifth Section, along lines laid out by leading extreme Liberal Protestants in their *science religieuse*, ought not to have surprised anyone.

The Durkheimians, with equally good credentials in the eyes of the anticlerical Third Republic, were, however, never able to wrest control of the Fifth Section from the Liberal Protestants despite the Christian theological dalliances of the Révilles. The Liberal Protestant theological agenda itself, however, fell victim to larger historical trends outside their control. Both Révilles, father and son, died within years of each other, Albert in 1906 and Jean in 1908, and in doing so, effectively deprived the section of a theological articulation of its future. But, again contrary to what most present-day students of the social study of religion might imagine, the failure of the theological program of the Révilles did not at the same time pave the way for the triumph of the Durkheimians in the Fifth Section of the École Pratique des Hautes Études. In the Fifth Section, oblivion also awaited the Durkheimian project for a sociological study of religion. The Durkheimians were only able to see two of their number elected to the faculty of the Fifth Section during Durkheim's lifetime—Henri Hubert and Marcel Mauss—and these in 1900 and 1901. Further progress infiltrating the Fifth Section was effectively curtailed by the decimation of the Durkheimian *équipe* during the First World War, and the persistence of the old historicism in the Fifth Section. In official circles, Durkheimian thought only seemed to have attained influential levels in the area of civic and moral education in the primary and secondary schools.[48] As the theological efforts of the Révilles died with them, the section then remained dominated by the old historicism of the Liberal Protestants, increasingly shorn of its once potent Deistic religious justifications. "Scientific" history had simply become common historical practice, even for Roman Catholic historians, and thus no longer an ideologically charged issue between French Catholics and Protestants. The Durkheimians, on the other hand, became "sociologists."

In order for the Durkheimians to exert the kind of influence we recognize today, they had in effect to abandon the Fifth Section after fighting so hard to place their people in it. Instead, they created new official structures, such as the Institut d'Éthnologie, founded by Marcel Mauss and Lucien Lévy-Bruhl. Failing in attempts to create other institutions of this sort, the work of the Durkheimians was taken over by new schools of historians, such as the

Annales group. While not formally associated with the Durkheimian *équipe*, they eagerly adopted the Durkheimian sociologizing lead and pioneered the ethnographic history of religion—history of religions "from the ground up," so to speak.[49] The works of Marc Bloch (1923) on the social determinants of royal sacred healing or Lucien Febvre (1942) on the sociology of unbelief reflect Durkheimian insights that were never so loyally followed up by the historians of the Fifth Section.[50] Significantly, in order to do this new history of religions, the *Annalistes* eventually had to secure an institutional home outside the historicist Fifth in the relatively newly Sixth Section.[51] Here, the *Annalistes* established themselves and dominated research in a way in which the Durkheimians never did or could in the Fifth Section. It was then left to individuals such as Marcel Mauss (Hubert died prematurely in 1927), rather than institutions and disciplines, to pass on the Durkheimian torch. Louis Dumont's contributions to the study of religion in India, as well his latest work on modern ideologies, for example, all reflect the direct personal tutelage he enjoyed under Mauss.[52] Durkheimian studies of religion first achieved their now familiar fame in England among the likes of Radcliffe-Brown or Evans-Pritchard (and students of theirs, like Mary Douglas). Dumont himself was moved to work in Oxford with Evans-Pritchard partly to reinforce the pre–World War II Durkheimian trajectory of his thought. It is worth recalling that today we pay heed to the Durkheimians largely, but ironically, because in the late 1960s, Lévi-Strauss celebrated Marcel Mauss—misleadingly as it happens—as a Lévi-Straussian structuralist before his own time. In fact, as Dumont shows, Marcel Mauss was in part committed to the same positivist historical work pioneered by the Protestants and which would be a target of Lévi-Strauss's polemics against history for years. Thus, it was not Marcel Mauss's scholarly successes in the discipline of *science religieuse* as practiced in the Fifth Section that Lévi-Strauss celebrated in his years there.[53] Instead, it was a mythical Marcel Mauss, fashioned in the service of advancing structuralism's prestige, whom Lévi-Strauss held up for admiration. Accordingly, although appointed to the Fifth Section as remote successor to Mauss, by way of direct succession to Mauss's student, Maurice Leenhardt, Lévi-Strauss took his first opportunity to flee the inhospitable disciplinary surroundings of the *science religieuse* of the Fifth Section for the independence of a chair outside standard French academic disciplinary boundaries, in that home of the intellectual virtuosi, the Collège de France.

NOTES

1. A spectacular case in point of the revolt against the disciplines came in 1947, when a new version of the Sixth Section—"economic and social sciences"—was

founded (see Terry N. Clark, *Prophets and Patrons: The French University and the Emergence of the Social Sciences* [Cambridge: Harvard University Press, 1973], 42–51). The Sixth is, of course, the institutional home of Braudel, Furet, Le Goff, and others—later, in 1975, to be renamed the École des Hautes Études en Sciences Sociales. Thus, the official yearbook of the Section states that it includes "divers domaines des sciences humaines (histoire, géographie, économie, sociologie, psychololologie, anthropologie, linguistique, etc)." Most importantly, the new Sixth stands for the interrelation of these various "domains of science." Thus, as its yearbook states, "Les relations entre ces divers domaines et les recherches à caractère pluridisciplinaires font partie de la vocation de l'école" (École des Hautes Études en Sciences Sociales, *Annuaire. Comptes Rendus des Cours et Conférences 1980–1981, 1981–1982* [Paris: Sofiacparis, 1983], 4).

2. Pierre Bourdieu, *In Other Words*, trans. Matthew Adamson (Stanford: Stanford University Press, 1990); Fritz Ringer, *Fields of Knowledge: French Academic Culture in Comparative Perspective, 1890–1920* (Cambridge: Cambridge University Press, 1992).

3. Ringer, *Fields of Knowledge*, 13.

4. Pim den Boer, *History as a Profession: The Study of History in France, 1818–1914* (Princeton: Princeton University Press, 1998), 54.

5. See Robert J. Smith, *The École Normale Supérieure and the Third Republic* (Albany: State University of New York Press, 1982).

6. Before the middle of the nineteenth century, there had also always been individual virtuosi of independent means who practiced what would later be declared by the state as the stuff of the "disciplines" right through the fin de siècle. The historian Jules Michelet at one time held a chair in the Collège de France as well as being *"conservateur"* of the National Archives. But, neither Charles Renouvier, the most important and influential philosopher of the Third Republic, nor Henri Berr, one of the epoch's most original historians, ever had official posts as "historians" in the universities or in the various state-sponsored institutions.

7. George Weisz, *The Emergence of Modern Universities in France, 1863–1914* (Princeton: Princeton University Press, 1983), 310.

8. Letter of Henri Hubert to Marcel Mauss, n.d. 1898. I thank Marcel Fournier for this citation. See also Marcel Fournier and Christine De Langle, "Autour du sacrifice: lettres d'Émile Durkheim, J. G. Frazer, M. Mauss et E. B. Tylor," *Études durkheimiennes/Durkheim Studies* 3 (1991): 2–9.

9. See Philippe Alphandéry, "Albert Réville," *Revue d'histoire des religions* 54 (1906): 419.

10. Albert Réville, quoted in [anonymous], "École Pratique des Hautes Études," *La Vie universitaire à Paris* (Paris: Colin, 1918), 189.

11. On the current state of French Protestantism see Grace Davie, "The Changing Face of Protestantism in 20th Century France," *Proceedings of the Huguenot Society* 24 (1987): 378–89.

12. See André Encrevé, "La première crise de la Faculté de theologie de Paris: la démission de Maurice Vernes," *Bulletin de la Société de l'Histoire du Protestantisme Français* 136 (1990): 83.

13. See Ninian Smart, *The Religious Experience of Mankind*, 3rd ed. (New York City: Charles Scribners' Sons, 1984), 364.

14. See André Encrevé, Jean Baubérot, and Pierre Bolle, "Les réveils et la vie interne du monde protestant," in *Histoire des Protestants en France*, by Robert Mandrou, Janine Estèbe, et al. (Toulouse: Eduoard Privat, 1977), 272. On "orthodox" views favoring the atonement theory of Jesus' death, see Jean Rivière, "La rédemption devant la pensée moderne," *Revue du clergé français* 70 (1912): 161–80 and 278–305.

15. Daniel Ligou and Philippe Joutard, "Les Déserts (1685–1800)," in *Histoire de Protestants*, 235.

Protestants of the period drew especially upon Rousseau, who was born and died a Protestant, even though he dallied with Catholicism in between (ibid., 234). The authors single out Protestant ministers David Lévade and François Jacob Durand for special mention as disciples of Rousseau in the years 1750–90. On Rousseau's Protestantism, see Ronald Grimsley, *The Philosophy of Rousseau* (Oxford: Oxford University Press, 1973), 71–73, 80–83.

16. See Grimsley, *The Philosophy of Rousseau*, 71–85.

17. Albert Réville, *Lectures on the Origin and Growth of Religion*, trans. P. H. Wicksteed (London: Williams and Norgate, 1905), 254. This humanism passed to the Protestant community of 1789 in several ways; one was through the ideal of tolerance, deriving primarily from Voltaire. See Stuart R. Schram, *Protestantism and Politics in France* (Alençon: Corbière et Jugan, 1954), 50; and Ligou and Joutard, "Les Déserts," which identifies Antoine Noël Polier de Bottens and Paul Rabaut-Saint-Étienne as mid- to late-eighteenth-century theologians especially influenced by Voltaire (234–37).

18. Schram, *Protestantism*, 34.

19. Ibid., 54.

20. A disciple of Alexandre Vinet, Colani studied theology at Tübingen, like the elder Réville, Schérer, and Pécaut. Tübingen was then the center from which the theory and practice of historical and critical study of the Bible emanated. Colani adhered to this standard of scientific study of the biblical documents, and, like Vinet, was led to deny standard orthodox doctrines, such as Christ's miraculous virgin birth, divinity, and resurrection, as well as original sin. See André Encrevé, "Les deux aspects de l'année 1876 pour L'Eglise réformée de France," in *Actes du colloque: Les protestants dans les débuts de la Troisième République (1871–1885)*, ed. André Encrevé et Michel Richard (Paris: Société de l'histoire du protestantisme français, 1979), 372. Although Colani had founded the leading periodical of the liberal movement, the *Revue de théologie et philosophie chrétienne* (later to become the *Revue de Strasbourg*), he quit publishing it (1869) before his open rejection of the 1872 orthodox Declaration of Faith. Shortly thereafter, he abandoned theology entirely and even ceased church attendance (ibid., 290, 293).

21. Schérer began his professional life as a professor of biblical exegesis in Geneva. After exposure to German biblical criticism, he broke with orthodoxy over questions of the inerrancy of scriptures, the incarnation and divinity of Jesus, original sin and Jesus's resurrection. Later he would become a leading light at the Paris newspaper *Les Temps* and in the politics of the foundation of the Third Republic. See Philippe Vigier, "Edmond Schérer, père fondateur de la Troisième République," in *Actes du colloque*, 183–97.

22. Pécaut resigned his pastorate only months after his assignment. While in the

service of the church, he had gained fame as an author of a book declaring Jesus an ordinary mortal, *Le Christ et la conscience* (1859) and, approaching the time of his resignation, took to writing on the "religion of the future" in his *De l'avenir du théisme chrétien considéré comme religion* (1864). Later he was appointed by the Protestant minister of public instruction, Jules Ferry, to be director of the École Normale Supérieure at Fontenay-aux-Roses. There he sought to define the bases of a "secular faith."

23. Albert was also the father of Jean Réville, whose work on the doctrine of the Eucharist in early Christianity we have cited as well.

24. Daniel Robert, "Les intellectuels non-protestants dans le protestantisme des debuts de la Troisième République," in *Actes du colloque*, 93.

25. Ringer, *Fields of Knowledge*, 216–19.

26. A Durkheimian member of the Fifth, Henri Hubert, had, for example, been trained as an archeologist and historian in the officially recognized schools and institutes created for this purpose. These qualifications won him membership in the Fifth Section. He was *"en enseignement"*—literally, he taught the *histories* of the religions of pre-Christian Europe aided by his archeological efforts under the rubric, "The Primitive Religions of Europe." Yet, as a member of the inner circle of Durkheim's sociological collaborators, Hubert would well be counted a sociologist as well.

27. For more on the Durkheimians' opposition to the scholarly methods used by Liberal Protestants, see Henri Hubert and Marcel Mauss, *Sacrifice: Its Nature and Functions* (1899), trans. W. D. Halls (Chicago: University of Chicago Press, 1964).

28. Compare, for example, Mauss's rather soft criticism of Auguste Sabatier's work while he was still seeking appointment to the Fifth Section with his much more outspokenly critical attack on the Protestant philosopher after having been safely awarded his post in the Fifth Section. In 1898, before election to the Fifth Section, Mauss complimented Sabatier's *Esquisse d'une philosophie de la religion* (1897) for having put the "social and external character of dogma into bold relief" (*Marcel Mauss, Oeuvres*, vol. 1, *Les Fonctions sociales du sacré*, ed. Victor Karady [Paris: Éditions de Minuit, 1968], 535). He likewise passes over the theologian's treatment of primitive religion. But in his never completed Ph.D. thesis, "La Prière" (1909), he calls Sabatier's treatment of primitive religions "cavalier" (ibid., 1:535). Similarly, in 1898, Mauss politely notes about Sabatier that the "preoccupations of the soul sincerely burning with his religious faith compromise the uses of method here" (ibid., 1:531). Yet, from the security of his post in 1909, Mauss damns Sabatier's entire discussion of prayer as "predetermined by the faith of the author" (ibid., 1:375). In 1909 Mauss also notes that Sabatier's progressivist story of religious evolution is "broad and facile" (ibid., 1:536).

29. Mauss, "La Prière," in ibid., 1:375.

30. Jean Réville, "The Role of the History of Religions in Modern Religious Education," *The New World* 1 (1892): 516.

31. Albert Réville believed in a common human evolution in which we were swept into a union of human unity and divine presence.

> In setting forth the intellectual and moral unity of mankind, everywhere directed at the same successive evolutions and the same spiritual laws, it brings into light the great principle of *human brotherhood.*

This common "evolution," in turn, forms a "basis of reason" for the "august sentiment of *divine fatherhood*. Brother-men and Father-God!—what more does the thinker need to raise the dignity of our nature?" (Albert Réville, *Lectures on the Origin and Growth of Religion*, 2nd ed., trans. P. H. Wicksteed [London: Williams and Norgate, 1905], 40–41).

32. Jean Réville, "L'histoire des religions. Sa méthode et son rôle, d'après les travaux récents de MM. Maurice Vernes, Goblet d'Alviella, et du P. van den Gheyn," *Revue de l'histoire des religions* 14 (1886): 352.

33. See Jean Réville, "Leçon d'ouverture du cours d'histoire des religions au Collège de France," *Revue de l'histoire des religions* 55 (1907): 189–207; his "Role of the History of Religions," 503–19; and "La Théologie partie intégrante du cycle de l'enseignement universitaire et fondement indispensable de la Réformation," reported in "Chronique," *Revue de l'histoire des religions* 39 (1899): 412. See also Jean Réville, *Les Phases successives de l'histoire des religions* (Paris: Ernest Leroux, 1909); and "L'Histoire des religions et les facultés de théologie," *Revue d'histoire des religions* 44 (1901): 428.

34. Jean Réville, "Role of the History of Religions," 518.

35. See William R. Keylor, *Academy and Community: The Foundation of the French Historical Profession* (Cambridge: Harvard University Press, 1975), 125–40; and den Boer, *History as a Profession*, 339–42 (my translation). Berr commissioned an article from Jean Réville for the inaugural number of *Revue de synthèse historique* on the first international congress of the history of religions (1900); see Jean Réville, "Congrès d'histoire des religions," *Revue de synthèse historique* 1 (1900): 211–13. Berr was proved right in his assessment of Jean Réville, given the plans Réville laid out regarding his own commitment to a thoroughly psychologized history reminiscent of Dilthey. With an *histoire historisante* apparently in mind, the younger Réville asserted that the "historian has not finished his task until, with the aid of the testimonies which he has preserved, he reconstitutes their exact tenor" ("Leçon d'ouverture," 202). To Jean Réville, the task of reconstructing the frame of mind of religious folk lays a special burden upon the historian, and calls forth, quite literally, a kind of "methodological Methodism." As if reclaiming part of the vital Methodist heritage of French Protestantism, Réville says that although he does not denigrate the many studies of religion done "from outside," one must now seek "the human soul" so that one can "find the underlying and true explanation of religious phenomena in the imagination, heart, reason, conscience, instincts and passions" (ibid., 203). Why this "methodological Methodism" is virtually absent from Albert Réville's writings is a question for further research.

36. See Émile Durkheim, *The Rules of Sociological Method and Selected Texts on Sociology and Its Method*, trans. W. D. Halls, ed. Steven Lukes (London: Macmillan, 1982), 175–240.

37. Émile Durkheim, "Débat sur l'éxplication en histoire et en sociologie," *Bulletin de la Société française de philosophie* 8 (1908): 229; *Émile Durkheim: Textes*, vol. 1, ed. Viktor Karady (Paris: Minuit, 1975), 199.

38. Norman Ravitch, *The Catholic Church and the French Nation, 1589–1989* (London: Routledge, 1990), 21.

39. Ibid., 52.

40. Ibid., 58.

41. Jean Réville's "L'influence sociale de l'histoire des religions," *Université de Paris* (1906): 22–25, cited in Weisz, *Emergence of Modern Universities*, 295.

42. Simon Schama, *Citizens: A Chronicle of the French Revolution* (Knopf: New York, 1989), 349–50.

43. Malcolm O. Partin, *Waldeck-Rousseau, Combes, and the Church: The Politics of Anti-Clericalism, 1899–1905* (Durham: Duke University Press, 1969).

44. Ravitch, *Catholic Church and the French Nation*, 21, 40.

45. Ibid., 21.

46. Dale Van Kley, *The Jansenists and the Expulsion of the Jesuits from France, 1757–1765* (New Haven: Yale University Press, 1975).

47. Louis Havet, "Section des Sciences Religieuses," in *La vie universitaire à Paris* (Paris: Colin, 1918), 188.

48. Ivan Strenski, "Sacrifice and Social Theory between Rome and Reform," in *Contesting Sacrifice: Religion, Nationalism and Social Thought in France* (Chicago: University of Chicago Press, 2002).

49. See my discussion of the links between the Durkheimians and *Annalistes* in my "Hubert and Mauss and the Comparative Social History of Religions," in *Religion in Relation* (London: Macmillan; Columbia: University of South Carolina Press, 1993).

50. Marc Bloch, *The Royal Touch*, trans. J. E. Anderson (New York: Dorset, 1989); and Lucien Febvre, *The Problem of Unbelief in the Sixteenth Century: The Religion of Rabelais*, trans. Beatrice Gottlieb (Cambridge: Harvard University Press, 1982).

51. See note 1.

52. On Dumont's relation to Mauss and modern ideologies, see Louis Dumont, "Marcel Mauss: A Science in Becoming," in *Essays on Individualism* (Chicago: University of Chicago Press, 1986). For Dumont's major contribution to religious studies, see his *Homo Hierarchicus* (Chicago: University of Chicago Press, 1970).

53. On the British appropriation of Durkheimian thought in advance of the French, see Claude Lévi-Strauss, *The Scope of Anthropology* (London: Jonathan Cape, 1967), 7–11. On Lévi-Strauss's self-serving reading of Marcel Mauss and the Durkheimian tradition, see Ivan Strenski, *Four Theories of Myth in Twentieth-Century History* (London: Macmillan; Iowa City: University of Iowa Press, 1987), 138–44.

Part III

DISCIPLINES OF THE SELF

CHAPTER 6

Subjecting English and the Question of Representation

GAURI VISWANATHAN

CHALLENGES IN THE WRITING OF ENGLISH STUDIES

How English became a university subject has probably the most convoluted history of any discipline that we know today. No two accounts are similar, which is no doubt an acknowledgment of the field's prodigious narrative capacity. Yet there is more convergence in the *manner* of telling the story of English than its *matter*. A number of critics have drawn attention to such varied topics as popular democracy,[1] moral and social missionizing,[2] Christian hermeneutics,[3] colonial management,[4] governmental control,[5] and credentialization[6] as major motivations in the growth of English studies since the nineteenth century. At best, these are given as discrete issues informing English literary instruction from its inception. Relative to each other, these developments would have to be understood as responses either to various historical pressures or changing social demands. This view emerges most sharply in Chris Baldick's *The Social Mission of English Criticism* (1983), an early work integrating literary criticism and educational history. Baldick's work set a certain style for writing the history of English studies, the allure of which has also been entrapping. Its chronological mode of narration and institutional focus notwithstanding, its reading of literary education as primarily a history of English criticism has kept discussion squarely focused on the fate of texts in the context of shifting schools of thought.

Charting the transformations in the field is no easy task, as the very nature of change is to produce new forms whose relation to earlier ones is rarely self-evident and indeed often so opaque as to counteract any suggestion of continuity or systematic development. One of the great challenges in writing the history of English studies is the sheer mass of detail confronting the critic and historian, who is obliged to attend simultaneously to policies, institutional requirements, curricular content, the universe of learners, pressures of the market-place (including publishing), and distribution systems, not to mention the vagaries of fashion and shifting standards of value. Correspondingly, the historian of English studies cannot simply invoke whatever theoretical approach happens to have currency at the time, but rather must enlist the help of a wide range of disciplines, including sociology, aesthetics, philosophy, literary criticism, pedagogy, politics, and history, in order to make sense of unpatterned developments in the field. Nor is the problem made any easier by the fact that the professional study of education (which attempts the integration of the afore-named approaches in some form or other) still remains somewhat outside the pale of scholarly attention in many disciplines.

This is not to say that, within English studies, the last decade has not witnessed impressive new work forcing an introspective gaze on the origins and growth of the field. As a number of critics have observed, English studies is a relatively young field with barely one hundred and fifty years behind it. But despite its youth, the beginnings of the discipline have always seemed somewhat opaque in the popular memory, as if English studies stretched back langorously to an origin identical with that of England. There is no reason why English scholars should be surprised that English study has a colonial connection, among other motivations, or that it might be implicated in the cultural management of other societies, including other parts of Greater Britain.[7] Yet what seems to some a fairly unexceptional finding has the blatant force of heresy for many others.

One reason for this may be that, to an extent, the discipline's cultural origins are subsumed within the current debates on canonical value, which in large part are a response to the challenge posed by social groups now gaining access to the rights of education. The presentism of such debates, while obviously crucial, deflects from an equally important focus on the historical processes by which these groups emerged from being the objects of moral pedagogy to becoming subjects of their own history. One overlooked instance, as pointed out by John Guillory, is the effect produced by the vernacularization of English literary study on constructions of value, cultural identity, and nationhood.[8] Perhaps more extreme are those, like myself and Robert Crawford, who have argued that English studies have been invented elsewhere, specifically, in colonial India and Scotland.[9] But whatever the orientation of those scholars adopting more historical approaches, much closer theorization is required to clarify the relation between these heterogeneous historical narratives and emerging norms of cultural citizenship. Equally urgent is more rigorous examination of the relation between the combined domestic and international circumstances shaping the discipline, on the one hand, and, on the other, literature's role in enabling its readers' insertion into—and their subsequent reclamation of—the civil structures of participatory democracy.

FROM MORAL PEDAGOGY TO CULTURAL CITIZENSHIP

The distance between a literary pedagogy that depends on a view of readers as inherently deficient and an educational agenda that expects literature to reflect social diversity is a huge one indeed. In the first instance, "representation" refers to an assessment of the moral status of readers, on the basis of which literary study develops functions that enhance readers' moral sensibilities through a process of discrimination and evaluation. This meaning persisted even with the advent of democratic mass society. Indeed, the moral function became even more pronounced when the English working classes entered mainstream education, as literature became a powerful tool for the containment of lower-class agitation. Matthew Arnold understood this all too clearly, and, by presenting political restiveness as a symptom of cultural anarchy, he extended the tradition of projecting literary goals as a response to the moral deficiencies of the citizenry.[10] That he could include the "savage" Irish in this project just as effortlessly as he did the English working classes showed how flexible was this meaning of representation. Significantly, Arnold reinforced the idea of literature as moral education at a time when the working classes were demanding the franchise and the Irish were agitating for rights of self-determination. This conjunction of developments suggests how close is the slippage between literature's representation of its constituency of readers and its transformation into a political demand for readers' rightful inclusion in the social world it portrays. In fact, the depiction of readers' inadequacies is not a finite activity, an early phase of literary education followed by a later moment, a second phase, when readers assert their political presence. Rather, representation of moral insufficiencies must be considered as an ongoing response to readers' claims to self-determination. This is clear in Chinua Achebe's famous denunciation of Joseph Conrad's *Heart of Darkness* for perpetuating racist portrayals of Africans.[11] Achebe's critique exposes the colonial pedagogy of the novel, even when the work was purportedly questioning the validity of the colonial enterprise. His criticism suggests that Conrad's physical representation of African natives as long-limbed and langorous neutralizes the threatening restiveness of Africans. An incipient agitation that would soon lead to independence movements all over the continent is turned into inert passivity, as the physical details of Conrad's descriptions rob his supposedly critical narrative of an "alternative frame of reference" by which to judge the actions of his characters.[12] Achebe's own reading therefore can be said to be political in this vital sense: it restores the context of upheaval and resistance to colonial rule by exposing Conrad's racialized language and dismantling its structure of racist stereotypes.

The meaning of representation as a purely political idea, referring to the presence of social groups in the decision-making democratic process, cannot easily be transferred to the literary curriculum, which can never presume to encompass the total social fabric or advance the interests of all its members simultaneously. At best the curriculum can reflect only the presence of social groups *in the university* (a crucial distinction), but demographic diversity cannot be equated with political representation. Nonetheless, literary study is newly marked for its potential to bear different class, gender, and racial interests, thus breaking the back of the Arnoldian curriculum, which asserts that education exists to filter the values of a dominant class downward to other classes. In part, the spread of class and other interests cuts into literature's historical role as a shaper and producer of moral selves, as the relativism of values dismisses the possibility that there can be such a thing as a consensual moral self. After all, whose values are to be disseminated when there are competing groups represented in the curriculum?

These opposed tendencies in literary pedagogy convince me more than ever that we need a workable theory of representation bridging two radically different conceptions of the reader. On one hand, we must contend with the historical genealogy of English literary study from its religious origins: that is, the construction of readers of English literature as inheritors of a scriptural legacy of original sin. The legacy is so strong as to posit literary study as an instrument of moral elevation, if not redemption. On the other hand, the second conception, which regards readers as encompassing the full range of social diversity, follows from the rise of the nation-state, and it requires the interpellation of readers as members of a community increasingly defined on national rather than religious or ethnic lines. The movement from *representation* to *representational politics* adduces a contingent relationship between literary education and its universe of readers who are often overlooked when texts are deemed to be the sole source of value. Indeed, by this calculation it should be possible to relocate value from texts to the enhanced bargaining power of readers, based on their access to the civil structures of participatory democracy.

I want to illustrate my approach to this issue by beginning with a contemporary memoir authored by a woman belonging to India's untouchable, or *dalit*, class. Kumud Pawde's "The Story of My Sanskrit" (1992)[13] is a remarkable work for several reasons. The memoir appeared at a time when untouchables, like other minority groups in the United States and elsewhere, were mobilizing themselves around a cultural identity to undo the erasure of their existence by their caste oppressors. Central to the act of self-reclamation were critiques of brahmanical literature as a cause of untouchables' oppression.[14] In this context it would appear that the route to dalit empowerment is a proportional devaluation of the literature produced by their antagonists, who are members of the upper castes. But interestingly, "The Story of My Sanskrit" traces a reverse trajectory, untypical though it may have been of other dalit writings. It describes the class aspirations of a dalit woman who persists in mastering Sanskrit, traditionally considered to be the preserve of India's upper-caste Brahmins, for whom Sanskrit as a Hindu scriptural language has a status analogous to that of Latin in Roman Catholic liturgies. Therefore, when a dalit woman, the "lowest of the low" whom "religion has considered vermin,"[15] masters the language and literature so successfully as to earn professional credentials to teach it, she attracts both admiration (from other dalits) and denunciation (by the upper castes). The admiration from her caste-members stems from their understandable pride in seeing one of their own gain access to forbidden knowledge. Yet their satisfaction is not simply because Pawde achieves the impossible and demonstrates superior literary skills, on a par with those who jealously guard Sanskrit. Rather, they see her access to Sanskrit as driven by the same momentum spurring dalits to gain entry into Hindu temples, assert claims to civic amenities such as common drinking water, and other such attempts to remove restrictions. It is as if to say, as Pierre Bourdieu suggests, that "there is no other criterion of membership of a field than the objective fact of producing effects within it."[16] In mastering Sanskrit, Pawde encouraged dalits to believe that, by disrupting Sanskrit's alignment with a select social group, she had paved the way for them to enter other forbidden spaces. So that even though Pawde's great desire to learn Sanskrit may appear assimilationist, she asserted the voice of a newly enfranchised untouchable community by thwarting Sanskrit's identification with the upper castes. And by staking her own claims to Sanskrit as an outcaste woman, she denied the boundaries that preserved Sanskrit in all its purity. In other words, she disentangled Sanskrit from the social group whose values it was presumed to reflect (yet Sanskrit is no more status-linked than any other language). The power of a new voice like Pawde's was that it presented a challenge to negative representations, not by throwing out the literature by which caste oppression was maintained, but by refuting its identification with an elite social group and the economic and symbolic capital it represented. Pawde's memoir suggests that if the object of the dalit struggle remained confined to discarding brahminical literature, it would not necessarily make any difference in the power relations between the upper castes and the untouchables. Indeed, it was very likely that the various social groups would remain intact in their separate spheres. As an ultimate gesture of nonessentialism, Pawde's desire to learn Sanskrit refuses the label of self-hating assimilationism.

John Guillory rightly points out that the canon debate in the United States has derailed educational reform from its real objective—ensuring equal access to cultural capital—by focusing exclusively on competing social representations as the primary issue that has to be worked through. In our contemporary preoccupation with making the curriculum as inclusive as possible to match the growing numbers of social groups entering education, we have opted for a curricular version of affirmative action, without the social goals of affirmative action. We have settled for representative coverage rather than aiming for social transformation through equitable distribution of educational resources, including cultural capital. When the curriculum is conceived as a micro-model of pluralist society, social heterogeneity is valued to the extent that it can be mirrored in the content of literary instruction. But representational claims suggest that literature can only be a simulacrum of social realities, not the site of social struggle itself nor the struggle for rights, the attainment of which marks the full inclusion of diverse social groups in civil society and the nation-state. Indeed, by a paradoxical quirk, when full rights are obtained, it becomes a moot question whether various social groups would turn to literature as the place where they would pursue the path to social equality and justice. In the realm of actual realization of rights, the function of literary education would be itself transformed, as a site perhaps of the historical memory of struggle.

CHRISTIAN KNOWLEDGE AND SOCIAL HETEROGENEITY

Christian hermeneutics appears to construct at least one bridge between history and canonical authority. A line of educational thinkers from Comenius and Erasmus to Milton established the close correspondence between word and Word, paving the movement from empiricism to revelation.[17] Indeed, Milton's key contribution in his seminal essay *Of Education* (1644) was to frame empiricist knowledge in the terms of rational Christian morality. This move freed him from being chained down to a concept of human nature as inherently depraved and enabled him to place postlapsarian humankind in a secular trajectory of progress. Milton's tractate on education showed how keen he was to resituate Adam not only as regenerate but also as having a place in the state. Historically, Christian knowledge has constituted an important rationale for literary study as the pursuit of morality, salvation, and self-knowledge. That these goals are then naturalized as inherent attributes of a body of canonical texts has everything to do with the fact that Christian knowledge is secularized and its religious functions usurped by literature, as Matthew Arnold presciently observed.

But even by characterizing English literature's moral impulses in terms of its derivation from Christianity, we entertain a number of false assumptions about the organic composition of the culture in which literature is taught. This was typically the fallacy driving missionary work in non-Christian societies, which were reorganized to correspond with a uniform English society pervaded by the influence of Christian culture shaping English conduct and thought. This construction encouraged many Christian missionaries to subscribe to a unitary theory of English civil society based on religion, influencing the full range of knowledge produced in that society. But such a construction also had strategic uses, particularly in the colonial context. When Western society is characterized as a perfect fusion of civil and sacred institutions with literary and religious knowledge, the description inevitably affects the way non-Western societies are delineated. The representation of Christian society as a unitary composition can hold true only by discussing non-Christian societies in antithetical terms, that is, as asymmetrical societies whose knowledge runs counter to established institutions and structures. Making societies Christian is as much a pedagogical as a political objective.

Literature's generic descent from scripture may have the force of descriptive fact, but it cannot account for literature's moral influence in an unevenly composed society Christian only in name, as is the case with England especially by the mid-nineteenth century. Its history of multiple sects highlights an Anglicanism eroded as much by dissent as by the rising tide of movements like secularism, freethought, and atheism. Moreover, social groups like Jews, Nonconformists, and atheists, who were hitherto excluded from participation in England's civic life, were brought into the fold by the third quarter of the nineteenth century.[18] Simultaneously, colonized subjects who embraced a range of religions from Hinduism and Islam to Sikhism and Buddhism were obliged to read English literature in schools funded by the British government.[19] That being the case, what does it mean to allude to English literature's Christian roots if the very society in which it is read and studied does not partake of a uniform Christian character? The heterogeneity of England's religious population set alarm bells ringing for William Gladstone, who fretted about the threat posed by religious plurality to governmental efficiency. It prompted him to advocate the yoking of temporal and spiritual interests in order to achieve a more uniform society in which, as Thomas B. Macaulay charged, "the propagation of religious truth is one of the principal ends of government, as government."[20]

Historically, the severest challenge to coherent objectives in literary instruction has come from the pluralistic *religious* composition of society. This is often lost sight of in our own contemporary debates, in which *ethnicity* figures more prominently as an index of a society's pluralistic character. An English population comprising not only Anglicans but also Jews, Catholics, Dissenters, Nonconformists, and other denominations militates against a composite characterization of literature's Christian motivation, or even against the notion that texts are open to private interpretation. Furthermore, when English literature is taught in the colonies, a heterogeneous colonized population that includes Hindus, Muslims, Buddhists, Sikhs, among other religious groups, poses a direct challenge to the expected purposes and outcomes of Christian instruction. With the scriptural antecedents of literature not being self-evidently persuasive in non-Christian societies, and in the absence of continuity between civil and sacred institutions, literary instruction reaches a point of crisis. Its resolution paradoxically entails that literature be taught precisely in order to Christianize. This forced motivation violently attempts to form a unity between the civil and the sacred where such unity does not exist—a replication of the colonialist move itself.

The question to ask, then, is this: What effect does a literary education with roots in Christian hermeneutics have on the construction of other communities of readers who are non-Christians (or more precisely, non-Anglicans)? To say that discrepancy among religious backgrounds of readers affects the response to that literature is to state the obvious. But the statement can be refined further to suggest that literature does not produce readings against the Christian grain so much as it creates the terms in which it is read as an ethics of self-improvement. In other words, as its functions shift relative to the increasing heterogeneity of readerships, literature is less important in its Christian effects than in producing the modern subject. So that ironically, by making strict Christian readings impossible, yet at the same time by not being able to jettison Christian roots altogether, pluralism prepares the way for literature to create the new self of modernity. The shift also amounts to a change in the very nature of representation. From a concept bearing Christian overtones, in which the reader is described as weighed down by original sin and hence inherently depraved, representation acquires political overtones through its construction of the reader as ready to assume a place in civil society and to accept the responsibilities and duties of citizenship.

CAN LITERARY THEORY RECOGNIZE A PLURAL READERSHIP?

If English studies helped produce the secular subject of modernity, its indirect investment in religious practices of reading and instruction is most forcefully revealed through its practices of criticism and theory. Although much has been written about literary education's scriptural roots, less discussed is theory's relation to an ethics of reading derived from Christian hermeneutics. Most recently, Ian Hunter has gone further than most critics in ascribing a religious motivation not only to literary education but also to literary theory, which he believes has grown out of an earlier tradition of moral self-questioning associated with Christian hermeneutics.[21] His essay on the place of literary theory in civil life makes a complicated, even austere, argument that defiantly returns poststructuralist theory to its religious origins. I begin with Hunter's essay to broach my speculation about representation, not because Hunter unveils the transition to representational politics—indeed he does not—but rather because his theorization of the theorist's role continues to assume a homogeneous literary readership that, in denying religious plurality, stalls theory's emancipatory trajectory.

We can agree in saying that English literary education has succeeded in setting up certain norms, such as civility, comportment, refinement, and sensibility. Clearly these requirements no longer pertain, and the interesting question is how English has shifted from a moral to an intellectual to an ideological function. Now we no longer read literature for moral transformation and not even for intellectual growth, but we read skeptically and with great suspicion of authors' motives, and we call this ideological critique. As Brian Doyle points out, the journals *Scrutiny* and *Review of English Studies* were ranged against each other in fierce debate over the shift in attitude toward authors. The shift amounted to casting doubt on authors, rather than celebrating their virtue or accepting their credentials as unassailable.[22] Today, of course, unassailability is a vanished concept, as much for authors as critics, and literary criticism as ideological critique is the prevailing norm. This has emerged in part through the mediating role of theory, but perhaps the only way it has been able to do that is by taking on the task of moral self-examination.

Hunter's account of literary theory's political investment returns to the self as the sole site of examination and transformation. By maintaining that theory aims at causing individuals to submit their own ethical presuppositions to continuous scrutiny, Hunter concludes that literary theory contrives political critique as an occasion for engaging with its real object: moral self-problematization as a technique of self-correction, derived from the broad brushstrokes of Christian hermermeutics. Hunter continues to work with an idea of representation as a characterization of the reader's moral status. An essential requirement for the Christian understanding of self, representation is a mode of objectification of human insufficiencies, without which the path to salvation is unbridgeable.

Ian Hunter regards reading as an ascetic practice, a spiritual discipline.[23] Since his intent is to link literary education with modern literary theory, he focuses on scripture as an exemplary text of opacity that makes meaning available only by forcing readers to examine themselves first. "It was the means by which the monk would be required and motivated to turn inward, deciphering and transforming himself by discriminating the inner meaning of the holy books from the false impressions left in the corrupted medium of their human understanding." By removing the husk from inner truth, writes Hunter, "the spiritual athlete can then purify and clarify his inner self, preparing it for contemplation of divine things."[24] Transparent texts, on the other hand, do not cause readers to work overtime in this manner and leave them virtually unchanged, not forcing them, as opaque texts do, to submit to self-scrutiny. Thus, opacity is a function of the corruptions of human nature. The texts produced by postlapsarian humankind partake of the same density that, through its incomprehension, thwarts humanity's ultimate salvation. The inscrutability of literature conjures up the reading subject as driven by a universal longing for insight into its operation.

When Hunter describes approaches to literature and politics prior to the advent of literary theory as "theoretically minimal and morally undecided,"[25] he concludes that theory *inherently* holds a political stance on literary issues *because* it commits one to a moral view of life. Other approaches apparently lack this moral intent and instead have only technical or historical value. The crucial difference, Hunter seems to suggest, is that historical approaches have no particular moral view toward the exercise of power, whereas theory unequivocally exposes power interests in literary texts. Hunter's opposition between literary theory and history is problematic, for one should surely be able to accept that literary theory may emerge from historical approaches, rather than viewing them as mutually exclusive.

Instead of asking how the truth of literature may be revealed, Hunter believes literary theory shifts the burden of examination from the text to the self so that latent literary processes are approached not as theoretical problems requiring clarification but as ethical self-problematizations. This form of ethical instantiation requires readers to redirect their investigation of texts virtually to a study of themselves: "The inscrutable character of literature arises not from theoretical reflection but from its pedagogical or 'psychological' use as a discipline shaping the comportment of the one who reflects."[26] As a rehearsal of Christian hermeneutics, literary theory is reduced to a form of self-cultivation. It is linked to the exercise of power not through a theoretical clarification of the unconscious or the ideological, but through the cultural qualification of the theorist as an ethical being who seeks clarification and, once illuminated, then proceeds to create an order of intellectual governance.

The one point at which Hunter attempts a transition to representational politics occurs with his suggestion that the political salience of theory lies less in its unmasking of power than in its placing the moral authority of the unmasking theorist in the service of social governance. In other words, the literary theorist is just as intent on bringing into being a certain kind of social and political order as were the literary elite of early modern Europe. This is quite a daring thought, and Hunter brilliantly evokes theory's deliberate construction of an order of management, which occurs by illuminating the dark spaces of the self and turning moral limitations into points of monitoring and self-regulation. To my mind, this constitutes the crucial linchpin for a theory of representation. The question of social representation is critical in the development of intellectual fields. Yet in tracing the power and prestige of literary theory to long-standing hermeneutic practices, Hunter inexplicably fails to relate the corruptions of human nature, which literary theory purports to correct, with the deployment of such understandings in the *mission civilisatrice*. Nor does he have much to say about the deliberate representation of learners as morally deficient: while he views such representations as implicit in Christian instruction, he does not go further to examine how they are put to use by administrators and missionaries alike for practices of colonial control and management. By this account, the literary theorist who attempts to fit readers into a political world made comprehensible by the severe disciplining insights of literary theory performs a function akin to that of a colonial administrator who catalyzes moral and political conscience.

Literary education employs the rhetoric of Christian amelioration when it assumes the state of readers to be burdened by the weight of original sin. But when readers do not share the Christian conviction of collective guilt at disobeying God's command, it is fair to ask why literature should have a purgatory function for these readers. However, Hunter's inability to acknowledge the heterogeneity of literary readerships allows him to constitute a common interpretive community of Christians. Indeed, his focus on private interpretation construes this community even more specifically as Protestant. However, the range of religious and sectarian distinctions in England's population, as well as in colonized societies, makes representation of such populations critical. Literary instruction cannot thrive without a proportional representation of its readers' inadequacies. Characterizing other societies as morally and intellectually deficient is possible only by foregrounding their bondage to original sin, which means, of course, that their religious difference is denied. This is precisely what is overlooked in Hunter's account, and the omission leaves his otherwise complex reading incomplete and open to further elaboration.

FROM REPRESENTATION TO REPRESENTATIONAL POLITICS

The concept of representation is crucial in the move beyond Christian and even *Christianizing* functions. There is a curricular nexus between two radically different notions of representation: the first, drawing on a rhetoric of Christian morality and Christian salvation, posits an understanding of human nature as diminished and seeking regeneration; and the second asserts claims on rights to full political participation. The move between the two has helped define the shape, content, and objectives of English literary instruction since its inception. The transition from representations of human nature as open to moral improvement, to the idea of representation as a political marker of citizenship can, on one level, be explained in the context of a shift from religious to secular worldviews. But on another level, the continuity between the two discourses establishes how necessary are educational programs to sustain both ideas of representation. The discrepancy between literary functions inherited from scriptural exegesis and the heterogeneous composition of England's religious population, not to mention that of colonized societies, makes representation of such populations of paramount importance in the continuing vitality of literature. Homogenizing the population to constitute one single (religious) culture is not an idle function of English literary study, and indeed is a significant part of its socializing mission.

Yet the examination of representational politics—or what in some quarters would be described today as identity-politics—in relation to representation as a discourse of human insufficiency has remained elusive. How does the

Christian rhetoric of moral depravity and elevation through literary study contribute to the development of citizenship criteria and the notion that literary education exists to adapt individuals to civic participation? Is the shift in function from Christian salvation to participatory democracy a wholly inevitable one, paralleling the replacement of religion by secular motivations? While I would agree that secularization diminishes the salvational rhetoric of English studies, I do not believe it fully explains the emergence of a new discourse of representational politics, especially if the latter is seen to abort the religious trajectory. The ideology of improvement marks its limits when those who are to be "improved" reach a level playing field, and improvement shades into assertions of equality. If Christian discourse objectifies those receiving literary instruction and describes them as inherently lacking in qualities required for their self-transcendence, representational politics asserts the claims of disparate groups to full participation in the moral and social universe of literary texts, proportionate to readers' participation in larger social processes. "Inadequacy" becomes a point against which political mobilization is ranged, as resistance to literary ideology also involves rejecting the unitary Christian values it transmits. The transition from religious to secular meanings coincides with a shift in the reader as object (of instruction) to the reader as subject (in the political process), a move that defies the "conscription" of the reader caught in a one-sided conversation in which it is believed he or she "can never talk back."[27] By the 1880s this move is complete, and the question we have to ask is how the possibilities of critique opened up by such a shift contribute to the ongoing transformation of English studies. If English is no longer studied as a repository of moral value and judgment, what (perhaps more utilitarian) purpose does it now serve that links it to the historical processes of legal inclusiveness and citizenship?

By the end of the nineteenth century English literary study had produced a new idea of the reader, mediated in part by the rise of modern bureaucracy and the nation-state.[28] In asserting this, I want to distinguish between the politicization of the reading subject and the insertion of the reader into civil society. The creation of the new secular subject of modernity is radically transformed by the attempt to adapt literary study to the demands of an increasingly complex English state responsible for both domestic and colonial governance. The moral and civic emphasis ascribed to literature enhanced the functioning of the state, providing civil subjects with the moral backbone required to ensure their integrity, loyalty, and duty. The new discipline of English literature created a consciousness of national and civic identity, while simultaneously recoding the (inherently deficient) modern subject as capable of improvement. The Christian rhetoric of moral enhancement blended perfectly with the new ideology of progress. Unlike anthropology, which yields a new knowledge of the other as romantically placed in the past, the subject of English contains the other within, even as that other is transcended through literary pedagogy. In more ways than one, the notion of "inherent moral deficiency" is the key to modern literary studies. Literary education's training of an enlightened but pliable citizenry is possible only by its insistence that readers are flawed but ultimately salvageable.

The rhetoric of conversion in all this is inescapable. Making readers "better" is making them think differently, adopting a viewpoint that is not theirs. The teaching of English for purposes of assimilating colonial subjects and adapting them to English political goals is akin to the eighteenth- and nineteenth-century conversion of Jews to Christianity so that England would be made uniform and cohesive.[29] Yet because reclamation of Jews as Christians had the unintended effect of driving Jews away and, instead, created a fierce sense of group cohesion and solidarity among them, Jewish conversions took a back seat to the pressure for legal emancipation of Jews. The movement for civil relief was driven by secular Anglicans as much as by Jews. If Jews would not become Christians, they were at least more likely to accept being English, if only to have existing civil disabilities against them lifted. However, though secular Anglicans may have aimed at reversing the separatism of Jews, the claims of Jews to full political participation offered by religious emancipation transformed a strategic English objective, which was largely confined to the absorption of Jews. Parliamentary acts, intended to assimilate Jews by removing exclusionary edicts, instead created a more radicalized political subjectivity among English Jews. Representation as a function of Christian salvation, which derogates the Christ-denying Jew as lying outside the pale of English society, metamorphoses into *representation* as the groundwork for asserting political legitimacy.

The picture is more sharply focused when moral self-problematization and the ethics of improvement are set in the context of nineteenth-century arguments for a new *politics*, rather than a morality, of representation. No figure in nineteenth-century letters expressed the full range of meanings of representation more powerfully than Thomas B. Macaulay, particularly in two seminal essays, the "Minute on Indian Education" (1835) and the less familiar but critically important essay, "Civil Disabilities of the Jews" (1830). In these two works, Macaulay shifted the moral terrain to rewrite the Christian discourse of moral regeneration and improvement into a call for the political inclusion of groups hitherto removed from English parliamentary process, such as Jews, Nonconformists, Catholics, and Dissenters.

Closely identified with the English education of Indians, Macaulay is perhaps less known as an advocate of Jewish emancipation. His clarion call to remove restrictions against English Jews had a major, if delayed, effect on absorbing Jews into the English state. Even when proposing the anglicization of Indian subjects, his political attention was squarely focused on the nebulous position of English Jews. Infamous on account of his "Minute on Indian

Education" for advocating that the British withdraw support of indigenous
learning and instead turn its sights on the promotion of English literature,
Macaulay also happened to be one of the most vocal proponents of Jewish
emancipation. At first glance it appears as if Macaulay's domestic and international agendas were at odds with each other. After all, his call for an
acknowledgment of Jewish civil presence might appear to have more in
common with a philosophy of cultural relativism, which he had himself cast-
igated when it was practiced in India as Orientalism.[30] But Macaulay was
motivated less by a culturalist argument than by a strictly political one,
which was in turn driven by secular goals. If he came to realize that the
making of good Englishmen was a more worthwhile objective than the
Christianizing of England, this was no doubt because he felt it was impracticable to aim for the making of either good Christians in India or good Anglicans in England. His support of Jewish civil emancipation had all the
earmarks of Whig liberalism, with its belief that English progress required
the absorption of excluded groups into the nation.[31] The fact remains that
Macaulay's plan to anglicize Indians was shaped from the same political
philosophy that advocated the emancipation of religious minorities in
England. This congruence establishes his colonizing mission of humanistic
education not as the antithesis but rather as the international counterpart to
the domestic agenda of incorporating Jews into the English nation-state.

Macaulay's espousal of Jewish civil relief was not a typical position
among the Clapham Evangelicals in whose community he grew up, and it
brought him into conflict with them on numerous occasions. Their eagerness
to reclaim Jews as converts to Christianity led the Evangelicals initially to
oppose Jewish civil emancipation. Yet they were not closed to reformist
tendencies in the culture, even though they themselves might have repudiated Macaulay's more radical intentions. Certainly the Evangelicals were
divided on the issue of Jewish emancipation. If even the more conservative
among them gave their nod to Jewish emancipation, it was because they
were convinced it would make the task of Christian conversions easier, since
removal of civil restrictions would make Jews feel less alienated from Angli-
can culture. Like many other Christian organizations, the Clapham Evangelicals reacted with alarm to the fierce cohesiveness of the Anglo-Jewish
community, strengthened in many ways by their marginality in English society. Evangelicals were open to rethinking England's exclusionary politics
only because they perceived that the policies created a separatist consciousness and pride in Jews, making Christian conversions virtually impossible.
When, therefore, in the 1830s, Sir Robert Grant presented a set of parliamentary bills proposing Jewish civil emancipation, the Evangelicals did not uni-
laterally withhold support. In fact, Lord Bexley, former chancellor of the
Exchequer, declared that admitting Jews fully into public life "will be a great

step to bring them back from the Talmud to Moses and the Prophets—from there to Christ the transition is comparatively easy."[32]

But though the Clapham Evangelicals may have conceded the importance of incorporating Jews into the English social system, Macaulay did not share their motivation in linking Jewish emancipation to Christian conversion. Conversion was less his goal than national consolidation. He was too pragmatic not to see the significant political gains in turning his liberal agenda to the extension of the franchise and the elimination of religious disabilities. Having written passionately on the destined international course of English history, he could now turn his attention to domestic reforms as a focal point of England's international expansion. In his extraordinary essay, "Civil Disabilities of the Jews," published in 1830 in the *Edinburgh Review*, he spared no punches, declaiming that in a period when Englishmen were spreading to the far corners of the world and establishing themselves as rulers and managers, England could not afford to turn its back on its own internal religious minorities, who were systematically excluded from civic participation.

> If there be any proposition universally true in politics, it is this, that foreign attachments are the fruit of domestic misrule. It has always been the trick of bigots . . . to govern as if a section of the state were the whole, and to censure the other sections of the state for their want of patriotic spirit. If the Jews have not felt towards England like children, it is because she has treated them like a step-mother. . . . Till we have carried the experiment farther, we are not entitled to conclude that they cannot be made Englishmen altogether. The English Jews are, as far as we can see, precisely what our government has made them.[33]

In this eloquent plea to admit Jews, Macaulay performed a rhetorical sleight of hand by denouncing as unpatriotic not the Jews but rather the English state. The state contributed to its own self-alienation by refusing to extend the virtues of good government to all sections of society. If Jews saw themselves first as Jews and only secondarily as English, their apparent lack of English feeling could be attributed to misguided actions by the state, which persisted in excluding them. The disloyalty of Jews could be argued, in short, as state-produced. By drawing attention to the Jews' separatism as an outcome of state policy, rather than a justification for excluding them from citizenship, Macaulay blew apart the hypocritical pretenses of the English state, which resorted to blaming the victim for the alienation it had in effect created.

But Macaulay had his own interests in promoting Jewish emancipation, and they were not confined to his wish to see the English state realize its liberal promise. Administrative efficiency remained his paramount goal, as is clear in the utilitarian language he used while urging Jewish civil relief. He was less interested in Jewish self-identity than in the usefulness of Jews to oil the machinery of government. His support of Jewish relief on utilitarian grounds was no different from his Anglicist philosophy of promoting English education to make colonized Indians "good" subjects of the empire. If we compare his views on Jewish civil disabilities and on the education of Indians, there is no doubt they appear to have been cut from the same fabric:

> On our principles all civil disabilities on account of religious opinions are inde-
> fensible. For all such disabilities make government less efficient for its main
> end; they limit the choice of able men for the administration and defense of the
> State; they alienate it from the hearts of the sufferers; they deprive it of a part of
> its operative strength in all contests with foreign nations.[34]

Now when we place this passage alongside its parallel one in "Minute on Indian Education," it is strikingly clear how Jews and Indians have value for Macaulay only insofar as they serve British commercial interests:

> In India, English is the language spoken by the ruling class. It is spoken by the
> higher class of natives at the seats of Government. It is likely to become the
> language of commerce throughout the seas of the East. . . . There is now in that
> country a large educated class, abounding with persons fit to serve the state in
> the highest functions, and in no wise inferior to the most accomplished men who
> adorn the best circles of Paris and London. There is reason to hope that this vast
> empire, which in the time of our grandfathers was probably behind the Punjab,
> may, in the time of our grandchildren, be pressing close on France and Britain in
> the career of improvement.[35]

Macaulay is evidently less interested in the cultural mission of English for its own sake, but rather imagines the day when the tissue of connection through the English language and literature will constitute the true empire, more lasting than an empire subject to the vagaries of military control.

Imperial though his motivation may have been, Macaulay believed administrative efficiency required that both colonized subjects in India and Jews in England be released from the suffocating hold of representations that cast them as pagans and Christ-killers respectively. However, he could not have foreseen that affiliation to England through its literature rather than religion opened the way for these very groups to stake a claim to a place in the English political process. Significantly, their claims would be made as Indians and Jews primarily, not as English subjects or English citizens. This development disturbs the typical description of anticolonial resistance as a benevolent legacy of English liberalism and education. The depraved self may need literature for elevation, but there is no way of ignoring the fact that reading literature effectively also requires a suitably elevated sensibility. The circularity of the argument leaves the relationship between literature and reader always unstable and volatile, and ultimately bidirectional. If former subjects are imbued with a desire for freedom, so the liberal argument goes, this demand must have been inculcated in them by the principles of English liberty enshrined in English literature. There is no greater testament to the value of literature than its emancipatory function, say its apologists. But read outside a Christian hermeneutic of depravity and salvation, literature could not sustain the myth that disparate groups would all subscribe to a common teleology of universal progress, as Macaulay mistakenly believed they would. And it is thus only appropriate that the misfit between Christian hermeneutics and the heterogeneous composition of society should unravel the myth of a common developmental purpose. Diverse social groups confirm the impossibility of reading literature as Christian knowledge, even though, ironically, it was through the acculturating intentions of literary study that the Christian motivation was both renewed and defeated.

I have argued in this essay that literature's shift in the making of modern selves occurs as a direct response to the pluralistic religious composition of society. Religious pluralism connects the societies of the colonizer and the colonized in special ways, since both face the challenges and problems created by a proliferation of faiths defying the official desire for a unitary society. The inescapable reality of religious pluralism creates possibilities for new kinds of definitions for literature, just as it also enables resistance to a single point of reference from which ensue values, dogmas, and principles. However much the English state, bent on consolidating its hegemony, may have aspired to will away religious difference, the variety of religious distinctions persisted to plague the effortless attainment of a flattened, homogeneous society, driven by universal values. When the religious motivation can no longer sustain literary education, because both English and colonial societies are too religiously diverse to accommodate a single ethic, literary study is itself transformed. At first, the transformation reflects the secular assimilation of various groups as national subjects, but from the site of "national subjects" readers further transform literature as the vantage point from which to stake claims to full political participation.

NOTES

1. Brian Doyle, *English and Englishness* (London: Routlege, 1989).

2. Chris Baldick, *The Social Mission of English Criticism* (Oxford: Clarendon Press, 1983).

3. Ian Hunter, "Literary Theory in Civil Life," *South Atlantic Quarterly* 95, no. 4 (Fall 1996): 1099–34.

4. Gauri Viswanathan, *Masks of Conquest: Literary Study and British Rule in India* (New York: Columbia University Press, 1989).

5. Ian Hunter, *Culture and Government: The Emergence of Literary Education* (London: Macmillan, 1988).

6. Gerald Graff, *Professing Literature* (Chicago: University of Chicago Press, 1987).

7. See Robert Crawford, ed., *The Scottish Invention of English Literature* (Cambridge: Cambridge University Press, 1998) for an overview of the contributions of Scottish educators like Hugh Blair, Adam Smith, and William Greenfield to the institutionalization of English.

8. John Guillory, *Cultural Capital* (Chicago: University of Chicago Press, 1993).

9. See Viswanathan, *Masks of Conquest*; Robert Crawford, *Devolving English Literature* (Oxford: Clarendon Press, 1994); Crawford, ed., *The Scottish Invention of English Literature*.

10. Matthew Arnold, *Culture and Anarchy* (1866), ed. John Dover Wilson (Cambridge: Cambridge University Press, 1981).

11. Chinua Achebe, "An Image of Africa: Racism in Conrad's *Heart of Darkness*," in *"Heart of Darkness": An Authoritative Text*, ed. Robert Kimbrough, 3rd ed. (New York: W. W. Norton, 1988).

12. Ibid., 256.

13. Kumud Pawde, "The Story of My Sanskrit," in *Poisoned Bread: Modern Marathi Literature*, ed. Arjun Dangle (Delhi: Orient Longman, 1992).

14. Indeed, the pages of the main dalit journal published by the Dalit Sahitya Akademi are filled with trenchant rereadings of mainstream Hindu texts like *The Bhagavad Gita* and *The Mahabharata*, most of which are intended to show the operations of Brahmin hegemony over dalits. Dalit Sahitya Akademi translates as the "Academy of Letters of Untouchables"—an ironic twist on the name of the national body, the Sahitya Akademi (National Academy of Letters). The function of the mainstream literary academy is to set the terms for the approbation and evaluation of the literary traditions of India. By appropriating the name, the Dalit Sahitya Akademi establishes its own intent in proposing an alternative literary canon.

15. Ibid., 97.

16. Pierre Bourdieu, *The Field of Cultural Production: Essays on Art and Literature* (New York: Columbia University Press, 1993), 42.

17. I explore the fusion of Platonic and Christian strains in English education in "Milton, Imperialism, and Education," *Modern Language Quarterly* 59, no. 3 (1998): 345–61.

18. See Gauri Viswanathan, *Outside the Fold: Conversion, Modernity, and Belief* (Princeton: Princeton University Press, 1998), which examines the legal emancipation of religious minorities as part of a larger process of national consolidation. Because of its leveling of religious differences, civil enfranchisement provoked the paradoxical response of conversion, especially to so-called minority religions, as a mode of salvaging the self-definitions of religious communities.

19. The thrust of Thomas B. Macaulay's "Minute on Indian Education" (1835) maintained that it was time for the British to stop funding Oriental learning and redirect its energies to the full support of instruction in English literature, to which "the whole native literature of India and Arabia" could not be compared. See "Minute on Indian Education," in *Macaulay: Prose and Poetry*, ed. G. M. Young (Cambridge: Harvard University Press, 1967), 722.

20. Thomas B. Macaulay, "Gladstone on Church and State," in *Macaulay: Poetry and Prose*, 613.

21. Hunter, "Literary Theory in Civil Life."

22. Doyle, *English and Englishness*, 80–81.

23. See also Geoffrey Galt Harpham, *The Ascetic Imperative in Culture and Criticism* (Chicago: University of Chicago Press, 1987).

24. Hunter, "Literary Theory in Civil Life," 1110.

25. Ibid., 1102.

26. Ibid., 1103.

27. Garrett Stewart, *Dear Reader: The Conscripted Audience in Nineteenth-Century British Fiction* (Baltimore: Johns Hopkins University Press, 1996), 13.

28. See Richard D. Altick, *The English Common Reader: A Social History of the Mass Reading Public, 1800–1900*, 2nd ed. (Columbus: Ohio State University Press, 1998), 207–12.

29. See Michael Ragussis, *Figures of Conversion: The Jewish Question and English National Identity* (Durham: Duke University Press, 1995).

30. This term, contrasted with Anglicism, has a specific meaning in eighteenth- and nineteenth-century British Indian history. It does not refer to Edward Said's now celebrated term to describe the encompassing uses of knowledge of the non-Western world to control and dominate colonized societies. In eighteenth-century India, Orientalism referred to the cultural philosophy of promoting study and translation of indigenous languages and literatures, which was then superseded by Anglicism, or the promotion of Western knowledge and culture. Macaulay was among the best-known figures in advocating the supercession of Orientalism by Anglicism.

31. See Israel Finestein, *Jewish Society in Victorian England* (London: Valentine Mitchell, 1993), 79–92.

32. Ibid., 85. See also David Katz, *Jews in the History of England 1485–1850* (Oxford: Clarendon Press, 1994), 293–95.

33. Thomas B. Macaulay, "Civil Disabilities of the Jews," *Edinburgh Review* (January 1830); reprinted in *Selections from the Edinburgh Review*, vol. 5, ed. Maurice Cross (Paris: Baudry, 1835), 207. See also Macaulay, "Parliamentary Reform, I: A Speech Delivered in the House of Commons on the 2d of March, 1831," in *Macaulay: Poetry and Prose*. In this speech, Macaulay makes an impassioned plea in behalf of the relief of civil disabilities imposed on Jews, but at the same time he opposes universal suffrage.

34. Macaulay, "Gladstone on Church and State," 656.

35. Macaulay, "Minute on Indian Education," 723–24.

CHAPTER 7

Dying Twice: Victorian Theories
of Déjà Vu

ATHENA VRETTOS

IN THOMAS HARDY'S 1873 novel *A Pair of Blue Eyes*, the heroine, Elfride Swancourt, whose romantic life demonstrates an inconvenient tendency toward repetition, is provoked to walk around the tower parapet of West Endelstow Church by the memory of the same "giddy feat she had performed the year before." This time, in the presence of a new lover, she loses her footing and falls a short distance onto the roof below. After being rescued, she discusses her feelings with her companion, Henry Knight (who knows nothing of either the earlier incident or the earlier lover):

> "You are familiar of course, as everybody is, with those strange sensations we sometimes have, that our life for the moment exists in duplicate."
> "That we have lived through that moment before?"
> "Or shall again. Well I felt on the tower that something similar to that scene is again to be common to us both." . . .
> "That such a thing has not been before, we know. That it shall not be again, you vow. Therefore think no more of such a foolish fancy."[1]

Envisioning these "strange sensations" as a temporal division, a feeling of living "in duplicate," Elfride describes a psychological state in which the perceived boundaries of time and space have become strangely blurred. But whereas Knight understands this state to consist of an uncanny feeling of repeating the past, a form of retrocognition, Elfride interprets her sensation as precognition, a prevision of the future. In Hardy's novel, both paradigms turn out to be true. Three weeks later, on a cliff overlooking the ocean, Elfride and Knight do indeed experience a dangerous repetition of this event, that, in turn, precipitates the revelation of their feelings for one another and an awkward second engagement for Elfride. More than a "foolish fancy," Elfride's strange experience, it seems, looks both backward and forward, marking (for Hardy and his heroine) the potentially disturbing intrusions of past and future into the experience of the present.

Twenty-two years later, in 1895, Elfride's drama of re-remembering was reenacted, this time in the annual Cavendish Lecture presented to the West

London Medical-Chirurgical Society by the Lord Chancellor's Visitor in Lunacy, physician and psychiatrist Sir James Crichton-Browne. (The lecture was subsequently published in the British medical journal *The Lancet*.) Taking as his subject the somewhat amorphous phenomena of "Dreamy Mental States," Crichton-Browne began his lecture with an exhaustive set of *literary* quotations (including a reading of Hardy's scene) that describe, as he put it, "the simplest form of these dreamy mental states—a sense of reminiscence it has been called by some, a sense of prescience by others."[2] He went on to note that "the application to it of such apparently contradictory names suggests that it is somewhat mysterious in nature and difficult of interpretation." Reading fictional passages from Sir Walter Scott, Charles Dickens, and Hardy, as well as excerpts from the poetry of Dante Gabriel Rossetti, Edward Dowden, William Wordsworth, Samuel Taylor Coleridge, James Russell Lowell, Coventry Patmore, and Lord Alfred Tennyson, Crichton-Browne catalogues the repetition of a type of uncanny experience that soon came to be called "déjà vu." Tracing its frequent appearances through the fiction and poetry of the nineteenth century, he observes that those who describe this disorienting state of mind "know well that it is no ordinary reminiscence, no error of memory, no mere poetical fancy, but an absolute identification of the present with the past."

Crichton-Browne's lecture was part of a flurry of interest in the experience of déjà vu in the 1890s. In England, Frederick Myers and Crichton-Browne published lengthy studies of the phenomenon in 1895, followed by Havelock Ellis in 1897; at least two studies appeared in America, and no less than ten articles on the subject appeared in French journals of philosophy and psychology between 1893 and 1898, followed by four medical theses and, over the following decade, at least twenty articles and numerous references in British, American, French, German, and Italian psychological and medical writings (including, of course, those of Freud).[3] The 1890s were also the decade in which the term "déjà vu" made its first official appearance in psychological treatises in France and England. Although it seems to have entered the French language in 1876, when E. Boirac described "*la sensation du déjà vu*" in a letter to the journal *Revue Philosophique*,[4] it did not emerge as part of the classificatory terminology of psychology until 1894, when it appeared in the title of an article by L. Dugas, also in the *Revue Philosophique*: "L'impression de 'l'entièrement nouveau' et celle du 'déjà vu'" [The Impression of "the Entirely New" and That of the "Déjà Vu"].[5] The first English citation seems to be in 1895, in Frederick Myers' lengthy study of retrocognition and precognition titled "The Subliminal Self," which was published in the *Proceedings of the Society for Psychical Research*, of which Myers was a founding member. Within a decade, "déjà vu" emerged as the dominant designation for this particular mental state, consolidating what had been referred to variously as paramnesia (a general term for disorders of memory), promnesia (memory beforehand), false recognition, false memory, memory of the present, memory illusion, hallucinations of memory, memory falsification, pseudo-reminiscence, dreamy mental states, voluminous mental states, double memory, double perception, and double illusion.[6] In addition, J. Hughlings Jackson had identified in 1888 the frequency of "intellectual aurae" (in effect, déjà vu experiences) as preludes to epileptic seizures.[7]

This definitional instability of the very concept of déjà vu corresponded to a broader disruption in conceptualizations of memory and mental structure that, I argue, became emblematic of the fin de siècle. In this chapter, I examine the debates surrounding déjà vu in the disciplines of psychology, neurology, and the emerging sciences of memory in the latter decades of the nineteenth century, focusing particularly on its appearance in the medical and psychological theories of four British writers: George Henry Lewes, Havelock Ellis, Sir James Crichton-Browne, and Frederick W. H. Myers. By studying the different explanatory models of déjà vu, its emergence as a distinct psychological phenomenon, its place in competing conceptualizations of memory, and its role in distinguishing between normal and pathological states of mind, we can see some of the contested disciplinary boundaries among literature, psychology, neurology, psychical research, and spiritualist belief in this period. We can, in addition, see how British psychologists attempted to enter into and claim a national stake in the field of experimental psychology, which was becoming increasingly dominated by continental theories and theorists at the century's end.

The debates about déjà vu emerged within a constellation of discourses of the self, at a moment when psychological conceptions of selfhood were becoming increasingly destabilized. If we look at a range of psychological writings—both in the area of medical psychology and in the tradition of introspective philosophy—we can see how the coherence of personal identity had already been substantially (though not systematically) challenged by the century's end, as psychological writings confronted questions about suggestibility, somnambulism, hypnotism, alternating or multiple personality, and crowd psychology (to name just a few). Such studies challenged traditional Enlightenment assumptions about the existence or necessity of a unified self, or a transcendental ego.[8] Debates about the phenomenon of déjà vu, while not addressing the more spectacular pathologies of memory that helped to define and codify the memory sciences, highlighted the conjunction of philosophical and medical uncertainty about the normal functioning of mind at the fin de siècle. They pitted psychologists who sought to stabilize the category of the "normal" by pathologizing déjà vu experiences against those who used déjà vu to explore the permeable boundaries of consciousness. These debates marked a transitional moment in conceptions of selfhood, as writers from various disciplines attempted to define normal versus abnormal memory and to establish its relation to the stability (or instability) of identity. Indeed, what was at stake in definitions of déjà vu was the very notion of a "normal" self. Thus, at a historical moment when the boundaries between past, present, and future were particularly charged with cultural and psychological significance, déjà vu not only emerged as an important object of study, but also came to represent a pervasive sense of disorientation in psychological conceptions of selfhood. In their common attempts to answer philosophical questions about time and space, about the identification of memory with identity, and about the proper (and possible) relationship between past, present, and future, studies of déjà vu confronted, in Crichton-Browne's words, "those ultimate scientific ideas—space, time, matter, motion, force, and the like—which are beyond the domain of certain knowledge, and, according to Herbert Spencer, unthinkable."[9]

THINKING ABOUT THE UNTHINKABLE

Before the 1890s, déjà vu seems to have been considered too fleeting and too familiar an experience to generate sustained inquiry. It was too common, too universal to be seen as a psychological problem in need of classification, treatment, or cure. Yet it was too far out of the ordinary realm of experience to be easily incorporated into normative theories of mind. It is precisely this definitional impasse that is foregrounded when déjà vu appears in medical and psychological writings, for as the one uncanny psychological experience that almost everyone could recognize (either as having experienced it oneself or hearing it described by other, seemingly normal people), it functioned as a kind of boundary line between the normal and the pathological, between the transcendental and the everyday. Its appearance in late-nineteenth-century psychological treatises seemed, like accounts of the experience itself, to open a door to another world, to invite spectral intrusions. In one sense it *had* to be accounted for in theories of normal psychology, precisely because of its presumed familiarity. Yet even proponents of the most resolutely physiological explanations (Arthur Ladbroke Wigan's and Henry Maudsley's theories of brain hemisphere asymmetry;[10] James Sully's and George Henry Lewes's analogies between optical illusions and mental echoes;[11] Crichton-Browne's speculations about hereditary brain lesions) often found themselves stepping into a realm of metaphysical conundrums and ontological doubts. Déjà vu immediately confronts us with questions about identity and temporality that seem mystifying. For writers like Crichton-Browne, it seemed to strike terror of a knowledge beyond scientific comprehension—a rupture between past and present. "Contrary to all experience," Crichton-Browne writes, such phenomena have yet apparently the highest experiential validity. They declare themselves now as tamperings with those intuitions that yield the consciousness of continued existence, and again as excursions into that infinite field that lies behind appearances and of which it is dangerous to affirm or deny anything. Plunges they are into these depths of outer mystery in which the certitudes of science lose themselves and out of which, it has been said, the certitudes of faith arise.[12]

For Crichton-Browne, as for a number of other psychologists and philosophers in this period, déjà vu marked the experiential borderland between science and faith. To explore the mysteries of memory and identity scientifically formed part of what many historians have seen as a more widespread project of nineteenth-century science, which was to explain and demystify phenomena that had previously been the domain of the supernatural and the subject of religious faith. Thus the "dangerous excursions" and "plunges" into "the depths of outer mystery" that threaten, in Crichton-Browne's description, to baffle scientific certitude, are, he concludes, "especially . . . worthy of medical observation and research."[13] They are of interest, Havelock Ellis similarly claimed, precisely because of their "real influence on belief" in "earlier stages of [human] culture . . . suggesting to primitive man that he somehow had had wider experiences than he knew of, and that, as Wordsworth put it, he trailed clouds of glory behind him."[14]

Before turning to the specific theories, I want to outline three problems of definition that they all faced—each offering slightly different conclusions—in confronting the phenomenon of déjà vu. First, the problem of temporal perception: what delimits the present moment and distinguishes it from past and future? Second, the problem of normality: what does normal memory consist of and can strange experiences nevertheless be considered normal? Third, the problem of ownership: where do our memories come from and can they be linked to a continuing sense of identity?

Precariously poised between looking forward and looking backward, déjà vu depends perhaps foremost upon the ability to define what is the present; for it is only by understanding the temporal experience of "presentness" that we can locate how the present is routinely distinguished from past and future, and identify states of mind in which such borders might break down. Thus we find numerous discussions of time and memory by late-nineteenth-century psychologists that offer comparative numerical calculations of the human experience of presentness, attempting to register through the almost mystical precision of numbers the intangible moments of transition when future becomes present and present becomes past. Frederick Myers claimed that "The true Present is an evanescent, an infinitesimal thing. It is the imaginary meeting-point between two eternities; and the more finely we divide Time the less is left which is not Past or Future."[15] "Let anyone try," writes William James, "I will not say to arrest, but to notice or attend to, the *pre-*

sent moment of time. One of the most baffling experiences occurs. Where is it, this present? It has melted in our grasp, fled ere we could touch it, gone in the instant of becoming."[16] In his attempt to "grasp" the concept of time, James must locate it in space, asking not *"When* is it, this present?" but rather *"Where* is it?" It is as if, by merely shifting the terms of the question, James seeks to give time substance and weight—to register the present's presence. It is perhaps significant that James, at this point, resorts to quoting poetry to register this sense of the ineffability of the present and its collapse of spatial and temporal dimensions of experience: "Le moment où je parle est déjà loin de moi" [the moment where I speak is already far away from me].[17] This conceptual shift from time to space becomes particularly acute in explanations of memory, as psychologists seek to locate the temporal sequences of memory in the spaces of the human mind. Thus Ellis explains how external sensations could be mistaken for internal ones—that is, for memories—as a result of mental exhaustion; and Myers speculates about the mind's absorption of subliminal perceptions—"of knowledge afloat, so to say, in the Universe"—and their conversion into the temporal disjunctions of déjà vu.[18]

In exploring the development of amnesia and hypermnesia as diagnostic categories in nineteenth-century French psychiatry, Michael Roth has argued that doctors and philosophers were confronting questions about the "normal or healthy relationship of past to present" at the same time that historians were posing similar questions about the national past in the professionaliza-tion of their discipline.[19] Unlike amnesia and hypermnesia, however, déjà vu did not pose questions about the quantity of memory (the dilemma of remembering either too much or too little) so much as it presented problems of spatial and temporal displacement and raised questions about the proper ownership of memory. Memories appeared to be in the wrong place or the wrong time, or even inhabiting the wrong person. "False memories," William James claimed, "distort the consciousness of the me. . . . [T]he *me* is changed."[20] Déjà vu threatened to disrupt the very category of "normal" in conceptualizing memory. It marked a fissure in the relation of past to present, and a potential gap between memory and identity, that was all the more confusing for being so widespread. Very few psychologists viewed déjà vu as a pathological condition, and those who did, like Crichton-Browne, placed it at the normal end of the spectrum; even Jackson stressed that although "intellectual aurae" often accompanied epilepsy, they could not be used as diagnostic criteria because of their frequency of occurrence in healthy peo-ple. It was precisely the familiarity of the experience that was disturbing (that is, both the familiarity of déjà vu as an experience and the inappropriate feeling of familiarity that constituted its defining feature). In effect, déjà vu forced psychologists to think about the unthinkable by virtue of its strange familiarity—its spectral intrusions into everyday life.

DYING TWICE

Although nineteenth-century psychologists offered numerous descriptions of déjà vu—gathered from friends, patients, poetry, novels, essays, travelogues, other psychologists' writings, and personal experience—there was one particular instance of déjà vu that seemed to haunt British psychology more than any other. Appearing repeatedly in treatises on memory (sometimes in brief references, sometimes in lengthy descriptions), it became, I would argue, one of the paradigmatic experiences of déjà vu in the nineteenth century. First appearing in 1844 in a book entitled *The Duality of the Mind* by the psychologist Arthur Ladbroke Wigan, it consisted of his first-hand account of a powerful feeling he had experienced twenty-seven years earlier, on 19 November 1817, while attending the funeral of Her Royal Highness the Princess Charlotte, heir to the British throne, in Windsor Chapel. Princess Charlotte's tragic death in childbirth, along with the death of her newborn child, caused a crisis of succession in the British monarchy and provoked a spectacle of mass mourning that Wigan's account both reacts to and participates in. Wigan describes how, in a state of grief and exhaustion, as he watched the coffin sink slowly and silently into the crypt, punctuated only by outbursts of tears from the bereaved husband, Prince Leopold, he was overcome by "not merely an *impression*, but a *conviction*, that I had seen the whole scene before on some former occasion."[21] Wigan's description came to function, through the cumulative effect of repetition, not merely as *a* description of déjà vu, but as *the* description of déjà vu. That is, I would argue that it became the British model for examining the phenomenon of false reminiscence in the second half of the nineteenth century. Two of its later appearances—in the final volume of Lewes's 1879 *Problems of Life and Mind* and in Ellis's 1897 "A Note on Hypnagogic Paramnesia" (which he later expanded upon in *The World of Dreams* in 1911)—are particularly extensive, each reinterpreting Wigan's experience according to the later author's own paradigm; yet each is haunted by the conjunction of memory and mourning that Wigan's experience evokes.

Lewes uses Wigan's account of déjà vu at Princess Charlotte's funeral to outline a theory of mental echoes. Envisioning memory as a reinstatement of emotions and perceptions that have not necessarily entered fully into consciousness, Lewes offers two scenarios in which mental echoing could produce the impression of remembering something that the individual had never actually experienced before. First, Lewes envisions the power of an emotional experience (such as the death of a princess and the spectacle of national mourning) to flood mental channels, thereby erasing the boundaries between past and present. Invoking the spatializing rhetoric that we see so often in theories of déjà vu, he claims that "the thrill of emotion diffuses itself over the field of consciousness, and obliterates the landmarks whereby new and old would be distinguished." Second, Lewes goes on to claim that once this "wave of feeling has swept through us . . . another similar though fainter wave succeeds, [and] this secondary feeling will naturally be mistaken for a vague remembrance."[22] In effect, Lewes envisions the mind as filled with orienting landmarks that separate past and present—landmarks that become disorienting (as they are erased or concealed) and produce mental echoes when powerful emotions flood temporal reference points.

In explaining this two-part wave of feeling, Lewes describes incidents of memory in which "there is proof positive" that they "could never have been experienced by us."[23] The most positive such proof, of course, is in the experience of another's death as having happened before. Lewes offers two such examples. The first is Wigan's account of Princess Charlotte's funeral. The second is from a German case study in which, upon hearing of the death of an acquaintance, a patient "was seized with indefinable terror, for it appeared to him that he had lived through this experience already." In the words of the patient, "I felt that I had once before been lying here, in this bed, and that K. had come to me and said, 'Müller is dead'; and I replied, 'Müller died some time ago; he can't die twice.' "[24] For Lewes, both of these accounts of "dying twice" seem to crystallize the ontological and epistemological disorientations of false memory. That is, while we can experience the perception of a particular place any number of times, and thus we might be uncertain whether we have seen a given landscape or locale before, read about it in a book, or viewed it in a picture, it is more immediately evident that we cannot have experienced another, particular person's death twice. Lewes's interest in the presence of powerful emotional experiences preceding déjà vu (as opposed to Wigan's interpretation of brain hemisphere asymmetry or Ellis's emphasis on hypnagogic fatigue) marks one of the few theories, before Freud's focus on the emotional content of déjà vu experiences, that conceptualized the power of emotion to produce disjunctions of memory. (And one might note here that Freud's explanation of déjà vu in *The Psychopathology of Everyday Life* as a remembrance of unconscious fantasies analyzes a young woman's experience of anticipating another's death and mourning).[25]

Wigan himself described the funeral of Princess Charlotte in terms of the contagious emotions it provoked: "One mighty all-absorbing grief possessed the whole nation, and was aggravated in each individual by the sympathy of his neighbour, till the whole people became infected with an amiable insanity . . . [a] universal paroxysm of grief which then superseded every other feeling."[26] By the time Wigan and, later, Lewes recalled Wigan's experience, Princess Charlotte's death had come to exemplify a quintessentially communal experience of mourning, a moment of national crisis in which assumptions about the private ownership of feelings were challenged by an insistently public experience and definition of grief. Although, in his actual

explanation of it, Wigan himself virtually ignored the emotional content of
the experience he described in such detail, developing instead a theory of
false reminiscence as a temporal disjunction between brain hemispheres,
Lewes's later interpretation seems haunted by the flood of emotions preceding and accompanying Wigan's scene of remembering. Both Esther Schor
and Adela Pinch have discussed some of the strange affective disjunctions
accompanying the spectacle of national mourning that surrounded the
funeral of Princess Charlotte.[27] Studying the tendency of emotions to be represented and understood as free-floating, "located among rather than within
people," Pinch notes that, "feelings may be most powerful . . . when they are
where they are not supposed to be."[28] Pinch locates this preoccupation with
the transmissibility of feeling in late-eighteenth- and early-nineteenth-century England, noting that by the late nineteenth century contagious emotions
came under increasing medical and psychological scrutiny.[29] We can see this
scrutiny at work in the appropriations of Wigan's experience by subsequent
Victorian psychologists. Indeed, déjà vu's challenge to the self-contained
nature of memory and emotion—to the very concept of a "normal" self—
becomes more explicit with each successive writer. For Lewes, the relationship between memory and identity is disrupted by the presence of anomalous
memories and emotional echoes. He claimed that because we are capable of
remembering things we may not have been conscious of feeling at the time
they occurred but are aware of only in retrospect, we should not identify
memory with consciousness. By using the funeral of Princess Charlotte as
one of his central examples, Lewes, in effect, envisions the communal overflow of emotional experience that had come to characterize the funeral as an
analogue of the emotional erasure of temporal boundaries (the "obliterated
landmarks of old and new") that produce the phenomenon of false or
repeated memory. In both instances, Lewes reveals the mental markers that
might be (and often had been) used to define an essential concept of
"self"—that is, feelings and memories—as unstable and subject to spectral
intrusions and repetitions.

Lewes goes on to define these moments of emotional overflow and their
consequent production of mental echoes as akin to visual, auditory, and
olfactory "after-sensations." In an attempt to link these more clearly physi-
ologically based hallucinations and optical illusions to comparable echo
chambers of memory, and thereby to establish even uncanny experiences of
memory as phenomena explainable through physiological psychology,
Lewes describes an astonishing variety of sensory "haunt[ings]."[30] These
include a man who was pursued for two days by an after-sensation of
swarming bees (293–94), a murderer who was haunted into confession by a
dazzling red after-image he took for a "bucketful of blood" (295), a patient
who was "troubled with . . . the appearance of phantoms having the form of
portraits of heads and faces with old-fashioned wigs" (296), a philosopher

haunted by spectral columns of numbers to add and by "phantasms" of "spinning teetotums" (302), and a physician who experienced a "Hallucination" of a corpse wearing a hat—the image of a dead man whom he had tended days before (303). Lewes concludes with two accounts of his own phantom sensations. These consist of "several weeks" of "violent" olfactory after-sensations of being sprayed by tiger urine at the zoo (298), and a vanishing and reappearing "transverse section" of a woman's spinal cord under a microscope that, he claims, "followed me in long country rambles" and "went to bed with me at night" (299–300). By linking false reminiscences with the after-sensations of sight, smell, and sound, Lewes attempts to ground memory in the material, defining it as a physiological process. Yet he simultaneously reveals the instability of experience, the spectral mysteries and echo chambers of the senses. In order to explain aberrations of memory, Lewes must define *all* after-sensations as spectral, as physiological hallucinations that chart the mind's power to haunt. The processes of memory thereby become invested in the spectral rhetoric and gothic imagery that Terry Castle has identified as characteristic of nineteenth-century psychology and its transference of the spiritual world to the human mind.[31] Yet what Lewes reveals is the slippage involved in the very project of explaining the supernatural. If nineteenth-century psychology sought to reinscribe (and thereby contain) the supernatural within a rationalist scientific discourse, it simultaneously disrupted the rationality of that discourse with the intrusion of haunting emotions and phantom sensations.

Ultimately, Lewes's account of anomalous memories, sensory hallucinations, and emotional echoes place him, conceptually, between psychologists who sought to stabilize the category of the "normal" by pathologizing déjà vu experiences, and those who challenged the very concept of a unified self by seeing the familiarity of déjà vu as evidence for the permeable boundaries of consciousness and identity. For Lewes, to invest the normal functioning of the mind with the trappings of the supernatural provided a way of explaining seemingly inexplicable and irrational experiences in scientific terms while simultaneously expanding accounts of normal mental processes such as sensation, emotion, and recollection to include the irrational and uncanny. In accounting for déjà vu experiences such as Wigan's, Lewes exposed the arbitrariness of the divide between the normal and the pathological, the scientific and the supernatural. He thereby helped to destabilize some of the conceptual and disciplinary categories through which selfhood had been defined.

If Lewes accounted for the mystery of false recollections—and Wigan's funeral episode in particular—by envisioning *all* processes of mental repetition as forms of spectral illusion, Havelock Ellis attempted to demystify déjà vu—and Wigan's experience—by explaining it as the consequence of hypnagogic fatigue. Ellis identifies Wigan's experience as "the earliest case of paramnesia recorded in detail by a trained observer,"[32] and goes on to describe the funeral scene in considerable detail. Yet this is a somewhat different scene than the one Lewes describes. For Ellis, it is Wigan's exhaustion that is paramount, his nights of disturbed sleep before the ceremony. It is not only his grief, but his want of food, his standing up for four straight hours and nearly fainting when taking his place by the coffin that explains his uncanny conviction of having seen the scene before. Ellis sets out to explain what he characterizes as a "simple" yet "much-discussed phenomenon" to "throw some light" on a condition that has led to "so many strange and complicated theories" (283–84). Yet Ellis seems unable to sustain, in part because of the example he has chosen, the simple, prosaic explanation he seeks to propose. Associating déjà vu with a trajectory that leads from fatigue to hypnagogic states and eventually to parallels with dreams, Ellis claims that the paramnesic state differs from the allied state of hypnotic trance in that "[i]nstead of accepting a representation as an actual present fact, we accept the actual present fact as merely a representation" (286). That is, déjà vu makes the present moment unreal, representational. It constitutes "an internal hallucination, a reversed hallucination" (286). And at this point, as perhaps by now we might expect, Ellis resorts to another form of representation and recollection—quoting poetry to make his point and letting literature have the last word. As if describing his own invocation of Princess Charlotte's funeral, Ellis explains how—in the experience of paramnesia—the present appears "in the enfeebled shape of an old memory—'like to something I remember / A great while since, a long, long time ago'" (286).

I would like to speculate here that this curious reappearance of Princess Charlotte's funeral in Victorian discussions of déjà vu performed a particular function toward the century's end. If the experience of déjà vu involves locating present feelings in the past or future, distancing the present moment from itself by making it representational, the end of the century is also a moment when the present takes on an unusually charged relationship to both past and future. The act of remembering Princess Charlotte's funeral—that is, psychologists' combined acts of remembering and re-remembering Wigan's memory of re-remembering the funeral—memorialized an unusually communal and national experience of mourning both the death of a princess and the death of the state, the end of a royal line and the end of an era. In confronting this almost infinite regress of memory (Princess Charlotte seems to die not just twice but many times), we might see the task of explaining déjà vu as a characteristically fin de siècle gesture. That is, accounting for Wigan's curious psychological response to the death of the princess may have offered a way for British psychologists to conceptualize the historically intensified relationship of the past to the present and the present to the future toward the century's end. The repeated recollection of this one example reproduced the effect of déjà vu in the very discourses that sought to explain it. In the process, these discourses also came to conceptualize déjà vu (as I will go on to show) as an increasingly prevalent phenomenon at the fin de siècle and—in at least one case—as a product of both evolutionary progress and social class.

REMEMBERING AT THE CENTURY'S END

By the mid-1890s, when Ellis, Myers, and Crichton-Browne published their studies of déjà vu and related mental states, memory had newly become, according to Ian Hacking, "an object of scientific knowledge" and the shape of that knowledge had taken on different forms in different national and cultural settings.[33] In Germany, it developed first as a science of measurement, of statistical analysis of recall, with Hermann Ebbinghaus's 1885 study *On Memory*. French studies focused more on pathology after the publication of Théodule Ribot's lectures on diseases of memory in 1881.[34] If, as Hacking has claimed, British psychologists were simply less interested in questions of memory—or at least in identifying pathologies of memory—than their French counterparts, a number of British psychologists nevertheless were, by the 1890s, aware of this national divide and concerned about British psychology and neurology falling behind in the emerging scientific and disciplinary terrains of the approaching century. It was not, however, the more spectacular pathologies of memory that interested writers like Ellis, Myers, and Crichton-Browne. Instead, they focused on the more familiar anomalies of memory that British poets and novelists had been writing about over the course of the century, those "mental conditions," according to Crichton-Browne, "that are encountered in daily life . . . which have not yet received in this country the amount of attention they deserve."[35]

For Crichton-Browne, literary accounts of anomalous memories testified to a pervasive psychological phenomenon that medicine and psychology needed to explain. Yet Crichton-Browne's literary quotations serve a double purpose in his lecture, both describing and, in a sense, enacting déjà vu. They mark an intrusion of the past into present; they are, he claims romantically, "culled from the faded leaves of an old notebook" (1). Functioning as a double reminiscence, they represent memories from Crichton-Browne's past (his old notebook) that are, nevertheless, not quite his own. As he recollects past acts of reading, returning to meaningful passages he has extracted over many years of his life, Crichton-Browne marks the eerie conjunction of reading and remembering, blurring the boundaries between having memories of reading about other's memories and having memories of one's own. The role of the quotation book—in particular, the popularity of collecting and compiling one's own favorite quotations—was part of a wider, virtually institutionalized "culture of quotation" in the eighteenth and nineteenth centuries in which, as Pinch has argued, emotions seem to circulate freely, displaced from individual ownership.[36] In the case of Crichton-Browne, writing at the end of the nineteenth century, not merely emotions but memories themselves seem to be free-floating. This displacement of ownership further crosses disciplinary boundaries, as literary quotations become the common intellectual property of medicine and psychology, at times mimicking the status of clinical evidence. Here the quotation book doubles as the case study, recording the reader's, the doctor's, and the poet's overlapping psychological "experience" of dreamy mental states. In a gesture that we find repeated with remarkable frequency in late nineteenth-century treatises on déjà vu, Crichton-Browne invokes literature as a privileged resource for understanding dreamy mental states, one which offers important intersections with medicine and psychology.[37] He invites his medical audience to "leave the bedside for a little and consider with me certain mental conditions that are encountered in daily life that have a literary and philosophical interest, and that are not, I believe, without great medical significance" (1).

For Crichton-Browne, the presence of so many fictional and poetic accounts of dreamy mental states seemed, on the face of it, to argue for their universality as a human experience. This had been, in fact, the assumption of almost every prior writer on the subject dating back to the ancient Greeks, a notable exception being Théodule Ribot, who briefly mentions false reminiscences as rare occurrences, believing only three or four cases to have been recorded.[38] Crichton-Browne offers the cumulative wisdom of Britain's "most gifted writers," who claimed to describe a feeling "with which everybody is familiar" (1). Yet what we learn from this collection of literary insight, according to Crichton-Browne, is that such states are neither normal nor universal:

> No doubt these dreamy states are very common amongst us at the present day, but it will, I am sure, be found on inquiry that they are by no means all-embracing, and that while they abound amongst the educated, the refined, and the neurotic classes, they are comparatively rare amongst the unlettered, the prosaic, and the stolid masses of our people (2).

In other words, dreamy mental states are a condition of the fin de siècle, a visible symptom of an increasingly over-refined, neurotic, educated—indeed poetic—population.[39] This construction of déjà vu as both a marker of class and a sign of widespread nervous decline demonstrates some of the tensions within the disciplinary project of defining memory—especially displaced memory. Crichton-Browne informs us that the reason eminent writers have written so much about dreamy states is that they are indeed authorities on them, that poetic genius is intimately linked to mental pathology and hereditary brain disease, and that these conditions are on the rise at the century's end. Indeed, Crichton-Browne sees them as a by-product of evolution. "[D]reamy mental states," he claims, "emerge only at a certain state of mental evolution, rarely occurring . . . in a man or woman of less than average mental development, and are not themselves a part of the evolutionary process, but one of the accidents by which it is attended" (2). Here, Crichton-Browne echoes a wide array of arguments that appeared toward the end of the nineteenth century envisioning the combined effects of evolutionary development and modernity on an increasingly nervous, intellectual population. Discussions of neurasthenia, for example, elaborated a similarly dangerous trajectory for the world's "brain workers," though Crichton-Browne's overwhelming emphasis on heredity draws at least equally from theories of genius, degeneration, and eugenics. A substantial portion of his lecture is devoted to a detailed case study that traces dreamy mental states through four generations of one family, chronicling a spectrum of experiences that ranged from "spells of absentmindedness" to topographical disorientation (a periodic inability to locate oneself in space), to temporary losses of personal identity, to epileptic seizures (4). Proposing a continuum from comparatively normal to distinctly pathological states of mind, Crichton-Browne is anxious to prove that even the "slightest and simplest form [of dreamy mental states] . . . occurring in presumably healthy persons, involve disorder of mind" (2). In this retrenchment of mental norms, Crichton-Browne attempts to ward off the encroaching dissolutions of memory, identity, and consciousness that déjà vu experiences seemed to evoke. Precisely because he envisions different kinds of dreamy mental states as interconnected, and false reminiscence as merely "the first step in a series" (2)—a slippery slope into the uncanny that ends with epilepsy and insanity—Crichton-Browne seeks to redefine the boundaries of the normal mind. In effect, by challenging the inclusion of unaccountable reminiscences within the category of the normal and universal, Crichton-Browne hopes to avoid the philosophical consequences of déjà vu's anomalous familiarity, and to resituate memory and identity on more stable ground.

In order to do this, Crichton-Browne argues that false reminiscences are not isolated events; rather, they may be the first dangerous symptoms of a dreamy temperament, potentially leading to "more elaborate manifestations" such as "double consciousness . . . a loss of personal identity . . . a deprivation of corporeal substance. . . . [I]t is impossible to put into words such strange and incomprehensible visitations" (2). He turns at this point to a poet, Tennyson, to express the inexpressible:

> Moreover, something is or seems,
> That touches me with mystic gleams,
> Like glimpses of forgotten dreams—
>
> Of something felt, like something here;
> Of something done, I know not where;
> Such as no language may declare.
>
> ("The Two Voices," 379–84)

Crichton-Browne invokes the wide range of dreamy states represented in Tennyson's poetry as his justification for tracing a progression from simple forms of false reminiscence to lost identity to epileptic seizure ("weird seizures," he notes, afflict the hereditarily nervous hero of Tennyson's "The Princess"). What is perhaps most striking here is that Crichton-Browne does *not* cite Hughlings Jackson as his authority for this leap, even though Jackson had made the connection between "intellectual aurae" and epileptic seizures a decade earlier. Instead, Crichton-Browne relies on poetry precisely because Jackson had cautioned against using this type of loose diagnostic trajectory from false reminiscence to epilepsy (though one might note here that Jackson himself quoted from Charles Dickens's description of déjà vu in *David Copperfield*).

In his attempt to redefine false reminiscences as pathological states of mind, to associate them with a dangerously effete fin-de-siècle population, and to identify them as threats to a stable conception of identity, Crichton-Browne repeatedly emphasizes case studies and memoirs that chronicle losses of identity as either accompanying false reminiscences or representing the next stage of mental dissolution. He describes the case of a young man—representing the fourth generation of a family of nervous sufferers—who experienced sudden feelings of "los[ing] hold of the universe and ceas[ing] to know who he was." He found he "could bring [these attacks] on by gazing intently at his own face in a looking-glass . . . [and if he became] 'abstract and metaphysical,' as he termed it. . . . If he asked himself, 'Who am I?' 'What am I?' 'Where do I come from?' 'How do I stand related to persons and things around me?' he inevitably had an attack" (4). For a population becoming progressively dreamier as a side effect of evolutionary development, Crichton-Browne suggests, even to ask metaphysical questions might pose a crisis of identity and a threat to the nerves. As a consequence, the medical profession must pay new attention to issues previously reserved for philosophy.[40]

Despite such medical forays into the metaphysical—indeed, having identified the very contemplation of metaphysics as dangerous to the nerves—Crichton-Browne ultimately seeks to contain such unthinkable questions (and those who persist in thinking about them) by classifying them in the domain of pathology. In the process, he identifies disruptions of memory (and the confusions of identity that they both embody and encourage) as the proper subject of medical study—as hereditary disorders of the brain. Crichton-Browne attempts to turn the attention of British medicine toward issues and conditions that had previously been the province of mental philosophy, introducing both a British voice and a medical agenda into debates that increasingly were becoming the disciplinary territory of psychology, particularly continental psychology. Offering strikingly prosaic medical advice for those suffering from too many psycho-poetic flights (he advocates the rest cure, vegetarian diet, and a "well-ordered education"), Crichton-Browne enters into the debate about déjà vu, confronts its abysses of time, space, and identity, in a bid to reclaim the proper ownership of memory and reestablish the coherence of identity as the defining criteria of mental health.

Whereas Crichton-Browne sought to retrench the category of the normal in the face of growing fin-de-siècle dreaminess, his contemporary Frederick Myers envisioned a competing continuum that not only embraced the universality of déjà vu sensations, but also extended it to include telepathy. As part of a wider effort to include psychical research in the emerging discipline of experimental psychology, Myers's study of promnesia sought to establish the scientific validity of transcendental states—to expand the category of the normal to explain psychic and spiritual phenomena. Myers and Crichton-Browne had clashed with each other well before they published their contrasting studies of déjà vu in 1895, both having participated in tests of thought transference sponsored by the Society for Psychical Research in 1883. Expressing skepticism and insisting on subjecting telepathic claimants to more rigorous tests than the Society members had scheduled, Crichton-Browne provoked Myers's anger, leading the latter to accuse Crichton-Browne of derailing the demonstration through his "offensive incredulity."[41] Crichton-Browne seems to have taken pride in this accusation, recording his memory of it in an account of the proceedings for the *Westminster Gazette* in 1908. Despite their shared interest in explaining uncanny psychological experiences such as déjà vu, Myers's and Crichton-Browne's different approaches chart some of the tensions between materialist and spiritualist accounts of the human mind, the status of psychical research in a period of disciplinary consolidation and professionalization, and the role of déjà vu as a representative site for shifts in disciplinary ground at the century's end.

One of the most striking aspects of the clash between Myers and Crichton-Browne's studies of déjà vu is how the far more theoretically marginal figure, Myers, draws upon a much more extensive body of psychological research, offering summaries of the latest continental debates on déjà vu, introducing the term to his British audience, and demonstrating a widespread knowledge of British, American, and continental psychology. (Myers's series of articles titled *The Subliminal Consciousness* [1891–95], in which his study of déjà vu or "promnesia" appeared, included the first introduction of Freud's and Brauer's studies of hysteria to an English audience.)[42] Myers summarizes previous explanations of déjà vu, dividing them into two camps. First, theories arguing that the reminiscence is a true one, arising either from past waking experiences or dreams. Second, theories that view the reminiscence as illusory, depending either on disruptions of perception and attention (such as fatigue, wandering attention, accelerations of thought, after-sensations) or on the asynchronism of cerebral hemispheres.[43] Myers pays particular attention to the French psychologist André Lalande, whose 1893 article

on déjà vu corresponded to the theory of subliminal consciousness Myers
had developed in his series of articles for the Society for Psychical Research,
beginning in 1891.[44] Grounding his work, in part, on studies of hypnosis,
Lalande posits the role of a powerful, unconscious hyperaesthesia, or subliminal perception, which he calls "telepathy," as the basis of paramnesic
experiences. That is, both Lalande and Myers conceptualize déjà vu as a
division of attention between conscious and subconscious modes of perception. Myers goes on to speculate that promnesia arises not only from our
heightened subliminal perceptions of the material world, but from subliminal
telepathic communications with other minds. That is, he argues that many
false reminiscences really *may* belong to someone else; they may constitute
intrusions of others' thoughts and others' reminiscences into our consciousness, providing instances of both retrocognition and precognition.

For Myers, the traditional concept of memory is called into question by
déjà vu experiences, as he explains in "The Subliminal Self."[45] Not only, he
speculates, do we have latent memories richer than even hypnosis can evoke,
those memories descend "deeply to gland and blood vessel" to the very
"germ-plasm" that links the generations (348–49). Under these circumstances, he claims, "memory must become no more than a metaphor" (348).
Noting that "[n]o one doubts" the transmission of maternal emotions to the
embryo in "children born during the alarms of a siege, or of the Reign of
Terror in France" (349), Myers suggests that even more local shocks to
maternal emotions may "imprint upon the child the organic memory of the
mother's emotion of admiration, disgust, or fear" (349). This organic memory may even reach into the distant past, and evolutionary ancestors "more
remote than Adam" may "even now influence our psychical life" (349).
These speculations lead Myers to propose that sensations of déjà vu may
actually be resurgences of ancestral memory, as we visit locales familiar to
our grandfathers, or even more primitive progenitors. Though he is careful to
admit that as yet there is no adequate scientific evidence to substantiate these
claims, he offers them as hypotheses that have the power to explain phenomena that seem "at first to be still more incredible" than the theories he proposes (351).

Myers, like Lewes, envisions the power of emotions to produce déjà vu
experiences, but for Myers these are neither false recollections nor echoes.
Rather, they are surfacings of subliminal perceptions, details that our subliminal selves have perceived but that we are not consciously aware of experi-
encing or remembering. Expanding upon Lewes's observation that we may
remember aspects of an experience that we were not conscious of at the time
they occurred, Myers conceptualizes a stratum of subliminal perceptions—
perceptions that include impressions of the world around us, as well as
unspoken and unintended signals received from other people. Powerful emotional experiences may bring these subliminal perceptions to the surface.

"Almost any mental tempest," Myers claims, "may bring remote impressions to light—as storms will wash up cannon-balls on a long-since bombarded shore" (354). Thus, sensations of déjà vu may, in many cases, be recollections of actual experiences—experiences we were only partially aware of at the time they occurred.

In his attempt to establish the normality of déjà vu experiences and their telepathic origins, Myers is careful to disassociate déjà vu from nervousness. Unlike Crichton-Browne, Myers claims that "the subjects of promnesia . . . do not seem to be specially morbid or nervous persons" (345). What they do seem to have in common is that "they have often also experiences of veritable telepathy or precognition" (345). Of course, for Crichton-Browne, this association between experiences of uncanny reminiscence and experiences of telepathy would serve to confirm the pathological trajectory of dreamy states. For Myers, however, this is a sign that those who frequently experience déjà vu have a greater ability to bring subliminal perceptions to consciousness. It is, in effect, a proof of the potential normality of both déjà vu and telepathy, insofar as both arise from the layered structure of the human mind.

Ultimately, Myers seeks to synthesize competing theories of déjà vu under a wider explanatory rubric. That is, he proposes not one theory of promnesia, but a number of possible explanations for different causes of promnesic experiences, each of which confirms his larger theory of subliminal perceptions. Thus, returning to his initial division between theories of déjà vu that see it as a product of false or displaced reminiscences and those that see it as a product of forgotten, but real, events, we can see how Myers accommodates both sides of the argument. Some sensations of déjà vu are, he claims, the surfacing of forgotten or latent perceptions of real events. Other déjà vu experiences can be explained by the presence of fetal or ancestral memories in the subliminal consciousness, or, alternately, by the power of subliminal perceptions to transfer the memories and experiences of others (either alive or dead) into ourselves—in effect, a process of telepathy. Even objects, Myers speculates, may have this power of transference, retaining traces of their contact with organisms that may be communicated subliminally.[46] Finally, Myers incorporates theories of brain hemisphere asymmetry, which had been dismissed in continental psychology but were still being discussed in Britain (342). Rejecting the physiological explanations of writers such as Wigan and Maudsley, Myers nevertheless proposes his own account of the duality of mind: "one among many causes of promnesia may lie in a double perception of the present moment by the subliminal and the supraliminal self" (342). For Myers, all of these theories converge to suggest that déjà vu is not merely a strangely familiar phenomenon, but rather the most tangible and recognizable evidence of a hidden stratum of consciousness—a subliminal selfhood or "secular soul."[47]

CONCLUSION

In this chapter I have argued that déjà vu emerged as a distinct and classifiable phenomenon in medical and psychological literature in the final decades of the nineteenth century, and that attempts to explain this phenomenon generated debates among doctors, psychologists, and psychical researchers as they tried to define both the normal function and proper ownership of memory and its relationship to both consciousness and identity. I have further suggested that the repeated quotations of fictional and poetic representations of déjà vu, as well as the repeated reminiscences of one particularly haunting déjà vu experience at the funeral of a princess, transformed psychological explanations of displaced memory into strange reenactments of the déjà vu experience itself. Finally, I have speculated that this intense flurry of interest in the phenomenon of déjà vu may have arisen because déjà vu seemed to manifest the heightened experience of temporal disorientation involved in contemplating the century's end. If déjà vu represents an intensified instance of the problem of identifying the present in relation to the past and the future, it may very well be that it offered an especially significant topic at a moment in history when anxieties about the passing of a century and the advance of a new era were crystallizing assessments of evolutionary development, national character, and the spiritual consequences of scientific progress. Certainly Crichton-Browne's and Ellis's associations between paramnesic phenomena and languid, anemic, or nervous temperaments—writers, dreamers, and the intellectual elite—suggest that the emergence of déjà vu as an object of study, and the competing attempts to normalize and pathologize it, arose in part from a shared set of cultural narratives about the state of society at the century's end. Like Crichton-Browne, we might see déjà vu as an appropriate emblem of the fin de siècle, the psychological paradigm for that sense of exhaustion and repetition, of having seen and done it all before, that pervades so much of the literature of the period and has come to characterize how we think about British (and much of European) culture at this time.

In the debates I have traced here, we can see the culmination of a century of challenges to philosophical conceptions of a unified self. If memory and consciousness constituted the basis of personal identity, déjà vu called into question the integrity of both. Crichton-Browne desperately attempted to stabilize this rift by pathologizing déjà vu in the interests of a coherent ontological norm. Myers embraced it by seeing the universality of déjà vu as evidence for the permeable boundaries of a subliminal consciousness. Both Lewes and Ellis charted the uneasy middle ground between these two positions. For all four writers, déjà vu marked a fissure in the relation between memory and identity. It became a fertile testing ground for competing conceptualizations of memory, and exposed the contested disciplinary territories at stake in psychology, neurology, and psychical research at the fin de siècle. To raise questions about the ownership of memories is to raise doubts about who "owns" the past and how it intrudes on the present or shapes the future. Ultimately these questions, which would seem crucial at any century's end, are about who has the right to interpret memory and history.

NOTES

1. Thomas Hardy, *A Pair of Blue Eyes* (1873; New York: Harper, 1896), 195.

2. Sir James Crichton-Browne, "Dreamy Mental States," *The Lancet* 3749 (July 6, 1895) and 3750 (July 13, 1895): 1. The next two quotations are from the latter source (1).

3. The majority of the French articles on déjà vu that appeared in the 1890s were published in the *Revue Philosophique*, with many of them appearing in an 1894 volume that framed the debate. These were subsequently summarized in the *Année Psychologique* for 1895. Both Frederick Myers and Havelock Ellis offer bibliographies of the déjà vu debates; see Frederick W. H. Myers, "The Subliminal Self: The Relation of Supernormal Phenomena to Time;—Retrocognition," *Society for Psychical Research Proceedings* 11 (1895): 334–407; Havelock Ellis, *The World of Dreams* (1911; reprint, Boston and New York: Houghton Mifflin, 1922). Sigmund Freud makes reference to the *Revue Philosophique* articles on déjà vu in his 1909 *The Interpretation of Dreams*, vol. 5, *The Standard Edition of the Complete Psychological Works*, trans. and ed. by James Strachey in collaboration with Anna Freud, assisted by Alix Strachey and Alan Tyson (London: Hogarth Press and the Institute of Psychoanalysis, 1960), 5:483. See also Vernon M. Neppe, *The Psychology of Déjà Vu* (Johannesburg: Witwatersrand University Press, 1983) for a bibliography of writings on déjà vu that extends through 1980.

4. E. Boirac, letter, *Revue Philosophique* 1 (1876): 430.

5. L. Dugas, "L'impression de 'l'entièrement nouveau' et celle du 'déja vu,'" *Revue Philosophique* 38 (1894): 41–46.

6. See Neppe, *Psychology of Déjà Vu*, 2; W. H. Burnham, "Memory, Historically and Experimentally Considered," *The American Journal of Psychology* 2, no. 3 (1889): 433, 439; Crichton-Browne, "Dreamy Mental States," 1.

7. J. Hughlings Jackson, "On a Particular Variety of Epilepsy," *Brain* 11 (1888): 179–207.

8. Ian Hacking cites an 1843 article by Thomas Wakely, the editor of *The Lancet*, as one of the first to address the philosophical (rather than strictly medical) implications of phenomena such as somnambulism and double consciousness, seeing them as a challenge to long-held philosophical assumptions about the unity of personal identity and the singularity of consciousness. See Ian Hacking, *Rewriting the Soul: Multiple Personality and the Sciences of Memory* (Princeton: Princeton University Press, 1995), 221.

9. Crichton-Browne, "Dreamy Mental States," 2.

10. See Arthur Ladbroke Wigan, *The Duality of the Mind* (1844; U.S. reprint, n.p.:

Joseph Simon, 1985); and Henry Maudsley, "The Double Brain," *Mind* 54 (1899): 161–87.

11. See James Sully, *Illusion. A Psychological Study* (London: C. K. Paul, 1881); and George Henry Lewes, *Problems of Life and Mind*, 3rd ser., vol. 12 (Boston: Houghton, Osgood, 1880).

12. Crichton-Browne, "Dreamy Mental States," 2.

13. Ibid., 75.

14. Havelock Ellis, "A Note on Hypnagogic Paramnesia," *Mind*, n.s., 22 (1897): 286.

15. Myers, "The Subliminal Self," 342.

16. William James, *Principles of Psychology*, 2 vols. (1890; reprint, New York: Dover Press, 1950), 1:608.

17. Ibid.

18. See Ellis, "A Note on Hypnagogic Paramnesia"; and Myers, "Subliminal Self," 362.

19. Michael Roth, "Remembering Forgetting: *Maladies de le Mémoire* in Nineteenth-Century France," *Representations* 26 (1989): 50, 64.

20. William James, *Principles of Psychology*, 1:373.

21. Arthur Ladbroke Wigan, *The Duality of the Mind*, 66.

22. Lewes, *Problems of Life and Mind*, 130.

23. Ibid., 129.

24. Lewes, *Problems of Life and Mind*, 130–31.

25. Freud discusses déjà vu and related psychological states most extensively in his 1901 *The Psychopathology of Everyday Life* (in *Complete Psychological Works*, 6:265–68), but also in two passages added to *The Interpretation of Dreams* in 1909 (5:399, 483). A related discussion of déjà raconté appears in his 1914 "Fausse Reconnaissance (Déjà Raconté) in Psycho-analytic Treatment" (13:201–207) and a discussion of memory and "depersonalization" that echoes some of Crichton-Browne's case studies appears in his 1936 "A Disturbance of Memory on the Acropolis" (22:239–48).

26. Wigan, *The Duality of the Mind*, 65.

27. See Esther Schor, *Bearing the Dead: The British Culture of Mourning from the Enlightenment to Victoria* (Princeton: Princeton University Press, 1994); and Adela Pinch, *Strange Fits of Passion: Epistemologies of Emotion, Hume to Austen* (Stanford: Stanford University Press, 1996).

28. Pinch, *Strange Fits of Passion*, 166, 192.

29. Ibid., 166, 214.

30. Lewes, *Problems of Life and Mind*, 295. All subsequent references to this source will be listed parenthetically by page number.

31. Terry Castle, "Phantasmagoria: Spectral Technology and the Metaphorics of Modern Reverie," *Critical Inquiry* 15, no. 1 (1988): 26–61.

32. Ellis, "A Note on Hypnagogic Paramnesia," 285. All subsequent references to this source will be listed parenthetically by page number.

33. Hacking, *Rewriting the Soul*, 155, 205. In Britain, Hacking claims, there was substantially less attention to questions of memory, at least in studies of multiple personality or double consciousness.

34. Ibid., 204–205.

35. Crichton-Browne, "Dreamy Mental States," 1. All subsequent references to this source will be listed parenthetically by page number.

36. Pinch, *Strange Fits of Passion*, 166–67,171.

37. See, for example, Jackson, "On a Particular Variety of Epilepsy"; Burnham, "Memory, Historically and Experimentally Considered"; James, *Principles of Psychology*; Ellis, "A Note on Hypnagogic Paramnesia."

38. Théodule Ribot, *Les Maladies de la Mémoire* (Paris: Ballière, 1881).

39. Ellis also associated déjà vu experiences with a characteristically fin de siècle temperament, claiming that they were particularly prevalent in the "languid and anaemic," people who are suggestible, and those prone to daydreaming and wandering attention. He notes that the French psychologist Dugas (who published a study of déjà vu in 1894; see note 5) had associated déjà vu with writers and others of "unusual mental capacity" (Ellis, "A Note on Hypnagogic Paramnesia," 285). There were, however, competing accounts of susceptibility to sensations of déjà vu, especially in France. André Lalande, for example, writing on déjà vu in 1893, associated the prevalence of déjà vu experiences with children and savages, claiming "with them . . . the senses are more subtle and impressionable than with developed men. Life blunts our sensibility little by little" (translated in Myers, "The Subliminal Self," 346).

40. Confirming his view that hereditary weakness, intellectual development, and the "refined" classes were associated, Crichton-Browne goes on to note that the late Lord Beaconsfield suffered from debilitating dreamy states that involved sensations of lost identity. Lord Beaconsfield claimed in his memoirs: "I was not always assured of my identity or even existence, for I sometimes found it necessary to shout aloud to be sure that I lived, and I was in the habit very often at night of taking down a volume and looking into it for my name to be convinced that I had not been dreaming of myself" (quoted in Crichton-Browne, "Dreamy Mental States," 5). Returning yet again to the linkage of reading and remembering, Lord Beaconsfield's description offers uncanny echoes of the opening scene of Jane Austen's *Persuasion*, in which, we might recall, Sir Walter Elliot repeatedly confirms his sense of identity (admittedly an inflated rather than a diminished one) by finding himself in his favorite book, the British "Baronetage." We might even recognize parallels between the self-affirming fictions of Lord Beaconsfield's library and Crichton-Browne's own notebook, in which acts of reading and rereading simultaneously confuse and constitute identity.

41. See Janet Oppenheim, *The Other World: Spiritualism and Psychical Research in England, 1850–1914* (Cambridge: Cambridge University Press, 1985), 286.

42. Ibid., 245.

43. Myers, "The Subliminal Self," 341.

44. André Lalande, "Des paramnésies," *Revue Philosophique* 36 (1893): 485–97.

45. All subsequent references to "The Subliminal Self" will be listed parenthetically by page number.

46. Sir Arthur Conan Doyle's short story "The Leather Funnel" explores this theory. Doyle, who was a devoted spiritualist and an initial supporter of psychical research, describes the power of objects to retain traces of powerful emotions that have been associated with them—even over centuries. In Doyle's story, a man is asked to sleep next to a leather funnel, knowing nothing of its history or purpose, and

to think about it before falling asleep. The man dreams of a scene of torture, the leather funnel placed in a woman's mouth to force her to swallow water until she confesses or dies. Upon waking and relating his terrifying dream to his host, he is informed that his dream was an accurate depiction of the object's history, and that the victim's terror—dating back to a murder trial in seventeenth-century France—has left such powerful emotional traces on the funnel that they can be transferred to receptive minds. See Arthur Conan Doyle, "The Leather Funnel," in *Tales of Terror and Mystery* (Garden City, N.Y.: Doubleday, 1977), 29–42.

47. I have taken this term from John J. Cerullo's study *The Secularization of the Soul: Psychical Research in Modern Britain* (Philadelphia: Institute for the Study of Human Issues Publication, 1982), which provides an excellent account of Myers's relationship to continental work on hypnosis (particularly that of Pierre Janet) and his participation (along with other representatives from the Society for Psychical Research) in the International Congresses of Experimental Psychology in 1889, 1892, and 1896.

CHAPTER 8

Oscar Wilde, Erving Goffman, and the Social Body Beautiful

JEFF NUNOKAWA

WHO WOULDN'T want it?

> "How sad it is!" murmured Dorian Gray, with his eyes still fixed upon his own portrait. "How sad it is! I shall grow old, and horrible, and dreadful. But this picture will remain always young. It will never be older than this particular day of June. . . . If it were only the other way! If it were I who was always young, and the picture that was to grow old!" (*The Picture of Dorian Gray*, 25–26)[1]

The difference, of course, between the general yearning to look forever young, a yearning as inescapable as the specter of Fashion that propels it, and the particular version of this desire uttered here is that unlike that of anyone else, the dream of Dorian Gray comes true. As "monstrous" as it is to "think," the "mad wish" he "uttered" "that he himself might remain young, and the portrait grow old" is "fulfilled" (78). And if the story of someone who secures the appearance of eternal youth merely by uttering the wish to do so is as fantastic as a child's sense that, simply by wanting it, he is responsible for a change in the weather or the death of his father, this fairy tale describes in condensed form a spirit of voluntarism that pervades the atmosphere of Wilde's society, and societies beyond, a spirit of voluntarism that crowds our own cosmetic counters, weight rooms, and elective surgery offices, the spirit of voluntarism which believes that the way we look to others can be decided by our own determinations.

The magic thinking of *Dorian Gray* has a less miraculous, but still impressive analogue in the control that Wilde's characters, at least those who inhabit what he calls "good society," exert over their appearance, characters such as the butler in *An Ideal Husband*, "a mask with a manner,"[2] or the dandy to whom he is attached, who even under the duress of international intrigue or domestic scandal, always seems to know that his buttonhole is adjusted to the best possible effect, or his feminine counterpart in society whose "affectation of manner has a delicate charm" (392). Such feats of self-presentation are familiar fixtures in Wilde's book:

Mabel Chiltern is a perfect example of the English type of prettiness, the apple-blossom type. She has all the fragrance and freedom of a flower. There is ripple after ripple of sunlight in her hair, and the little mouth, with its parted lips, is expectant, like the mouth of a child. She has the fascinating tyranny of youth, and the astonishing courage of innocence. To sane people she is not reminiscent of any work of art. But she is really like a Tanagra statuette, and would be rather annoyed if she were told so (*An Ideal Husband*, 393).

Mabel Chiltern and her kind are as well-composed and well-known as the aphorisms their author assigns them to ventriliquize. What distinguishes the one from the other, though, is that while we can but recognize the aphorism as the work of a remote author, we can only regard the character as a performance entirely self-fashioned. If a character like Mabel Chiltern would be "rather annoyed if she were told" that "she is like a Tanagra statuette," that is only because such a characterization would give the credit for her work to someone else. Can anyone imagine that such a type has left any aspect of her appearance to chance, especially those aspects which seem least culti-vated?—anyone, that is, who has read a word of Wilde, or who senses, even without reading him, simply by partaking of the culture that he helped to define, that "[b]eing natural is simply a pose" (*Dorian Gray*, 10). Only someone as jejune as the designated straight man in a Wilde routine would think that the least element of this well-wrought figure was unintended by her, someone as jejune as the observer naive enough to think that there is really anything about the dandy's "mode of dressing" that he has not designed, except, of course, what he has designed as such:

His mode of dressing, and the particular styles that from time to time he affected, had their marked influence on the young exquisites of the Mayfair balls and Pall Mall club windows, who copied him in everything that he did, and tried to reproduce the accidental charm of his graceful, though to him only half-serious fopperies (*Dorian Gray*, 100).

Of course such fashionings of the self differ in more than degree from the alchemy that Dorian Gray accomplishes. As impressive as they are, the art-ful self-presentations that are the signature style of high society in Wilde's book can never hope to achieve the miracle of Dorian Gray, by which the most recalcitrant element of appearance suddenly bends to the will of its subject, the element of appearance that even the quickest and brightest can-not hope to govern. Even the most resourceful presentations of the self must stop, as if for death, at the limits of the body. Thus, the most important element of this presentation in the world that Wilde describes is the one least susceptible to the agency of the self; the most vital element of this presenta-tion is that which the self is least able to *present*. No one, apart from Dorian Gray, can will for himself the good looks that "make princes of those who have it." Such beauty is "higher than Genius. . . . It is one of the great facts of the world, like sunlight, or spring-time, or the reflection in dark waters of that silver shell we call the moon. It cannot be questioned. It has its divine right of sovereignty. It makes princes of those who have it" (*Dorian Gray*, 23). For those who know Wilde, these lines are as much a surprise as the sight of a libertine who all of sudden makes the sign of the cross. For here, the most illustrious of prophets for the priority of the cultural hails the body beautiful as a primal fact of nature before which all the powers of human contrivance fall silent. This lustrous body makes its entrance less like a figure on stage than the dawning of a heavenly light; the show-stopping incandescence of the lovely face can no more be willed by the self who is blessed by it, or by one who is not, than a season or a planet can be brought into being by aesthetic fiat; the divine prerogatives of good looks can no more be acquired, even by the most cunning sense of style, than a man can crown himself king.

But if Dorian Gray's willed transfiguration is beyond the scope of mere mortals, his example nevertheless describes an avenue by which the presentation of the self is able to evade the obduracy of the body. Well before the advent of cosmetic interventions invasive enough to reshape it, Wilde suggests a means not of reforming the body but rather of replacing it with a preferred one. It would be difficult to overestimate the stakes involved in this act of surrogacy, at least by Oscar Wilde's count. As we will see, the strategy of substitution by which the self is able to undo the limits imposed by his own natural physique, the strategy of substitution by which the self exchanges a decaying, defective body for one youthful and beautiful, enables him to escape from the exterminating exclusions that Wilde's society visits on those whose appearance fails to meet the standards of physical acceptability.

We will return to assess this strategy, but first I want to notice that the sense of theatrical agency that reaches its terminus ad quem in the miracle of Dorian Gray extends well beyond the rarified region of Wilde's society. The knack for self-presentation that Wilde attributes to his characters may appear at first glance as far removed as the steps of a ballet from our own pedestrian walks, but by the lights of a theorist most closely associated with the concept of self-presentation, such power of self-fashioning is the stuff of everyday life in the modern social world. We can take the measure of the agency that Erving Goffman grants the self to orchestrate the way he appears to others by contrasting his subject to the subject of surveillance that another social theorist has made far more famous in recent years. Compare the way Goffman describes the broad effects of the mild or traumatic surprise that routinely arises "[w]hen an individual feels he is sheltered from others' view, and suddenly discovers he is not," to the subject Foucault describes. Here is Goffman:

[A]t such moments of discovery the discovered individual is likely to assemble himself hurriedly, inadvertently demonstrating what he lays aside and what he puts on solely for others. In order to guard against these embarrassments, and in order to generate within himself other persons' view of him, the individual may maintain presentability even when alone (*The Presentation of Self in Everyday Life*, 41).[3]

For those schooled in the contemporary disciplines of literary and cultural studies, it is easy at first glance to confuse Goffman's subject here with that of Foucault. The subject whose good behavior is underwritten by the sense of an audience from whom he can never fully shield himself is as familiar to us as the blueprint of the panopticon—as familiar as the pressure of potential surveillance that works to enforce the intricate rules and regulations that define proper conduct in "social gatherings," a pressure of potential surveillance persuasive enough to induce its subject to toe the line even when he is home alone.

Less familiar though to the disciplines that have taken to heart Foucault's model of the subject who internalizes the expectations of an effectively omniscient audience is Goffman's appreciation for the power of this subject to shape what others see. The actor at home on the broad stage Goffman calls the social world exerts a degree of autonomous artistic control over the performance he is compelled to produce that his most accomplished theatrical counterpart would be proud to own.

To invoke one of Goffman's own key terms, the stress he places on the autonomy of "[t]he individual . . . constrained to sustain a viable image of himself in the eyes of others" may be illuminated by the frame of his study. For however eloquent his eccentricities, however delicate and original his local insights, Goffman, after all, inhabits the broad context of a mid-century American sociology, concerned to define the sphere of social determination as the backdrop for the drama of individual freedom, rather than the pessimistic structuralism inclined to regard the drama of individual freedom as little more than a prop in the theater of social determination.

By Goffman's lights, the demands of propriety enforced by the specter of uncontainable surveillance are less the form of the individual's oppression than the condition of his creativity, less like the shades of the prisonhouse than the theatrical script or the musical score. In Goffman's admiring eyes, the conformity of this subject to the often exquisite exactions that govern his appearance in society is matched or even eclipsed by his power to arrange it. Thus, for example, the subjection of this subject to the complex rules of engagement that govern his behavior before a real or phantom audience—rules that dictate the precise degree as well as the proper occasion for the show of "involvement"—is difficult to notice next to the éclat with which he satisfies their dictates. "A [general] rule against 'having no purpose,' or being disengaged [in public], is evident in the exploitation of untaxing involvements to rationalize or mask desired lolling," Goffman observes. The "veneer of acceptable visible activity" such as "minimal 'recreational' activities" serves as "cover for disengagement, as in the case of 'fishing' off river banks where it is guaranteed that no fish will disturb one's reverie" (*The Presentation of Self*, 58). The more specific obligation to lock one's step with the "proceedings" that define what Goffman calls "focused gatherings"—church, weddings, funerals, conferences—is visible only in the dance performed to uphold the letter while evading the spirit of the law. "Thus, in some urban public libraries, the staff and the local bums may reach a tacit understanding that dozing is permissible as long as the dozer first draws a book and props it up in front of his head" (55).

Like the high-wire artist whose grace becomes vivid in the face of the disaster that interrupts it, the general competence of those who enact the prescribed performances of everyday life is thrown into relief when someone falls from the not-too-much-not-too-little tightrope that is the path of propriety:

> Whatever the prescribed . . . involvement, and whatever [its] approved intensity, we usually find, at least in our middle-class society, that the individual is required to give visible evidence that he has not wholly given himself up to this main focus of attention. Some slight margin of self-command and self-possession will typically be required and exhibited. This is the case even though this obligation often must be balanced against the . . . obligation to maintain a minimum of an acceptable main involvement (*Behavior in Public Places*, 37).[4]

> Ordinarily the individual can so successfully maintain an impression of due disinvolvement that we tend to overlook this requirement. When a real crisis comes, which induces his complete absorption in a situated task, the crisis itself, as a new social occasion, may conceal, exonerate, and even oblige what would otherwise be a situational delict. During minor crises, however, when the individual has cause to withdraw from the general orientation of the gathering but has no license to do so, we may witness wonderfully earnest attempts to demonstrate proper disinvolvement in spite of difficulties. Thus, when a man fully invests himself in running to catch a bus, or finds himself slipping on an icy pavement, he may hold his body optimistically stiff and erect, wearing a painful little smile on his face, as if to say that he is really not much involved in his scramble and has remained in situationly appropriate possession of himself (60).

Like any failed performance, the "wonderfully earnest attempts" that Goffman reviews here illuminate by contrast the accomplishment of a successful one. The "body optimistically stiff and erect, wearing a painful little smile" falls below a standard that the subject of surveillance, charged with what Goffman calls the presentation of self in everyday life, is usually able to sustain, a standard of performance refined enough to require that the act it elicits efface any sign that it is compelled at all: "Ordinarily the individual can so successfully maintain an impression of due disinvolvement that we tend to overlook this requirement."

But to the extent that the subject in Goffman's account is the master of his performance, he is determined by the social protocols that script it. To take the measure of this subjection, we need only compare the intentionality that Goffman attributes to the subject of performance with the agency that contemporary accounts ascribe to subjects who parody the social scripts that establish the identities of gender and sexuality. While taking care to complicate the concept of what she calls "theatrical agency," care to measure the limits of volition that can be attributed to the subject of such performances, Judith Butler suggests where such agency may be still be found:

> It is in terms of a norm that compels a certain 'citation' in order for a viable subject to be produced that the notion of gender performativity calls to be rethought. And precisely in relation to such a compulsory citationality that the theatricality of gender is also to be explained. Theatricality need not be conflated with self-display or self-creation. Within queer politics, indeed, within the very signification that is 'queer,' we read a resignifying practice in which the desanctioning power of the name 'queer' is reversed to sanction a contestation of the terms of sexual legitimacy. Paradoxically, but also with great promise, the subject who is 'queered' into public discourse through homophobic interpolations of various kinds takes up or cites that very term as the discursive basis for an opposition. This kind of citation will emerge as theatrical to the extent that it mimes and renders hyperbolic the discursive convention that it also reverses. The hyperbolic gesture is crucial to the exposure of the homophobic 'law' that can no longer control the terms of its own abjecting strategies.[5]

Quite unlike the transgressive agency that Butler sketches here, the intentionality that Goffman attributes to the presentation of self in everyday life is enlisted not to reject or resist society, but rather to secure its acceptance. When his subject makes a mockery of the social role he reiterates, he does so unwittingly; he does so not because, as with the counterdiscursive strategists of a new social movement whom Butler pictures in this passage, he has successfully prosecuted his intentions, but rather because he has failed to do so. Thus, for example, Goffman observes the ordeals undertaken by the inmates of an insane asylum to meet the demands for involvement that defines proper behavior in public:

> Sometimes the patient gives the impression that he knows he cannot hope to contain himself in the situation and is now concerned merely with giving others some impression of being properly present. In Central Hospital, I observed one patient who would walk from one end of the day-room to the other, where there

was a doorway leading out to the porch, bravely attempting to give the impression that there was something on the porch he had to see to, and then, without entering the porch, retrace his steps and repeat the cycle. Another patient, a young psychotic woman, with the incredibly rapid tempo of a patient with motor excitement, seemed to attempt to squeeze herself back into the situation by dumping one ashtray into another, one bowl of water into another, one plate of food into another, apparently in the vain hope that it would look as though she were doing something acceptable and meaningful (*Behavior in Public Places*, 54–55).

These farcical or tragic repetitions of more ordinary presentations of the self are enacted without the glorious costumes of political purpose. The actors who perform them are queer in the old-fashioned sense of one whose earnest efforts to imitate normality has been baffled rather than the renovated sense of the rebellious hero who, by means of a hyperbolic embrace of the abnormal identity assigned to her, manages to upset the regime that dispenses such assignments.

Goffman has his own word for the awkwardness routinely covered up by the glamour that mantles contemporary rehabilitations of the queer. His word, of course, is stigma, the "spoiled identity" of the social loser made to bear a mark of disgrace that disqualifies her from membership in society. Some who bear this mark are able by the ingenuity of their self-presentation to pass as normal, like the mulatto, the homosexual, and the "ex-mental patient" who can sometimes "conceal information about [their] real social identity," and can thus exchange the exclusions visited on the abnormal for the fear that others "may discover that they are in the company of what in effect they demand but . . . haven't obtained,"[6] or, in the language of the melodrama that Oscar Wilde wrote and lived, for the terror that "every moment" the "mask" could be "stripped from one's face."[7]

Elsewhere, though, the stigma that disqualifies its subject from the privileges of social membership is too obtrusive to be hidden by any feat of self-presentation. First among the species of stigma whose recalcitrant visibility defeats the theatrical agency that would conceal it are bodily marks impossible to hide or change, marks of ethnicity, disability, or deformity that recall the etymology of the term. As Goffman writes, "The Greeks . . . originated the term *stigma* to refer to bodily signs. . . . [T]he bearer was a . . . blemished person, ritually polluted, to be avoided, especially in public places" (*Stigma*, 3).

Goffman's catalogue of spoiled identity features a range of bodily stigmas that even the most artful presentation of the self can do little to obscure. But along with the indelible marks of illness, accident, or ethnic difference there is another stigma, one that this catalogue omits, a stigma less drastic and thus more elusive than those that the society we inhabit, or that at least inhabits us, associates with a missing or a slanted eye: the stigma attached to any woman's face that fails to meet a standard of sexual attractiveness in a society where youth is beauty, and beauty youth. Silent on this topic in his full-scale study of spoiled identity, Goffman lightly touches on it elsewhere:

> An interesting fact about the proper composition of the face is that the ease of maintaining it in our society would seem to decline with age, so that, especially in the social class groupings whose women long retain an accent on sexual attractiveness, there comes to be an increasingly long period of time after awakening that is required to get the face into shape, during which the individual in her own eyes is not 'presentable' (*Behavior in Public Places*, 28).

The uncomposed face of the aging woman bears a passing but profound resemblance to the disfigured one that Goffman takes up in *Stigma*: "Before her disfigurement Mrs. Dover had . . . enjoyed traveling, shopping, and visiting her many relatives. The disfigurement of her face, however, resulted in a definite alteration in her way of living . . . she seldom left her . . . home, preferring to remain in her room."[8] In both cases its deformation is radical enough to bar the blemished face not only from public acceptance, but from public view. Such derogation extends beyond the downcast or denigrating eyes of others; it extends to include the revocation of the opportunity to be mocked or avoided by these eyes in the first place.

For Wilde, as for Goffman, the theatrical agency of the self stops at the border of the body; for Wilde, as for Goffman, the consequences of a body that fails to meet the standard of social acceptability are often grave. In Wilde's book, this standard is at once more broadly exacting, and more exact than the one that keeps only the aging woman at home in Goffman's account: the demand that she fails to fulfill is a universal requirement in the world that Wilde inhabits and describes. Predicting the tendency of our own culture to put both sexes through the gauntlet of the fashion runway designed more often for one only, the care his text takes to rank men's bodies is no less assiduous than the trouble that others take on behalf of its female counterpart alone. If Wilde's habit of remarking which man's face makes the grade and which does not ("you—well, of course you have an intellectual expression, and all that. But beauty, real beauty, ends where an intellectual expression begins" [*Dorian Gray*, 24]) is still able to startle us slightly, that is due at least as much to its deviation from the custom of exempting men from such judgments as to the homosexual imagination that this deviation brings to the surface.

More widely applied in Wilde's book, the standard that defines public presentability as the "sexual attractiveness" of youth is also more strictly interpreted there: the criteria that circulates in *The Picture of Dorian Gray* specifies not merely the young body, but more particularly "the slim thing, gold haired like an angel," the rose white youth that, in Eve Sedgwick's words, "stood at the same time for a sexuality, a sensibility, a class, and a narrowly English national type."[9]

If in the glamorous world that Wilde helped to write, "there is absolutely nothing . . . but" the narrowly English national type he calls "youth," at least not for very long, that is not because those who fail to meet this mark decide to stay away. It is rather because the integrity of this charmed circle is assured by external forces, such as a habit of narrative representation that regularly excludes anyone who dwells outside it from the scene of the story. Thus in *The Picture of Dorian Gray* nobody who falls very far from a bodily standard represented by the "young man of extraordinary personal appearance" (24) whose portrait stands at the center of the room as the story begins and ends lasts for very long in the novel's field of vision. Like the "rough uncomely assistant" (94) who comes to transport the picture of Dorian Gray and then quickly disappears, those who fail to meet the specifications of beautiful youth set out by the novel are removed as quickly as possible, thus clearing the field of any sight but "the glamour of rose-white boyhood" (9). At its most avid, this narrative tendency cancels the appearance of the unpreferred body the very moment it arrives on stage. The artist whose "rugged strong face" and "coal black hair" (9) is no match for "the ivory and rose leaves" (9) of his subject disappears from view even before he is introduced to it: "in front of [the portrait], some little distance away, was sitting the artist himself, Basil Hallward, whose sudden disappearance some years ago caused . . . such public excitement" (50). Less fantastic than the magic force that enables the hero to conceal the sight of his decomposing face while sustaining a public aspect forever young and beautiful, the policy of population control prosecuted by *The Picture of Dorian Gray* works more quietly to promote the same end.

Sometimes as discreet as an eye that never wanders far from a body type projected by Hollywood or the House of Windsor, the inclination to police the boundaries of a society whose visible emblem is the fair-haired youth that Wilde and his heirs never tire of celebrating elsewhere takes form in a more violent impulse to remove all others. Consider the fate of the unlovely outsider in "Lord Arthur Savile's Crime,"[10] the fortune-teller who appears like the "sight of the Gorgon's head" to the eyes of one who "had lived the delicate and luxurious life of a young man of birth and fortune, a life exquisite in . . . its beautiful boyish insouciance" (26). The murderous fate that the fortune-teller reads in the hero's hand is no more horrible than his own face and fingers while he does so: "A shudder seemed to pass through him, and his great bushy eyebrows twitched convulsively, in an odd, irritating way they had. . . . Then some huge beads of perspiration broke out on his yellow forehead, like a poisonous dew, and his fat fingers grew cold and clammy" (26). Like the killer Wilde celebrates in "Pen, Pencil and Poison" ("When a friend reproached him with the murder of Helen Abercrombie he shrugged his shoulders and said, 'Yes; it was a dreadful thing to do, but she had very thick ankles' "),[11] Lord Arthur is driven to execute the fortune-teller as much for his "fat, flabby face," "sickly feeble smile," and "sensual mouth" as to fulfill the destiny he has predicted for him. Literalizing the underworld euphemism, killing this sorry specimen is a matter of making him disappear:

> In a moment he had seized Mr. Podgers by the legs, and flung him into the Thames. There was a coarse oath, a heavy splash, and all was still. Lord Arthur looked anxiously over, but could see nothing. . . . Once he thought that he caught sight of the bulky misshapen figure striking out for the staircase by the bridge, and a horrible feeling of failure came over him, but it turned out to be merely a reflection, and when the moon shone out from behind a cloud it passed away. At last he seemed to have realized the decree of destiny (49).

Like that of another Arthur, the decree of destiny that this one fulfills extends beyond the scope of a single individual: by arranging the disappearance of "the bulky misshapen figure" of his "Nemesis," Lord Arthur removes his like from a world of "beautiful boyish insouciance." The mixed society in which he meets the palm reader at the start of the story, a "reception . . . even more crowded than usual," where "pretty women" in "their smartest dresses," mingle with "a heavy Tartar-looking lady, with tiny black eyes" and "stout prima-donna[s]," yields to an unbroken vision of a purer one at the end of the story, after "the bulky misshapen figure" has been forced out of it:

> When [Lord Arthur's] wedding took place, some three weeks later, St. Peter's was crowded with a perfect mob of smart people . . . everybody agreed that they had never seen a handsomer couple than the bride and bridegroom. . . . Some years afterwards, when two beautiful children had been born to them, Lady Windermere came down on a visit to Alton Priory, a lovely old place . . . [she] looked wonderfully beautiful with . . . her large blue forget-me-not eyes, and her heavy coils of golden hair. Or pur they were—not that plate straw colour that nowadays usurps the gracious name of gold, but such gold as is woven into sunbeams or hidden in strange amber. . . . [She sat] with Lady Arthur . . . one of the most beautiful girls in London . . . watching the little boy and girl as they played up and down the rose-walk, like fitful sunbeams (50–51).

"Passing away" like the shadow of a cloud, the thing of darkness that pollutes the atmosphere of "rose-white youth" takes his entire race with him, clearing the way for the aryan pastoral that is the story's final image: a society from which all but the most authentic blonde hair and blue eyes have sunk from view.

Wilde could hardly do more to show that protecting a "world where there is absolutely nothing but the body of blonde youth" involves methods

broader than the merely personal qualms that deter anybody else from showing up there. At the same time, though, that he amplifies the objective force
of the protocol that determines public presentability, he also extends the
capacity of those subjected to this force to satisfy its requirements. A subject
whose physical features fail to satisfy the ruthless demands of what, with
little risk of hyperbole, we might call a regime of body fascism can still
qualify as a member by substituting for his own physical aspect a surrogate
one, like the picture of Dorian Gray, or, closer to home, the rhetorical figures
fashioned by Lord Henry. His own face, with its "olive complexion" (*Dorian
Gray*, 19) and lines of age, while "interesting," is hardly the ticket for admission to the high society of the body beautiful which is the only one that
counts in Wilde's book, or Lord Henry's own ("youth is the one thing worth
having" [9]). With only the genius of his speech to declare, Lord Henry
enters the company of beautiful youth in an access of eloquence by which
his own defective body gives way to one fully qualified to join that company
without flinching:

> He played with . . . [an] idea, and grew willful; tossed it into the air and trans-
> formed it; let it escape and recaptured it; made it iridescent with fancy, and
> winged it with paradox. The praise of folly, as he went on, soared into a philoso-
> phy, and Philosophy herself became young, and catching the mad music of Plea-
> sure, wearing, one might fancy, her wine-stained robe and wreath of ivy, danced
> like a Bacchante over the hills of life, and mocked the slow Silenus for being
> sober. Facts fled before her like frightened forest things. Her white feet trod the
> huge press at which wise Omar sits, till the seething grape-juice rose round her
> bare limbs in waves of purple bubbles, or crawled in red foam over the vat's
> black, dripping, sloping sides. It was an extraordinary improvisation. He felt that
> the eyes of Dorian Gray were fixed on him, and the consciousness that amongst
> his audience there was one whose temperament he wished to fascinate, seemed
> to give his wit keenness, and to lend colour to his imagination. He was brilliant,
> fantastic, irresponsible. He charmed his listeners out of themselves, and they
> followed his pipe laughing. Dorian Gray never took his gaze off him, but sat as
> like one under a spell, smiles chasing each other over his lips, and wonder
> growing grave in his darkening eyes (37–38).

In an exercise of theatrical agency that Goffman's "heroes of dissimulation" might well envy, the heroes of dissimulation whose facility for passing
allows them, against all sorts of odds, to "mix with the crowd," Lord Henry
joins the ranks of the body beautiful, exchanging the "worn expression" of
his face for the fresh figures of his rhetoric. The spellbinding power of his
speech manages not only to transform Folly, Philosophy, and Pleasure into
bodies as "fleet, joyous" and youthful as the picture of Dorian Gray, it manages as well to make Lord Henry one with those bodies. It's not just that he
praises the soaring figure of folly, he merges with it: "The praise of folly, as

he went on, soared into a philosophy, and Philosophy herself became young." By the power of his speech, Lord Henry not only incarnates Philosophy, he makes that body his own: who is it but he who makes facts flee like frightened forest things. What is the enchanting thing from which Dorian Gray cannot withdraw his gaze but the renovated aspect of Lord Henry himself, not the "olive-coloured face and worn expression," but rather the ravishing figure of "Philosophy herself [become] young," whose "white feet trod the huge press . . . till the seething grape-juice rose round her bare limbs in waves of purple bubbles."

More than most aspects of self-presentation, "[l]inguistic messages are felt to be voluntary and intended," Goffman remarks (*Behavior in Public Places*, 14). They are surely more so, at least by Wilde's lights, than the "wrinkled, worn and yellow face" and "coal-black hair" that mark the denigrated physique not only with the signs of age, but with unpreferred designations of class and race. "Linguistic messages" are surely more "voluntary and intended" in Wilde's book than the body of the author occulted by it, the body whose shape and tone, unlike those of his words ("My Irish accent was one of the thing many things I forgot at Oxford"[12]) could hardly be purged of an ethnic element intolerable in a society of "rose-white youth." By means of this new figure, Oscar Wilde, and others besides, conspires to soar above a limit no less steep than that of the body itself, a limit that describes not only the difference between life and death, health and illness, but as well the difference between those who make the social scene and those who are regularly exterminated from it. Such presentations of the self, by no means everyday, may be seen to join the metaphysical achievement of theatrical agency celebrated by queer theory as a triumph over the rule of the social. Shows as artful as Lord Henry's performance or the transvestite masquerades that celebrate sexual difference even in the act of suspending it are at least as committed to gaining admittance to a society whose rules they evade as to upsetting its premises. In the case of the labor that Wilde and his kind undertake to be beautiful, far more so: a labor that seeks to fashion a body as glamorous as the one they desire, the body that social forces, as great as any, count as the only one fit to be seen.

NOTES

1. Oscar Wilde, *The Picture of Dorian Gray* (1891), ed. Donald L. Lawler (New York: Norton, 1988). All citations of *Dorian Gray* will refer to this edition.
2. Oscar Wilde, *An Ideal Husband*, act 3, in *The Oxford Critical Edition of Oscar Wilde* (Oxford: Oxford University Press, 1989), 439. All citations of *An Ideal Husband* will refer to this edition.

3. Erving Goffman, *The Presentation of Self in Everyday Life* (New York: Double-day, 1959). All citations of *The Presentation of Self* will refer to this edition.

4. Erving Goffman, *Behavior in Public Places: Notes on the Social Organization of Gatherings* (New York: The Free Press, 1963). All citations of *Behavior in Public Places* will refer to this edition.

5. Judith Butler, *Bodies That Matter: On the Discursive Limits of "Sex"* (New York: Routledge, 1993), 232.

6. Erving Goffman, *Stigma: Notes on the Management of Spoiled Identity* (New York: Simon & Schuster, 1963), 73. All citations of *Stigma* will refer to this edition.

7. Oscar Wilde, *Lady Windermere's Fan*, act 3, in *Collected Plays* (London: Meth-uen, 1988) 77.

8. F. Macgregor et al., *Facial Deformities and Plastic Surgery* (Springfield, Ill.: C. Thomas, 1953), quoted in Goffman, *Stigma*, 12.

9. Eve Kosofsky Sedgwick, "Nationalisms and Sexualities: As Opposed to What?" in *Tendencies* (Durham: Duke University Press, 1993), 151.

10. Oscar Wilde, "Lord Arthur Savile's Crime," in *Complete Shorter Fiction*, ed. Isobel Murray (New York: Oxford University Press, 1995). All citations of "Lord Arthur Savile's Crime" will refer to this edition.

11. Oscar Wilde, "Pen, Pencil and Poison," in *Complete Works of Oscar Wilde* (New York: Harper & Row, 1989), 1006.

12. See Richard Ellmann, *Oscar Wilde* (New York: Vintage, 1988), 38.

PART IV

DISCIPLINE AND THE STATE

Character and Pastorship in Two British "Sociological" Traditions: Organized Charity, Fabian Socialism, and the Invention of New Liberalism

LAUREN M. E. GOODLAD

> Perhaps no characteristic of the present efforts for social reform [is] more hopeful and more important than the deepening emphasis now placed . . . on the moral element in social reform. . . . Today the key-word in reform is "cooperation" and in economics "character." If this may seem to some too optimistic a view, we remind them that individualist, socialist, and even anarchist reformers all seek cooperation, while in economics the reason why individualist economists fear socialism is that they believe that it will deteriorate character, and the reason why socialist economists seek socialism is their belief that under individualism character is deteriorating.
>
> The Encyclopedia of Social Reform *(1897)*

"ENERGY OF WILL—self-originating force—is the soul of every great character," wrote Samuel Smiles in 1871. In so doing he reiterated the main theme of his enormously popular *Self-Help* (1859), presenting "character" as the rock-solid foundation of Britain's liberal constitutional consensus during a century of tumultuous change.[1] Through the powerful and often chauvinistic language of character, Britons were encouraged to imagine themselves as a nation of self-governing individuals and communities. Inseparable from this mythology was its material underside: the informal collectivism of countless philanthropic, voluntary, and self-help organizations. The 1834 Poor Law Amendment Act (or New Poor Law) is understandably regarded as the dawn of modern administration in Great Britain. Nevertheless, the law was devised to strengthen local government and self-reliance—not to supplant them. Throughout the nineteenth century, private philanthropy not only supplemented but also outstripped the activities of the New Poor Law.

Whereas England's Continental rivals were ruled by powerful centralized bureaucracies, in Victorian Britain, "most of the functions performed by government in other societies were . . . performed by coteries of citizens governing themselves."[2] According to the author of *Self-Help*, "it is every day becoming more clearly understood, that the function of Government is negative and restrictive, rather than positive and active." Indeed, the determination to minimize centralized intervention and promote local autonomy was reaffirmed by the unpopularity of the Public Health Act (1848) and the subsequent collapse of Edwin Chadwick's notoriously "un-English" Board of Health.[3]

That said, my purpose in the present essay is to address the crisis of character and the backlash against liberalism that began in the fin de siècle and culminated in the New Liberalism of the pre–World War I era. After decades as the world's leader in industry and empire—a supremacy unquestioningly linked to the nation's character—Britain was forced to acknowledge the importance of efficient "pastorship."[4] Both members of the Charity Organization Society (COS) and Fabian Socialists sought to meet this demand by imposing new forms of authority over what had long been mythologized as a nation of self-reliant individuals. In actuality the COS's voluntary casework approach had a great deal in common with the Fabians' emphasis on bureaucratic expertise. Nevertheless, the COS drew on idealist philosophical foundations and sought to enlarge organized private initiative, while the Fabians drew on materialist philosophy and aimed to justify state intervention. Hence, COS and Fabian proposals emerged from within two disparate cosmologies—including two different conceptions of character.

Beginning in the 1890s, Idealist proponents of the COS clashed with Fabian Socialists in ways that prepared the ground for the New Liberal middle course of David Lloyd George and Winston Churchill.[5] These debates over social policy reached a head in the 1905–1909 Royal Commission on the Poor Laws. The subsequent stalemate between supporters of the Majority and Minority Reports eventually gave rise to the invention of a new national tradition to support the flagging myth of self-reliant character: the National Insurance Act of 1911. As we shall see, the *Encyclopedia of Social Reform* was not exaggerating when, in 1897, it described the political divisions of the day as, in effect, a contest over the meanings and condition of character. These same divides affected the emerging discipline of sociology.

The contest between organized charity and the Fabians' statist agenda can be represented through the careers of two prominent married couples: the COS's Helen and Bernard Bosanquet, and the Fabians' Beatrice and Sidney Webb. The chief goal of the Charity Organization Society, founded in 1869, was to promote individual and family self-reliance by voluntary means. District by district, COS committees would organize Britain's labyrinthine charities, providing individualized assistance for the deserving and eliminating the "pauperizing" effects of indiscriminate handouts. The Fabians, by contrast, sought to eradicate Britain's unsystematic philanthropic legacy, replacing it with a "rationalised two-way relationship between the individual and the state."[6] The COS thus harked back to the negative (deterrent) function of the 1834 New Poor Law. Minimal public provision for the destitute was "a necessary evil" that must never be permitted to encroach upon the norm of the self-maintaining family.[7] The Fabians drew instead on the long-suppressed positive (technocratic and interventionist) aspects of the Benthamite tradition—aspects that had been in abeyance since the mid-century failure of Edwin Chadwick's sanitary reforms.

These oppositions crystallized in the landmark divisions of the 1905–1909 Royal Commission on the Poor Laws. The COS-dominated Majority Report urged rigorous application of the deterrent policies set forth in 1834. This public strategy would be supplemented by scientific charitable assistance for the "helpable" poor, based on "careful study of the characters and circumstances" of each "case."[8] The Fabian-dominated Minority Report instead urged dissolution of the existing Poor Laws and foresaw no meaningful role for philanthropy. Social problems must instead be broken down, classified, and systematically remedied by means of specialized intervention and institutional rehabilitation.

Significant though they are, the differences between the COS and the Fabians do not, as they might appear, solidify lines between entrepreneurial individualism and professionalized collectivism.[9] On the contrary, the difference between the COS and the Fabians is better understood as that between two strains of self-consciously "sociological" but manifestly paternalistic thinking, *both* of which mandated collective and professionalized responses of some kind. Both groups addressed themselves to what the 1897 *Encyclopedia* described as the "moral element in social reform," invoking "cooperation" in order to ameliorate "character." In so doing, both presented a distinctive vision of national pastorship yoked to the authority of modern science, including a discernibly post-individualist philosophy of the state and an evolutionary paradigm predicated on collective moral purpose. Nevertheless, to a remarkable extent, the COS and the Fabians represent two distinct fin-de-siècle cosmologies, with competing claims to the emerging discipline of sociology.

BRITISH SOCIOLOGY

> I do not . . . belittle material conditions or deny that insuperable misfortune may destroy the industrial qualities and drag a man down among the invertebrate Residuum. Still less, in maintaining the main evil to be moral, do I suggest the indolent and vulgar evasion—'It is all their own fault.'

> On the contrary, the fault, I am persuaded, lies in great
> measure at *our* door; but the suffering—the suffering is
> *inevitably* theirs
>
> *Bernard Bosanquet, "Character in Its Bearing*
> *on Social Causation" (1895)*

> What we have to do is apply the scientific method to facts
> of social life.
>
> *Beatrice Webb,* Sociological Papers *(1905)*

Britain's idiosyncratic sociological development—its failure to produce a "classical sociology" such as that of Émile Durkheim or Max Weber—has long been a "commonplace" among scholars.[10] The present essay bears on this question because the COS's casework approach to poor relief, and the Fabians' non-Marxist variety of socialist analysis represent a substantial part of what Britain *did* produce when it was not producing a theoretical and ostensibly apolitical sociology such as Weber's.[11] The subject is complicated by the fact that while the British academy was exceedingly slow to institutionalize the discipline, a wide variety of figures, inside and outside of the academy, characterized their work as "sociology."[12] This idiosyncratic disciplinary history testifies to late-Victorian Britain's as yet fluid epistemological foundations.

Although both the Fabians and the Charity Organization Society frequently described their respective activities as "sociology," their place in the complicated history of that discipline has become somewhat obscure. In 1903 the COS established the School of Sociology for the systematic training of charitable volunteers. In so doing, they considered collaborating with the Fabian-controlled London School of Economics.[13] Yet, in his illuminating exploration into the Idealist contribution to British sociology, Stefan Collini describes the COS as "anti-sociological," while devoting one footnote to Beatrice and Sidney Webb. Clearly to speak of "sociology" in Britain during this period is, in effect, to speak of sociologies.[14]

Collini's reference to the COS's "anti-sociological" tendencies concerns two disparate but well-established aspects of Britain's diverse sociological precedents. The most popular exponent of mid-Victorian "sociology" was Herbert Spencer—editor of *The Economist* and architect of a wide-ranging positivist, evolutionary, and radically individualist theory of the social organism.[15] From the Fabian point of view, Spencer's laissez-faire political deductions, but not the evolutionary theory on which they were premised, had long ceased to be valid. By contrast, for Idealists such as Bernard Bosanquet, Spencer's opposition to state paternalism was welcome, but his atomized and depersonalizing evolutionary theory was unacceptable. Hence, neither position is entirely compatible with Spencerian sociology.

When Britain's idiosyncratic presociology is not aligned with Spencer's positivism, it is instead equated with the "crude empiricism" and "narrow" reformist agenda of the "Booth-Rowntree tradition of social enquiry."[16] Charles Booth's seventeen-volume *Life and Labour of the People in London* (1889–1903) and Seebohm Rowntree's York-based *Poverty: A Study of Town Life* (1901) are widely recognized as having innovated important methods for social-scientific analysis.[17] From a modern disciplinary perspective, however, these ad hoc surveys lack the sociologist's explanatory and theoretical rationale—charges that have been similarly leveled at the Webbs.[18] Indeed, Beatrice Webb's "apprenticeship" as one of Booth's social investigators, and her subsequent affiliation with the COS point to the strong affinities between Booth's and Rowntree's social inquiry, COS casework, and Fabian social analysis. Despite many differences, all were concerned to provide moral guidance—that is, pastorship—and, for the very same reason, all claimed sociological legitimacy while diverging from the theoretical and ostensibly apolitical criteria that were defining the discipline outside of Britain.

Insofar as the COS was "anti-sociological" in Collini's terms, what the organization objected to was not Booth's and Rowntree's casework methods, but the environmentalist interpretive frame and interventionist politics to which their results were soon harnessed. Evidence that as much as one-third of Britain's population lived in a state of grinding poverty tended to discredit the position that self-reliant character, aided by organized philanthropy alone, was a sure path to social progress. Yet it is important to recognize that, in battling the environmentalist camp, what the COS opposed was not collectivism per se, but the depersonalizing (statist and materialist) collectivism envisioned by the Fabians. In this respect the COS looked back to an important pre-Victorian precursor: the early-nineteenth-century scheme of neighborhood-visiting introduced by Dr. Thomas Chalmers, "almost the patron saint of the COS." Chalmers had sought to abolish the poor laws entirely, arguing that neighborhood charity would build laboring-class character and encourage self-help.[19] For Chalmers, a Glasgow clergyman and moral philosopher, charity was fundamentally pastoral: a gift of "judgment," "time and attention," as well as monetary aid.[20] Like Chalmers before them, members of the COS believed that this personal element was crucial to improving character.

Chalmers's moral legacy was not, however, unique to Britain's philanthropic Idealists. The Fabians also sought to provide pastorship in order to forward a progressive liberal society. In so doing, they too rejected the atomism and hedonism of Manchester school political economy.[21] Nevertheless, while Beatrice Webb admired the "persistent service" and "personal responsibility" of the COS, it was not primarily to this Chalmers-inspired citizen ethic that Fabian Socialism was tied.[22] Instead, the Fabians' comparatively impersonal and technocratic utopia looked back to Edwin Chadwick's ambitious public health agenda. Hence, while the Webbs claimed zealously to uphold the character-building mission, their environmentalist approach to improving the nation's moral and physical condition tended to reduce character to a determined effect.

LIBERALISM DURING AND AFTER THE FIN DE SIÈCLE

> None of the strong men in the strong ages would have
> understood what you meant by working for efficiency.
> *G. K. Chesterton,* Heretics *(1905)*

In forwarding competing claims to sociological authority, both the COS and the Fabians thus drew on the past in order to envision the future. The "scientific charity" of the COS originated in the pastoral mission of an early-nineteenth-century clergyman. The technocracy urged by the Fabians had, in Chadwick's day, been rejected by a generation of Britons who believed with Smiles that "Heaven helps those who help themselves."[23] But the fin de siècle world in which these ideas reemerged was dramatically unlike that of Chalmers or Chadwick. The late-Victorian and Edwardian eras were periods of intense massification: liberalism's core mythologies were subjected to pressures generated by the increasing scale of commercial enterprise, the growth of a mass reading culture, the introduction of advertising, and, of course, the advent of mass politics. Just as liberal claims to a genuinely deliberative democracy were undermined by the rise of party discipline, so the myth of individual progress was challenged first by demands for (male) working-class enfranchisement and then for a labor-oriented political agenda.[24] Demographically, these massifying trends expressed themselves in a shift away from provincial communities and toward the metropolis. No longer synonymous with Smiles's self-made entrepreneurs, Britain's middle classes were increasingly composed of corporate professionals, commuting from London's booming suburbs.[25]

These dynamic shifts coincided with a steady ebbing of Britain's uncontested position as the nineteenth century's preeminent world power. As Geoffrey Searle has argued, mid-Victorian liberalism depended on a national supremacy that most ruling-class Britons simply took for granted. Only while the nation dominated world markets, outstripped competitors, and ruled the seas could strict adherence to liberal principles simultaneously operate as moral imperative and sound national policy. Britons were rudely awakened to the nation's declining standing by trade depression in the 1880s, Booth's and Rowntree's disturbing revelations, and the humiliating military blunders of the Boer War in 1899. The truth, however, is that British predominance had already been challenged by 1875 when, under the systematic pastoral state of Otto von Bismarck, the newly unified Germany became a serious contender for world dominance.[26]

Searle describes the subsequent backlash against mid-Victorian liberalism as a mandate for "national efficiency." Rather than liberalism's amateurish and minimalist government, proponents of efficiency urged a corporatist approach that—like Germany's—would actively promote military power, imperial expansion, social welfare, technological progress, and industrial prosperity. The "State" they envisioned would, in the words of one Edwardian enthusiast, institute "savoir faire," not "laisser faire."[27] Such an agenda appealed to Fabian Socialists, some conservatives, imperialists (including many liberals), eugenicists, Broad Church clergy, technophiles, large-scale industrialists, Darwinian evolutionists, and professional experts of many kinds. Nevertheless, such an agenda amounted to an about-face on liberal principles that had become synonymous, even for many conservatives, with Britain's national identity. Efficiency discourses tended to promote state intervention of the kind Britain had long abjured; collectivist notions antithetical to self-help; and technocratic specialism at odds with Britain's entrepreneurial and gentlemanly ideals. Unsurprisingly, many Britons opposed and/ or were made anxious by these un-English proposals, even as they lamented the national decline that had precipitated them.

These national concerns led to renewed interest in reforming a Poor Law system that had been fashioned according to stringent liberal economic principles. In their respective approaches to reform, both the Charity Organization Society and the Fabians offered a means to satisfying the popular demand for efficient pastorship in some form. As we shall see, "character" was an operative category for each position, but, at the same time, a telling sign of disparate cosmological foundations.

"MIND AND WILL"

> When we say . . . that the problem is moral rather than economic, we are not to be understood as adopting any vulgar answer to the vulgar question, "Did this man sin, or his parents, or society?" A moral point of view does not to us mean a point of view which holds a question as solved by apportioning blame to the unfortunate; it does mean a point of view which treats men not as economic abstractions, but as living selves with a history and ideas and a character of their own.
>
> *Bernard Bosanquet, "Character in Its Bearing on Social Causation" (1895)*

> Your incapable person is like a London garden, it takes a
> most extravagant amount of attention to get absurdly small
> results, but we are very proud of what we do get.
>
> *Helen Dendy (later Bosanquet), "Meaning and*
> *Methods of True Charity" (1893)*

As a gradual convert to collectivism, John Stuart Mill was an important precursor for the Fabians. But as the propounder of a humanistic utilitarian ethic, and a major influence on T. H. Green and later exponents of the British Idealist school, Mill also was a crucial figure for members of the Charity Organization Society. Green's Kantian and Hegelian critique of Mill, further developed in Bernard Bosanquet's *Philosophical Theory of the State* (1899), promulgated the crucial transitional notion of *positive* freedom. According to this view, government is morally charged to promote human liberty in active fashion. Yet while Idealists thus repudiated orthodox laissez faire, neither Green (an advanced Liberal), nor Bosanquet (an ardent voluntarist) advocated the investiture of a tutelary and interventionist state. Hence, in retrospect, Idealism looks more like a late-Victorian extension of Mill's humanistic liberalism than the radical break postulated by contemporaries.[28] Bosanquet ambiguously insisted on the state's "moral purpose," but argued that it is only through "consciousness" that the "best life" is chiefly realized. Thus, for Bosanquet, Fabianism's delight in state intervention, and socialism's more general determination to redistribute wealth, fundamentally misunderstood human character. Such material improvements avail nothing, argued Bosanquet, unless they are "charged with mind and will."[29]

In revising utilitarianism, Mill had forged a synthesis between a too-deterministic Benthamite materialism, and a too-metaphysical "Germano-Coleridgean" tradition. To improve on these antitheses, Mill had experimented with Comtean positivism, including Comte's "sociology," in an attempt to create an empirical but nondeterministic foundation for social progress. The Idealist tradition revised this humanist project, demoting empirical criteria to secondary importance, and drawing on Darwin and Hegel to supplement the classical teleology that had been so important to Mill. Hence, the society whose interrelations Mill had theorized in revised utilitarian terms, and for which he had sought a positive basis in Comtean sociology was, in Bosanquet's Idealist view, a "social organism" that endows each member with "a function which is the essence of his being."[30] Bosanquet's German-Romantic and evolutionary influences, along with his debts to Chalmers's charitable ethos, imbued his writing with a teleological certitude that Mill, a steadfast critic of "a priori" assumptions, was unable to achieve.

This teleology was evident in the Bosanquets' practical proposals for Poor Law reform. Writing in 1893, Helen Dendy (later Bosanquet) "picture[d] humanity as a great army pressing on towards an invisible goal, and guided by a wisdom not its own." Organized charity must aid the weak and selfish, not by minimizing the pain of falling, but by enabling them to "keep step with their comrades." The key to achieving this disciplinary aim was the COS's famed casework method: the germ of modern professional social work. Trained to investigate "the difficult question of character," the C.O.S. caseworker recognized that a "little wholesome starvation" at the onset of defective conduct was preferable to the "moral degradation" of dependence.[31]

These tenets assumed a more up-to-date Darwinian cast in the contemporaneous writing of Bernard Bosanquet. The continued advance of civilization, he warned, was threatened by any scheme that "suppresses" the "personal struggle for existence." For this reason, organized charity enhances nature, while a socialistic state obstructs it. The latter, by discouraging family self-reliance, commits "an abuse fatal to character," undermining community "efficiency." Left to itself, "natural selection" is inherently progressive. That is, in the absence of state interference (or, for that matter, unscientific charity), only those willing to assume the moral and material responsibilities of bourgeois domestic life will marry and, consequently, reproduce the species. Here, by alleging the individual's freedom to choose between respectable domesticity and celibacy, Bosanquet recast what was at bottom the old Malthusian precept that those too poor to maintain a family had better practice "moral restraint."[32] The principles of 1834 facilitate this process, further deterring the reproduction of "uncompetitive" "stock." Organized charity plays a pastoral rather than primarily humanitarian role. Its chief purpose is to distinguish between the helpable and the incorrigible pauper, facilitating the former's self-reliance, while relegating the latter to the tender mercies of the workhouse.[33]

It would be a mistake, however, to reduce Bosanquet's poor law philosophy to a mere application of laissez-faire economic principles. Scientific charity involved a full-blown bureaucratization of philanthropy, including the preparation of *Annual Reports*, the collection of statistics, and the training of caseworkers in "the 12 principles of relief." Writing in support of the Majority Report in 1910, Bernard Bosanquet called for "an army of social healers to be trained and organised."[34] Indeed, COS goals were so systematic that it is possible to argue that the Society sought simply to consolidate in private hands the pastoral powers that the Fabians would appropriate for the state.

But here, too, would be a serious misrepresentation. Central to the Society's philosophy was a devout belief in the Chalmers-inspired premise that charity—however necessarily scientific—preserved individual and family autonomy in a way that state interference could not. Bosanquet's voluntary army would be trained to approach economic failure as a fundamentally "moral" problem—"a defect in the citizen character" that affects the entire community.[35] Hence, while the COS envisioned a nationwide network of caseworkers, invested with multifarious pastoral powers, and cooperating with Poor Law authorities on a semi-official basis, they simultaneously believed that the relation between workers and their "cases" was *personal*. Invidious comparisons between the inert, even harmful agency of the public "official" and the attentive pastorship of the charitable caseworker surfaced repeatedly in COS writings.[36] Ironically, the COS's foremost defense against Fabian technocracy was the personality of an organized corps of Dickensian Mrs. Pardiggles.

It seems clear therefore that the late-Victorian and Edwardian organized charity movement was less a bona fide individualism than a professionalized and quasi-collective paternalism, cloaked in the defense of a venerable liberal rhetorical tradition. Enshrined in the COS's distinctive point of view was mid-Victorian Britain's popular conviction of the special qualities of civil society, galvanized by what Smiles had described as the "self-originating force" of character. This still cherished liberal myth, and the moral assumptions that sustained it, legitimated the COS's confident distinctions between the state's inability to "consider the needs of the individual," and the charitable caseworker's unique capacity to "foster" family "character."[37]

To be sure, the COS's claims on behalf of caseworkers were not purely rhetorical. COS methods strove to deliver a level of individualized service that might conceivably exhaust even the Victorians' formidable voluntary resources.[38] Octavia Hill, a long-standing member of the COS Central Commission and a signatory of the Majority Report, urged caseworkers to cultivate "deep sympathy for the poor," lest the Society devolve into "a dry, ineffectual machinery for enquiring about people."[39] Rather more imperiously, but no less in earnest, Helen Dendy warned that charity work requires "months of patient care, and a determination that if we are to fail it shall not be for want of either time or money."[40] Nevertheless, the fact remains that the Fabians sought to establish comparable (and arguably greater) pastoral agencies in the specialized services of the state. Hence, it is significant that, in sparring with its Fabian rivals, the COS did not, by and large, adopt the traditional liberal-individualist defense against state intervention. Rather than insist on the unconstitutionality of Fabian designs, COS members preferred directly to impugn the relation between the government official (whether local or national) and the poor. Virtually ignoring the Fabians' terrific emphasis on specialized training, the COS dogmatically held that state officials were incapable either of understanding or relating to the family and the personal questions of character that sustain it.

This ardent rhetorical privileging of personality was part of a more ambitious attempt to cordon off cherished spheres of social knowledge—to claim the burgeoning field of "sociology" for organized charity. The COS envisioned sociology as a science of civil society, emphasizing the sacrosanct domestic and moral relations between individuals, families, and communities. Hence, the charitable caseworker was an expert insofar as she was scientifically trained and rationally organized. But she was also a bulwark *against* bureaucratic impersonality insofar as charity itself remained anchored to a vehemently antimaterialist Victorian cosmology.[41]

For the COS, long-venerated concepts such as the neighborhood, the home, the family, and, of course, character, thus retained their capacity to signify the truth of human autonomy. That is why the attack on Fabianism rarely took the form of a polemic against the general principle of collectivism. On the contrary, organized charity was itself envisioned as a collectivizing force: a corporate voluntarism of sorts, that offered a superior alternative to statist bureaucracy. Like John Stuart Mill before them, COS members perceived the diminution of individual power in a mass society; but unlike Mill, they retained sufficient faith in civil society's unique moral qualities to see organized charity as a transcendence of modern isolation and a return to vitalizing character-building.[42]

Employing classical republican ideas much like Mill's, Bosanquet described fin-de-siècle civilization as a "modern wilderness of interests." Unlike the ancient Greeks who recognized their positive duty to govern, modern Britons find their citizenship undermined by multiple "divisions and estrangements." To overcome this fragmentation, Britons must put aside class differences, professional affiliations, regional identities, and even, when required, domestic obligations. Most of all, they must dismiss the pernicious distinction between "official" government—a mere simulacrum—and the self-government that ought properly to realize itself from within civil society. In its current semidormant condition, the latter is reduced to a "mass of unofficial persons who . . . regard themselves as mere units among millions of their like."[43] Against such pictures of pastorless, liberal dysfunction, the COS positioned the corporate voluntarism alone afforded by organized charity.

This utopian stance was epitomized by C. S. Loch, Secretary of the Society between 1877 and 1913, self-styled sociologist, and another member of the Royal Commission. Writing in 1903, Loch explained,

> If I were asked why I joined the Society I should answer that through its work and growth I hoped that some day there would be formed a large association of persons . . . who, disagreeing in much, would find in charity a common purpose and a new unity. . . . Such an organisation might bear on the removal and prevention of evils a combined force that would far exceed in weight and influence any yet existing. It could make legislation effective, could see that it was enforced. Apart from all legislative interference and with the use of means and

influences more far-reaching it could renew and discipline the life of the people by a nobler, more devoted, more scientific religious charity. . . . It would open to many a new path for the exercise of personal influence.[44]

Hence, while individual agency is clearly constrained, the "combined force" that Loch imagined is personalized, charismatic, pluralist, and voluntary. It is "a large association of persons," rather than Bosanquet's fragmented "units" or, for that matter, the comparatively anonymous evolutionary juggernaut envisioned by the Fabians. Minimizing the importance of "legislative interference," Loch's formulation promised to indemnify "the exercise of personal influence." In this way, organized charity secured much-needed pastorship ("the removal and prevention of evils") in a form that neither subjugated, homogenized, nor dehumanized the individual members of the social organism.

In effect, the COS attempted to create a pastoral agency that would overcome the paradox of institutionalized authority in a society of putatively self-reliant individuals. Because the relationship between the caseworker and the family was personal and voluntary, rather than official and prescribed, organized charity's "combined force" could have its cake and eat it too. As described by various proponents, it was, on the one hand, systematic, rational, efficient, and affirmative, and, on the other, personal, moral, humanizing, and liberating. Fulfilling a vision that had, for Mill, remained tellingly incomplete, the Idealists rejected the latter-day determinism of their Fabian rivals, while simultaneously warranting a positive basis for human progress. Bosanquet's teleology married evolutionary forces with human mind and will, repudiating any program that privileged one without the other. Neither the individualist's laissez faire nor the determinist's "mechanical pressure of circumstances" availed until the Idealist's synthesis was *first* asserted. For Bosanquet, positive liberty, the actuation of "some plan or value in the circumstances that press upon us, in relation to which we can assert ourselves," completed the teleology sketched by Mill.[45] Character, what George Behlmer describes as "that aspect of mind which enabled the [Idealist's] individual to impose order on social circumstances," was the human medium of such progress.[46] Citizen-pastorship—an army of "social healers," specially trained but "disciplined and animated with a single spirit and purpose"—was the unique corporate agency capable of translating Idealist philosophy into social policy.[47]

"UNCONSCIOUS SOCIALISM"

It is surely the worst of all forms of national waste to allow the ravages of preventable sickness to progress unchecked; and this not merely because it kills off thousands of producers prematurely (burdening us, by the way, with the

widow and the orphan), but because sickness levies a toll
on the living and leaves even those who survive crippled,
debilitated, and less efficient than they would otherwise
have been.

The Minority Report of the Royal Commission
on the Poor Laws, 1905–1909 (drafted by Beatrice and
Sidney Webb)

Of course, from the Fabian point of view, what the Bosanquets proposed
was a retrograde philosophical mystification. Practically speaking, Idealism
like that of Bernard Bosanquet obstructed the state's modern pastoral potential and promoted old-fashioned moralizing and inefficient policy in its stead.
Just as the COS never seriously acknowledged Fabian determination to
install qualified social workers in the state, so the Fabians ignored COS
determination to achieve a similar end through organized voluntarism.
Hence, any analysis of these alternative approaches to social welfare must
look beneath programmatic differences, and query basic assumptions.

Although I have already suggested that the Webbs were heirs to Edwin
Chadwick's long-suppressed technocratic interventionism, it is important to
recognize that the Fabians envisioned themselves within a much broader
historical narrative. In contrast to Bernard Bosanquet's evolutionary cosmology, attendant on the "personal struggle for existence," Fabian evolution was
forwarded by "blind social forces," and staged at the mass level of societies
and nations. Writing in 1889, Sidney Webb credited Comte, Darwin, and
Spencer with demonstrating the perpetual "dynamism" of civilization. The
ideal of socialism, he argued, is immanent in late-nineteenth-century developments, but it is not the end of history.[48] Be that as it may, Webb's quite
specific present-day purpose was to account for and justify collectivist measures that a previous generation of liberals (including Spencer) had repudiated. With this polemic in mind, Webb narrated a history of "irresistible
progress." Just as feudalism was dissolved by the laissez-faire tenets of the
industrial revolution, so this "creed of Murdstones and Gradgrinds" would
be superceded as a matter of course. Individualism, with its undesirable tendency to produce anarchy and atomism, must be and, in fact, *already was*,
displaced by a new "intellectual and moral revolt."[49]

Webb traced the decline of individualism in a panoramic sweep including
references to the Romantic poets, as well as Thomas Carlyle, Charles
Dickens, and, of course, John Stuart Mill, whose gradual shift from laissez-
faire political economy to collectivism represented a veritable microcosm of
evolutionary forces at work.[50] Yet so far from exalting these proto-socialist
heroes, Webb's ultimate purpose was to subordinate their efforts to the determination of supra-individual forces. In a passage that elucidates the cardinal
differences between COS and Fabian philosophies, Webb conceded that the

"Zeitgeist" cannot itself "pass Acts of Parliament," or "erect municipal libraries":

> Though our decisions are moulded by the circumstances of the time, and the environment at least roughhews our ends, shape them as we will; yet each generation decides for itself. It still rests with the individual to resist or promote the social evolution, consciously or unconsciously, according to his character and information. The importance of complete consciousness of the social tendencies of the age lies in the fact that its existence and comprehensiveness often determine the expediency of our particular action: *we move with less resistance with the stream than against it* [emphasis added].[51]

Here Webb offered a bare minimum of free will. Individuals retained the power either to promote or resist progress; to render their actions expeditious or obstructive. Unsurprisingly, Webb's strategy was not to insist on the importance of such negligible advocacy, but to win support by very different means. Webb's far more controversial premise was that socialism was already a fait accompli: immanent in the era's large-scale municipal projects, and in the expanded purview of state and local government. "Such is the irresistible sweep of social tendencies," argued Webb, that the most ardent liberals have worked *unconsciously* "to bring about the very Socialism they despised."[52] Thus Webb solicited support for Fabianism, not because civilization's progress depended on active mind and will, but because skepticism in a universe determined by larger forces was all but meaningless.[53]

Interestingly, the Webbs' Chadwick-like environmental determinism most clearly emerged when they attempted to prove that they did not, as their critics alleged, ignore "personal character."[54] After acknowledging the great extent to which indigence is caused by "personal defects," the Webbs proceeded to connect these defects to a prior combination of infant neglect, disability, and unemployment. Of course, this broad line of reasoning translated individual character from the *cause* of pauperism, into the *effect* of theoretically preventable circumstances.[55] From there the Webbs were situated to invoke their corporatist notion of joint responsibility, an "indissoluble partnership" between the individual and the community. In this Fabian version of the social contract, liberalism's hallowed boundary between civil society and government entirely evaporated, as "new and enlarged obligations," "unknown in a state of *laisser faire*," were imposed on individuals.[56]

In essence, what the Webbs proposed was a preventive as well as curative pastorship, enjoining individuals either to measure up to minimum standards or submit themselves to the state's vigorous tutelage. As historians have often noted, this turn-of-the-century Fabianism had more to do with rationalizing social welfare than implementing socialism.[57] Needless to say, the Webbs' deterministic stance implicitly dismissed Idealism's stress on character as a potentially autonomous force. Rejecting charity's inefficiency, the Webbs detailed a totalizing disciplinary program. Assuming that character may, when necessary, be engineered through timely intervention, the Webbs urged preventive strategies too invasive for all but the most zealous enthusiasts of efficiency.[58]

NEW LIBERALISM

> While the problem of 1834 was the problem of *pauperism*, the problem of 1893 is the problem of *poverty* [emphasis added]; that a man ought not to be allowed to live in a bad home, that extreme poverty ought to be regarded, not indeed as a crime, but as a thing so detrimental to the State that it should not be endured.
>
> *Alfred Marshall, testimony before the Royal Commission on the Aged Poor (1893)*

> Parallel with this progressive nationalization or municipalization of industry, there has gone on the elimination of the purely personal element in business management. . . . [N]ow every conceivable industry, down to baking and milk-selling, is successfully managed by the salaried officers of large corporations of idle shareholders. More than one-third of the whole business of England, measured by the capital employed, is now done by joint stock companies, whose shareholders could be expropriated by the community with no more dislocation of the industries carried on by them than is caused by the daily purchase of shares on the Stock Exchange
>
> *Sidney Webb, "Historic" (1889)*

> If I had to sum up the immediate future of democratic politics in a single word I should say "Insurance." That is the future.
>
> *Winston Churchill, "The Budget and National Insurance" (1909)*

The 1905–1909 Royal Commission's failure to produce *any* legislative response remains "one of the major mysteries of Edwardian political history."[59] What is nonetheless clear is that the Minority Report—much like Chadwick's Sanitary Report of yore—was simply too un-English to win popular confidence. L. T. Hobhouse exemplified the kind of core liberal resistance that helped to defeat Fabian technocracy. Challenging the era's cult of expertise, Hobhouse may have subtly alluded to the fall of the Sanitary Idea when he reprobated those who believe "that the art of governing

men is as mechanical a matter as that of laying drain-pipes."[60] Yet if Britons
recoiled from Fabian plans to engineer character through state pastorship,
they simultaneously expressed ambivalence toward the Majority's proposal
to build character through the combined efforts of deterrent laws and organized voluntarism. Clearly, Alfred Marshall, Cambridge professor of political economy (and disciple of John Stuart Mill), had enunciated a growing
perception when he distinguished between the blamable *"pauperism"* of
1834 and the compassionable *"poverty"* of 1893 (see epigraph for this section). By the same token, Marshall's remarks suggest the extent to which
Britain's liberal mythology had been damaged since the fin de siècle.

In retrospect it is clear that the nation's liberal constitutional consensus
had depended on an unquestioned correlation between the self-originating
force of character and material prosperity. Britain's declining world-standing
weakened this foundational myth. Thus, Marshall's new politico-economic
construction of the impoverished masses reflected the growing perception of
individual powerlessness and the increasing sway of environmentalism. Marshall pronounced a subtle but decided shift from the morally culpable universe of 1834 (wherein "pauperism" signaled defective character), to the
morally neutral universe of 1893 (wherein "poverty" was determined by
social forces beyond the individual's control). Like the Fabians, in other
words, Marshall located individuals in an environment dominated by impersonal forces, a condition of impotence from which only the state's intervention might rescue them.

To counter this anathematic political economy, C. S. Loch returned to the
logic of the early nineteenth century, arguing that nonstigmatic provision for
the relief of poverty would, like the Old Poor Law of yore, "weaken moral
obligations."[61] More than a decade later, the Majority Report, which he
signed, insisted that "[t]he causes of distress are not only economic and
industrial; in their origin and character they are largely moral."[62] Britons
raised to believe that "Heaven helps those who help themselves," may well
have felt a powerful predisposition to favor such arguments. To be sure, few
of them were likely to join Sidney Webb in rejoicing at the prospect of the
vanishing "personal element" in business or in any other aspect of everyday
life. Nevertheless, the material prosperity and global dominion on which
moral claims like Loch's had once securely rested had visibly deteriorated.
While fantastic fictions such as Bram Stoker's *Dracula* (1897) and H. G.
Wells's *War of the Worlds* (1898) dramatized Britain's vulnerability to foreign invasion, realist novels such as George Gissing's *The Nether World*
(1889) implied the irrecuperability of Smiles's mythic character, at once a
self-generating force and a secure moral foundation.[63] Given these uncertain-
ties, the COS's vision of corporate voluntarism could not but appear to offer
Idealist abstractions when what was wanted were practical programs to
improve national efficiency and ensure national security.

Here in other words, in the widening gulf between unrealizable moral ideal and ominous material reality was a mandate for the invention and mass-production of a new turn-of-the-century tradition: the revamped liberalism of Winston Churchill and David Lloyd George.[64] Churchill's Edwardian speeches were a rhetorical triumph, playing off Fabian and COS antitheses in order to evoke buoyant New Liberal syntheses. Speaking in 1906, Churchill married liberalism to socialism, vowing simultaneously to preserve the "vigour of competition" and "to mitigate the consequences of failure." Civilization, he argued in Bosanquet's evolutionary vein, depends upon "competitive selection." But, he insisted, that is no reason to object to the Liberal Party's provision of (politically popular) old-age pensions. Such measures would not interfere with self-reliance but merely "strap a lifebelt around" the laborer, the "buoyancy" of which, "aiding his own strenuous exertions, ought to enable him to reach the shore."[65]

Old-age pensions and school meals were the means by which New Liberalism proposed "to spread a net over the abyss" without hazard to Britain's mythic entrepreneurial spirit.[66] Nevertheless, the centerpiece of what was "new" in this reconstructed liberalism was the (German-originated) notion of national insurance: a social security measure rhetorically amplified to suggest a quasi-collectivist foundation for national progress. The landmark National Insurance Act of 1911 was not a compromise between the two rival Poor Law Reports, but a maneuver, in the words of one contemporary, to "render . . . both unnecessary."[67] Offering guaranteed unemployment benefits in exchange for workers' compulsory contributions, the Act was not, as it might seem, a "half-way house to socialism," but rather a bulwark for private property. By providing nonstigmatic support for the unemployed, the Act established a minimal basis for national efficiency.[68] It thus appeared to obviate Fabianism's pastoral state, and even radical socialist demands for the collectivization of wealth. Yet, for the very same reason, the Act "cut the ground" from beneath the COS's call for stiffened deterrence and rigorous self-reliance. Indeed, both Lloyd George and Churchill argued that the notion of "undeserving poor" was irrelevant to the premise of "universal entitlement earned by contributions." Churchill in particular declared himself unwilling to mix up "moralities and mathematics"—a point to which I will return.[69]

Historians sometimes attribute the Liberals' preference for National Insurance to Lloyd George's opportunism and political savvy. Be that as it may, the conflicts I have described were the underlying context for that calculated move. The politics of the day pitted individual liberty against social equality, self-help against national efficiency. Yet, as Marshall's remarks suggest, many leading authorities saw formal collectivism of some kind as the only viable means to countering the individual powerlessness of a mass commercial society. Edwardian policymakers were thus charged simultaneously to promote prosperity and preserve character when, in fact, the integrity of the latter had long been questionable. Precisely because they proposed a cure for something ailing, both of the Commission's Reports betrayed the vulnerable condition of the Victorian era's most hallowed myth.

By contrast, New Liberal rhetoric might pay lip service to character without constituting it as a direct object of state action. Rather than officious pastorship in any form, New Liberalism offered a comparatively unobtrusive link between the individual and the state—much like the early-Victorian ideal of strong but disinterested government. Indeed, Churchill might have said "Whig" when, in 1909, while campaigning on an Insurance platform, he defined a Liberal as "a man who . . . stand[s] as a restraining force against . . . extravagant policy."[70] If National Insurance lacked the paternalistic embrace of Fabian technocracy or COS casework, it did not pry, visibly coerce, or moralize. Not the dawn of a new philosophy, but a restrained approach to the play of contrary extravagances was the significance of the measure.[71]

"A man of his day" like George Gissing's Jasper Milvain, Lloyd George may well have seized upon the New Liberal agenda at least partly for political gain. In so doing, he penetrated the logic of liberalism as elucidated by the later essays of Michel Foucault. In opting for National Insurance's balanced check between voluntarism and compulsion, Lloyd George recognized "that if one governed too much, one did not govern at all." Like Foucault's revised theory of power, New Liberalism encouraged social welfare comparatively indirectly: neither as tutelary state nor as personal benefactor but as "a mode of action upon the action of others."[72]

Campaigning in 1908, Winston Churchill argued that "Socialism assails the maximum pre-eminence of the individual," whereas New Liberalism "seeks to build up the minimum standard of the masses."[73] In the slippage between the individual preeminence that socialism putatively destroys, and the standardized mass that liberalism explicitly promotes, John Stuart Mill's 1836 analysis of modernity—in which power passes from individuals to masses—became the policy of Edwardian government.[74] The turn-of-the-century rhetoric of insurance was, in this respect, fundamentally unlike the Victorian rhetoric of self-generating character.[75] Nevertheless, in distinguishing between morality (the subject of personal relations in civil society) and mathematics (the properly impersonal object of state initiative), Churchill created the basis for a *new* liberal mythology without necessarily dismantling the old:

The wonderful century which followed the . . . downfall of the Napoleonic domination, which secured to this small island so long and so resplendent a reign, has come to an end. We have arrived at a new time. Let us realise it. And with that new time strange methods, huge forces, larger combinations—a Titanic

world—have sprung up around us. The foundations of our power are changing.
. . . We must go forward. . . . We will go forward into a way of life more
earnestly viewed, more scientifically organised, more consciously national than
any we have known.[76]

The progressive "way of life" to which Churchill pointed was predicated on
insurance: "Insurance against dangers from abroad, Insurance against dangers scarcely less grave and much more near."[77] By thus taking full advantage of the word's rhetorical force, Churchill invented a foundation to
replace (at least for a time) the flagging symbolic power of character in a
world of "combined forces." An invented tradition in an age of mass politics, insurance was conspicuously national and morally neutral. In this form
it promised to protect workers against fatalities beyond their control without
impinging upon liberties that were the hallowed birthright of every Briton.[78]
     Nevertheless, if Churchill's "Titanic world" seems to anticipate a more
ambitious "organisation" than that afforded by a modest unemployment benefit, that is probably because he privately recognized that a "tremendous
policy in Social Organisation" might eventually be built under the New Liberal banner.[79] Lloyd George's pre-1914 measures were but the rudiments of
an efficiency state that, prior to the war, cautious and self-reliant Britons
remained reluctant to endorse. Although the New Liberal agenda consigned
the Poor Law to gradual desuetude, insurance did not even profess to provide intrusive state pastorship.[80] Britain's eventual readiness to authorize an
institutional basis for social management—in essence, the close of a liberal
era based on the putative self-reliance of individuals—did not, by and large,
develop until after the debacle of another World War. The welfare state that
emerged, a triumph of social policy over socialism, owed much to the governing-class visiting practice that originated with Thomas Chalmers and
climaxed in the Charity Organization Society. In particular, the protosociological charity work of women such as Helen Bosanquet and Beatrice Webb
facilitated the momentous transition from a moral pastorship predicated on
the symbolic capital of the *personal* to a modern pastorship predicated
on the symbolic capital of the *professional*.

NOTES

This essay was supported by a grant from the Walter Chapin Simpson Humanities
Center at the University of Washington and by a University of Washington President's Junior Faculty Fellowship. A shorter version was presented at the Northeast
Victorian Studies Association conference on "Victorian Breakdowns" in April 2000.
George Behlmer, Kathleen Blake, Marshall Brown, and John Toews were kind
enough to provide comments on an early draft. Thanks are also owing to Tim Dean,

Tabitha Sparks, and Mark Sammons. I am especially indebted to Amanda Anderson and Joseph Valente for their superb editorial advice.

The passage from *The Encyclopedia of Social Reform* is cited in Stefan Collini, *Liberalism and Sociology: L. T. Hobhouse and English Political Argument, 1880–1914* (Cambridge: Cambridge University Press, 1979), 49, n. 124.

1. Samuel Smiles, *Character* (1859, reprint, New York: A. L. Burt, n.d.), 27–28. Here and throughout this essay, my sense of liberalism is that of a cumulative and multifaceted national mythology, a comprehensive worldview, rather than a narrow political agenda. What historians have described as the liberal constitutional "consensus" was consolidated in the mid-Victorian period and withstood the late-Victorian and Edwardian pressures I describe later. See Geoffrey Searle, *The Quest for National Efficiency* (Oxford: Oxford University Press, 1971), 15–16; and José Harris, "Society and the State in Twentieth-Century Britain," in *The Cambridge Social History of Britain, 1750–1950*, vol. 3, *Social Agencies and Institutions*, ed. F.M.L. Thompson (Cambridge: Cambridge University Press, 1990), 68.

2. José Harris, "Society and the State," 68. According to F. K. Prochaska, throughout the Victorian period nearly twice as many paid workers were employed by charitable organizations as were employed by the Poor Law. As late as 1911, the gross annual receipts of registered charities (excluding self-help organizations such as friendly societies) exceeded Poor Law expenditures; see Prochaska, "Philanthropy," in *The Cambridge Social History of Britain*, 3:384–85. See also George K. Behlmer, *Friends of the Family: The English Home and Its Guardians, 1850–1940* (Stanford: Stanford University Press, 1998), especially 31–73; Anne Summers, "A Home from Home: Women's Philanthropic Work in the Nineteenth Century," in *Fit Work for Women*, ed. Sandra Burman (London: Croom Helm, 1979), 33–63; and Simon Gunn, "The Ministry, the Middle Class and the 'Civilizing Mission' in Manchester, 1850–80," *Social History* 21, no. 1 (January 1996): 22–36.

3. Cited in Derek Fraser, *The Evolution of the British Welfare State,* 2nd ed. (London: Macmillan, 1984), 268. On the failure of Chadwick's sanitary reforms, see Anthony Brundage, *England's "Prussian Minister": Edwin Chadwick and the Politics of Government Growth, 1832–1854* (University Park: Penn State University Press, 1988), 79–156. On the subsequent retreat from Benthamism, see Searle, *Quest for National Efficiency*, 16; Jonathan Parry, *The Rise and Fall of Liberal Government in Victorian Britain* (New Haven: Yale University Press, 1993), 114; and José Harris, *Private Lives, Public Spirit: Britain, 1870–1914* (Harmondsworth: Penguin, 1993), 18.

4. The notion of "pastorship" as the means by which a society governs its citizens, both inside and out of formal state mechanisms, is developed in Foucault's late thinking on governmentality, especially in "The Subject and Power," in *Michel Foucault: Beyond Structuralism and Hermeneutics,* ed. Herbert L. Dreyfus and Paul Rabinow (Chicago: University of Chicago Press, 1983), 208–26. See also Colin Gordon, "The Soul of the Citizen: Max Weber and Michel Foucault on Rationality and Government," in *Max Weber, Rationality and Modernity*, ed. Sam Whimster and Scott Lash (London: Allen and Unwin, 1987), 297; and Foucault, "Governmentality" in *The Foucault Effect: Studies in Governmentality*, ed. Graham Burchell, Colin Gordon, and Peter Miller (Chicago: University of Chicago Press, 1991), 87–104. Although Foucault never completed a revised model as such, the essays on governmentality clearly aim to provide alternatives to the objectivizing disciplinary paradigm articu-

lated in *Discipline and Punish: The Birth of the Prison,* trans. Alan Sheridan (New York: Vintage, 1979). Nevertheless, the present essay does not profess to provide an orthodox Foucauldian account of any kind.

5. Stefan Collini describes Idealism as the dominant philosophy of late-Victorian and Edwardian Britain, a philosophy characterized by thoroughgoing rejection of empiricism in favor of Kantian and Hegelian metaphysics. See his "Sociology and Idealism in Britain, 1880–1920," *Archives Européenes de Sociologie* 19, no. 1 (1978): 4. Compare with Sandra M. den Otter, *British Idealism and Social Explanation: A Study in Late-Victorian Thought* (Oxford: Clarendon, 1996), 1.

6. See Harris, "Society and the State," 63.

7. Bernard Bosanquet develops this point from an evolutionist standpoint in "Socialism and Natural Selection," in *Aspects of the Social Problem,* ed. Bernard Bosanquet (1895; reprint, New York: Kraus, 1968), 303–304. The New Poor Law attempted to impose uniformity and politico-economic rationality on Britain's 15,000 parishes in the matter of poor relief. Influenced by Edwin Chadwick, a disciple of Jeremy Bentham, the law proposed to deter pauperism by eliminating all but punitive and stigmatic assistance inside the workhouse. The history of the law's passage and uneven implementation is extremely complicated. For the Webbs' interesting account of variations in post–1834 Poor Law practice, see Sidney and Beatrice Webb, *English Poor Law Policy* (London: Longmans, 1910), 257–73. For a sample of modern scholarship on the subject, see Fraser, *British Welfare State,* 31–55; M. A. Crowther, *The Workhouse System, 1834–1929: The History of an English Social Institution* (Athens: University of Georgia Press, 1982); and Peter Wood, *Poverty and the Workhouse in Victorian Britain* (Phoenix Mill: Alan Sutton, 1991).

8. See Helen Dendy (later Bosanquet), "Meaning and Methods of True Charity," in *Aspects of the Social Problem,* 169–70. No less than six of the Commission's nineteen members were prominent COS members, including C. S. Loch, Octavia Hill, and Helen Bosanquet. Both Sidney Webb and Bernard Bosanquet published supportive arguments for, and were acknowledged exponents of, the Minority and Majority Reports respectively. Nevertheless, neither of the husbands was a formal member of the Royal Commission.

9. Harold Perkin has argued that Britons' allegiance to an entrepreneurial middle-class identity (such as that extolled by Smiles) was supplanted by a professional alternative (stressing meritorious service rather than capitalist competition); see his *Rise of Professional Society: England Since 1880* (London: Routledge, 1989). The COS offers an interesting addendum to Perkin's argument since, as I argue, they advanced proto-professional methods through entrepreneurial rhetoric. The Fabians, by contrast, perfectly illustrate the professional ideal at work, as Perkin himself argues (125).

10. Perry Anderson approached the question from a Marxist perspective in "Components of the National Culture," *New Left Review* 50 (1969): 1–57. Stefan Collini noted the "commonplace" in "Sociology and Idealism in Britain," tracing the observation back to the U.S. sociologist Talcott Parsons in 1937, (3, n. 1). Since that time, M. S. Hickox is among those scholars to reassess the question, "The Problem of Early English Sociology," *Sociological Review* 32, no. 1 (February 1984): 1–17. For additional sources and her own contribution to the debate, see chapter 3 in den Otter, *British Idealism.*

11. See, for example, the epigraph above, cited by den Otter from a published

address given by Beatrice Webb to the London Sociological Society. As though to disqualify Idealist philosophy, Webb went on to argue (in den Otter's paraphrase) that "sociology is about observation and experience, not about ends and purposes" (den Otter, *British Idealism*, 136).

12. In the 1920s, while credentialed sociologists proliferated in Continental and North American universities, L. T. Hobhouse, a respected but out-of-date figure, was Britain's *only* professor of sociology; see Collini, *Liberalism and Sociology*, 248–49.

13. See Charles L. Mowat, *The Charity Organization Society, 1869–1913: Its Ideas and Work* (London: Methuen, 1961), 72, 112–13. C. S. Loch, Secretary of the COS from 1875 to 1913, held an academic post in economics and statistics. It was Loch who wrote the entry on "sociology" for the eleventh edition of the *Encyclopedia Britannica*; see Mowat, *The Charity Organization Society*, 65, 71. See also Collini, "Sociology and Idealism in Britain," 23–24; and T. S. Simey, "The Contribution of Sidney and Beatrice Webb to Sociology," *British Journal of Sociology* 12, no. 2 (June 1961): 106.

14. Collini, "Sociology and Idealism in Britain," 44, 45, n. 128. On sociology's multiple meanings see den Otter: "Political science, economics, social philosophy, social surveys, social work, psychology, and sociology spilled into each other" during this period (*British Idealism*, 121; see also 123–24).

15. Another and prior positivist influence in sociology was Auguste Comte, the Frenchman who had invented the term. Spencer's and Comte's theories shared much in common but differed dramatically on the role of the state. On Comte's influence over British ideas, see den Otter, *British Idealism*, 124–27.

16. Hickox, "Problem of Early English Sociology," 2.

17. See Fraser, *British Welfare State*, especially 135–36.

18. See Simey, "Contribution of Sidney and Beatrice Webb," 106.

19. Mowat, *The Charity Organization Society*, 10. Compare with A. F. Young and E. T. Ashton, *British Social Work in the Nineteenth Century* (London: Routledge, 1956), 70–71, 74–75.

20. Cited in Young and Ashton, *British Social Work*, 78.

21. See Simey, "Contribution of Sidney and Beatrice Webb," 120.

22. Beatrice Webb, *My Apprenticeship* (London: Longmans, 1926), 199.

23. Cited in Fraser, *British Welfare State*, 268.

24. On the postmodern representational characteristics of late-Victorian society, see Regenia Gagnier, *Idylls of the Marketplace: Oscar Wilde and the Victorian Public* (Stanford: Stanford University Press, 1986), 9–10. On the rise of party discipline, see R.H.S. Crossman's introduction to Walter Bagehot, *The English Constitution* (Ithaca: Cornell University Press, 1963), 1–57. On the eventual demise of the Liberal Party, see Perkin, *Rise of Professional Society*, 40–53, 100–101.

25. Harris, *Private Lives*, 19–20. On the accelerated rise of the late-Victorian professional middle classes, see Perkin, *Rise of Professional Society*, especially 26–61.

26. See Searle, *Quest for National Efficiency*, especially chapters 1 and 3. On the growing awareness of poverty, see Fraser, *British Welfare State*, 132–45 and Perkin, *Rise of Professional Society*, 166–67.

27. Searle is citing a 1905 lecture by J. L. Garvin (*Quest for National Efficiency*, 97).

28. Compare with Peter Nicholson, "The Reception and Early Reputation of Mill's Political Thought," in *The Cambridge Companion to Mill*, ed. John Skorupski (Cambridge: Cambridge University Press, 1998), 485–88.

29. Cited in Mowat, *The Charity Organization Society*, 72–73. Den Otter shows that Bosanquet's theory of the state was often misunderstood by traditional liberals. Bosanquet was strongly influenced both by the Kantian notion that "will, and not force, is the only legitimate basis" of a state, and by Hegel's view of *Sittlichkeit*, a moral community within civil society, including special emphasis on the family (see den Otter, *British Idealism*, 23, 30).

30. Bernard Bosanquet, "Character in Its Bearing on Social Causation," 113.

31. Dendy, "Meaning and Methods of True Charity," 171–79.

32. On Malthus and the strategic repression of laboring-class sexual desire, see Thomas Laqueur, "Sexual Desire and the Market Economy During the Industrial Revolution," in *Discourses of Sexuality: From Aristotle to AIDS*, ed. Donna C. Stanton (Ann Arbor: University of Michigan Press, 1992), 185–215.

33. See Bernard Bosanquet, "Socialism and Natural Selection," 289–307.

34. Bernard Bosanquet is cited in Sidney and Beatrice Webb, *English Poor Law Policy*, 280.

35. Cited in Sidney and Beatrice Webb, *English Poor Law Policy*, 280.

36. From the COS's 1895 *Annual Report*, cited by Mowat, *The Charity Organization Society*, 101. When a 1906 Act provided school meals the COS exhorted volunteers to carry out the state's new responsibilities. Otherwise, they warned, these functions "will be managed by officials, *and must almost inevitably lose most of the characteristics that will make them useful to society*" [emphasis added], cited in Mowat, *The Charity Organization Society*, 154–55.

37. 1895 *Annual Report*, cited in Mowat, *The Charity Organization Society*, 101.

38. COS casework was remarkably particularized: the Society might seek pensions for the "respectable" elderly, subsidize emigration, make loans, purchase clothes, apprentice children, acquire surgical boots for the handicapped, and so forth. See Mowat, *The Charity Organization Society*, 100.

39. Hill's 1869 inaugural address to the Society is cited in E. Moberly Bell, *Octavia Hill* (London: Constable, 1942), 108; and Nancy Boyd, *Josephine Butler, Octavia Hill, Florence Nightingale: Three Victorian Women Who Changed Their World* (London: Macmillan, 1982), 112.

40. Dendy, "Meanings and Methods," 301. Compare with epigraph at the beginning of this section.

41. Perkin illuminates the irony of the COS's unintentionally self-defeating strategy. The COS's scientific approach to charity, he explains, eventually led, "despite their dislike of state intervention, to the development of the professional, and eventually state-employed, social worker" (*Rise of Professional Society*, 124).

42. Mill challenged the liberal myth of autonomous individuality in works such as "Civilization" (1836) and *On Liberty* (1859). So far from a self-governing nation mobilized by Smiles's "energy of will," what Mill perceived was a superficial democracy in which individuals unwittingly ceded their liberties to mainstream norms. See "Civilization" and *On Liberty*, both in *Collected Works of John Stuart Mill*, vol. 18, *Essays on Politics and Society*, ed. J. M. Robson (Toronto: University of Toronto Press, 1977), 119–47, 213–310. I emphasize this aspect of Mill's legacy in my forthcoming book on Victorian literature and governance.

43. See Bernard Bosanquet, "The Duties of Citizenship," in *Aspects of the Social Problem*, 2–4.

44. Cited in Mowat, *The Charity Organization Society*, 81.

45. Bernard Bosanquet, "The Duties of Citizenship," 5–6.

46. See George K. Behlmer, "Character-Building and the English Family: Continuities in Social Casework, c. 1870–1930," in *Singular Continuities: Tradition, Nostalgia and Identity in Modern British Culture*, ed. George K. Behlmer and Fred Leventhal (Stanford: Stanford University Press, 2000), 63.

47. Cited in Beatrice and Sidney Webb, *English Poor Law Policy*, 280.

48. Sidney Webb, "Historic," in *Fabian Essays in Socialism*, ed. George Bernard Shaw (1889; reprint, Boston: Ball, 1911), 27–28.

49. Sidney Webb, "Historic," 28–40.

50. Ibid., especially 40–41.

51. Ibid., 44.

52. Ibid. The tendency to equate "collectivism" with "socialism" was not unique to the Fabians; see chapter 1 in Collini, *Liberalism and Sociology*, especially 17.

53. See also Raymond Williams, *Culture and Society, 1780–1950*, 2nd ed. (New York: Columbia, 1983), 181–85. According to William Morris, whom Williams cites, Webb "overestimate[s] the importance of the *mechanism* of a system of society apart from the *end* towards which it may be used" (183). Although Morris was not associated with the Idealists, his distinction between "mechanism" and "end" would have been familiar to the Bosanquets.

54. Sidney and Beatrice Webb, *English Poor Law Policy*, 304.

55. Ibid., 305.

56. Ibid., 270.

57. Perkin points out that the Fabians "were not motivated by the working-class ideal of a society based on egalitarian labour but by the professional ideal of an elitist society run by professional experts" (*Rise of Professional Society*, 130). See Searle on Beatrice Webb's desire to establish "minimum standards" to enable Britain to compete with the efficient Germans and Japanese (*Quest for National Efficiency*, 238).

58. According to Searle, "[T]he Minority Report brutally ignored all liberal susceptibilities" (*Quest for National Efficiency*, 241, compare to 242–43). The Report proposed that appropriate authorities not only treat "the neglected child, the sick wife, and the maltreated feeble-minded child," but that they also actively "search out" and prevent these cases of "incipient destitution" *before* they arise. Hence, "the drinking head of the family would . . . [be] called to book long before he found himself in the comfortable quarters of the workhouse." The Webbs also called for the "systematic prevention and cure" of chronic alcoholism and for the establishment of "detention colonies" for the treatment of the irremediably unemployable. See Sidney and Beatrice Webb, *English Poor Law Policy*, 306–307.

59. Searle, *Quest for National Efficiency*, 237. According to Fraser, "Never can so important a Royal Commission have produced so little in the way of immediate action." Even moderate measures, recommended by *both* the Majority and Minority, were not implemented for another twenty-five years (Fraser, *British Welfare State*, 161).

60. Hobhouse's comments were published in *Democracy and Reaction* (1904), cited in Searle, *Quest for National Efficiency*, 82.

61. C. S. Loch, "Some Controverted Points in the Administration of Poor Relief," in *Aspects of the Social Problem*, 244. Loch argued point by point with extracts from Marshall's articles in the March and September 1893 issues of the *Economic Journal*.

62. Cited in Fraser, *British Welfare State*, 160.

63. In a longer version of this essay, part of my forthcoming work on Victorian governance, I explore the connection between dueling social policies and contemporary literature.

64. On the notion of the "mass-generation of traditions" in Europe between 1870 and 1914, see Eric Hobsbawm, who defines them as "new devices to ensure or express social cohesion and identity and to structure social relations" ("Mass-Producing Traditions: Europe, 1870–1914," in *The Invention of Tradition*, ed. Eric Hobsbawm and Terence Ranger (Cambridge: Cambridge University Press, 1983), 263.

65. See Winston Spencer Churchill, "Liberalism and Socialism" (1906) and "Unemployment" (1908) published in *Liberalism and the Social Problem*, 2nd ed. (New York: Haskell, 1973), 82, 208, 210.

66. Churchill, "Liberalism and Socialism," 82–83.

67. Fraser, *British Welfare State*, 163. Searle, however, notes that Lloyd George did not, as the same contemporary put it, deliberately "dish the Webbs." Rather, National Insurance, modeled after a Bismarckian precedent, was more attractive than either of the Royal Commission's Reports (*Quest for National Efficiency*, 252–53).

68. Paul Thompson emphasizes that both the nationalized unemployment insurance of 1911 and the health insurance that followed in 1913 "helped those best able to help themselves." Sick women, children, and old people, as well as the typical unemployed casual worker remained dependent on poor relief. See Paul Thompson, *The Edwardians: The Remaking of British Society,* 2nd ed. (London: Routledge, 1992), 220. The working-class politician Keir Hardie described the measure as a refusal to "uproot the cause of poverty" and instead to give workers "a porous plaster to cover the disease that poverty causes" (cited in Fraser, *British Welfare State*, 164). The Webbs objected that "[i]t's criminal to take poor people's money and use it to insure them, if you take it you should give it to the Public Health Authority to prevent their being ill again" (cited in Fraser, 168). Compare with Collini, who argues that "it was . . . the peculiar achievement of New Liberalism" to undermine socialism's "intricate blend of moral and economic arguments from within" (*Liberalism and Sociology*, 26).

69. Cited by Fraser, *British Welfare State*, 162, 172; compare with Searle, *Quest for National Efficiency,* 253. Churchill's insistence that insurance be operated on "actuarial" rather than moral principles was not entirely antithetical to COS principles, since it was based on the COS-like premise that workers *earned* entitlements through contributions (the compulsory rather than voluntary nature of which the COS, of course, repudiated). In the end, Churchill was overruled and a compromise made: workers dismissed for misconduct were deprived of benefits but on actuarial rather than moral grounds (see Fraser, *British Welfare State*, 162, 172).

70. Winston Spencer Churchill, "The Budget and National Insurance," in *Liberalism and the Social Problem*, 303. On Churchill's temporary alliance with the Webbs and his abrupt shift to the New Liberal agenda, see Searle, *Quest for National Efficiency*, 248–56.

71. Compare with Harris, "Society and the State," 69–70.

72. Michael Foucault, "Space, Knowledge, and Power," in *The Foucault Reader,* ed. Paul Rabinow (New York: Pantheon, 1984), 242; see also Foucault, "The Subject and Power," in *Michel Foucault*, 220 –21.

73. Cited in Fraser, *British Welfare State*, 163.

74. See Mill, "Civilization," in *Collected Works*, 119–47.

75. That is not, however, to suggest that either the language of character or the Smilesean myth entirely disappeared at the fin de siècle; only that the particular exigencies of the prewar period required a different rhetorical ground. As I have elsewhere noted, contrasts between British and Continental character are a regular feature of the United Kingdom's contemporary Euro-politics and, as recently as 1996, Smiles's *Self-Help* was lauded in *The Observer* as a "lodestar" for the twenty-first century; see Lauren M. E. Goodlad "'A Middle Class Cut into Two': Historiography and Victorian National Character," *ELH* 67 (2000): 168.

76. Churchill, "The Budget and National Insurance," 317.

77. Ibid., 309.

78. Hobsbawm implies that mass-produced traditions in and of themselves supplied the "social cement" of mass societies, legitimating the social bonds and ties of authority that liberalism failed to provide. In this sense, the New Liberal insurance platform can be understood both as a tradition in Hobsbawm's sense as well as a specific social policy that, in effect, mandated working-class thrift ("Mass-Producing Traditions," 268–69).

79. Cited in Fraser, *British Welfare State*, 173.

80. See Searle, *Quest for National Efficiency*, 205. Behlmer writes that "at no time prior to the Second World War did English social casework offer anything resembling a coherent 'programme' for disciplining the working-class family" ("Character-Building," in *Singular Continuities*, 70).

CHAPTER 10

Victorian Continuities: Early British
Sociology and the Welfare of the State

SIMON JOYCE

IN THINKING about some of the ways that we might reflect back on the late-nineteenth century from the end of the twentieth, I am drawn to that familiar constellation of themes—about unemployment, crime, poverty, social pathology, and institutional responsibility—that surfaced in the 1880s, as well as to the forms of analysis and observation that attended them: journalistic exposés, ethnographic and statistical surveys, experiments and debates about the efficacy and limitations of charitable philanthropy. But having read and written about such mechanisms of late-Victorian self-analysis,[1] I am also aware of just how easy it is to critique their underlying assumptions, by now the academic equivalent of shooting fish in a barrel. Thus, I think it hardly extends or challenges our understanding of the period to uncover racist or social Darwinist attitudes at work in presentations of the poor; to castigate the new social sciences as naively in thrall to the perils of determinism, positivism, and empiricism; or to view their programmatic recommendations as woefully inadequate—which is simply another way of saying that the problems they addressed remain with us, and a good enough reason for studying them.

But if this might seem to go easy on the social sciences—by which I have in mind that broad alliance of sociology, psychology, ethnology, and the mass media that was brought to bear on the urban poor—then let me emphasize that each area (and more particularly the grounds of their interaction) is a valuable focus of study. It is just that the usual conclusions, which I have briefly elaborated here, seem depressingly predictable. Besides, I want to come at this from another angle, which seeks to make distinctions rather than tracing out some underlying mindset. Perhaps the most surprising of the continuities in my title is the state, which would seem to have developed and mutated beyond recognition in the past hundred years; nonetheless, I want to take it as a yardstick for analyzing the discourse on poverty in the 1880s and to see if and where policy suggestions and conclusions anticipate the modern welfare state, as opposed to more individual or voluntarist solutions.

This emphasis is in part strategic. As recently as 1994, Martin Wiener

remarked on the declining interest in the state on the part of Leftist as well
as conservative historians in Britain, echoing the political climate of the
Thatcher years: the state, he notes, was seen almost by consensus as paternalistic, manipulative, and coercive, and deemphasized in favor of private
initiative on the Right and forms of popular empowerment on the Left.[2]
These attacks have continued especially from the Right since that time,
deploying a particular view of the Victorian period that is well worth contesting; and the result is that the welfare state must be diagnosed as in critical condition at best. Summarizing recent policy debates in Britain, which
have been dominated by Prime Minister Tony Blair's vague pursuit of a
"Third Way" between or beyond socialism and free-market capitalism, Will
Hutton notes, for example, a new "politics of pessimism," within which
"[t]he best that the state can offer is to help people to better accommodate
themselves to a capitalist reality that is no longer to be shaped by public
action." "It is a philosophy," he concludes,

> that would never have permitted, for example, the launch of the National Health
> Service or even the establishment of the BBC; the best that could be offered in
> today's climate would be some mix of regulation and tax incentives to persuade
> the private sector to do part of the job, but only if it chose. The creation of new
> public institutions is off limits. But this is only part of a wider trend in which
> public action is regarded as self-defeating and necessarily inefficient.[3]

This self-limitation of public discourse is a depressing feature of modern
politics, at a time when a renewed debate about the possible forms and
functions of the state is urgently called for. Such a debate, which might
represent one possible site of intervention for a policy-oriented cultural
studies, is, however, hamstrung by a critical tendency to consider the state in
the abstract as an ahistorical, Orwellian nightmare acting on and against the
subject, and thus to elide the distinctions among its various forms—even as,
quite separate from academic practice, we know those distinctions to be
under debate and may find ourselves actively supporting a version of the
liberal state against conservative assaults. As David Norbrook has argued in
a forceful critique of literary studies under the influence of Foucault, "At a
time when there are powerful ideological pressures to see such institutions as
the British welfare state as part of a terroristic apparatus of total control, the
new historicist assault on the Benthamite panopticon of modernity has
equivocal political implications."[4]

This is not to suggest that the welfare state is beyond criticism: to defend
it against conservative attacks is something very different from giving total
support. In many respects, this apparent choice, which seems so often to
come down to an all-or-nothing proposition, can blind us to the history that I
want to trace out in this chapter—a history in which the ideal of a welfare
state system was itself developed in dialogue with a broader range of com-

peting positions, some of which can still find echoes in contemporary political discourse. In particular, a language of personal morality and responsibility had shadowed the welfare state from its inception, and has coexisted uneasily with a more value-neutral conception of cradle-to-grave support that would be available irrespective of circumstances. If the last decades of the nineteenth century mark the origins of the interventionist state, then it would seem useful to investigate the debates out of which it grew; to ask how a new liberal consensus on public policy helped to legitimate it, in part by drawing upon the emerging social sciences for support; and then to analyze some of the conditions and limits of the new political configuration that emerges in the early years of the twentieth century.

What is immediately striking in this respect is how much more frequently (and almost universally) analyses of late-Victorian poverty argue the necessity for central governmental action. The consolidation of power and decision making in a state bureaucracy, which has become the focal point of conservative criticism as well as a cliché of twentieth-century dystopias, was anticipated by welfare advocates more than a hundred years ago. Indeed, it was often precisely the facelessness of the machinery of welfare support that appealed to the architects of the modern state, who saw the main alternative line of thinking—the belief that individuals, charities, or the free market can cope—as wholly inadequate to the task at hand. If we consider the Utopian novels that appeared at the end of the nineteenth century, it is apparent that the society of the future was invariably imagined as one in which the government organizes all systems of commodity production, distribution, and the provision of services—the exception that proves the rule here being William Morris's *News from Nowhere* (1890), which sees this as only the transitional phase of "State Socialism" along the way to a decentralized society with devolved and consensual decision making.[5] When the Victorians imagined the future, it was almost always in the recognizable form of a centralized state, even if what came into being in this century was something less than even "State Socialism" as people like Morris or Edward Bellamy imagined it, and was limited by late-Victorian assumptions about government, the market, and the individual (as well as the range of possible interrelations among all three), which continue to set the horizon of policy debates and options.

THE STATE OF WELFARE:
VICTORIAN REFORMERS AND THE NEW RIGHT

These preliminary thoughts were derived from a reading of Gertrude Himmelfarb's *The De-Moralization of Society* (1994). This book is really the culmination of a series of studies of Victorian poverty and the moral imagination, in which Himmelfarb has increasingly sought to demonize the critical readings of the period produced by Left historians, and to lay out a political agenda that is captured in the subtitle of her book: "From Victorian Virtues to Modern Values."[6] Thus, in a bizarre final chapter that selectively maps rates of crime and illegitimacy in Victorian England and in the present day to trace out what she terms a "U-curve" of antisocial deviance, in which today comes to resemble, and even surpass, the bad old days of the early nineteenth century, she can argue not only for the supposed failures of the modern welfare state but also for a return to those Victorian virtues trumpeted by Margaret Thatcher and William Bennett.[7] The book has had a quite surprising impact on public policy, considering its historical focus. Speaking at the height of the Republican Contract with America in 1995, then House Speaker Newt Gingrich commented to the National League of Cities that the Victorians "changed the whole momentum of their society. They didn't do it through a new bureaucracy. They did it by re-establishing values, by moral leadership;" when asked if similar tactics might work for contemporary America, he replied, "Read Himmelfarb's book. It isn't that complicated."[8] In this essay, though, I am less concerned with identifying the political lineage of her argument or in explicating how it rewrites the nineteenth century as an endorsement of a neoconservative agenda (the war on drugs, the shift from welfare to workfare, "moral education" in the classroom),[9] than to emphasize what I take to be the silent center of the book: its implied critique of the welfare state.

Thatcher's celebration of Victorian values, which both opens and closes *The De-Moralization of Society*, is inseparable from her assaults on the welfare state as inefficient, intrusive, and essentially lacking in value—either in moral or economic terms, since it is also conceived as a bad bargain, especially when compared to the minimalist state of the Victorians.[10] For Himmelfarb, similarly, the welfare state is elided with socialism in general, perhaps to the surprise of those European liberals, social democrats, and even one-nation Tories who have supported it over the years: take, for example, the following passage on Toynbee Hall, in which the terminological slide is hard to miss:

> [T]he creation or implementation of a welfare state was not the intention of the founders of Toynbee Hall; nor was it the practical function of the hall in its early years. Although neither Toynbee nor [Samuel] Barnett had any aversion to social legislation in principle—they both advocated specific measures of reform—they were wary of anything resembling "continental socialism" (as Toynbee referred to Marxism) or "paternalistic socialism" (*De-Moralization*, 159).

The welfare state here gets confused with something it is considerably less than: the specter of socialism and Marxism against which it was developed in the first place. Meanwhile, what gets left unanswered is its implied connection to the general principle of social legislation, which it is surely more than.

As I shall argue in a moment, the founders of Toynbee Hall were not only not averse to government action to combat poverty, but actively advocated it; it is far less clear, though, that Himmelfarb herself favors it. She admits that the voluntary sector cannot entirely take the place of the welfare state, being better equipped (as were the mutual aid societies of the 1880s) for providing short-term relief than the equivalent of a living wage in periods of high unemployment;[11] and yet she also insists that state provision is counter-productive, encouraging a pathology of "welfare dependency" that the Victorians successfully discouraged by distinguishing (in Henry Mayhew's famous phrase) "those that will not work" from "those that cannot." In this, she reveals a surprising affinity for the thinking behind the 1834 New Poor Law, which aimed to replace the simple structure of the earlier Speenhamland System of relief—whereby public assistance made up any financial shortfall from a fixed minimum wage—with a more punitive version that sought to stigmatize those on public relief. Her influence on contemporary neoconservative "welfare reformers" begins to make sense, then, even if it is based on a tendentious misreading of the nineteenth century.

It is ultimately unclear whether the welfare state provides even a relative benefit for Himmelfarb, as it gets inextricably identified not only with socialism but also with the state itself as the source of secular relativism and site of the erosion of Victorian values—indeed, at the furthest limit with government in general.[12] There are, of course, a host of admirable values that are articulated by and through the welfare state, ranging from collective responsibility to the removal of the cash nexus from the provision of human services, but there is a more fundamental point here about the necessity of such services themselves that Himmelfarb consistently sidesteps. This is because she is caught between two polar images of the late-Victorian period: a rose-tinted one in which crime, violence, drunkenness, and illegitimacy are all on the decline; and a far gloomier one in which vast armies of private benefactors and charities are called upon to redress the social conditions we more typically associate with the period. Read together, it is as if this spirit of giving existed entirely outside of the conditions themselves, and was valuable in spite of its own frequent protestations of inadequacy. Indeed, it gets reified as a kind of Hegelian "time-spirit," linking up a range of social actors with widely divergent analyses of the period; thus, for the socialists in the Social Democratic Federation (SDF),

> it meant the rational, planned organization of the economy and society. For social workers (in the Charity Organisation Society) it meant the rational, planned organization of charity and relief. For settlement-house workers (in Toynbee Hall), it meant the education and edification of the working-classes. For social reformers (like Charles Booth or Seebohm Rowntree), it meant the systematic investigation and analysis of the different classes of the poor, their material and moral conditions, their problems and prospects of improvement (*De-Moralization*, 147).

But this unified "time-spirit" glosses over important differences. In fact, its components can be redrawn with the SDF at one pole of collective public provision and the COS, which tried to discourage "indiscriminate almsgiving" and instead organize charitable relief on the principles of political economy, at the other. My point is that we need to view this as a debate occurring among late-Victorian reformers and social scientists, instead of imagining an idealized past in which both positions—as well as incompatible views of the period—are able to coexist.

There was certainly no welfare consensus in the period, even though the general direction of public policy and public sentiment tended to lead away from those principles that Himmelfarb and others would like to see revived. In reality, the socialist analysis proved both more accurate and significant for developments that would follow, whereas that of the charity organizations proved to be ineffective for much the same reasons that Himmelfarb applauds it: because it insisted on treating poverty as a self-inflicted character issue that was best addressed either by highly selective relief or by the iron laws of the marketplace, and failed to see that the principles which underwrote the 1834 Poor Law were no longer sustainable. As the century progressed, and especially under the impact of economic recession in the 1870s and 80s, it became increasingly difficult to uphold the principle of "lesser eligibility" under which the able-bodied were considered less qualified for relief than the aged and ill, not to mention the draconian measures (including the separation of families, the institution of a minimal diet, and the requirement that workhouse inmates perform useless work) that followed on from it. While the U-curve of Himmelfarb's conclusion seeks to parallel the present with pre-Victorian England, thereby providing the basis for turning back the clock to a time of moral censure and the workhouse, the more significant continuity connects the present to the turn of the century when the terms of the modern welfare state were being worked out. As Gareth Stedman Jones has argued, the massive reforms of 1945 were not in any fundamental sense new, but instead "testified to a continuity of assumptions from the days of pre-1914 progressive liberal imperialism. Globally and nationally," he concludes, "the post-war Labour government was the last and most glorious flowering of late Victorian liberal philanthropy."[13]

From Charitable Philanthropy to State Provision

For Himmelfarb, the Victorian past has to be made to justify the assault on the welfare state in the name of private enterprise and charity, even when the evidence would seem to make the opposite case. Some of the ensuing confusion can be seen in her discussion of Charles Booth, who emerges from her book as an unlikely precursor of Thatcherism.[14] Booth began publishing his major work *Life and Labour of the People in London* in 1889, in order to present an exhaustive statistical analysis of poverty in the capital (divided into eight classes from A to H) and to define a more workable "poverty line" that pegged the criteria significantly higher than the subsistence level applied by the workhouse test of 1834. Originally undertaken in order to contest the provocative claim by H. M. Hyndman of the SDF that a quarter of Londoners lived under conditions of extreme poverty, Booth simultaneously challenged and confirmed this assessment. First, he found that only 7.5 percent of Londoners lived a hand-to-mouth existence—designated as class B—alongside a smaller hardcore of the vicious and criminal class A, of about 1 percent. With these findings, "[t]he hordes of barbarians of whom we have heard, who, issuing from their slums, will one day overwhelm modern civilization" were shown to be mythical.[15] But then, having rejected these more lurid prophecies, Booth proceeded to offer statistics that were in fact more troubling, with the calculation that the number below the poverty line creeps up above Hyndman's figure to around 31 percent when the number of irregular wage earners (classes C and D) is added.

It is hard, on this basis, to accept Himmelfarb's claim that Booth "refuted" charges of a "submerged tenth" of the population, made by, among others, General William Booth of the Salvation Army, whom she dismisses as "sensationalist."[16] Even less sustainable is her conclusion that the New Poor Law had substantially decreased levels of pauperdom and was in little need of reform, especially when reading passages like the following: "[I]n view of all the evidence to the contrary, it is not too fanciful to suppose that the alarm about physical and moral deterioration was itself a reflection of the rise in aims and expectations among the people as a whole and more especially among social commentators" (*De-Moralization*, 44). This strikes me as the mirror inverse of the vulgar Foucauldian criticism highlighted by David Norbrook, which can find the evils of panoptic surveillance hiding beneath the most innocuous forms of Enlightenment rationality; here instead, the recognition of social dysfunction is adduced as testimony that happy days are here again. Interestingly, Booth himself cautioned against such a position as a possible "bias" for his studies, and tried in particular to avoid the moralizing tone which held "that the poor are often really better off than they appear to be" when their lives are considered in terms of real needs rather than "extravagances."[17]

Reading Booth admittedly can be frustrating, because he can be made to line up with so many of the strands of early British sociology, which I shall discuss later in this essay. He was, for example, reluctant to abandon the moral principle underwriting the 1834 measure, even though his research and testimony before the Royal Commission on the Poor Law and the Relief of Distress helped bring about its decisive modification; like a good ameliorist, he believed in the category of character as a decisive factor in human development, and shared the suspicions against indiscriminate almsgiving, which drove the COS and other welfare reformers of the period. Sometimes he can read like a typical Victorian moralist, backed with a Darwinian theory of natural selection, and working back from prior assumptions to empirical evidence; at others, like a rigid statistician who refuses to privilege theory over facts, and who suspected that his studies proliferated at such length due to his own failure to reach any definitive conclusions. We can see each of these tendencies represented in the conclusion to Booth's final volume, with its opening invocation of "the dark side of the picture" in which lives are "cursed by drink, brutality, and vice, and loaded down with ignorance and poverty," which both religion and administrations have been incapable of ameliorating. Booth outlines twin aims—both "to raise the general level of existence" and also "to increase the proportion of those who know how to use aright the means they have"—before seeming to privilege "Individual Responsibility" as the key factor in improvement; but the stress immediately shifts away from the particular and toward the most generalized efforts of governmental administration, in support of which "facts are still needed." Somewhat defensively, and in the guise of the pure statistician, he closes by commenting,

> I have sought, however imperfectly, to show what is being done to ameliorate [poverty's] conditions, and have suggested some directions in which advance might be made; but this last was no part of the original design, which was, solely, to observe and chronicle the actual, leaving remedies to others. To this attitude I would now revert. For the treatment of disease, it is first necessary to establish the facts of its character, extent and symptoms.[18]

It is as if Booth is consciously backtracking from even the modest solutions he has proposed, while also acknowledging that the form of the inquiry itself has led him to propose them. In doing so, I would argue, he also undercut the emphases on moral character and personal responsibility with which he began.

We might also consider his decision to focus on the street rather than the family as the unit of analysis, or his progressive extrapolation of larger social patterns from more limited empirical evidence: the basis for his break-down of poverty ultimately rests, for example, on the reports of sixty-six School Board visitors in East London, on the assumption of consistent ratios of married men with and without children of school age in particular occupations, and of proportionate numbers of older and younger children, and that each of these calculations will hold for the rest of the population. The resulting sense of scale is a deliberate choice on Booth's part, on the principle that "the facts should be reduced to some common measure of validity by being passed, as it were, through a sieve which should make it possible not only to reject the false and hold back the improbable, but also to tone down exaggeration" by relying "first and chiefly on mere average and consensus resulting from the great number and variety of my source of information."[19] In this sense, the sheer size of these studies—magnified street-by-street and borough-by-borough—militated against a moral reading of poverty, which usually worked in collusion with more localized philanthropic efforts, and it is also understandable that Booth was increasingly drawn to the analysis of large-scale factors in the internal structure of the professions themselves as the key indicators of poverty, and to an impersonal bureaucracy as the best solution to social problems that resisted face-to-face solutions. While still maintaining that lack of employment and personal habit were both contributing factors in the causation of poverty, he consistently endorsed governmental action at the expense of individual initiatives or religious efforts, suggesting that for the eradication of structural problems in society, "voluntary effort is almost useless, for unless the inquiries spring from genuine energy of administration grounded in goodwill, no benefit can result." At best, he argued, voluntary associations might draw attention to their existence.[20]

Booth's poverty line is another important element distinguishing his studies either from those of Mayhew forty years earlier or from the thinking of the New Poor Law, both of which obsess in different ways over persons in extreme poverty. Booth is by contrast—and surprisingly, given the prevailing discourses of the time—relatively uninterested in what was then being termed "the residuum" or underclass.[21] If this is the category that gives force to the Poor Law, by providing the baseline against which the eligibility of others would be tested and also embodying the shameful stigma of irresponsible dependency, then Booth is mainly concerned to take it out of the equation for economic reasons. In order to safeguard persons in the immediate proximity of the underclass and thus at risk—that more sizable group of irregular wage earners—he proposed that those in category B poverty (casual earners, "the very poor") be removed from the job market and placed "under State regulation." Although still allowed to live in families, they would not compete for scarce jobs and be allowed to earn lower wage rates in the process; instead, they would be trained and encouraged to build their own dwellings, cultivate the land, make clothes and furniture, using materials provided by the state at a considerable public expense, which would necessarily exceed the going rates of pay for their work. It is a program Booth referred to as "limited Socialism," with an acute awareness of its potential unpopularity as well as the possible benefits: the ability to focus attention more closely on the hardened criminals of class A, the opening up of new opportunities and greater pay for those struggling in C and D, and the chance to improve and uplift those in B. The scheme seems abhorrent until we contrast it with one that was simultaneously proposed (but also never implemented, despite widespread support) by the Salvation Army, which would resettle "the residuum" first in farm colonies outside of the city before transporting them abroad to oversee colonial plantations.[22] My point is not, in any case, to defend Booth here, but to stress that he viewed poverty as primarily an environmental problem, which needed to be redressed through state intervention, and not a moral one that could be handled by the private sector. Repeatedly in *Life and Labour*, he advocated governmental involvement in industry and job creation, the extension of public education, and the state provision of old-age pensions.

I would argue that all of this places Booth closer to prevailing opinion than Himmelfarb might allow. The critique of almsgiving set out by the COS and others, for example, also took the intermittent laborer as its touchstone: according to Whitechapel clergyman Brooke Lambert, for example, such a figure is pauperized by charity, and "becomes in nine cases out of ten, a whining supplicant, ready to cringe for all he can get."[23] This demoralization thesis echoed the principle of "lesser eligibility" earlier in the century, and was a key component of both evangelical and liberal approaches, but where the former favored a combination of local action and Benthamite financial orthodoxy, the latter were increasingly pointing to the need for far-reaching economic intervention. One of the more influential exposés of poverty that acted as another spur to Booth's study, Andrew Mearns' *The Bitter Cry of Outcast London* (1883), argued for an environmental rather than a moral etiology for the recent upsurge in crime, saying that "[t]here can be no question that numbers of hardened criminals would never have become such, had they not by force of circumstances been packed together in these slums with those who were hardened in crime."[24] That same year, *How the Poor Live* by George Sims closed with a chapter entitled "Legislation Wanted, Not Almsgiving," which praised the 1870 Education Act and concluded, "I have been grievously misunderstood if anything I have said has led to the belief that all Englishmen have to do to help the denizens of the slums and alleys is to put their hands in and pull out a sovereign or a shilling."[25]

In all of these ways, the late-Victorian discourse on poverty offered up a critique of forms of private charity, at the same time that it was also eroding the framework of the New Poor Law. The Liberal (and later Unionist) politician Joseph Chamberlain first set out a revised rationale in a circular of 1886, which argued that relief should be granted to the able-bodied during periods of deep recession, in the form of "work which will not involve the stigma of pauperism," as was the case for stone-breaking or oakum-picking under the earlier system.[26] In doing so, he placed the responsibility for unemployment with society rather than the individual, thereby charging the authorities with the task of understanding local and national economic trends; indeed, the 1905 Unemployed Workmen Act, which grew out of the Chamberlain Circular, specifically mandated that local distress committees "shall make themselves acquainted with the conditions of labor in their area" as a basis for judging applications for relief, with the understanding that unemployment was often beyond the control of the unemployed themselves.[27] During the first decade of this century, other measures protecting children and the elderly, and mandating school meals and workers' insurance all similarly undermined the basic principle of the Poor Law, and effectively prepared the ground for the modern welfare state.

The Settlement Movement, Sociology, and the New Liberalism

It is telling to note that many of the architects of the British welfare state were themselves the products of an alternative tradition of private charity work that modern neoconservatives would like to see supplanting or supplementing welfare. Himmelfarb's endorsement of Toynbee Hall, for example, is preceded in her book by a passage from T. H. Green, who was a formative influence on the university settlement movement, in which he criticizes "paternal government" for narrowing the social spaces within which individuals are able to embody a personal morality "consisting in the disinterested performance of self-imposed duties."[28] Toynbee Hall and the larger movement that it represented are praised by Himmelfarb for giving Oxbridge undergraduates the opportunity to live and work in the poorest areas of London, and thus to demonstrate "a self-sacrificing, even self-abasing spirit, a belief that the 'privileged,' no less that the poor, had spiritual needs, that they had to 'give' . . . as much as the poor had to receive, and that what they had to give was of themselves."[29] But this neither gives the entire picture of Toynbee Hall nor a suggestion of its lasting importance, which consisted in the training of an entire generation of politicians and social legislators who would oversee the development of the twentieth-century welfare state: people like Hubert Llewellyn Smith, first head of the Labour Department at the Board of Trade; E. J. Urwick, director of the London School of Sociology (later the London School of Economics); Cyril Jackson, who served on the London County Council and advocated child welfare legislation; and especially William Beveridge, who piloted unemployment insurance and the first Labour Exchanges and would later provide the blueprints for the sweeping legislation enacted by the Labour government after 1945, through which the National Health Service, family allowance, and national insurance were introduced within that government's first year.

Philosophically, the influence of Green has to be set against that of Arnold Toynbee, who—in Standish Meacham's account of the history of the institution that shared his name—"pressed the case for state intervention further" than Green's limited conception of its possible use in developing bonds of community, arguing that "[w]here people are unable to provide a thing for themselves, and that thing is of *primary social importance* [Toynbee's emphasis] . . . the State should interfere and provide it for them."[30] If we see Samuel Barnett and Toynbee Hall as the products of these twin influences, then we might also analyze the institution's history as moving away from a mainly individualist focus on personal responsibility and face-to-face contact, and as recognizing in its place the increasing priority being granted to governmental action by Booth and growing sections of the Liberal Party. As Meacham notes, while Barnett began his work in Whitechapel in full accord with the principles of the COS, and continued to concentrate his own efforts locally, "he grew increasingly to believe that the problems of poverty and unemployment were not local problems, but ones demanding the attention and intervention of the state." The insistence on ascribing "at least a portion of the misery in East London to environment rather than to individual moral failing alone" brought him into increasing conflict with the COS throughout the 1890s, as did his support for proposals for the centralized provision of health, education, and welfare relief (including old-age pensions and unemployment benefits). Beveridge, who served as subwarden at Toynbee Hall from 1903 to 1905, extended Barnett's move away from the strict localism of face-to-face connection, proposing to see "the welfare of the state as a whole . . . in a scientific way," while rejecting "the saving power of culture and mission and isolated good feeling" as entirely inadequate responses to large-scale social problems.[31]

Another who shared this growing dissatisfaction with the original settlement house model was C.F.G. Masterman, who would be a rising politician in Asquith's New Liberal government, which came to power in 1908. Seven years earlier, while still living in the Albany Dwellings in Camberwell, which were connected with the Cambridge University Settlement, Masterman contributed to a collective New Liberal statement called *The Heart of the Empire*, which hoped to capitalize on concerns about the disastrous Boer War campaign to focus attention on poverty at home. The first essay, Masterman's "Realities at Home," delivers a devastating critique of the university settlements, which it characterizes as an idea whose time has passed, somewhere between "the Age of Slumming" and "the Age of Philanthropy." "For my own part," he noted,

> I realise that the call has failed. The Universities and the cultured classes, as a whole, care little about the matter. The wave of enthusiasm which created the modern settlement has ceased to advance; the buildings remain and a few energetic toilers, and the memory of a great hope. . . . In all the London settlements, among over four million of toilers, there are not a hundred resident male workers; of these many will not stay for less than a year's residence. I cannot believe that this is the machinery destined to bridge the ever-widening gulf between class and class, and to initiate the new heavens and the new earth.[32]

The Heart of the Empire is notoriously thin on positive counterproposals, but the best indication of what Masterman saw as taking the place of the settlement movement can be found in the political work he engaged in while in government: working alongside Lloyd George and Winston Churchill in developing model legislation for unemployment and health insurance programs.

The general shift I have been tracing toward a public policy of centralized provision is one element that undermined what Meacham terms "the Toynbee ethos," as it would have originally developed out of the influence of Green and Matthew Arnold, but he also cites as contributing factors the revival of Christian Socialism and the emergence of the new discipline of sociology. The history of the latter is hard to reconstruct, however, because it was effectively formed out of the collision of a number of divergent practices and beliefs, many of which I have already noted in my discussion of Booth: among them, the quintessentially mid-Victorian mania for gathering and tabulating information, which had an institutional home in the Statistical Society (in which Booth was a dominant figure); a countermovement that stressed the vitality of ameliorative efforts and focused more closely on the question of personal character in place of numerical abstractions; and a more theoretical position that wanted to generalize about the historical trends in human society, often backed by a social evolutionism inspired by Darwin. The amalgamation of such disparate forces and agendas into a single discipline occurred through a lengthy sequence of compromises and deferrals, which were further compromised by the remarkable availability of public funds in the wake of Booth's studies. As Philip Abrams notes in this context, "[I]f ameliorism was one's real commitment, politics was open and in the process of redefinition; government was sponsoring the ad hoc statistical investigation of social problems on an unprecedented scale; the whole structure of political conflict was shifting and energies devoted to hammering out new political ideologies and programs seemed assured of quick returns."[33] This means that when discussions finally took place concerning those institutional supports that would typically help to legitimate a new discipline—like the formation of the Sociological Society in 1903, or the first Department of Sociology, organized at the University of London four years later—key figures like Booth, Beveridge, and Beatrice and Sidney Webb played little or no part.

Sociology in Britain lacked a stable disciplinary base until the early years of this century, and can more usefully be viewed as a broad church of positivists, philanthropists, statisticians, social evolutionists, and anthropologists each of which tended to pull in different directions. There was no real consensus about its future orientation, in other words, but an availability of funds and projects, especially emanating from government, which established a provisional sense of unity in advance of the more traditional disciplinary foundations. Indeed, L. T. Hobhouse, the holder of the first British chair in sociology and an influential New Liberal theorist, chose to make virtue out of a necessity, arguing in 1907,

[I]t is clear that the definition which is to satisfy everybody must come not at the beginning but at the end of discovery. We must know what we are investigating only in the sense that we must have a rough and provisional outline of the field of work. If this imperfect and broken knowledge be ruled out, it remains that we can only know what we are looking for when we have found it.[34]

Thus, when Meacham lists sociology as a challenge to the philanthropic ethos of the late-Victorian settlement movement, it is mainly to the extent that it emphasized the positivist "what is" of statistical investigation at the expense of the moral "what ought" of ameliorative action; although, as already noted, it suffers from the same drain of energies and resources into government-sponsored projects that weakened the settlements in the early years of this century.

In effect, the fledgling discipline of sociology worked in tandem with the New Liberalism of the period to provide an ideological rationale for the interventionist state, and even its internal tensions find a parallel in government's stated aims to harmonize the individual with the state, and personal morality with economic or environmental determination. This is recognizably the position of the Liberal administrations under Asquith and Lloyd George, driven in part by the need to head off the nascent Labour movement, and it also describes the dominant school of sociology during the early years of this century, which favored a collective solution framed in terms of morality and character. Thus, according to Hobhouse, a "joint obligation" links the individual with the state, with the former being charged to secure "the contingencies of life" as far as possible and the latter being authorized to step in when required. With few exceptions, it seems that early sociology complemented the New Liberalism—in Philip Abrams' phrase—as "theory and practice of a last stand against socialism."[35] This helps to explain the piecemeal reformism of the Liberal government and also accounts for the frustrations of even a moderate Left-leaning sociologist like Sidney Webb, whose Fabian Socialism shared many of the statist concerns of the New Liberalism; after urging a more dramatic overhaul of the Poor Law, he was forced to conclude "that it would be easier and more profitable to remake the political system than to spend further energy on the sociological education of the present incumbents."[36]

CONCLUSION: THE WELFARE OF THE MODERN STATE

The interventionist state that begins to emerge under the New Liberalism also played a much greater role than its Victorian predecessors in organizing the market itself, by directing and safeguarding the labor force through insurance schemes, benefits for the temporarily unemployed, and the piloting of labor exchanges beginning in 1908. In this sense, the state acts, at least on the surface, against capital's immediate interests, partly under pressure from a resurgent labor movement and the suffrage campaigns, which articulated a more inclusive vision of politics and a universalizing discourse of human rights. The New Liberal conception of citizenship is predicated on a teleological vision of social harmony and progress, in which abstract social rights dominate over class interests, much as they do in the sociological writings of the period. Hobhouse again clarifies the respective roles of the individual and the welfare state, arguing that in theory,

> [t]he function of the State is to secure conditions upon which its citizens are able to win by their own efforts all that is necessary to full civic efficiency. It is not for the State to feed, house, or clothe them. It is for the State to take care that the economic conditions are such that the normal man who is not defective in mind or body or will can by useful labour feed, house, and clothe himself and his family.[37]

Here we can see the socioeconomic contract as predicated on a free-market model, which charges the state with safeguarding (and where necessary, *engineering*) conditions within which those who want to can find work and provide for themselves.

As Stuart Hall has argued, this is really a negative conception of rights seeking "to compensate those who visibly suffered gross privation on account of their being unable, for whatever reason, to participate fully in market relations."[38] Hobhouse's statement still assumes a norm of productive citizenship, in other words, against which welfare recipients can be regarded as functionally inadequate—even if their "failure" is no longer conceived of as their own fault or a basis for refusing aid. In Beveridge's version of this contract, whereby each citizen is offered a "place in free industry," which is in turn predicated on "full employment and average earnings up to a definite minimum," the punitive language of the Poor Law reemerges when he argues that those who refuse this offer "are not citizens in fact and should not be so in right"—disenfranchisement being "in this view . . . part of the 'stigma' of pauperism."[39] Thus, it is not clear exactly how far the New Liberal thinking of the early years of the twentieth century managed to dispense with the high-Victorian moralism of the New Poor Law, which retained a residual force even for those who helped to fashion the postwar welfare state.

Beveridge's advocacy of a targeted disenfranchisement of those who resist this ideal of citizenship did not find support, of course, as Britain belatedly moved toward universal suffrage after World War I. In a sense, though, that very universality—which is equally fundamental to the principles of the welfare state—helped to discourage more active participation in either politics or the economy. In political terms, universal suffrage represented a victory for labor and the women's movement, but also foreclosed on the possibilities of a more direct involvement in the process of government by binding the Labour Party in particular to the structures of Parliamentary democracy. An analysis of class interests disappears, as we have seen in the previous examples of New Liberal and sociological rhetoric, or is subsumed within a more abstract conception of universal rights: as Perry Anderson has argued, "The economic divisions within the citizenry are masked by the juridical parity between exploiters and exploited, and with them the complete *separation* and *non-participation* [his emphasis] of the masses in the work of parliament. This separation is then constantly presented and represented to the masses as the ultimate incarnation of liberty: 'democracy' as the terminal point of history."[40]

This highlights a possible fissure within current neoconservative thinking. For if Anderson is correct, then the modern state that Himmelfarb, Thatcher, and others have subjected to a vigorous critique in recent years also embodies that endpoint of history which Francis Fukuyama suggests has emerged with the end of the Cold War. Because it has no more external enemies or competing ideologies (at least on a global scale), Western liberal democracy seems to Fukuyama capable of extending itself across the globe, and thereby putting a halt to the processes of conflict and synthesis that are the motor-force of history. In doing so, it generalizes a vision of the state that "is liberal insofar as it recognizes and protects through a system of law [the] universal right to freedom, and democratic insofar as it exists only with the consent of the governed."[41] As Himmelfarb herself points out in an equivocal response to Fukuyama's thesis, central among the main victories of liberal democracy has been its success "in resolving the 'class issue,'" even if it now has a considerable "underclass" to deal with.[42]

It is important to note these fault lines in modern neoconservatism, and to consider how they might help in the development of a convincing defense of the welfare state. The historical analysis I have attempted here gives little support to the Thatcherite position, which requires the return to a mid-Victorian minimalist state with priorities in defense, domestic order, and international trade. Indeed, as I have tried to indicate, what is noticeable is how quickly the idea of an impersonal and bureaucratic state gets enshrined as the only available option for dealing with large-scale social problems, especially if the other options are private charity and philanthropic moralism. Given that such Left-liberal alternatives as communitarianism and decentralized local government initiatives have yet to be tested without the welfare safety net, it seems worth revisiting the debates of a century ago and holding them up as a salutary caution against knee-jerk antistatism, which, as Martin Wiener notes, has infected both ends of the political spectrum.

The other implication of this historical inquiry is that we need at the same time to consider the negative implications of the interventionist state that emerges out of the fin de siècle: the limiting effects of its universalist rhetoric of rights and responsibilities; the cooption of the progressive social sciences to a liberal political vision that remains dominant; and the reluctance to investigate fully the conditions and origins of poverty or to propose any radical social change. In all of these ways, the modern state remains a compromise between the "limited socialism" proposed by Booth and an aggressive capitalist economy that still struggles to resolve "the class issue" or to acknowledge its responsibility for poverty and unemployment. As its name suggests, "neoliberalism" is not all that far from the New Liberalism of a century ago, which already anticipated many of the features of the "third way" now being touted by Tony Blair's "New Labour" and the centrist Democratic leadership caucus in the United States. Put simply, the difference is that the earlier version emerged in competition with Left alternatives and in reaction to a discredited philosophy of laissez-faire conservatism, while its modern variant faces the opposite case, in which free-marketeers like Thatcher, Gingrich, and Himmelfarb can pose themselves as the only rival in town.

NOTES

1. See my "Castles in the Air: The People's Palace, Cultural Reformism, and the East End Working Class," *Victorian Studies* 39, no. 4 (1996): 513–38.

2. Martin J. Wiener, "The Unloved State: Twentieth-Century Politics in the Writing of Nineteenth-Century History," *Journal of British Studies* 33 (1994): 283–308. For an influential version of the liberal antistatist position in Britain, see Jonathan Freedland, *Bringing Home the Revolution: How Britain Can Live the American Dream* (London: Fourth Estate, 1998), which elaborates a range of U.S. alternatives to the central state (including communitarianism, voluntary work, and devolved government) as models for post-Thatcherite Britain.

3. Will Hutton, "The State We Should Be In," *Marxism Today* (1998, special issue on "The Blair Project"): 34–37.

4. David Norbrook, "Life and Death of Renaissance Man," *Raritan* 8, no. 4 (1989): 107. I am indebted to Jim Holstun for this reference, and for his insightful comments on an earlier version of this essay.

5. See William Morris, *News from Nowhere, and Other Writings*, ed. Clive Wilmer (Harmondsworth: Penguin, 1993), especially the pivotal chapter on "How the Change Came." Morris's objections to State Socialism are also outlined in his critical review of Edward Bellamy's *Looking Backward* (1889), the Utopian text that inspired *News from Nowhere*; see *News*, 353–58.

6. Gertrude Himmelfarb, *The De-Moralization of Society: From Victorian Virtues to Modern Values* (New York: Random House, 1994).

7. It is hopefully unnecessary to point out here that a very different graph would emerge if, say, literacy rates or life expectancy were selected as the determining

factors for comparison, and indeed, that just about any letter of the alphabet can be traced out depending on the choice of which variables to plot.

8. See "Gingrich Looks to Victorian Age to Cure Today's Social Failings," *New York Times*, 14 March 1995, p. A19.

9. For critical reviews of Himmelfarb that take up these issues, see David Bromwich, "Victoria's Secret," *The New Republic*, 15 May 1995, 28–33; and Marilynne Robinson, "Modern Victorians: Dressing Politics in the Costume of History," *Harper's Magazine*, July 1995, 72–77.

10. This is not to suggest that Thatcherism was merely attempting to turn back the clock. As Raphael Samuel argues, with perhaps an echo of Stuart Hall's description of its "regressive modernism," the ideological appeal of Thatcher's "Victorian values" went hand-in-hand with an antitraditionalist project of modernization, which it partly helped to camouflage. See Samuel, "Mrs. Thatcher's Return to Victorian Values," in *Victorian Values: A Joint Symposium of the Royal Society of Edinburgh and the British Academy*, ed. T. C. Smout (Oxford: Oxford University Press and British Academy, 1992), 9–29; and Stuart Hall, *The Hard Road to Renewal: Thatcherism and the Crisis of the Left* (London: Verso, 1988).

11. See for example Himmelfarb, *De-Moralization*, 246–48, where the admission is disguised in part by being couched in terms of *values*, so that "[a]gainst such a pervasive system of state-supported and state-sanctioned values, the traditional conservative recourse to private groups and voluntary initiatives may seem inadequate" (247). This inadequacy is conceded even by a conservative advocate of a return to mutual aid societies, Stephen Davies, who proposes that they administer welfare payments funded by governmental taxation. See Davies, "Beveridge Revisited: New Foundations for Tomorrow's Welfare," in *Policies of Thatcherism: Thoughts of a London Thinktank*, ed. Richard Haas and Oliver Knox (Lanham, Md.: University Press of America, 1991), 123–59.

12. It is perhaps more accurate to characterize Himmelfarb as advocating a minimalist state, with the reluctant acknowledgment that its functions cannot entirely be assumed by the private sector. Speaking to Mark Gerson, for example, she notes that "[w]e are children of the Depression, and are committed to the New Deal kind of welfare state—by present terms, a very minimal welfare state. Nevertheless, Social Security is something we regard as a very good thing." See Gerson, *The Neoconservative Vision: From the Cold War to the Culture Wars* (Lanham, Md.: Madison Books, 1996), 243–44.

13. Gareth Stedman Jones, "Why Is the Labour Party in a Mess?" in *Languages of Class: Studies in English Working-Class History, 1832–1982* (Cambridge: Cambridge University Press, 1983), 246.

14. On my reading, Booth is actually more of a collectivist than a comparable figure like Mayhew, who seems in many ways to be a more likely hero for modern conservatives. As David Englander and Rosemary O'Day note, there is a spirit of political partisanship that underwrites Himmelfarb's consistent attacks on Mayhew, who "might reasonably have been included as a fair specimen of the compassionate middle classes" that she looks to; however, they continue, he "receives a battering less, one suspects, because of what he wrote and more because of the way in which he has been taken up and lionized by those whose politics Himmelfarb abhors," especially E. P. Thompson. See the introduction to *Retrieved Riches: Social Investi-*

gation in Britain, 1840–1914, ed. David Englander and Rosemary O'Day (Aldershot: Scolar Press, 1995), 32.

15. See *Charles Booth's London: A Portrait of the Poor at the Turn of the Century, drawn from his "Life and Labour of the People in London,"* ed. Albert Fried and Richard M. Elman (New York: Pantheon, 1968), 12. All references to Booth are taken either from this volume or a similar collection, *Charles Booth on the City: Physical Pattern and Social Structure*, ed. Harold W. Pfautz (Chicago: University of Chicago Press, 1967).

16. Himmelfarb, *De-Moralization*, 37. Later, the tortuous argument runs like this: "[I]t is against the background of these statistics that one must consider the much publicized finding by Charles Booth, in the late 1880s, of 30 percent of the population of London in poverty. His 'poverty' was clearly not that of the early- or mid-Victorian periods. A better basis for comparison would be his class of the 'very poor,' which included not only paupers but also those who were employed irregularly and at low wages" (137–38). Through this sleight of hand, 30 percent is magically reduced to 7.5 percent!

17. Pfautz, ed., *Charles Booth on the City*, 180–81.

18. Fried, ed., *Charles Booth's London*, 338–39.

19. Ibid., 284–85.

20. Ibid., 287–88.

21. For a useful account of Booth's attitudes toward "the residuum" in the context of the period, see José Harris, "Between Civil Virtue and Social Darwinism: The Concept of the Residuum," in *Retrieved Riches*, 67–87.

22. The Salvation Army's plan was set out in (General) William Booth, *In Darkest England, and the Way Out* (London: International Headquarters of the Salvation Army, 1890), and received surprising support from prominent liberals and Fabian Socialists, including Beatrice Webb, Samuel Barnett of Toynbee Hall, and W.J.T. Stead of the *Pall Mall Gazette*; opposition came from Hyndman, William Morris (who denounced the scheme as "Workhouse Socialism") and the trade unions. For a discussion of these responses, see Victor Bailey, " 'In Darkest England and the Way Out': The Salvation Army, Social Reform and the Labour Movement, 1885–1910," *International Review of Social History* 29, no. 2 (1984): 133–71.

23. Brooke Lambert, *East End Pauperism* (1868), cited in Gareth Stedman Jones, *Outcast London: A Study in the Relationship Between Classes in Victorian Society* (Oxford: Clarendon, 1971), 247.

24. Andrew Mearns, *The Bitter Cry of Outcast London*, reprinted in *Into Unknown England, 1866–1913: Selections from the Social Explorers*, ed. Peter Keating (Manchester: Manchester University Press, 1976), 97.

25. George R. Sims, *How the Poor Live*, reprinted in *Unknown England*, 85–86.

26. Cited in Michael E. Rose, *The English Poor Law, 1780–1930* (New York: Barnes and Noble, 1971), 259.

27. Rose, *English Poor Law*, 261–62. These developments are discussed in Derek Fraser, *The Evolution of the British Welfare State: A History of Social Policy since the Industrial Revolution* (New York: Barnes and Noble, 1973), chapter 7.

28. Green, *Lectures on the Principles of Political Obligation* (1882), cited in Himmelfarb, *De-Moralization*, 152.

29. Himmelfarb, *De-Moralization*, 157–58.

30. Standish Meacham, *Toynbee Hall and Social Reform, 1880–1914: The Search for Community* (New Haven: Yale University Press, 1987), 17, citing Toynbee's lecture "Are Radicals Socialists?"

31. See Meacham, *Toynbee Hall*, 69–71 (on Barnett) and 137 (on Beveridge).

32. C.F.G. Masterman, ed., *The Heart of the Empire: Discussions of Problems of Modern City Life in England* (Brighton: Harvester Press, 1973), 35.

33. Philip Abrams, *The Origins of British Sociology: 1834–1914* (Chicago: University of Chicago Press, 1968), 101.

34. Cited in Abrams, *Origins of British Sociology*, 108. It is tempting to compare this inter- or antidisciplinary nature with that of contemporary cultural studies, which similarly prides itself on forming situational alliances among the disciplines instead of formulating definitive and self-regulating protocols, which would help to determine exactly what cultural studies *is* (and *isn't*). For an influential endorsement of this refusal, see the introduction to Lawrence Grossberg, Cary Nelson, and Paula Treichler, eds., *Cultural Studies* (New York: Routledge, 1992).

35. Abrams, *Origins of British Sociology*, 60.

36. Cited in Abrams, *Origins of British Sociology*, 144.

37. L.T. Hobhouse, *Liberalism* (1911), cited in Stefan Collini, *Liberalism and Sociology: L.T. Hobhouse and Political Argument in England, 1880–1914* (Cambridge: Cambridge University Press, 1979), 137.

38. See Stuart Hall and Bill Schwartz, " State and Society, 1880–1930," in Hall, *The Hard Road to Renewal*, 111.

39. William Beveridge, "The Problem of the Unemployed" (1907), and "Unemployment in London" (1905), both cited in Meacham, *Toynbee Hall*, 149–50.

40. Perry Anderson, "The Antinomies of Antonio Gramsci," *New Left Review* 100 (1976–1977): 28.

41. See Francis Fukuyama, "The End of History?" *The National Interest* (1989): 5.

42. The hesitation is telling here: on the one hand, Himmelfarb supports the idea of a final victory, especially over those ideological opponents who stress "the class issue," but on the other hand she is committed to a vision of the modern West as being undermined by the same social problems she elaborated in *The De-Moralization of Society*. Hence, I see her invocation of the underclass as gesturing toward a problem that "does not fit the old 'class' model, the kind familiar to classical economists and Marxists"—presumably because she sees it as an issue of morality as much (or more) than of economics. See "Responses to Fukuyama," *The National Interest* (1989): 26.

Part V

DISCIPLINARY CONTESTS AND
THE PRESENT HORIZON

The Arnoldian Ideal, or Culture Studies and the Problem of Nothingness

CHRISTOPHER LANE

Estote ergo vos perfecti! [Be ye therefore perfect!]
Matthew Arnold, Culture and Anarchy

Say, what blinds us, that we claim the glory
Of possessing powers not our share?
Matthew Arnold, "Self-Deception"

CULTURE WARS

One of the ironies of Arnold's *Culture and Anarchy* (1867–68, 1869)—lost on neither its author nor its many critics—is that the book's thesis about our "best self," its key to promoting excellence, failed to establish a conclusive, universal aesthetic.[1] Alluding to this failure, several detractors asked at the time why Arnold need look to ancient Greece and Rome for signs of this aesthetic. Two of his successors, Walter Pater and Oscar Wilde, questioned wryly what our "best self" perceives and of what it consists.

Doubts about Arnold's theory—circulating in reviews of *The Strayed Reveller and Other Poems* (1849), the 1853 *Poems*, and *Merope* (1858)—first arose as criticism from friends such as Arthur Hugh Clough and James A. Froude.[2] Pater's implicit rebuttal of Arnold appeared in his now famous review of William Morris's poetry, just two months after the *Cornhill* published the final issue of Arnold's "Anarchy and Authority," the last of six essays that would be published together as *Culture and Anarchy*.[3] And Wilde's parody of Arnold's claims appeared much later, in "The Critic as Artist" (1890, revised 1891).[4] But Pater and Wilde, exaggerating Arnold's confidence, downplayed his debt to a tradition with which all three figures in different ways identified.[5] And following Pater and Wilde, many twentieth-century Arnold critics—including T. S. Eliot and Raymond Williams—have bestowed on him an authority he fell short of achieving, ironically eclipsing his most interesting, doubt-ridden moments.[6]

Although this brief summary reminds us that Arnold's poetry and prose were often critically received, a cursory look at his intellectual role today suggests that this hostility is not about to end.[7] As David DeLaura recently observed, "Arnold has become a sort of ideological football or touchstone— almost 'talismanic,' as he might have said—in the successive waves of the culture wars, especially since the 1960s."[8]

What can we learn from this impulse to praise or berate Arnold? Although politics is one factor dividing critics, the division itself is misleading, permitting a symptomatic misprision of Arnold's claims.[9] While the conservative defense of *Culture and Anarchy* is largely untenable, because Arnold advocated state education and his cultural "touchstones" are too nebulous to support a reactionary agenda, the Left perception of Arnold as woefully blind to social ills is equally implausible. Social inequalities and mass illiteracy appalled Arnold, who scorned the "incomparable self-satisfaction" of the Victorian middle class that permitted both.[10] Spending much of his career trying to reform Britain's elitist education system, he attacked "the hideous and grotesque illusions of middle-class Protestantism" in order to diminish its "pedantry, bigotry, and narrowness."[11]

Literary criticism and disciplinarity may also explain a near-visceral disdain surrounding Arnold's work, yet here, too, the judgment seems hasty.[12] Just when we're ready to dismiss Arnold as a staunch traditionalist, we recall his disdain for British parochialism, his admiration for European and Asian thought. And as often as we read about Arnold the antitheorist and champion of practices anticipating New Criticism, we find counterevidence proving that he favored parody over snobbery, debate over demagoguery, flux over rigidity, and inquiry over philistinism.

I propose another explanation for this hostility. Cultural studies is configured today in such a way that it misunderstands a central Arnoldian preoccupation: the ineffable or nonreferential. Generally tied to positive questions of value, cultural studies cannot assess what eludes representation in Arnold's and others' work. I refer to aspects of experience that resist meaning, because they are "extradiscursive" or beyond representation.[13] Arnold's repeated engagement with these elements nonetheless makes clear that the ineffable is not a transcendent category in his work and cannot be dismissed as a Romantic notion of sublimity.

Given these fault lines in Arnold's poetry and criticism, his fascination with obstacles to meaning—and with the impact of these obstacles on culture—highlights why the ineffable is a blind spot for cultural criticism. As such criticism has no viable means of engaging with this phenomenon, Arnold's ideal points to the shortcomings of cultural studies, its limited tolerance for what resists meaning and discursive processing.[14]

THEORY AT THE EXPENSE OF SELFHOOD

Arnold's aesthetic theory—preceding his earliest poems—ultimately evolved at the expense of his poetic endeavor and commitment to disinterestedness. While his account of perfection stemmed from ancient Greek and Roman philosophy, it advanced an anti-Romantic notion of subjective failure that some critics have ignored and others have exaggerated as proof of his inconsistency, both limiting his work's heuristic value. When, in the second edition of *Matthew Arnold*, Lionel Trilling defended Arnold from the charge of inconsistency, he not only rejected this assessment, but turned it against Arnold's accusers. Asked Trilling, "Does this [inconsistency] matter and is it not a symptom of our confusion to remark it—an evidence of our losing the sense of human limits, therefore of human powers, therefore of human processes, of our turning to the desperate absotion of his ideal?"[15]

Notwithstanding Trilling's emphasis, failure is central to Arnold's dialectical understanding of culture and selfhood, for it highlights the limits of ontological harmony and the trauma arising from the poet's periodic confrontations with nothingness. As Morris Dickstein explains when discussing Arnold's rhetorical strategies, "at times the effect . . . becomes so intense, the world so ludicrous, that it's a wonder he stops short of nihilism."[16] And though I began with Arnold's claims about the "best self," diverse, sometimes contradictory, claims about this phenomenon pepper his writing with changing intellectual consequences. Hence the mistake of reading Arnold chiefly for consistency or berating him for falling short of this goal. Both sets of judgment account for a strange oscillation in Arnold scholarship, as critics alternate between apologia and reproach. By contrast, I shall argue that Arnold's poetry and criticism illustrate a "self-cauterizing" dynamic[17] that promotes disinterestedness through the "best self" while undercutting the autonomy of the individual incorporating wisdom into his or her daily life. In light of Arnold's conflicted impulses and aims, it is inevitable that this dynamic would recur throughout his work.

Signs of this dynamic appear in a letter that Arnold wrote to his sister Jane in September 1858:

> [P]erfection of a certain kind may there be attained, or at least approached, without knocking yourself to pieces: but to attain or approach perfection in the region of thought & feeling and to unite this with perfection of form, demands not merely an effort and a labour, but an actual tearing of oneself to pieces, which one does not readily consent to (although one is sometimes forced to it) unless one can devote one's whole life to poetry.[18]

Although Arnold did not devote his entire life to poetry, in associating perfection of form, thought, and feeling with "tearing . . . oneself to pieces" he made self-laceration central to his theory of culture. Biographical details amplify this argument, but the repercussions of my thesis about the non-referential extend far beyond biography. While Arnold avowed in March 1849, "I am fragments, . . . [and] the whole effect of my poems is quite vague & indeterminate . . . [they] stagger weakly & are at their wits end,"[19] he pushed these concerns into an impersonal register, in this way sounding wider claims about Victorian theories of knowledge, disciplines, and cultural tradition and about the possibility of sustaining disinterestedness. (See Figure 11.1, "Sweetness and Light," in which the journal *Once a Week* [12 October 1872] burlesques Arnold leaping, as perhaps a dilettante, from "Criticism" to "Poetry," and thence to "Philosophy.")

Additionally, the failure of Arnold's arguments cannot be reduced to a single cause, and Arnold veiled his conceptual difficulties by more than one method. Especially in his earliest work, he was openly quizzical, even morbid in embracing despair; in his later criticism, he strove rhetorically for clarity but fell short of achieving authority. Sometimes his critics indulged his flights of fancy and grandiloquence. More often, he was upbraided for literary rigidity and excessive interest in theory, accused of "trifl[ing] with the public by versifying dreamy, transcendental excuses for laziness" and writing "clever, systematic madness."[20]

These different registers of doubt—psychological, philosophical, and rhetorical—do not surface consistently in his work. But, overall, Arnold's cauterizing dynamic defeated his cultural advocacy by voicing an argument against aesthetic certainty. Pointing inadvertently to what belies meaning, his work tells us much about the aims and disappointments of disciplinarity at mid-century, for Arnold's practical and intellectual relationship to knowledge influenced the Victorians' professional concerns about education and culture.[21] (I am referring to his "second career" as a critic, between roughly 1860 and 1885—from the time he wrote *On Translating Homer* to the publication of his *Discourses in America*.) By representing perfection as the goal of knowledge, Arnold's project tried to surpass selfhood. Yet his cauterizing dynamic—flourishing in his poetry and criticism—hobbled this argument in ways that Arnold's opponents have not convincingly explained.

UNIVERSALITY AND THE ARNOLDIAN IDEAL

These broad conceptual and biographical details should correct our misshapen fantasies of Victorian zeal. Cultural authority is a vague, sometimes troubling category in Arnold's work; and almost all of his famous dicta about *Bildung* (inherited partly from Goethe, Carlyle, and Emerson) are

Figure 11.1

ambiguous. Yet his thesis isn't entirely ruined by its internal fault lines. In advancing this claim, we simply restate a problem about universality and the ideal that preoccupied Arnold for many years. To put this more stringently, it is wrongheaded to dismiss Arnold's failure to resolve these problems as intellectual deficiency or political and psychic conservatism. In turning radical skepticism, class consciousness, or alternative terms such as performativity into guidelines, many critics today ignore not only Arnold's interest in the function of ideals, but also the perhaps surprising fact that we continue needing them.[22]

By acknowledging the conceptual leap needed to link the ancients and the Victorians in a credible way, Arnold realized that judgment and perception ceaselessly compromise disinterestedness, one of his ideals. And so despite its symbolic power, the ideal in Arnold's work has limited cultural efficacy. In his inaugural lecture at Oxford in November 1857, "On the Modern Element in Literature," Arnold argues that our intellectual

> deliverance consists in man's comprehension of this present and past. It begins
> when our mind begins to enter into possession of the general ideas which are the

law of this vast multitude of facts. It is perfect when we have acquired that
harmonious acquiescence of mind which we feel in contemplating a grand spectacle that is intelligible to us; when we have lost that impatient irritation of mind
which we feel in presence of an immense, moving, confused spectacle which,
while it perpetually excites our curiosity, perpetually baffles our comprehension
(*CPW*, 1:20).

The emphasis here on harmony is Burkean, but Arnold would discover that
the "grand spectacle" of history often defies understanding, culminating in
the opposite of "harmonious acquiescence of mind," and he was not alone in
reaching this conclusion. William Hazlitt had argued in "On Knowledge of
the World" (1827) that "see[ing] things divested of passion and interest, is to
see them with the eye of history and philosophy." It is "difficult to arrive at
the same calm certainty in actual life," Hazlitt added, "because the passions
and interests are concerned, and it requires so much more candour, love of
truth, and independence of spirit to encounter 'the world and its dread
laugh,' to throw aside every sinister consideration, and grapple with the
plain merits of the case."[23]

Although we still lack consensus on the merits of Arnold's case, his perception of cultural relevance changed subtly over the course of his career. In
spite of himself, his evaluations of poetry and culture were often idiosyncratic and later revised. Then, as now, many critics argued that Arnold's secular
ideal was spawned by a fantasy of human perfectibility. *"Estote ergo vos
perfecti!"* [Be ye therefore perfect!] (Matthew 5:48) is the epigraph he chose
for *Culture and Anarchy* (*CPW*, 5:86), an ideal Pater's narrator would echo
frequently in *Marius the Epicurean* (1885).[24] Arnold hoped this imperious
command would combine with *"a disinterested endeavour to learn and
propagate the best that is known and thought in the world* [his emphasis],"[25]
one of his most misquoted lines, but the command instead identified a traumatic deficiency in humankind, and it heralds overall an aesthetic paradise
that the Victorians were not capable of attaining. Why?

Arnold's ideal is the "sweetness and light" that apparently prevailed in
ancient Greece, later determining the role of *Bildung*, or self-development, in
the Victorian age. "How salutary a friend is culture . . . !" he declares
in *Culture and Anarchy* (*CPW*, 5:97). In the late 1850s and throughout the
1860s Arnold stressed that this "friendship" would help the Victorians
renounce materialism and egotism, leaving them susceptible to the "true
grace and serenity . . . of which Greece and Greek art suggest the admirable
ideals of perfection."[26] The ecumenical, quasi-messianic thrust of this grace
appears in his famous conclusion to "The Function of Criticism at the Present Time" (1864): "There is the promised land, towards which criticism can
only beckon. That promised land it will not be ours to enter, and we shall die
in the wilderness: but to have desired to enter it, to have saluted it from afar,

is already, perhaps, the best distinction among contemporaries; it will certainly be the best title to esteem with posterity" (*CPW*, 3:285).

That this ideal could emerge from idiosyncratic preferences is either so obvious or risible to us today that its mechanics seem to warrant little discussion. We have tended to accept at least the first half of T. S. Eliot's claim that "the total effect of Arnold's philosophy is to set up Culture in the place of Religion, and to leave Religion to be laid waste by the anarchy of feeling."[27] What we then uphold or dismiss are the repercussions of this ideal, which turn *Bildung* into a redemptive entity, capable of "usurp[ing] the place of Religion," as Eliot foresaw, while trying to ward off the worst that persists in us as thought and speech.[28] In approaching this last concern, however, we must ask (as Arnold did), what it means to be "laid waste by the anarchy of feeling," and what this "anarchy" tells us about the nonreferential and extradiscursive.

We learn most about Arnold's ideal, as we'll see, by focusing on what it is meant to protect us from and to prevent from happening. This is partly because his emphasis on deficiency and reparation alternates violently in his writing, generating punitive, ascetic, and self-lacerating consequences for his aesthetic theory. As Arnold once exclaimed to Clough in self-exasperation, "I have never yet succeeded in any one great occasion in consciously mastering myself: I can go thro: the imaginary process of mastering myself & see the whole affair as it would then stand, but at the critical point I am too apt to hoist up the mainsail to the wind & let her drive."[29] This observation points to more than Arnold's and others' concerns about his fecklessness, his leaning toward dandyism for much of his twenties.[30] Repeating the emphasis on reparation that often recurs in his criticism, Arnold adds that he hopes "praxis" and "a clear almost palpable intuition" will "mend" him. All the same, his self-goading makes this outcome unlikely: "I must try how soon I can ferociously turn towards England."[31]

Some of the coercive, "Hebraic" elements of Arnold's ideal not only distinguished imperfectly between the best and worst of *Bildung*, but also ensured that such extremes would clash repeatedly in his work. This outcome bears on subsequent literary and cultural studies, determining both the "place" of selfhood in this context—the "object" that literature apparently must elevate—and the class and psychic violence accompanying this transformation, which stitches individuals into "tradition" on condition that they reject their former selfhood. While F. R. and Q. D. Leavis—disdaining "academic intellectualism"—wrote largely for "the would-be self-improver,"[32] F. R. Leavis would still insist that "it is impossible to question the clear fact: only a minority is capable of advanced intellectual culture." "The triumph of democratic egalitarianism," he added in a later essay, "is disastrous for humanity."[33]

As the Leavises' statements are so tendentious, the origins of English literary criticism may seem damaged beyond repair. Nevertheless, it would be a serious mistake to reject the discipline because we eschew its early tenets; and there are still vast amounts to learn from this history. While for F. R. Leavis the Great Tradition fostered "continuity" among Jane Austen, George Eliot, Henry James, Joseph Conrad, and D. H. Lawrence, it also linked these figures—however incongruously—to the Bible and not to ancient Greece.[34] The Leavises built their edifice on strains of Arnoldian messianism, but they lopped off much of his Apollonian idealism and brought to the study of literature the very Hebraism that Arnold tried to check in Victorian culture. To put this in Arnoldian terms, they advanced Hebraism's *"strictness of conscience"* by scaling back what Arnold hoped to foster: Hellenism's *"spontaneity of consciousness"* (*CPW*, 5:165). And they did so to hinder piety without "Christian discrimination," clearly a non-Arnoldian formulation.[35] As Leavis tartly explained in *The Great Tradition*, correcting Lord David Cecil's evaluation of George Eliot's relationship to Puritanism:

> I had better confess that I differ (apparently) from . . . Cecil in sharing these beliefs [in heaven, hell, and miracles], admirations [of truthfulness, chastity, industry, and self-restraint], and disapprovals [of loose living, recklessness, deceit, and self-indulgence], so that the reader knows my bias at once. *And [these beliefs] seem to me favourable to the production of great literature* [emphasis added]. I will add (exposing myself completely) that the enlightenment or aestheticism or sophistication that feels an amused superiority to them leads, in my view, to triviality and boredom, and that out of triviality comes evil.[36]

Although critics coupling Arnold with Leavis have viewed their messianism as repressive and coercive, and as failing to abort literature's fascination with evil, Arnold's criticism too often is conflated with Leavis's "Christian discrimination." Gerald Graff claims that Arnold "forms a bridge between romantic predecessors like Carlyle, Wordsworth, and Chateaubriand, and subsequent modernists like Friedrich Nietzsche, T. S. Eliot, F. R. Leavis, D. H. Lawrence, and W. B. Yeats." "For writers in this tradition . . . ," he explains, "the condition of modernity is one of profound sickness, the cause of which lies in the crisis of belief provoked by Enlightenment science, individualism, and liberal democracy."[37] This summary not only elides profound differences among these thinkers (consider Nietzsche's disdain for the "consummate cant" of Carlyle and other "English flatheads"),[38] but also ignores Arnold's and others' interest in asking whether Victorian cultural ideals were viable, and why they often failed. Such questioning is the flip-side of Arnold's religionizing of culture in the 1860s, which derived in part from the volatile gap between Protestantism and Catholicism in the 1820s and 1830s.[39] Before the 1829 Emancipation Act, British politicians were required to take an anti-Catholic oath, and Irish and English Roman Catholics lacked full franchise and admission to all civil offices, a situation leading in 1828 to the threat of a nationwide revolt in Ireland. I am therefore suggesting that his inquiry into the symbolic status of ideals tells us much about the status of literary criticism at midcentury. Defining anarchy as both a mass revolt and a phenomenon internal to selfhood, Arnold's tendency to view culture as salvific had profound conceptual repercussions that are worth reexamining. Culture apparently must protect us from the "catastrophes of history and sexuality," and save us from ourselves, yet Arnold (unlike Leavis) continues to stress the limits of meaning.[40]

CULTURE AND NOTHINGNESS

Because some of these details are well known, the consequences of Arnold's argument seem deceptively clear. We apparently know what went wrong with his cultural project, and dismiss him accordingly. But concluding the argument with Arnold's redemptive expectation ignores his frequent—and invaluable—confrontation with culture's antiredemptive strains, his preoc- cupation with what resists meaning and certainty. Strange to say, the extent of Arnold's interest in these elements might *prevent* us from disparaging his endeavor as a false reification of culture. While T. S. Eliot was correct in bringing to our attention Arnold's "ecumenical and hierarchical impulses,"[41] Eliot tended to minimize Arnold's struggle to produce a cultural ideal that could withstand nothingness.

"The anarchy of feeling [that lays] waste to Religion" and other matters of faith remains a neglected and misunderstood component of cultural criticism. That this component is resurfacing with growing popularity today, not only in recuperations of Victorian mesmerism, but also in widespread popular discussion of the soul and the spirit, attests to the haunting underside of Arnold's project. Indeed, that Arnold's ideal failed to suppress its own prob- lem with absences, voids, and nothingness gave it a secret life that troubled him as much as it revisits us today. This partly explains why he tried to emulate Thomas à Kempis's recommendation to "frequently do violence to yourself" [*frequenter tibi ipsi violentiam fac*]. "I intend not to give myself the rein in following my natural tendency [being 'aimless and unsettled']," Arnold explained to his sister, "but to make war against it till it ceases to isolate me from you and leaves me with the power to discern and adopt the good which you have & I have not."[42]

Had Arnold's thesis about the ideal not replicated this rhetorical violence, these biographical statements would have only limited relevance. But as Ian Hamilton notes in his lively study of Arnold, "the deepest impulse" in Arnold's poetry and criticism is "towards repudiation."[43] This is one reason the speaker of "Courage" (1852) begins by insisting that "we must tame our rebel will . . . / Must learn to wait, renounce, withdraw," and ends by admitting that "Our bane, disguise it as we may, / Is weakness, is a faltering course" (*PW*, 481.1, 4; and 482.25–26). This is also why the speaker of "Self-Dependence," first published in the same year, claims to be "Weary of myself, and sick of asking / What I am and what I ought to be" (239.1–2). We learn most about the failure of Arnold's cultural project, in this respect, by addressing what *resists* redemption and reference in his poetry.

In his 1853 Preface, Arnold famously navigated this self-berating impulse while hoping to create an antidote for "the bewildering confusion of our times" (*PW*, xxx). He tried to help men "succeed in banishing from [their] mind[s] all feelings of contradiction, and irritation, and impatience; in order to delight [themselves] with the contemplation of some noble action of a heroic time, and to enable others, through his representation of it, to delight in it also" (xxx). For Nietzsche—writing in the 1870s and 1880s, when Arnold's "second career" began to wane—change was an opportunity to sweep aside the stale, the archaic, and the anachronistic. However, Arnold lamented this "ëpoch of dissolution and transformation." "The present age makes great claims upon us," he remarked; it often creates a "continuous state of mental distress" (xxviii, xviii).

Above all, Arnold hoped to resist a defining characteristic of modernity: "the dialogue of the mind with itself" (*PW*, xvii). Clearly, there was something about this internal conversation or chatter—superseding Arnold's departing religious faith—that disturbed his contemplative poise, generating interest in "the most utter calamity, . . . the liveliest anguish" (xviii). Again, because this interest stressed Arnold's preoccupation with passion, form, and knowledge (including self-knowledge), it is not reducible to biographical concerns. In his 1863 essay on Heinrich Heine, for example, Arnold declared that "the awakening of the modern spirit" derived in part from "the sense of want of correspondence between the forms of modern Europe and its spirit" (*CPW*, 3:109).

While refusing to depict anguish as a simple effect of social pressure, Arnold also ridiculed the argument made in David Masson's 1853 review of Eneas Sweetland Dallas's *Poetics: An Essay on Poetry* (1852) and Alexander Smith's *Poems* (1853, later retitled *A Life-Drama and Other Poems*), in which Masson argued that a "true allegory of the state of one's own mind in a representative history . . . is perhaps the highest thing that one can attempt in the way of fictitious art" (*PW*, xxiv).[44] "An allegory of the state of one's own mind, the highest problem of an art which imitates actions!" Arnold scoffed. "No assuredly, it is not, it never can be so: no great poetical work has ever been produced with such an aim" (xxiv). In contradicting so vehemently Masson's claims, Arnold tried to avoid solipsism and nihilism, yet he could not elude psychic life so easily.[45] He appealed to the ancients with a view to displacing crass materialism and transcending individuality, arguing that the poet is "most fortunate when he most entirely succeeds in effacing himself" (xxiii). Hoping such self-effacement would help readers "rediscover" tranquillity and disinterestedness from ancient Greece, Arnold resurrected these factors for those wanting "a steadying and composing effect" in Victorian England (xvii, xxviii).

Just as few twentieth-century Hellenists would sum up ancient Greece with terms such as "noble serenity," "radiancy," "dignified freedom," and "true grace" (*CPW*, 1:28, 3:378, and 5:125),[46] so few later Romanists would entirely corroborate Pater's account of Roman life in *Marius the Epicurean*. Arnold's Apollonian assessment of Delphic thought spurns the manic, Dionysian passion that Alcibiades threatens to unleash on Plato's *Symposium*, the unruly force that the charioteer must harness in Plato's *Phaedrus*.[47] Nietzsche, born twenty-two years after Arnold, considered such perspectives on the ancient world "consummate cant," and to his liking found many darker, antiredemptive impulses in Euripides's tragedies.[48] But Nietzsche was not alone in implying retrospectively that Victorian Hellenists, in idealizing Greece, had failed to obscure its preoccupation with passion and the "daemonic." Later still, in 1933, Eliot observed that "the vision of the horror and the glory was denied to Arnold,"[49] and in amplifying this claim, David DeLaura remarks that "Arnold's idealized and simplified Hellenism was in part a product of personal need and temperamental affinity."[50]

DeLaura's assessment of this "temperamental affinity" highlights the dramatic vicissitudes of Arnold's identifications and critical career, and it is worth noting some of these. Despite siding generally with his father in their joint differences with John Henry Newman's religious orthodoxy, Arnold seemed to have little difficulty in the late 1830s and early 1840s in incorporating Newman's contemplative relationship to art and literature into his vision of perfection. (There are many possible reasons for this, some involving a quite conventional anxiety of influence from Arnold's father, Thomas; Matthew Arnold's own rivalry with Arthur Hugh Clough for Dr. Thomas Arnold's approval; and his different relationship to religious doubt and to poetry's ostensibly salvific potential.) In Arnold's criticism, for instance, we hear echoes of *The Idea of a University* (1852), in which Newman famously praises "the repose of a mind which lives in itself, while it lives in the world."[51] One of Newman's primary aims was to "put . . . the mind above the influences of chance and necessity, above anxiety, suspense, unsettlement, and superstition, which is the lot of the many."[52]

While traveling alone in Sicily in May 1833, however, Newman—in DeLaura's words—"subjected himself to an intense examination of his own spiritual 'hollowness.'"[53] The last noun in this sentence is Newman's, referring partly to a traumatic exchange between Newman and Arnold's father. The exchange stemmed from the latter's bitter suggestion to A. P. Stanley, in May 1836, that "Newman and his party are idolaters."[54] "I do not call them bad men," he told Stanley in this letter, "nor would I deny their many good qualities; . . . but fanaticism is idolatry, and it has the moral evil of idolatry in it; that is, a fanatic worships something which is the creature of his own devices, and thus even his self-devotion in support of it is only an apparent self-sacrifice."[55]

The religious division that this and other texts—including Thomas Arnold's 1836 indictment of the "Oxford Malignants"—came to signify profoundly influenced nineteenth-century aesthetics, as the division helped generate secular demands for a culture that would repair the breach caused by the "departing gods."[56] The letter also points to an anxiety about faith and its "hollowness" that Newman obviously was not alone in voicing. In the same year that Newman traveled to Sicily, Thomas Carlyle began publishing *Sartor Resartus* in *Fraser's Magazine* (1833–34). Pretending to have recovered the thoughts of the imaginary professor Diogenes Teufelsdröckh (Born of God, Dung of the Devil), Carlyle's narrator responded to the question, "Why am I not happy?" by writing that the universe "was all void of Life, of Purpose, of Volition, even of Hostility: it was one huge, dead, immeasurable Steam-engine, rolling on, in its dead indifference, to grind me from limb to limb."[57] "Always there is a black spot in our sunshine," laments Carlyle through Teufelsdröckh; "it is even, as I said, the *Shadow of Ourselves*."[58]

Carlyle's now-famous concerns about the ineffable emerged four to five years after his more confident assertion in "Signs of the Times" (1829) that the individual's wisest response to the "mechanical" age is to cultivate "the mysterious springs of Love, and Fear, and Wonder, of Enthusiasm, Poetry, Religion, all [of] which have a truly vital and *infinite* character." The difference in these responses is instructive. Carlyle's earlier rationale stemmed from a belief that "the only solid . . . reformation, is what each begins and perfects on *himself*."[59] But as *Sartor* demonstrates, Carlyle's emphasis on self-solidity would not last. To help explain why, we note that three years earlier still, in *Vivian Grey* (1826), Benjamin Disraeli's eponymous hero declared that "self is the only person whom we know nothing about."[60]

Although it would be wrong to present these antecedents as a seamless genealogy, the thoughts entertained by Carlyle's, Newman's, and Disraeli's protagonists on self-solidity and egoic inadequacy predate Arnold's related concerns about "mental distress," highlighting their relationship to the non-referential (*PW*, xviii). To put this slightly differently, the peculiar incongruity of Arnold's cultural ideal—its ability to combine "sweetness and light" with heraldic resilience—displays more than anxiety about its dissolution into political anarchy. This ideal is a defensive plea against nothingness, the Arnoldian counterpart to Newman's fear of "hollowness" and Carlyle's dread of a universe that is "void of Life." The repercussions of this difficulty surface in Arnold's poetry, in a corresponding alternation between his speaker's calling Shakespeare "[s]elf-school'd, self-scann'd, self-honour'd, self-secure," in an 1849 sonnet (*PW*, 3.10), and Callicles' declaring in *Empedocles on Etna* (1849, 1852) that

There is some root of suffering in [Empedocles],
Some secret and unfollowed vein of woe,
Which makes the time look black and sad to him.

                                        (*PW*, 411.151–53)

POETRY AND DOGMA

Although by Oxford standards Arnold's departing faith was not especially dramatic, he lacked Newman's capacity to soothe this loss with Catholicism. Indeed, Arnold was aware that the space made available by challenges to orthodox Christianity increased the need for a secular ideal that could stave off related experiential crises of meaninglessness. As he later famously declared in his preamble to "The Study of Poetry" (1880), "There is not a creed which is not shaken, not an accredited dogma which is not shown to be questionable, not a received tradition which does not threaten to dissolve. Our religion has materialised itself in the fact, in the supposed fact; it has attached its emotion to the fact, and now the fact is failing it" (*CPW*, 9:161). In "Literature and Science" (1882), too, while stating his disdain for Victorian anti-intellectualism, he remarked, "There arises [in humankind] the desire to relate . . . pieces of knowledge to our sense for conduct, to our sense for beauty,—and there is weariness and dissatisfaction if the desire is baulked" by external or internal limits.[61]

Repeatedly in Arnold's 1850s and 1860s writing, this drama (inherited from Carlyle) recurs as the positing and partial dismantling of existing ideals. In "The Function of Criticism," Arnold speaks of the English Divorce Court as "an institution which perhaps has its practical conveniences, but which in the ideal sphere is . . . hideous" (*CPW*, 3:281). Yet despite focusing repeatedly—sometimes relentlessly—on what is least elevating about Victorian materialism (the tag phrase "*Wragg is in custody*," in "The Function of Criticism" and *Culture and Anarchy*, is surely his best-known example), Arnold looked for a way out. In his essay on "Wordsworth" (1879), he claimed that "the best cure for our delusion is to let our minds rest upon that great and inexhaustible word *life*, until we learn to enter into its meaning" (9:46). Fewer signs of this detachment manifest in his work from the 1860s. Although "The Function of Criticism" also promotes this "disinterested mode of seeing" (3:282), in this case alternating between detachment and paralysis, Arnold reminds us there that "the great safeguard is never to let oneself become abstract, always to retain an intimate and lively consciousness of the truth of what one is saying, and, the moment this fails us, to be sure that something is wrong" (3:283).

Although this sentiment recurs throughout Arnold's writing, owing to the vagaries and duplicities of speech, it is most prominent in his poetry, and assessing why helps convey my principal thesis about the nonreferential. As many commentators of "Dover Beach" have shown, the conclusion of Arnold's most famous lyric highlights this "tremulous cadence," "the turbid ebb and flow / Of human misery" (*PW*, 211.13, 17–18). More important, the poem's preoccupation with history's "withdrawing roar" complicates the "sweetness and light" that allegedly prevail in *Culture and Anarchy*, making clear that the ideal of that book is partly ineffective because it eludes reference. Although published in 1867, the year "Culture and Its Enemies" appeared in the *Cornhill*, "Dover Beach" was written in the summer of 1851. The poem represents the malaise of two lovers who are unable properly to join the world, "which seems / To lie before us like a land of dreams," offering "neither joy, nor love, nor light, / Nor certitude, nor peace, nor help for pain." Deprived of these ideals and defenses, Arnold's couple is perilously vulnerable "on a darkling plain / Swept with confused alarms of struggle and flight" (*PW*, 211.30–31, 33–34, and 212.35–36).

This "darkling plain" lacks the metaphysical power to prevail over chaos and war; in Arnold's poetry it is the flip-side of the sublimity of mountains.[62] Even as the speaker laments the lovers' vulnerability, he insists that there is no higher ideal to shield or guide them, only "vast edges drear." And though Arnold later declared that "we have to turn to poetry to interpret life for us, to console us, to sustain us,"[63] the well-known paradox of Arnold studies is that his poems consistently disable this redemptive expectation. Hence the "nameless sadness" that circulates in "The Buried Life" (1852), "the eternal note of sadness" sounded in "Dover Beach," and what Arnold called the "morbid" tone of *Empedocles on Etna*, whose protagonist—"dead to life and joy"—is a "prisoner . . . of [his] consciousness" (*PW*, xviii, 438.321, 439.352). These factors are haunting reminders of what escapes representation in Arnold's writing; they add a corrosive dimension to his thoughts on culture and perfectibility, with which critics today are generally unfamiliar.

"Oh, that I could glow like this mountain!," declares a weary Empedocles,

But mind, but thought—
. . . .
. . . never let us clasp and feel the All
But through their forms, and modes, and stifling veils.
And we shall be unsatisfied as now;
And we shall feel the agony of thirst,
The ineffable longing for the life of life
Baffled for ever . . .

(*PW*, 438.323, 439.345, 353–58)

In this and other poems by Arnold, we witness how "ineffable longing" clashes with materialism. Although the speaker fears being "baffled for ever," his yearning complicates Arnold's later discussion of our "best selves." Empedocles' realization that his ideals foster only "ineffable longing" also puts in relief the self-cauterizing dynamic that we find in Arnold's criticism. This dynamic recurs throughout his poetry in the 1850s, and it is one factor influencing the alternating collapse and resurrection of his ideal as it turned more consistently "outward" toward society in the 1860s and 1870s. In other words, while in his critical works Arnold skews his assessment of Hellenic ideals to make them more culturally amenable, his poetry announces the price of this ideal—its ascetic requirement that we sacrifice greater but more volatile passions on earth. Arnold's poetry also comes close to calling this belief in perfectibility a snare that, despite its richer, biblical resonance in *Culture and Anarchy*, conflicts with psychic life, and thus with much of his later criticism.

SELF-LACERATION, THE TRUE AUTHORITY AND LAW OF BEING?

"*[A]ll things seek to fulfil the law of their being*," declares Arnold in *St. Paul and Protestantism* (1869, 1870), but his departing faith and growing awareness of psychological factors corrupting ontological harmony make this statement profoundly equivocal (*CPW*, 6:10). In *Culture and Anarchy*, too, the establishment of our "*best self*" is meant to nudge us beyond class concerns and self-interest; it calls upon the "*power not ourselves which makes for righteousness*" to help us forget petty concerns.[64] However, this power is a source of Arnold's difficulty. The impersonality that he wants for beneficent purposes is never wholly devoid of coercive, occasionally despotic traits. As he explains in *Culture and Anarchy*, such power must be "capable of affording a serious principle of authority" (5:135), since it "enjoins us to encourage and uphold the occupants of the executive power, whoever they may be, in firmly prohibiting . . . [the] tumult and disorder [of] multitudinous processions . . . meetings [and] demonstrations" (5:136). Such moments highlight the ramifications of Arnold's more abstract claims in *Culture and Anarchy*, which surface slightly earlier in the book:

> By our *best self* we are united, impersonal, at harmony. We are in no peril from giving authority to this, because it is the truest friend we all of us can have; and when anarchy is a danger to us, to this authority we may turn with sure trust. Well, and this is the very self which culture, or the study of perfection, seeks to develop in us; at the expense of our old untransformed self, taking pleasure only in doing what it likes or is used to do (*CPW*, 5:134–35).

While inspiring the individual's pursuit of perfection, the best self also joins forces with an impersonal will to eclipse individuality entirely, "controlling individual wills in the name of an interest wider than that of individuals," as Arnold puts it slightly earlier (*CPW*, 5:117). This idea applies to all citizens, and Arnold comes close to saying that such overriding is necessary, as we would otherwise be left to our own devices, taking "pleasure . . . in doing what [we] like" (5:135), a direct rejoinder to John Stuart Mill's *On Liberty* (1859). Arnold is not, however, forging a simple opposition between freedom and restraint; his argument here also diverges from essays where he identifies the ideal more in class and ethnic terms (see especially *On the Study of Celtic Literature* [1866, 1867], in *CPW*, 3:291–395).[65] If there is any prejudice in Arnold's urging against "doing as one likes," it is voiced at bourgeois philistin-ism, as self-interest fosters complacency and indifference to others.

Arnold appeals to "the Eternal *not ourselves* which makes for righteous-ness," as he puts it in *Literature and Dogma* ([1871, 1873], in *CPW*, 6:311), because individuality is—regardless of class—the problem. "By our every-day selves . . . we are separate, personal, at war," he candidly declares in *Culture and Anarchy*. "We are safe from one another's tyranny when *no one* [emphasis added] has any power" (5:134). Revealing much more than Arnold's political concerns, this statement raises a profound ethical difficulty about our relationship to others. Arnold insists that "taking pleasure" only in what we like "expos[es] us to the risk of clashing with every one else who is doing the same!" (5:135). Materialist critics focusing largely on his well-known fear of mobs and insubordination tend to ignore this extra dimension of *Culture and Anarchy*, which really is the crux of its thesis on chaos. Because it promotes "our animality," pleasure puts us "at war" (5:94, 134). A secular ideal can end this "dead-lock" (5:135) only by displacing our "ordinary selves," so disrupting our habits and complacency (5:134).[66]

Arnold repeatedly confronts the problem of establishing a higher authority sufficiently benign to help us attain what is best, and sufficiently strict to "conquer . . . even the plain faults of our animality" (*CPW*, 5:101, 99). His best illustration of humans' "internal canker" (5:103–104) may be "Self-Deception" (1852), a much earlier poem in which he highlights many different forms of authority and an equal number of wills defying its strictures. The poem antici-pates the semantic and conceptual burdens that Arnold would later place on power, God, and inspiration. "Before we woke on earth," the speaker remarks,

> . . . this tremulous, eager being
> Strain'd and long'd and grasp'd each gift it saw;
> Then, as now, a Power beyond our seeing
> Staved us back, and gave our choice the law.
>
> (*PW*, 209.4, 210.9–12)

Although the moral authority of this poem is akin to God's, Arnold's loss of faith by this point renders uncertain the beneficence of this guidance, instead asking "a Power" to repair man's internal, self-directed damage.[67] And even if we knew little about Arnold's departing faith, his poem's fascination with man's inheritance of "powers" apparently inimical to the "Power beyond our seeing" might still disturb us:

> Ah, whose hand that day through Heaven guided
> Man's new spirit, since it was not we?
> Ah, who sway'd our choice, and who decided
> What our gifts, and what our wants should be?
>
> For, alas! he left us each retaining
> Shreds of gifts which he refused in full;
> Still these waste us with their hopeless straining,
> Still the attempt to use them proves them null.
>
> And on earth we wander, groping, reeling;
> Powers stir in us, stir and disappear.
> Ah! and he, who placed our master-feeling,
> Fail'd to place that master-feeling clear.

> (*PW*, 210.13–24)

That Arnold's poem concludes with veiled accusations at this "Power" for failing to "place" our "master-feeling" underscores why, despite his grasping imperfectly what is socially and psychically hostile to redemption, he later viewed culture as the best repository of faith. As in *Empedocles*, Arnold's speaker announces that his secular ideal must protect us from "hopeless straining" and ontological anxiety. Culture, in Arnold's later work, therefore is the subject's anchor, instantiating meaning that now lost faith formerly set adrift; it halts our "wander[ing], groping, reeling." But it does so by reproducing internally a Hebraic judgment that Arnold wanted to curb in *Culture and Anarchy* and elsewhere. As he declares in this last text, "It is all very well to talk of getting rid of one's ignorance, of seeing things in their reality, seeing them in their beauty, but how is this to be done when there is something which thwarts and spoils all our efforts?" (*CPW*, 5:168). Although today we might call this factor the unconscious, for Arnold this "something is *sin* [his emphasis] . . . and the space which sin fills in Hebraism, as compared with Hellenism, is indeed prodigious" (5:168). As Arnold implies, the "thrall of vile affections" far exceeds our interest in conformity. His "something" is inimical to ontological unity and religion, for it leads us astray from ideals, corrupting us internally with contrary impulses.

VICTORIAN PROSE AND THE SPLIT SUBJECT

When Arnold began to grapple with the repercussions of a split subject, torn between oughts and wants, he resurrected the notion of a higher authority to transcend the resulting confusion. Yet as he ruefully conceded, "The matter here opened is so large, and the trains of thought to which it gives rise are so manifold, that we must be careful to limit ourselves scrupulously to what has a direct bearing upon our actual discussion" (*CPW*, 5:176).

This "scrupulous . . . limit[ing]" helped Arnold juxtapose Hebraism's moral laws with "the group of instincts and powers which we call intellectual."[68] In this way, he elegantly reduced Delphic thought to Apollonian precepts, and as Norman O. Brown remarked sardonically in *Life against Death: The Psychoanalytical Meaning of History* (1959), Apollo for the Greeks was "the god of sublimation."[69] Formerly an analogue for the "something which thwarts and spoils all our efforts" (*CPW*, 5:168), "Dionysian power," as Nietzsche would later call it, has almost entirely vanished from the discussion, though its effects still trouble Arnold's work when passion corrupts judgment.[70] In his poetry, passion destroys disinterestedness and conceptions of the "best self." Recall William Hazlitt's observation, cited earlier: "Because the passions and interests are concerned . . . it [is] so difficult to arrive at . . . calm certainty in actual life" ("Knowledge of World," 296).

Many critics claim that the end point of this "corruption" in Victorian culture is Wilde's violent inversion of Arnold's hierarchy, which asserts the rule of criticism over authorial creations.[71] In "The Critic as Artist," Ernest paraphrases the thoughts of his friend Gilbert thus: "The highest Criticism . . . is more creative than creation, and the primary aim of the critic is to see the object as in itself it really is *not*" ("Critic," 368–69). With this statement Ernest archly rescinds Arnold's dictum—first raised in his second lecture on Homer (1861; reprinted in *CPW*, 1:140), later made the basis of his opening sentences in "The Function of Criticism" (1864)—that our aspirations as critics should be objective, disinterested, impersonal. We should aim, Arnold says (again paraphrasing Hazlitt), "to see the object as in itself it really is" (*CPW*, 3:258). Among other things (and echoing the 1853 Preface), this aim asks us to efface personality, so demolishing the arrogance of selfhood that would put the critic on par with the creator.[72] Arnold's near sacralizing of culture, his deliberate substitution of creativity for the creator, tried to turn the author into a progenitor of the world of culture, even as Arnold would later reintroduce a version of Jesus and Christianity into the mix. It is this vision of culture—changing, contradictory, and fundamentally pious—that Gilbert, in "The Critic as Artist," calls "a very serious error" ("Critic," 366).

Wilde joined the fray in 1890 by piggybacking on Pater's much earlier response to Arnold, and—embarrassing Pater—he rendered solipsistic elements of hedonism in Pater's work that undermined disinterestedness and thus the possibility of sustaining objectivity and detachment.[73] But although the story of these well-known details tends to end here, with Wilde serving as a martyr for "art for art's sake," the details themselves remain equivocal.

Wilde intensified Arnold's difficult appraisal of judgment, but he never resolved the debate and sometimes merely extended its reach. Despite bringing to the fore a similar drama about voided ideals, Wilde could not erase from his own writing the most Hebraic elements of Arnold's thought. Instead, like Arnold, he promoted and then recoiled from the ensuing voluptuousness, in part because he failed to control the psychic repercussions of this endeavor—both in his work and, more disturbingly, in the wider culture. Indeed, in a move that many critics either misunderstand or dismiss as politically embarrassing, he famously condemns the pursuit of ecstasy in *De Profundis* (1905), insisting: "The final mystery is oneself. . . . Who can calculate the orbit of his own soul?"[74] Here, as before, desire poses a profound question about knowledge, extending from selfhood to the ineffable and extradiscursive.

Basil Hallward echoes Arnoldian idealism in *The Picture of Dorian Gray* (1890, revised 1891), chapter one, when rashly declaring that Dorian "defines for me the lines of a fresh school, a school that is to have in it all the passion of the romantic spirit, all the perfection of the spirit that is Greek."[75] But the statement implicitly redefines Arnold's Hellenism, as is clear when Hallward continues: "The harmony of soul and body—how much that is! We in our madness have separated the two, and have invented a realism that is vulgar, an ideality that is void" (17). The ideal no longer can function as such, Hallward implies, without reincorporating those aspects of Hellenism—including physical passion—that Arnold tried to elide or control.

Yet in a sinister confirmation of Arnold's thesis, passion—betraying meaning—also undercuts the "best self" in Wilde's novel. And Wilde's novel is not alone in representing this menacing drive when it derails bids for personal and cultural perfection. In Hardy's contemporaneous *Jude the Obscure* (1894, 1895), the narrator also points up the cruel, impersonal vicissitudes of an "Immanent Will" (to borrow a later metaphor from his poetry), which combines joylessly with class prejudice to shatter, once and for all, Jude Fawley's stubborn ideals about culture and education.

If this were all that Hardy's novel accomplished, it would remain an intelligent commentary on his predecessors, such as Arnold, Benjamin Jowett, Mark Pattison, Newman, John Keble, and Edward Pusey, the last three of whom the novel invokes as "well-known" Tractarian ghosts: respectively, "the enthusiast, the poet, and the formularist."[76] Like Wilde's *Picture of Dorian Gray*, however, Hardy's last novel raises concerns about the ineffable and unsayable—nebulous elements that haunt the characters while driving them blindly into the future. As *Jude* lurches toward its harrowing conclusion, it gradually downplays the force of class consciousness and social prejudice as external determinants. Neither force vanishes entirely, to be sure, but what "wins" is a punitive element that seems partly allied with the

Immanent Will, while lacking its disinterestedness. The narrator describes Jude's actions as "self-harrowing" (396), and Jude himself avows to a group of his acquaintances, "I am in a chaos of principles—groping in the dark—acting by instinct and not after example" (399). Before Father Time hangs himself, having killed Sue and Jude's other children, Sue invokes Matthew Arnold directly as one of Jude's "Christminster luminaries," saying that although they have "one immediate shadow"—the plight of Father Time—before them, she "feel[s] that we have returned to Greek joyousness, and have blinded ourselves to sickness and sorrow" (366). Had Sue read Arnold more carefully, we are tempted to respond, doubt would have accompanied her belief in personal redemption.

Although Sue's comments seem sardonic in light of the novel's bitter conclusion, they signify traces of an argument put forth by Arnold and others which Hardy's protagonists cannot evade. Even as *Jude* anticipates psychoanalytic arguments about "screen memories," fantasy, and the death drive, the novel makes clear why Arnold's interest in the nonreferential persists as a nagging question about the apparently salvific power of culture. This interest seeps into Hardy's and Wilde's writing, framing especially the former's interest in the nonreferential while adding a bleak, even morbid quality to his arguments about consciousness, history, and progress.

Wrapping Up: Corrosive Voluptuousness

More could be said about Jude's subsequent chaos of principles, as well as the relevance of his being named after the saint of lost causes.[77] My point is that Wilde's and Hardy's characters meditate on the failure of disinterestedness, and thus on the problems besetting Arnold in the 1850s and 1860s. Substituting elements of psychology for Arnold's Hebraism, both writers push these strictures into a register concerned less with conscience, obedience, and even with what Jude eventually calls "something wrong somewhere in our social formulas" (399), than with the organism's peculiar tolerance for "self-harrowing" injury.[78] Especially for Hardy, the nonreferential is inimical to his protagonists' happiness, because it is capable of destroying these characters internally, given their desire to find freedom in an ideal they can neither define nor attain.

In this respect, Hardy and Wilde raise fascinating questions about the ideal which belie Arnold's repeated attempts at casting this element in a sublime, impersonal form. The self-effacement that Arnold advocated in his 1853 Preface manifests itself in later fiction as a cauterizing principle, giving protagonists little "repose" because his ideal points only to their deficiency. Yet considering the hostility to Arnold that exists today, it seems necessary to stress that Arnold was truly "modern" in highlighting this problem with referentiality in the 1850s and 1860s.

The irony of this outcome seems lost on many of Arnold's recent detractors, who view his writing as seamless elements of conservative thought, destined to limit what we now call "critical theory" and "cultural studies" to a strictly philological understanding of literature. Yet as we've seen, many Victorians criticized Arnold's 1853 Preface and other works for being excessively theoretical and for placing too much emphasis on different cultures and historical periods (emphases for which today he is considered lamentably deficient). Certainly, Arnold's comparative, historical emphases were selective, designed to praise aspects of classical philosophy in ways that even his contemporaries thought idealist. W. R. Roscoe's 1858 commentary in the *National Review* is a good example that returns us to my opening claims: "Mr. Arnold thinks . . . he can dig up the dusky olive from the plains of Attica, and plant it in our English wheatfields; that he can take in its fullest development in the most purely indigenous and the most intensely and narrowly national literature the world ever saw, and bid it find new springs of life some two thousand years later in a nation which has already found its expression in a dramatic literature evolved by itself. Did such an attempt ever succeed?"[79]

Roscoe was mistaken in confusing Arnold's interest in classicism with a neoclassicism that to both critics lacked depth and complexity. His claim that Arnold promoted only "the most purely indigenous and the most intensely and narrowly national literature the world ever saw" also ignores Arnold's debt to German Romanticism and Idealism; to novelists George Sand and Étienne de Senancour, poet Maurice de Guérin, and critic Sainte-Beuve; and to Celtic literature and Eastern thought. Arnold had a keen interest in the *Bhagavadgītā*, the Koran, and travel books, an interest partly recorded in his 1871–72 essay "A Persian Passion Play."[80]

However, Roscoe alludes convincingly to the historical disjuncture between the ancients and the Victorians that Arnold alternately acknowledged and tried to veil. Wanting the past to take root in the nineteenth century (to reproduce Roscoe's metaphor), Arnold found that he could not "transplant" this age without performing violence on accepted narratives of both historical periods. As Clough declared, in a devastating review of Arnold's early poetry, what Arnold tried to revitalize (with only limited success) was a "dismal cycle of . . . rehabilitated Hindoo-Greek theosophy."[81]

I have argued that we should appreciate Arnold's explanation for this failure and its ongoing cultural repercussions. By addressing antiredemptive elements of cultural and psychic life even as he tried to surpass them, Arnold complicated Carlyle's and Newman's interest in the relationship between culture and nothingness. And rather than breaking with this model, as many critics assume, Pater's, Wilde's, and Hardy's works often extended Arnold's preoccupation with the ineffable.

Although cultural studies today pays little attention to these concerns, the latter still determine, and undermine, what we expect from culture and ourselves. In refusing to engage with the nonreferential and extradiscursive, cultural studies paradoxically ensures the centrality of these categories, while depriving us of viable means of discussing them beyond limited claims about the transcendent. In short, the "extradiscursive" is a blind spot for culture critics today; and despite our assertions to the contrary, Arnold haunts us still. Although we have ample reason to discredit his speaker's conclusion to "Self-Dependence" (1852)—that "he, / Who finds himself, loses his misery!"—we continue to nurse, as traces of Arnoldian fervor, the speaker's belief that knowledge and culture drive us "Forwards, forwards, o'er the starlit sea." Doubtless, we hope to define progress quite differently from Arnold, appearing to release it from Enlightenment goals, but Arnold knew why this desire for progress rarely stabilizes our forward aim, and thus cannot "calm [us], ah, compose [us] to the end!" (*PW*, 239–40).

NOTES

For their astute comments on an earlier draft, I thank Amanda Anderson, Mark Bauerlein, Wayne Booth, David DeLaura, Jason Friedman, Walt Reed, Julia Saville, Ron Schuchard, and Joseph Valente.

The statement from Matthew 5:48 (Vulgate version) serves as Matthew Arnold's epigraph to *Culture and Anarchy* (1867–68, 1869), vol. 5 of *The Complete Prose Works of Matthew Arnold*, ed. R. H. Super (Ann Arbor: University of Michigan Press, 1965), 86. Subsequent references give pagination in main text after the abbreviation *CPW*.

The next statement is from Arnold, "Self-Deception" (1852), in *The Poetical Works of Matthew Arnold*, ed. C. B. Tinker and H. F. Lowry (London: Oxford University Press, 1950), 209.1–2. Subsequent references to this collection of poems and essays give pagination and line numbers in main text after the abbreviation *PW*.

1. "Hardly a day passes without the *Telegraph* having some fling at me," declared Arnold on 14 August 1867, referring to the *Daily Telegraph*'s allusion to "sweetness and light" in a leading article on the Reform Law, "but generally in a way that is not at all vicious" (*CPW*, 5:415). He was nonetheless aware of harsher criticism to "Culture and Its Enemies" from the likes of Henry Sidgwick and Frederic Harrison (see 5:410 for details). And Francis Mulhern declares in *The Moment of "Scrutiny"* (1979; reprint, London: Verso, 1981): "For the duration of [T. H.] Green's ascendancy [as a neo-Idealist in the 1880s], Arnold's project survived only as an idea, active in the work of individuals, but never finding that social anchorage in the stratum of 'disinterested' intellectuals, without which the passage from aspiration to action was inconceivable" (18). For elaboration on Green and his influence on late-Victorian England, see Melvin Richter, *The Politics of Conscience: T. H. Green and His Age* (London: Weidenfeld and Nicolson, 1964), especially 13–32.

2. An exhaustive list of references would be very long, but representative ones include the following reviews reprinted in *Matthew Arnold: The Poetry*, ed. Carl Dawson (London: Routledge and Kegan Paul, 1973): Charles Kingsley, unsigned

review of *The Strayed Reveller* in *Fraser's Magazine*, May 1849 (41–46); G. H. Lewes, "Schools of Poetry, Arnold's Poems," *Leader*, 26 November and 3 December 1853 (77–84); W. R. Roscoe, *National Review*, April 1858 (154–55); A. H. Clough, "Recent English Poetry," *North American Review*, July 1853 (71–76); and J. A. Froude, unsigned review in *Westminster Review*, 1 January 1854 (85–95).

3. Walter Pater's Conclusion to *The Renaissance* first appeared as the conclusion of an unsigned review of "Poems of William Morris," *Westminster Review* 31 (October 1868): 309–12. When incorporated into *Studies in the History of the Renaissance* (1873), the text was radically revised; it was later omitted from the second edition of the book (1877), but published in the third edition, renamed *The Renaissance: Studies in Art and Society* (1888), and in the fourth edition (1893). For details, see Samuel Wright, *A Bibliography of the Writings of Walter H. Pater* (New York: Garland, 1975), 166. Subsequent references to Pater's work are to *The Renaissance: Studies in Art and Poetry: The 1893 Text*, ed. Donald L. Hill (Berkeley: University of California Press, 1980), and give pagination in main text after the shortened title, "*Renaissance*." See also David Bromwich, "The Genealogy of Disinterestedness," *Raritan* 1, no. 4 (1982): 62–92; and David J. DeLaura, *Hebrew and Hellene in Victorian England: Newman, Arnold, and Pater* (Austin: University of Texas Press, 1969), 177: "Pater's Hellenism was a deliberate response to, and modification of, Arnold's view of the Greeks. Pater adopts the fervor, the sensuousness, some of the implicit sexuality, and a good deal of the anti-Christian tone of certain parts of German Hellenism." For an interesting commentary on these issues, see U. C. Knoepflmacher, "Arnold's Fancy and Pater's Imagination: Exclusion and Incorporation," *Victorian Poetry* 26, nos. 1–2 (1988): 103–15. Arnold's *Culture and Anarchy*, published in book form in 1869, had appeared beginning in July 1867 as six articles in the *Cornhill*: "Culture and Its Enemies" and five more essays under the title "Anarchy and Authority," which came out in January, February, June, July, and August of 1868. The collection of essays thus appeared over the course of a thirteen-month span, and was written in rather an antiphonal fashion.

4. Oscar Wilde, "The Critic as Artist" (first published in July and September 1890, and much revised for its 1891 publication in the collection *Intentions*), in *The Artist as Critic: Critical Writings of Oscar Wilde*, ed. Richard Ellmann (1969; reprint, Chicago: University of Chicago Press, 1982), 340–408. Subsequent references give pagination in main text after the shortened title, "Critic."

5. This tradition includes Thomas Carlyle and John Keats as well as Charles-Augustin Sainte-Beuve, Johann Wolfgang von Goethe, Johann Gottfried von Herder, Gotthold E. Lessing, Alexander von Humboldt, and Heinrich Heine. Many of Arnold's debts to these thinkers are evident in *Culture and Anarchy* as well as in his essays "Heinrich Heine" (1863) and "The Literary Influence of Academies" (1864), both in *CPW*, 3:107–32 and 232–57.

6. See T. S. Eliot, *The Sacred Wood: Essays on Poetry and Criticism* (1920; reprint, London: Methuen, 1948), especially xi–xiv and 1–2; and "Arnold and Pater" (1930), *Selected Essays, 1917–1932* (New York: Harcourt, Brace, 1932), 346–57. See Raymond Williams, *Culture and Society* (1958; reprint, Harmondsworth: Penguin, 1984), 124–36. For related examples, see Geoffrey H. Hartman, *Criticism in the Wilderness: The Study of Literature Today* (New Haven: Yale University Press, 1980), 14–15, 46, and 203–204; Chris Baldick, *The Social Mission of English Criticism*

1848–1932 (1983; reprint, Oxford: Clarendon, 1987), 18–58; and Robert J. C. Young, *Colonial Desire: Hybridity in Theory, Culture, and Race* (New York: Routledge, 1995), 55–89.

7. Partly to correct this trend, in 1994 Yale University Press reprinted *Culture and Anarchy* in its "Rethinking the Western Tradition" series, adding four commentaries to the text. Other, measured criticism on Arnold includes Clinton Machann and Forrest D. Burt, eds., *Matthew Arnold in His Time and Ours: Centenary Essays* (Charlottesville: University Press of Virginia, 1988); a special issue of *Victorian Poetry* 26, nos. 1–2 (1988); and "The Function of Matthew Arnold at the Present Time," a special issue of *Critical Inquiry* 9, no. 3 (1983): 451–516.

8. David DeLaura, "Review of *The Essential Matthew Arnold: An Annotated Bibliography of Major Modern Studies*, by Clinton Machann," *Analytical and Enumerative Bibliography* 8, no. 2 (1994): 141.

9. In *The Function of Criticism: From* The Spectator *to Post-Structuralism* (London: Verso, 1984), for instance, Terry Eagleton—"summarizing" Arnold—writes: "Culture must be 'classless,' and 'the men of Culture the true apostles of equality,' because the proletariat now exists; and the language of criticism must be ill-defined enough to encompass them. Ruling-class values must be modulated into metaphors open-textured enough to conceal their class-roots and take effect as much in the East End as in the West. It is the very urgency of the political situation which forces Arnold into his vague poeticism, the depth of his anxiety which breeds his apparent blandness" (63). One page earlier, however, Eagleton is obliged to recognize Arnold's "programme of social practice and educational reform. . . . For Arnold as much as for Addison and Steele, criticism is directed towards class solidarity, the creation of a society of enlightened equals" (62). Rejecting such "naive" interest in the educational opportunities of the working class, Eagleton is forced to downplay Arnold's practical initiatives, calling them "a strenuous social force" that fits uncomfortably with Arnold's "pious abstraction[s]" (62); Eagleton uses a similar sleight of hand in *Literary Theory: An Introduction* (Oxford: Blackwell, 1983), 24. Here again he minimizes Arnold's willingness to advocate on behalf of a disenfranchised class, and risks trivializing the Victorians' religious and epistemological crises. Given the structure of this society, Arnold's advocacy necessarily came close to paternalism, though it almost seems as if Eagleton would be happier had Arnold left alone the public sphere entirely, in this way making his middle-class anxiety all the more vulnerable to ridicule. I stress that Eagleton trivializes this crisis only in these passages from *The Function of Criticism* and *Literary Theory*; elsewhere—even elsewhere in *The Function of Criticism*, he is adept at interpreting the collapse of the "public sphere" in the nineteenth century. Indeed, in *Literary Theory*, Eagleton frames this collapse in Victorian culture in a way that Arnold would largely have supported: "In England, a crassly philistine Utilitarianism is rapidly becoming the dominant ideology of the industrial middle class, fetishizing fact, reducing human relations to market exchanges and dismissing art as unprofitable ornamentation" (19).

10. Arnold, cited in Morris Dickstein, "Arnold Then and Now: The Use and Misuse of Criticism," *Critical Inquiry* 9, no. 3 (1983): 495.

11. *CPW*, 5:107; Arnold, "The Incompatibles," in *Mixed Essays, Irish Essays and Others* (New York: Macmillan, 1883), 329.

12. Donald D. Stone's *Communications with the Future: Matthew Arnold in Dia-*

logue (Ann Arbor: University of Michigan Press, 1997) is one of the most recent attempts to sound intellectual and conceptual resonances *between* Arnold and Sainte-Beuve, Ernest Renan, and Henry James, as well as such contemporary philosophers as Michel Foucault, Richard Rorty, and John Dewey. The book is admirable in establishing a context for the creation and reception of Arnold's claims, and in touching briefly on Arnold's and Foucault's perhaps comparable fascination with nothingness (72), but its principal claims about Foucault's intellectual rapport with Arnold—potentially useful in highlighting Arnold's relationship to Victorian disciplinarity—are highly implausible. Stone's claim for this rapport lies in his insisting that Foucault's antihumanism has been massively overstated (67) and is anyway "not, I think, to [his] credit" (9); that both thinkers came from elitist backgrounds, Foucault much more so than Arnold (69); that they wrote sometimes contradictory claims (67), often with Romantic underpinnings (73); were indebted to literature (73); invented "quotable phrases" (74); and have been consistently misunderstood (67). The same, of course, could be said of an embarrassingly large number of disparate intellectuals.

13. For a superb account of this argument, see Joan Copjec, *Read My Desire: Lacan against the Historicists* (Cambridge: MIT Press, 1994), especially 1–14; but see also Slavoj Žižek, *The Sublime Object of Ideology* (New York: Verso, 1989); and Cathy Caruth, *Unclaimed Experience: Trauma, Narrative, and History* (Baltimore: Johns Hopkins University Press, 1996).

14. See, for instance, Gerald Graff, "Arnold, Reason, and Common Culture," in *Culture and Anarchy*, ed. Samuel Lipman (New Haven: Yale University Press, 1994), 188. I appreciate Joseph Valente's assistance with this argument.

15. Lionel Trilling, "Preface to the Second Edition," in *Matthew Arnold*, 2nd ed. (1939; reprint, London: Unwin University Books, 1963).

16. Dickstein, "Arnold Then and Now," 484. Later sections of this essay are greatly indebted to Dickstein's argument.

17. The phrase is Joseph Valente's, voiced in response to an earlier draft of this essay.

18. Arnold to Jane Martha Arnold Forster, 6 September 1858, reprinted in Cecil Y. Lang, ed., *The Letters of Matthew Arnold*, 5 vols. (Charlottesville: University Press of Virginia, 1996), 1:402.

19. Arnold to Jane Martha Arnold, 17 March 1849, *Letters*, 1:143. See also Arnold's letter to Thomas Arnold (his brother), 11 February 1858, *Letters*, 1:385.

20. Kingsley, unsigned review, *Fraser's Magazine* (May 1849), in *Matthew Arnold: The Poetry*, 45; William Alexander, "Matthew Arnold and MacCarthy," *Dublin University Magazine* 51, no. 304 (March 1858): 336.

21. See, for instance, Arnold's "Character of Discipline and Instruction in the French Secondary Schools" and "Superior or University Instruction in France" (1868) in *CPW*, 4:112–27 and 128–38, as well as "A Few Words about the Education Act" (1871), in *CPW*, 7:1–5.

22. For elaboration on this point, see Eugene Goodheart, "Arnold at the Present Time," *Critical Inquiry* 9, no. 3 (1983): 460–68.

23. William Hazlitt, "On Knowledge of the World" (1827), in *The Complete Works of William Hazlitt*, ed. P. P. Howe (London: Dent, 1933), 17:296. Subsequent references give pagination in main text after the shortened title, "Knowledge of World."

See also Bromwich, "The Genealogy of Disinterestedness," 70; and D. G. James, *Matthew Arnold and the Decline of English Romanticism* (Oxford: Clarendon, 1961), 31–33.

24. Walter Pater, *Marius the Epicurean: His Sensations and Ideas* (1885; Harmondsworth: Penguin, 1985), 117: *"Be perfect in regard to what is here and now"* (original emphasis). See also p. 65: "[Marius] was acquiring what it is the chief function of all higher education to impart, the art, namely, of so relieving the ideal or poetic traits, the elements of distinction, in our everyday life—of so exclusively living in them—that the unadorned remainder of it, the mere drift or *débris* of our days, comes to be as though it were not."

25. Arnold, "The Function of Criticism at the Present Time" (1864), *CPW*, 3:283.

26. *CPW*, 5:125. This point repeats almost verbatim Arnold's earlier claim that Sophocles' "energy," "maturity," "freedom," and "intelligent observation" are "idealized and glorified by the grace and light shed over them from the noblest poetical feeling" (1:28).

27. Eliot, "Arnold and Pater," 351.

28. Eliot, "Arnold and Pater," 349. The narrator of Edward Bulwer-Lytton's satire *Paul Clifford* puts this idea archly when declaring, "Perhaps it is not paradoxical to say that we could scarcely believe perfection in others, were not the germ of perfectibility in our own minds" (*Paul Clifford* [1840, 1848; Kila, Mont.: Kessinger, 1942], 393). The sublime archness of this idea—the insistence that we read it not ingenuously, but as a commentary on ubiquitous narcissism—is clearest in the context of this radical novel, which considers gentlemen and criminals quite indistinguishable. The narrator has just explained, too, how reluctant we are to find fault with those whom we love.

29. Arnold to Clough, 23 September 1849, *Letters*, 1:156.

30. For instance, Arnold told Clough on 5 [?] March 1845: "I am a reed, a very whoreson Bullrush . . . listless when [I] should be on Fire" (*Letters*, 1:65).

31. Arnold to Clough, 23 September 1849, *Letters*, 1:156.

32. F. R. Leavis, "The 'Great Books' and a Liberal Education" (1953) and "'Believing in' the University" (1974), in *The Critic as Anti-Philosopher: Essays and Papers*, ed. G. Singh (Athens: University of Georgia Press, 1982), 163, 165, 171.

33. Leavis, "The 'Great Books' and a Liberal Education," 162. The best account of the Leavises' work is still Mulhern's *Moment of "Scrutiny"*; on moral self-improvement, see p. 134: "[For *Scrutiny*], qualities that had once been instinct in a whole social order, and then, through a process of radical change, been displaced, were to be recovered and sustained in an action whose essence was *moral*." The Leavises arguably were influenced by Arnold's humanistic studies *St. Paul and Protestantism* (1869, 1870), *Literature and Dogma: An Essay Towards a Better Apprehension of the Bible* (1871, 1873), and *God and the Bible* (1875), but they appeared to disregard his most Hellenistic pronouncements on *Bildung*.

34. See F. R. Leavis, *The Great Tradition: George Eliot, Henry James, Joseph Conrad* (1948; reprint, Harmondsworth: Peregrine, 1983), 18.

35. F. R. Leavis, "The Logic of Christian Discrimination," *The Common Pursuit* (London: Chatto and Windus, 1952), 248–54.

36. F. R. Leavis, *The Great Tradition*, 23, n. 2.

37. Graff, "Arnold, Reason, and Common Culture," 193.

38. Friedrich Nietzsche, *The Twilight of the Idols; Or, How One Philosophizes with a Hammer* (1888), in *The Portable Nietzsche*, ed. and trans. Walter Kaufmann (New York: Viking, 1954), 521, 515.

39. Arnold's oft-cited argument about poetry's religiosity appears in the preamble to "The Study of Poetry" (1880): "Our religion has materialized itself in the fact, in the supposed fact; it has attached its emotion to the fact, and now the fact is failing it. But for poetry the idea is everything; the rest is a world of illusion, of divine illusion. Poetry attaches its emotions to the idea; the idea *is* a fact. The strongest part of our religion today is its unconscious poetry" (*CPW*, 9:161).

40. For elaboration on this argument, see Leo Bersani, *The Culture of Redemption* (Cambridge: Harvard University Press, 1990), 1–4. The quotation is from the jacket blurb to Bersani's book.

41. See Goodheart, "Arnold at the Present Time," 465.

42. Arnold to Jane Martha Arnold Forster, 25 January 1851, *Letters*, 1:189.

43. Ian Hamilton, *A Gift Imprisoned: The Poetic Life of Matthew Arnold* (New York: Basic Books, 1998, 1999), xii.

44. David Masson, "Theories of Poetry and a New Poet," *North British Review* 19, no. 38 (American Edition; August 1853), 180. Arnold misquotes Masson here, substituting "poetry" for "fictitious art."

45. For elaboration on these arguments, see Ekbert Faas, "Matthew Arnold and Psychology," *Retreat into the Mind: Victorian Poetry and the Rise of Psychiatry* (Princeton: Princeton University Press, 1988), 131–34. Faas writes, "Clearly, Arnold did not lack psychological insight. If anything, he had more of it than he wished to. Be that as it may, contemporary mental science never attracted his special attention" (132).

46. I am deliberately excluding the line of German Romanticism and Idealism represented by Johann Joachim Winckelmann, Goethe, and Friedrich Schiller.

47. According to David DeLaura, in personal correspondence with me, Arnold's "view of the Greeks in the 1853 Preface [also] relies on a 'misprision' on Goethe's part, during the latter's classical period in the late 1780s and 1790s." A useful reference is Josephine Maillet Barry, "Goethe and Arnold's 1853 Preface," *Comparative Literature* 32, no. 2 (1980): 151–67.

48. See Nietzsche, *The Twilight of the Idols*, 521. For valuable elaboration on Nietzsche's perspective, see Steven Marcus, "Conceptions of the Self in an Age of Progress," in *Progress and Its Discontents*, ed. Gabriel A. Almond, Marvin Chodorow, and Roy Harvey Pearce (Berkeley: University of California Press, 1982), 440–41.

49. T. S. Eliot, *The Use of Poetry and the Use of Criticism: Studies in the Relation of Criticism to Poetry in England* (1933; reprint, London: Faber and Faber, 1968), 106.

50. DeLaura, *Hebrew and Hellene in Victorian England*, 172.

51. John Henry Newman, *The Idea of a University, Defined and Illustrated*, ed. Charles Frederick Harrold (1852; reprint, New York: Longmans, Green, 1947), 158.

52. Ibid., 122.

53. Newman, cited in DeLaura, *Hebrew and Hellene in Victorian England*, 10.

54. Thomas Arnold to A. P. Stanley, Esq., on 24 May 1836, in Arthur Penrhyn Stanley, *The Life and Correspondence of Thomas Arnold* (New York: Scribners,

1895), 2:47. DeLaura quotes relevant parts of this letter in *Hebrew and Hellene in Victorian England*, 10, and I am indebted to his study for this and other references.

55. Thomas Arnold to A. P. Stanley, Esq., on 24 May 1836, *The Life and Correspondence of Thomas Arnold*, 2:46–47.

56. Thomas Arnold, "The Oxford Malignants and Dr. Hampden," *Edinburgh Review* 63, no. 127 (April 1836): 225–39. DeLaura reminds us that Thomas Arnold did not coin this term.

57. Thomas Carlyle, *Sartor Resartus* (1833–34, 1836), ed. Charles F. Harrold (New York: Odyssey, 1937), 164.

58. Ibid., 190.

59. Carlyle, "Signs of the Times," in *Critical and Miscellaneous Essays, II*, vol. 27 of *The Works of Thomas Carlyle*, ed. H. D. Traill (London: Chapman and Hall, 1896–99), 68, 82; original emphases. The essay first appeared in the *Edinburgh Review* 49, no. 98 (June 1829): 439–59.

60. Benjamin Disraeli, *Vivian Grey* (1826; reprint, New York: Century, 1906), 22. Such statements were not, of course, original in nineteenth-century fiction, but they recur in its literature with notable frequency and intensity. Thus, Captain Wentworth asks Anne Elliot in Jane Austen's *Persuasion* (1818; Harmondsworth: Penguin, 1985), "A question has suggested itself, whether there may not have been one person more my enemy even than that lady [Lady Russell]? My own self" (248).

61. Arnold, "Literature and Science" (1882), in *Matthew Arnold*, ed. Miriam Allott and Robert H. Super (Oxford: Oxford University Press, 1986), 463. Subsequent references to this collection of poems and essays give pagination in the main text after the abbreviation *MA*.

62. See Hamilton, *A Gift Imprisoned*, 151.

63. Arnold, "The Study of Poetry," *CPW*, 9:161. Elsewhere, he speaks of poetry as being able to offer "higher truth and . . . seriousness" (*CPW*, 9:171), and "solace" ("Literature and Science," *MA*, 466).

64. Cited in Goodheart, "Arnold at the Present Time," 454.

65. For elaboration on this text's discussion of class and ethnicity, see Vincent P. Pecora, "Arnoldian Ethnology," *Victorian Studies* 41, no. 3 (1998): 355–79.

66. Written the year after *Culture and Anarchy* appeared in book form but not published until 1879, Anthony Trollope's novella *An Eye for an Eye* is a useful example of this "rift" because it demonstrates the difficulty of sacrificing will or pleasure for a greater good. The "good" is presented to the protagonist, Fred Neville, as the prize of financial security and material well-being. The novella is particularly interesting, however, because it pits self-destructive passion against the imperative to protect one's relatives, future, and even personal comfort. Self-destructive passion "wins."

67. DeLaura cogently remarks that the bulk of Arnold's poetry is "unintelligible except as the expression of [his] struggle to clear some standing room in a world where he can accept neither past, nor present, nor future. With regard to that past, which is in large part Christianity, Arnold may feel intense regret at the departure of faith, but never in this period does he hesitate in his rejection of Christianity, nor does he make the slightest movement toward reconciliation" (*Hebrew and Hellene*, 19).

68. *CPW*, 5:177. As DeLaura remarks, "The ideal is everywhere 'moral' and

smacks more of Herder's ethical humanitarianism than of Goethe's or Schiller's more aesthetic humanism. Above all, Arnold's Greece is invested with a Winckelmannian calm and leans toward the statuesque, a sunlit Apollonianism" (*Hebrew and Hellene*, 171).

69. Norman O. Brown, *Life against Death: The Psychoanalytical Meaning of History* (1959; reprint, Middletown, Conn.: Wesleyan University Press, 1985), 174.

70. Friedrich Nietzsche, *The Gay Science, with a Prelude in Rhymes and an Appendix of Songs* (1882, 1887), trans. Walter Kaufmann (New York: Vintage, 1974), 327. See also 109 and 328–31.

71. See Marcus, "Conceptions of the Self in an Age of Progress," 446–47; Bromwich, "The Genealogy of Disinterestedness," 84–86.

72. As Bromwich points out, however, Arnold is himself adapting Hazlitt here. In "On Knowledge of the World," first published in *The London Weekly Review* in December 1827, Hazlitt argued that "if any one has but the courage and honesty to look at *an object as it is in itself* [emphasis added], or divested of prejudice, fear, and favour, he will be sure to see it pretty right." His aim was partly to speak about "cunning" and "wisdom," while showing how judgment can have its "seat in the heart rather than the head." "The difference depends on the *manner* of seeing things," he explains. "The one is a selfish, the other is a disinterested view of nature. The one is the clear open look of integrity, the other is a contracted and blear-eyed obliquity of mental vision" (296).

73. Pater claims that he omitted the Conclusion from the second (1877) edition of *The Renaissance* because he "conceived it might possibly mislead some of those young men into whose hands it might fall" (*Renaissance*, 186n).

74. Wilde, *De Profundis* (1905; reprint, New York: Putnam, 1906), 95. Wilde's text refers to Pater and Arnold, Carlyle and Goethe. Indeed Wilde's most Arnoldian *and* Paterian moment—retracting both the jocular style and substantive claims of "The Critic as Artist"—is when he declares: "What one had felt dimly, through instinct, about art, is intellectually and emotionally realised with perfect clearness of vision and absolute intensity of apprehension" (36).

75. Wilde, *The Picture of Dorian Gray* (1890, revised 1891; Harmondsworth: Penguin, 1982), 16–17. Subsequent references give pagination in the main text.

76. Thomas Hardy, *Jude the Obscure* (1894, 1895; Harmondsworth: Penguin, 1983), 126. Subsequent references give pagination in the main text.

77. See Liz Trotta, *Jude: A Pilgrimage to the Saint of Last Resort* (San Francisco: HarperCollins, 1998).

78. Consider also Michael Henchard, the miserable protagonist of Hardy's earlier novel, *The Mayor of Casterbridge* (1886; Harmondsworth: Penguin, 1985), who cannot "help thinking that the concatenation of events . . . was the scheme of some sinister intelligence bent on punishing him" (197).

79. Roscoe, cited in *Matthew Arnold: The Poetry*, 151.

80. Arnold, "A Persian Passion Play" (1871–72), in *CPW*, 7:12–39.

81. Clough, "Recent English Poetry," *North American Review* (July 1853), cited in *Matthew Arnold: The Poetry*, 76.

CHAPTER 12

Notes on the Defenestration of Culture

JAMES BUZARD

> Culture is a deeply compromised idea I cannot quite do
> without.
>
> *James Clifford*

A FUTURE historian of late-twentieth-century trends in the *Geistes-wissenschaften* will not fail, I think, to be struck by a couple of coincidences taking place at the frontier of the social sciences and the "softer" humanities.

It will be noted, for example, that the discipline of anthropology, which had emerged in the second half of the nineteenth century, had, by the middle of the twentieth, acquired a distinctively prominent place among its neighboring disciplines, in part because of the evident determination shown by a few of its most charismatic practitioners to maintain channels of communication with large, nonacademic audiences. It will be noted that this discipline then began a new phase, whose richest period of activity was during the 1970s and 80s, in which the entire conceptual and representational apparatus, not to mention the historico-political affiliations, of anthropology were subjected to a withering critique, both by accredited anthropologists and by a handful of outsiders only too willing to help. In this process, it was scarcely to be expected that the central, the *foundational* anthropological idea of "culture" would be spared, and it was not spared. Yet the retrospective interpreter of our activities—if we are lucky enough to be considered *important* enough to have one—will be sure to ponder over the fact that, just when this remorseless dissection and discounting of past anthropological glories was going on, a new movement, emerging just down the hall or across campus, was promising to grant a new lease on life to some of anthropology's tarnished notions, was offering shelter especially to that battered refugee called "culture," by provocatively, perhaps even impishly, styling itself "cultural studies." This was a movement—nothing so *Establishment* as a "discipline," it would hasten to assure you—very self-consciously imported to America from Britain and some of its other former colonies: its arrival on these shores was definitively celebrated—and its future fate in the American university system much worried about—at a mammoth interdisciplinary conference held at the University of Illinois in 1990, which gave rise to a comparably mammoth volume of essays called, simply (and, despite protestations to the contrary, *authoritatively*), *Cultural Studies*.[1] Whatever happened among the anthropological tribe, the concept of "culture," with all its charming inconsistencies, its serendipitous equivocalities, its picturesque morasses, could be kept alive—some might say, on life support—in this discipline-which-was-not-one, this moveable feast of a "field of study" whose chief principle seemed to be the studied avoidance of disciplinary self-definition.

The imagination of our chronicler in days to come will also be exercised by this second coincidence. Another imported movement, called "poststructuralism" or "deconstruction," will be shown to have disseminated itself (the future historian will no doubt enjoy the pun) widely among the human sciences, though its seeds sprouted best in the field of literary studies, from about the middle of the 1970s on. In fact, it is possible, though a little reductive, to pinpoint an "arrival" or at least a "harbinger" conference, in this case, too: the 1966 conference at Johns Hopkins University that yielded the volume of essays titled *The Structuralist Controversy: The Languages of Criticism and the Sciences of Man*. This dazzling and insouciant movement had many arrows in its quiver, but insofar as it can be said to have had a *target* or center—and, like the later "cultural studies," it would strenuously deny that it had one—that core principle demanding adherence was to be found in the eschewing of a "metaphysics of presence," itself founded upon appeals to the Speaking Voice of a Transcendental Subject presumed to be "really there," outside of language's endlessly sidewinding signifiers. Yet the historian will also detect that arising during these very same years was a powerfully influential body of critical historiography, literary criticism, and ethnography, quite cognizant of, and more often than not partially animated by, the poststructuralist afflatus, that nevertheless sought to reorganize the entire discursive environment of the humanities around the commitment to combat the ethnocentrism of the past, and of the present's construction of the past, with the *xenocentric* master-trope of "letting the hitherto silenced speak." No single conference, perhaps, but a handful of books (Edward W. Said's *Orientalism*, Elaine Showalter's *A Literature of Their Own*, Sandra Gilbert and Susan Gubar's *The Madwoman in the Attic*, and others) had ushered in an era in which the traditionally prestigious act of telling one's own tale—think of Odysseus among the Phaiakians—was retooled as the nearly unavoidable model of self-authorization for individuals and communities. For some years, cultural criticism became something of an echo chamber in which heretofore silenced Voices claimed the right to Speak for Themselves for the first time; everywhere there were Histories of Their Own, Empires Writing Back, People (formerly) Without History demanding the Permission to Narrate. To be sure, a certain care was taken, by some who worked at the boundary of these two movements, to bring deconstruction's critical edge to bear upon these inspiring metaphors and to caution that, however much one might like to think so, the Subaltern could *not* Speak. But for the most part, the work of even those scholars who openly repudiated "essentialism" or "identity politics" or the still more sinister-sounding "identitarianism" was characterized by an awkward gap between the declared opinions: between the *intentions* of the authors (something that, by poststructuralist standards, ought not to have counted at all) and the story told by the tropes and grammatical structures that continued to frame the texts. What might be called an unacknowledged *asseverationism* became the identifying mark of such work, a tacit insistence to the effect that "I tell you I *am* avoiding metaphysics," or, "yes, it *does* deconstruct phallogocentrism." In the "critical ethnography" and cultural studies of the era, the unspoken asseverationist creed could variously be rendered as "yes, we *can* achieve [or even *are achieving*] the noncoercive, intersubjective, cross-cultural encounter," "yes, we *are* producing the dialogic successor to the monologic monograph," "no, they *aren't* co-opted by the power structures that inscribe and circumscribe them," and so forth. The myriad publications ringing the changes upon these themes in several areas of humanistic inquiry inevitably had the result that an equally tacit, though less energetic—and, if the truth be told, rather *bored*—"if you say so," became a not uncommon reaction of their readers.

There was a time (our historian may observe) when one could find American anthropologists taking untroubled pride in what their discipline had wrought. Halcyon days! Textbooks and readers in the discipline could refer with satisfaction to the widespread reliance on the concept of "culture" to be found throughout the humanities and "all of the social sciences," not to mention, as one of them pointed out, just about everywhere in "the vocabulary of ordinary life outside the realms of professional scholarship." The pervasive culture idea was "primarily the child of anthropology," after all, and "unquestionably anthropology ha[d] done the most to formulate the concept and use it to gain an understanding of man's nature and ways of life."[2] It was true enough that the "pluralistic," "relativistic" culture concept of Bronislaw Malinowski's and Franz Boas's disciplinary descendants had achieved a stupendous currency and an authority so automatic and unquestioned that one can, for example, find the author of a turn-of-the-twenty-first-century novel set in the anthropological circles of the mid-nineteenth century putting the lingo of "cultures" and "a culture of their own" in the mouths of Victorian explorers and scientists. The 1850s characters in Andrea Barrett's historical fiction *The Voyage of the Narwhal* (1998) instruct each other in the pieties of the post-Boasian dispensation, saying such things as, "All the arctic peoples build a culture around the available food sources . . . [a]nd those cultures may be very different"; even the worst of these characters might diarize, in heroic participant-observer fashion, to the effect that "[w]ith their help [i.e., that of the 'Esquimaux'] I can convey to others the interest and wonders of their culture."[3] But within the academic world, how fatally complacent the anthropological self-congratulations seem, at a time when the enemy guns were being wheeled into position, and an energetic fifth column had begun its work of undermining the bulwarks and setting the dynamite in place at all the load-bearing walls.

Once the coup had begun, anthropological ideas previously held to be above reproach now had to produce their papers, and many had their good names besmirched. That once pedestalled notion of culture, most indispensable gadget in the anthropological kit, now stood liable to the charge of being (as Lila Abu-Lughod put it) "the essential tool for making other," an implement for giving the differences, separations, and inequities among groups of people "the [specious] air of the self-evident."[4] The "discourse of culture" (Daniel Cottom asserted) operated "through [a] metaphor of totality [that] represses the reality of political differences and historical change."[5] It was openly speculated that (in Nicholas Dirks's words), "the anthropological concept of culture might never have been invented without a colonial theater that both necessitated the knowledge of culture [or cultures] (for the purposes of control and regulation) and provided a colonized constituency that was particularly amenable to 'culture.'"[6] Accused of being an instrument of power/knowledge wielded at the behest of imperial governments, "culture" was now seen as corralling diverse peoples into epistemological packets so as to make them more easily digestible by administrators and bureaucrats. Anthropology's so-called cultural relativism was made (by Stanley Diamond) to assume the most unflattering construction of being but "the bad faith of the conqueror, who has become secure enough to become a tourist."[7] Whereas professionals in the field as well as interested amateurs had once devoted themselves to the task of achieving a definition of culture (see the many attempts collected in A. L. Kroeber and Clyde Kluckhohn's *Culture* [1952]), or at least to the task of assembling *Notes towards the Definition of Culture* (T.S. Eliot, 1948), their late-twentieth-century followers were aiming in the direction of a *defenestration*, a final heaving out of the window of that cumbersome vestige of the discipline's early successes.[8]

It became incumbent upon the new ethnographers, or post-ethnographers, to write (according to Abu-Lughod) "against culture," to set their sights on conceptual territories (as Akhil Gupta and James Ferguson, echoing Lionel Trilling, put it) "beyond culture."[9] The culture-centered enterprise of ethnography now appeared guilty of subjecting the actual people met in "the field" to (what Paul Rabinow called) a "symbolic violence" that emptied them of subjectivity and turned them into nothing more than representatives *of* their cultures; had not Malinowski himself blithely admitted that, "We are not interested in what A or B may feel *qua* individuals, in the accidental course of their own personal experiences, we are interested only in what they feel and think *qua* members of a given community"?[10] Anthropological understanding, it was now suspected, entailed the plunging of living communities into a vast imaginary vat for (what Arjun Appadurai labeled) "metonymic freezing," trapping them forever in (what James Clifford and others referred to as) the "ethnographic present" tense in which (what George Marcus and Dick Cushman denoted) "the common denominator people" of anthropological discourse—"the Trobrianders," "the Nuer," etc.— described the same "typical" motions endlessly.[11] Anthropology produced an effect of (what Johannes Fabian exposed as) "allochronicity," a "denial of coevalness" by which practitioners separated themselves from their objects of study, to whom they denied any such open-ended, living temporality as they and their Western, history-possessing and history-making cohorts enjoyed.[12] Anthropology cut peoples off from the larger world, in fact condescending to them for their isolation and backwardness even as it professed to celebrate them for their supposedly uncontaminated authenticity. And if one adds to the list of indictments cited here the contributions of nonanthropologists (such as Walter Benn Michaels or Robert J. C. Young) who, wholly unimpressed by Franz Boas's disciplinary platform statements disjoining "culture" from "race," were arguing that "culture" covertly *relies* on racism, it becomes all the more easy to see why so many had come to believe that the time for "recapturing anthropology" (as Richard Fox termed it) had arrived. The rescue narrative this phrase implied might begin with the brisk and remorseless defenestering of "culture," followed by extensive rituals of purification and atonement.[13]

And some thought this still not enough. In an essay on anthropology and its interlocutors, one of those only-too-helpful outsiders (Edward W. Said) pointed out that however much the producers of anthropological autocritique had problematized their discipline, not one of them had "explicitly called for an end to anthropology."[14] But this may have been because of an understanding among the young and restless practitioners that anthropology *must* survive, after the fashion of certain corporations unlucky in civil litigation, precisely in order to continue paying punitive damages to the many plaintiffs ranged against it. They had perhaps been inspired by deconstruction's example of how to prolong the life of a discipline by eviscerating its fundamental concepts and proclaiming its demise. They began to test out various alternative ideas, taking them for a spin to see how they might handle the road down which a contrite and reoriented—an *un-orientalized*—anthropology might now be permitted to travel. Admittedly, it *was* difficult to feel confident that a term like "global ethnoscape" would ever trip so lightly off the tongue as "culture" had once done, but it was the right thing to do.[15]

While anthropology was thus engaged, another sort of defenestering of culture was afoot, not the "tossing out of window" variety but the "taking out of confinement," the "freeing from old limitations" brand. In this other context, culture received, not a death sentence, but a new lease on life. More than one critical anthropologist of the period must have wondered at cultural studies' "commitment to deploy culture at a time when anthropologists [were] suspicious of its referentiality or validity." "Why," they must have asked themselves, "when the concept of culture has such an elitist history, would sympathetic anti-elitists contribute to its discursive objectification by trying to argue *in terms of it*?"[16] Especially in its newly Americanized form, "cultural studies" promoted itself as a movement that tore open the shutters and threw up the sash in order to cast a once-cooped-up concept of "culture" so widely among human practices that it appeared to contain them all. Yet it can certainly appear that, in arriving on the American academic scene just in time to receive the mangled baton of culture from its previous disciplinary carrier, cultural studies picked up a lot of the increasingly unclaimed, not to say positively shunned, anthropological baggage. Its general disposition toward "presentism," for instance, the operant principle that the only culture worth talking about was the culture of the *now*, can be seen as mimicking and even exaggerating a similar absence of historical dimension in so-called "functionalist" or "synchronic" ethnography.

The bearing of cultural studies toward its literary or bellelettristic precursors on "culture" was also reminiscent of various anthropological constructions of authority by contrast. In cultural studies rhetoric, the adjective "Arnoldian" was a handy term of abuse affixed to the ritualistically shattered illusion that culture had a circumscribed, limited area of applicability, that it denoted an elite space apart from *interest*, from politics and the market. Here one can look as far back as the opening of E. B. Tylor's epochal study *Primitive Culture* (1871), which does not explicitly take on Arnold, but which gives every impression of intending to subject the wayward, amateurish thought-cluster of "culture" to the rigors of scholarly definition. The book speaks of a new "wide ethnographic sense" in which culture comprises "that complex whole which includes knowledge, belief, art, morals, law, custom, and any other capabilities and habits acquired by man as a member of society."[17] The post-Boasian, post-Malinowskian anthropology of the twentieth-century university repeated Tylor's rejection of a limited sphere for culture, tirelessly emphasizing that (as one version has it), "[c]ultures are wholes. Everything is somehow related to everything else. The problem of investigation is that of finding the point of entrance in a circle. Whether you start with witchcraft or the exchange of goods or the graphic arts, you ought to end up in about the same place if you followed out your data in every direction in which they lead."[18] Yet this anthropology rejected also what Tylor and Arnold appeared to share: the idea that culture is one for all humanity, is equivalent to "Civilization." The new fieldworking ethography, which in Britain was hijacked by heretics wary of "culture" and turned into

"social anthropology," but which thrived in America as "cultural anthropology," approved of Tylor's dogma that culture was to be looked for in all, not
just some, areas of social life, and added to it the novel idea that "culture"
required an "s." It was a major theme of *the* major anthropological text of
the early twentieth century, Malinowski's *Argonauts of the Western Pacific*
(1922), that culture went "all the way down" in tribal life, that representation
or display pervaded this life to such a degree that—in an analysis of the *kula*
exchange-cycle (or of the seemingly worthless trinkets, the *soulava* and
mwali, traded in that cycle, or even of the canoes made for and used in it)—
to attempt to delineate "cultural" or "symbolic" elements from "material" or
"economic" or even "natural" ones would be to impose a set of "artificial
categories, foreign to the native mind."[19] Twentieth-century anthropology
was the discourse, not just of culture, but of "their own culture."

   Now, that ill-treated Arnold had, to be sure, written in universal-sounding
and value-laden terms of how culture gave access to "the best that has been
thought and said" and would "let reason and the will of God prevail," but,
then again, he had also invoked a "right reason" that was "*national*," as if
standards of rationality could not be applied across national—we would call
them "cultural"—lines.[20] But the point is not simply that post-Arnoldian students of culture erected their authority as so many other founders of movements and schools have done, in opposition to a partial and tendentious
portrait of their precursor. It is, rather, that in becoming the apparently indispensable tool of modern thinking about human affairs, the pluralist and supposedly "nonjudgmental" revisionist concept of culture merely displaced
judgment onto another plane: for to recognize the existence of "another culture" was to pay some set of people and practices the *compliment* of thinking
of it as organized rather than random, worth attending to rather than ignoring, significant rather than senseless. For Malinowski's children, "culture"
remained as much an honorific as it had been for Arnold: it could be
bestowed or withheld; to acknowledge the presence of "a culture," to say
nothing of setting out to study it, was to give people and practices credit for
having cleared the bar suspended over "pointless behavior," over mere appe-
titive aimlessness or (what once had been called) "savagery."

   Like its anthropological forebears, cultural studies operated according to
an implicit rescue narrative, in which the movement would liberate "culture," a righteously indignant madwoman in the attic, from the airless Victorian lumber-room in which it languished, packed up in tissue paper and
mothballs. The insistence that culture was "everywhere" meant that it was
everywhere entwined, in struggle or in complicity (or a bit of both), with
power. The Marxist framework from which the movement had emerged,
with its "superstructure" and its seemingly inexorable economic determinism, was revised beyond recognition, and to all intents and purposes
replaced, by fresher sociological approaches trading in concepts like the

"market of symbolic goods" and "cultural capital." The meanest, most apparently trivial elements of quotidian life, or "practice"—the meaner the better, it sometimes seemed—were now endowed with the dignity once so haughtily reserved for the quasi-sacred doings of "artists," "poets," "philosophers," and the like. Read as signs of popular "agency"—which generally meant implicit resistance, embryonic rebellion—the microscopic shiftings and makings-do of daily living acquired a moral grandeur as engagements in the never ending war pitting mighty Oppression against an outgunned but ceaselessly resourceful aristocracy of the plucky. Michel de Certeau was one inspiration here: he had outlined a poetics of quotidian subversions, "tactics" for undermining authority that he saw exemplified in the repertoire of opportunistic and shirking activities that French factory workers called *la perruque*, "the wig."[21] It is a subject matter that can start to appear positively highbrow in comparison with that found in some later applications of the method, in which one might read, for instance, that a poor family's leaving the TV on all day and cluttering its apartment with cheap bric-a-brac represented "not a sign of [its] having bought into the system [of consumer capitalism]" but rather "a way of filling [its life] with a variety of multiplicity of experiences"—a potent gesture, if we read it aright, showing how "the everyday culture of the oppressed takes the signs of that which oppresses them and uses them for its own purposes."[22] The example is worth dwelling upon, for the dwelling place it envisions, the domestic space of the Really Underprivileged, is after all one of the premiere stages on which the modern study of "cultures" enacted its primal scene.

It is here, behind the closed doors of the disadvantaged—if they *have* doors to close—that the weight of oppression comes down, that systemic oppression in which critical consciousness knows itself to be implicated. It is here that we will find the cradle, or day-care center at least, of that not entirely unpraiseworthy ("liberal") guilt which engendered the compliment of "cultures." Striking hard at the abashed bourgeois, perhaps even harder at the working-class man or woman who joins the intellectual caste (consider the entire career of Raymond Williams here), this *agenbite of inwit*[23] makes the poor family's hearth the altar on which it transubstantiates what *they* do, how *they* act, what *they* have, into "a culture of their own." In this setting, the producer of cultural studies rehearses a standard piece of the anthropological repertoire, the idea that (as Ernst Cassirer put it), "[people] can construct [their] symbolic world out of the poorest and scantiest materials."[24] Other borrowings have sources a century more remote, suggesting a sizable Victorian unconscious in the cultural studies "imaginary"—an unconscious in which, we shall see, even the reviled Arnold has his place. The late-twentieth-century student of culture might have taken a motto from Jane Eyre, with her declaration, "Nobody knows how many rebellions beyond political rebellions ferment in the masses of life which people earth."[25] Eliza-

beth Gaskell could have offered a model: taking her presumed-to-be-bour-
geois readers into a working-class home at the beginning of *Mary Barton*
(1848), Gaskell is at pains to show workers' private lives as participating in
a positive structure of custom, evaluation, and interrelation. She solicits
respectful attention for matters that she expects her readers will consider
beneath notice, implicitly arguing that those readers should reserve their
impatient judgment on each mean item in the Barton household (inhabitants
included) until they have appreciated its place in the meaning- and value-
bestowing network in which it functions.[26] Henry Mayhew might also have
afforded instruction. Chaperoning readers on a more harrowing tour in *London Labour and the London Poor* (1861–62), he was driven, if intermit-
tently, by an urge akin to Gaskell's. "The more closely we read Mayhew's
text," one very close reader observed, "the more 'animal passions' and biological needs among the poor tend to resolve into chains or clusters of
unconscious signifiers . . . and to call for a mode of interpretation that draws
the most disparate-seeming elements of street life . . . into a stylistically
coherent 'complex whole.' "[27]

   As was typical in cultural studies, the writer who conjured up that knick-
knack-and-noise-filled apartment of the poor was no doubt motivated by a
generosity of spirit that ought not to go uncelebrated. The assertion he makes
is not wholly wrong, either, if unsurprising: one feels sure that such refunc-
tionings of given structures or technologies go on all the time, in all walks of
life.[28] But the passage exudes the perennial, and perennially frustrated, long-
ings of the left-leaning intellectual, with this eager ascription of agency and
political impact to the subjects expressing the intellectual's *own* desire to
"make a difference," to trade in something stronger than words. Consider
"filling [its life] with *a variety of multiplicity of experiences*." One feels sure
that this constitutes but another of the myriad copyediting blunders lamentably so characteristic of academic volumes of the period, but even so, it is a
happy accident, since it so perfectly manifests the writer's earnest wish to
give—to give not just a variety, but a multiplicity, too. The phrase ought
probably to read "variety *or* multiplicity," but even if emended, will more
words make *mere words* into difference-making tools, devices, implements?
The writer is striving, like Keats's Autumn, to add "more, / and still more";
he wants to convert linguistic largesse into an enriched experiential world
for his subjects. It is a case of language wishing it were *matter*: the passage,
so redolent of the cultural studies spirit, is reminiscent of the song that ends
W. H. Auden's *The Sea and the Mirror*, "Ariel to Caliban" ("Desperately in
love with you . . ."). It's an old, old song: language wishing it *would* matter.
In the *Cultural Studies* anthology, Stuart Hall, the movement's visibly reluctant lion, found it necessary to remind his audience that "if you work on
culture, or if you've tried to work on some other really important things
[read: "politics," "activism," "the Real World"] and you find yourself driven

back to culture [query: with a billy club?], . . . you have to recognize that you will always be working in an area of displacement."[29] Amphion raised the walls of Thebes with his lyre, but the foundation of cultural studies' New Jerusalem would not be laid with laptops.

While on one level it is true enough to say that twentieth-century anthropology, as the discourse of "their own culture," operated on the principle that *everybody* had culture or was a member of *some* culture, on another level, a differential logic seemed to apply, according to which the contents of the global basket of putative cultures could be divided into "genuine and spurious."[30] And the burden of playing goat to the genuine culture's sheep was usually assigned, implicitly at least, to the anthropologist's *us*, the anomic, commodity-fixated, industrialized, bureaucratized West's sad excuse for the rich totality of a social existence in which "meaning and value [were] all-pervasive . . . lodging themselves somehow even in the most trivial-seeming and opaque-seeming materials of quotidian life."[31] On this level, culture was *elsewhere*, in fields whose contours were shaped at least in part by romance desire. And, bearing the *ambivalence* of romance desire, this elsewhereness of culture presented itself as something that, upon reflection, was not altogether regrettable. For if, in one moment of the ethnographic imagination, the juicy grapes of the genuine culture were always receding, Tantalus-fashion, from the grasping Western hand, in another, the disappointed fieldworker could take solace in the assurance that the fruit was sour: for, really, who would choose to inhabit a life-world so wholly permeated by cultural dictates as ethnography made "cultures" out to be—a domain in which, in John Stuart Mill's phrase, "the despotism of Custom [was] complete"?[32] T.S. Eliot had recognized that culture so conceived would give such weight and significance, such fatefulness, to every passing act or datum of living that it "could not be long contemplated without the horror of nightmare."[33] Who would choose to live "incarcerated" in one's culture, hemmed in on all sides by a relentless social "law" that would leave nothing, not even the most seemingly "spontaneous and motiveless phenomena . . . untouched on the score of remoteness or complexity, of minuteness or triviality"?[34]

And while it is true enough to say of this cultural anthropology—which reigned for much of the twentieth century and which exported its vision and vocabulary (and its ambivalence) so far afield—that from the very firing of the starter's pistol its practitioners hotly debated the status of "culture," poked holes in it, and occasionally set it on the windowsill in preparation for defenestering, it is also true that culture carried the day. Though some of the most influential early voices—A. R. Radcliffe-Brown, Robert Lowie, Edward Sapir—expressed misgivings about the "totalizing" or "reifying" tendency of the emergent idea, anthropologists increasingly showed, "in their procedures of study," how "explicit rejectors are often implicit acceptors."[35] Now, ethnographic field-workers had long been instructed not to attend to the articulated social ideas of their subjects, but to the behavior of those subjects, from which the ideas truly animating the culture could be inferred; as R. R. Marrett had put it, one needed to ask not the "why" question, but the "what."[36] (If the anthropological subject *could* articulate his or her own culture, what need the anthropologist?) Applying the same dose of pragmatism to the professional culture of anthropology itself, one can set aside the plentiful meta-commentaries and ontological inquiries and observe, as was sometimes noted then, that "[i]n the actual conduct of research and the presentation of interpretations . . . , [both] idealists and realists [on the question of culture] . . . generally proceeded as if culture were indeed 'real.' "[37]

There are numerous explanations—professional, sociological, and, more broadly, historical or philosophical—why this was so. All have their merit, but, taking the longest view, it seems not unlikely that "culture" had managed to get itself accepted as the name for that "horizontal" epistemological framework that began to displace a "vertical," typological one during the Renaissance. One argument, whose sweeping dualism seems, in this context, a fitting tribute to Arnold (with *his* impossibly ambitious categories of "Hebraism" and "Hellenism") maintained that the epistemology animating medieval art regarded the field of human experience, the fallen world, as "a set of discrete instances that had no interesting relations to each other" but only to the typological code that separately, and without regard for continuity, linked each detail to its figural counterpart; in contrast, the vision underlying post-Renaissance realism was that of a field in which the details of human experience derived their meaning and value from relations among each other, so that the identity of an object became "series-dependent," "discovered by comparing particular cases to each other," by separating essential from accidental data. The discontinuous space and time of medieval paintings gave way to a homogenized field in which identity "can be fully grasped only as an abstraction," experience yielding only "mere concretia that owe their significance to the invisible inner reality they register."[38] These "concretia" could be Malinowski's "imponderabilia"—the minute bits of everyday data about the native culture that must be sifted in the ethnographer's pan. The culture-seeking, field-working science that went "on the lookout for symptoms of . . . hidden and mysterious ethnographic phenomena behind the commonplace aspect of things" seems to have understood itself implicitly as heir to that dynasty of the Horizontal that had toppled heavenward-tending Verticality in the quattrocento.[39]

The ethnographic model of culture could not have emerged *until* the details of experience were seen to derive their meaning and value from horizontal relations rather than vertical ones. Once on the scene, what this model delivered that anthropologists and others "could not quite do without" was, above all else, the hermeneutic framework of pertinence that gave to everything "inside" it all the sense and worth it could expect to acquire in this world, since it now could look to no other (transcendental) source. Every culturally embedded object was less an "object" than a node or point of intersection in a network, acting upon and acted upon by every other node, joined in one web. Each factor in a culture was "a corollary of, consubstantial with, implied by, immanent in, all the others": the concept aimed at an effect that was the very opposite of capitalist "reification." But to de-reify the "contents" of a culture meant that the culture *itself* had in turn to be reified and concretized, had to be treated "as if [it] were indeed 'real.' "[40] To adapt a phrase of Thomas Carlyle's to this different (though not entirely different) context, the metaphoric "foam" of organic wholeness had "hardened into a shell," and the specter that the anthropologists had summoned would not depart at their bidding.[41] Never mind the frequent disclaimers, long before the 1990s' hype of "transnationalism" or "hybridity," to the effect that "[n]o specific culture is truly autonomous or independent of all other specific cultures,"[42] in practice culture was endowed with the quasi-magical power to yoke together and make sense of huge heaps of seemingly disparate material, so long as those heaps were demarcated from others seen to pertain not to *this* context of interpretation but to some other one, over *there*. As if inscribing in its conceptual apparatus one of the main themes of the late-Victorian science it superceded, the relativistic ethnography of the twentieth century invested the culture idea *itself* with the capacities ascribed to "cult" objects by the "primitive" peoples studied by anthropologists. This lived and practiced belief in the powers of "culture"—this "superstition of culture"[43]—bore comparison with those "survivals" that earlier theorists like Tylor and James Frazer had recorded, the vestiges of precivilized habits of thought that were manifested with alarming regularity all across the late-Victorian scene (especially, they thought, by children, women, and the working classes). Even in the new global reality that received so much press in the final years of the twentieth century, there was still a tendency to insist— and how could there not have been?—upon the *cultural specificity* of different "diasporas" or "migrations": an acknowledgment of the need to know into the context of *which* particular migration or diaspora one was to place the talismanic Coke bottle of delocalized globality in order to "understand" it. All the energetic fetishizing of "border regions" ("contact zones," "intercultures," *und so weiter*) characteristic of premillennial thinking could not dispel, but clearly *depended* upon, the idea of nonborder regions, which border regions were borders *between*. Having *become* the framing window— rather like the "magic casement" Keats imagined in the "Ode to a Nightingale," which opened onto "fairy lands forlorn"—"culture" could scarcely be thrown out of itself.

One result of culture's apparent escape from "Arnoldian" confinement, one upshot of its becoming traceable in *every* dimension of social life, might be the loss of that *critical* function Arnold had so prized in the idea. Once culture was *everywhere*, it could no longer provide that "space elsewhere" from the vantage point of which members could judge the shape of their collective life; it could no longer furnish what Arnold termed a "criticism of life" or what Raymond Williams called a "court of human appeal." This crowding-out of the critical faculty left modern, Malinowskian ethnography open to the sorts of charges we have already considered. Cultural studies, of course, would have no truck with the notion that culture meant consensus. Its theater of everyday operations staged no tacit togetherness, no group hug of the mind; its culture was constant *contest*, in which "the everyday culture of the oppressed [took] the signs of that which oppresse[d] them and use[d] them for its own purposes."[44] Yet cultural studies retained ethnography's insistence on the plurality of cultures, making vital use of that notion in its invocation of "subcultures"—a device by means of which cultural studies simply displaced the despised uniformitarian, one-making aspect of "culture" onto another plane. In the interest of denying that some large (say, national) culture was simply *one*, subcultures were introduced as the containers of difference and contestation; but the subculture *itself* was one, imagined solely in terms of its contesting function vis-à-vis the mainstream culture and not treated as if it contained any internal divisions worth noting. In this, cultural studies echoed the critical anthropology that (as Sherry Ortner pointed out) was disinclined to see indigenous cultures as anything *but* responses to or rebellions against the coercion of prior Western representations. Ortner rightly complained that this tendency deprived other peoples not of any "culture" of their own, but of any *politics* of their own—any politics, that is, not based first and foremost on reaction to the West.[45] Of course, one could subdivide the subculture into spheres of "dominance" and "difference," and then subdivide the subdivision (and so on). Such a process can, in fact, be discerned in the disciplinary evolution of the 1970s to 1990s, during which, for example, feminist critiques of "patriarchal society" eventually became the targets of newer feminist critiques distinguished by their commitments to such additional criteria as race, class, sexual orientation, and so forth, elements of difference that, it was argued, had been glossed over or "occluded" by the prior critiques. An enormously productive disciplinary engine had been discovered, one that dispensed a new and narrower clientele with each turn of the crank, each new version reproducing the oppositional logic of the first. It was turtles all the way down.

Critique based on gender
Gender plus race
Gender and race plus class
Gender, race, and class plus sexual orientation
etc.

Like many other features of late-twentieth-century thought, this mitotic tendency toward ever more specific identifications of "critical difference" had its secret Victorian sharer, perhaps most strikingly manifested in Charlotte Brontë's *Shirley*, in which we can watch the scream of rebellion that rises up against Robert Moore's textile mill devolve by stages into an appeal on behalf of the narrowest of constituencies, the very antipodes of the class-transcending national unity Brontë is at pains to advance: the "rioter's yell" becomes "a North of England—a Yorkshire—a West-Riding—a West-Riding-clothing-district-of-Yorkshire rioters' yell," reenacting the fragmentation of English culture that Brontë aims to diagnose and treat.[46] An ironist might have pointed out that such a tendency would ultimately lead late-twentieth-century thinkers back to a place few of them would have wanted to revisit: the very doorstep of "The Unique Individual," with the Holy Grail of difference finally being located, of all places, in that icon of Humanist ideology thought to have been demolished many levels back. The 1990s' efflorescence of academic memoirs might have appeared, to such an ironist, tacit confirmation for this conjecture. ("But enough about *your* positionality; let's talk about *my* positionality.")

In cultural studies no less than in anthropology, commitment to the plurality of cultures was bound to lead, sooner or later, to the question of whether one was an "insider" or an "outsider" of the particular culture under investigation—these perversely persistent designations testifying to the staying power (even after cultures had been shown to "travel," to overlap and intermingle) of the supposedly debunked illusion that cultures were bounded sites, mappable units, such that the language of spatial relation could still satisfy those who inquired about someone's relation to a culture. Just as difficult to dispense with as this spatial framework for conceptualizing culture was the category of identity.[47] To exchange consensus for contestation, to read the signs of struggle into every last little facet of culture, was not to elude the question, "what *counts* as a contestation?"—which was really just another way of asking *"whose culture* is it to contest?" This was the unavoidable question about where the boundaries are that divide one horizon of pertinence from another. Nothing I could do would ever count as a legitimate "contestation" in a culture to which I did not belong; it would count as "meddling" (if I had any power to produce an effect), or it would count as nothing (if I lacked such power). On the other hand, A and B could disagree about almost everything, but their disagreements might be seen as *constituting* their shared-and-contested culture, so long as A and B were recognized as members of the same culture and credited with authority to speak about it. In other words, as was argued by the author of a witty pamphlet entitled *Waiting for Foucault* (1993), "In order for the categories to be contested at all, there must be a common system of intelligibility, extending to the grounds, means, modes, and issues of disagreement."[48] Always downplayed, such cultural facts of life were yet made plain in every sort of forum, whenever "insiders" closed ranks against "outsiders" who presumed to interfere. Cultural studies itself, as the 1990 conference and 1992 volume amply attested, might set itself up as an "intervention" into the customary rule- and boundary-making operations of all cultures (including disciplinary ones), might aim at the utopia of a culture that is everywhere and *for everyone*, but there would be times when it had to be prepared to say to trespassers—to say along with Matthew Arnold, of all people—"force till Right is ready."[49]

There is one area, though, in which the new studies of culture appeared markedly different from the old. The early-twentieth-century discipline builders, including anthropologists, evinced an unembarrassed interest in securing authority by carving out space for their nascent programs, an interest that led them to articulate their fields' distinctive methodologies and objects of inquiry (in writings like Émile Durkheim's "What Is a Social Fact?" Alfred Kroeber's "The Superorganic," and I. A. Richards's *Principles of Literary Criticism*). In contrast, the late-twentieth-century discipline revisers exhibited an "anti-professionalism" and a dread of "co-optation" for which they were occasionally called to account, though such scoldings had little lasting effect.[50] Authoritative disavowals of authority became a common feature of the inter- or postdisciplinary landscape.[51] That 1990 University of Illinois cultural studies conference yielded a massive (788-page) volume of essays capable of dominating the desktop, its bulk and title effectively conveying the message *[Here is] Cultural Studies*; yet its editors and contributors seemed intent upon maintaining that they had "no distinct methodology," no mandatory subject matter, no natural constituency. Such methodology as it had, readers were told, "ambiguous from the start, could best be seen as a bricolage." "Although cultural studies work is often occasioned by an examination of specific cultural practices," the editors cautioned, "it should not be identified with any particular set of cultural practices." A reader would learn that "[t]he significance of 'the popular' in cultural studies involves the observation that struggles over power must increasingly touch base with and work through the cultural practices, languages, and logics of the people—yet 'the people' cannot be defined ahead of time." Stuart Hall insisted that "[c]ultural studies is not one thing[;] . . . it has never been one thing." Another observer found cultural studies to be "a whirling and quiescent and swaying mobile which continuously repositions any participating subject" (who hasn't felt like that, after a strenuous session of "Twister"?)— "a project whose realization . . . is forever deferred."[52]

Was there a hope that avoidance of specific conceptual or even procedural claims would be an aid to longevity in a marketplace of ideas even more remorselessly "presentist" than was cultural studies itself? After all, it had only been three years earlier, in 1989, that the publisher Routledge had influentially anthologized a critical movement ("the New Historicism") marked by what seemed an excessive emphasis on the ideological or discursive production of subjectivities and recontainment of rebellious energies; and now, in 1992, that same house's canny impresarios were marketing a movement characterized by what appeared an excessive emphasis on the "weapons of the weak." The "gallows Foucauldianism"[53] of the New Historicists, a gloomy frisson achieved with each new demonstration that purported acts of resistance or spaces of autonomy were, in fact—presto!—strands in the cunning web of power, was counterbalanced by the giddy up-beat-ness, the by-golly optimism that could result from cultural studies' repeated retrievals of popular "agency." In such an environment, where "all new-formed [ideas] become antiquated before they can ossify,"[54] a group of like-minded intellectuals might understandably have striven for a condition of permanent incipience, of protodisciplinarity, even as professional exigencies were driving them toward hefty *volumehood*.

And yet, if these strategies were defensive in nature, they seem likely to have had their aggressive side, too. If, on page 285 of *Cultural Studies*, Stuart Hall was to be found urging remembrance of the "necessary modesty of cultural studies," the book in which he did so offered a much-exampled paradox of monumentalized modesty. In their refusal to stake out their territory more explicitly, the spokespersons asserted the kind of semiotic self-sufficiency that some anthropologists used to ascribe to the "cultures" they studied: as in participant-observer ethnography, one needed to have "the insider's point of view" to make sense of the goings-on. They also asserted that cultural studies' future could not "be wholly constrained by its own heritage of cultural investments": the editors of *Cultural Studies* saw their enterprise as "[c]onstantly writing and rewriting its own history to make sense of itself, constructing and reconstructing itself in response to new challenges, rearticulating itself in new situations, discarding old assumptions and appropriating new positions."[55] Shaking off the dead hand of the past, this was to be a movement forever on the move, in directions and toward goals not to be foreseen, unfettered in its self-reinventions. It becomes possible yet once more to detect a certain parroting of the pariah here, as cultural studies envisioned a perfection that is (quoth Arnold) "not a having and a resting, but a growing and a becoming":[56] not a critique of disciplinarity, but a *super*-disciplinarity. There is nothing in the program statements of early-twentieth-century disciplines to compare with this titanic aspiration for a professional *Bildung* without end: it was an end-of-history goal appropriate to the age of the global market, a free and clear future to match the boundless domain of "the cultural."

NOTES

1. Lawrence Grossberg, Cary Nelson, and Paula Treichler, eds., *Cultural Studies* (New York: Routledge, 1992). Henceforth cited as *CS*.

2. Frederick C. Gamst and Edward Norbeck, eds., introduction to *Ideas of Culture: Sources and Uses* (New York: Holt, Rinehart and Winston, 1976), 3.

3. Andrea Barrett, *The Voyage of the Narwhal* (New York: Norton, 1998), 119–20, 315.

4. Lila Abu-Lughod, "Writing Against Culture," in *Recapturing Anthropology: Working in the Present*, ed. Richard G. Fox (Santa Fe: School of American Research Press, 1991), 143.

5. Daniel Cottom, *"Ethnographia Mundi,"* in *Text and Culture: The Politics of Interpretation* (Minneapolis: University of Minnesota Press, 1989), 54.

6. Nicholas Dirks, "Introduction: Colonialism and Culture," in *Colonialism and Culture*, ed. Nicholas Dirks (Ann Arbor: University of Michigan Press, 1992), 3.

7. Stanley Diamond, *In Search of the Primitive: A Critique of Civilization* (New Brunswick, N.J.: Transaction, 1974), 110.

8. See A. L. Kroeber and Clyde Kluckhohn, *Culture: A Critical Review of Concepts and Definitions*, vol. 47, no. 1 (Cambridge: Papers of the Peabody Museum of American Archaeology and Ethnology, Harvard University, 1952); T.S. Eliot, *Notes towards the Definition of Culture* (1948), reprinted in *Christianity and Culture* (New York: Harcourt Brace Jovanovich, n.d.), 72–202. For a spirited defense of "culture" that acknowledges how numerous are the concept's detractors, see Ulf Hannerz, "When Culture is Everywhere: Reflections on a Favorite Concept," in *Transnational Connections: Culture, People, Places* (New York: Routledge, 1996), chapter 3.

9. Abu-Lughod, "Writing Against Culture"; Akhil Gupta and James Ferguson, "Beyond 'Culture': Space, Identity, and the Politics of Difference," *Cultural Anthropology* 7, no. 1 (1992): 6–23.

10. Paul Rabinow, *Reflections on Fieldwork in Morocco* (Berkeley: University of California Press, 1977), 129–30; Bronislaw Malinowski, *Argonauts of the Western Pacific* (1922; reprint, Prospect Heights, Ill.: Waveland Press, n.d.), 23.

11. Arjun Appadurai, "Putting Hierarchy in Its Place," *Cultural Anthropology* 3, no. 1 (1988): 36; James Clifford, "On Ethnographic Authority," in *The Predicament of Culture: Twentieth-Century Ethnography, Literature, and Art* (Cambridge: Harvard University Press, 1988), 32; George Marcus and Dick Cushman, "Ethnographies as Texts," *Annual Review of Anthropology* (1982): 32.

12. Johannes Fabian, *Time and the Other: How Anthropology Makes Its Object* (New York: Columbia University Press, 1983), 31–32 and throughout.

13. For Franz Boas, see, for example, his *Anthropology and Modern Life* (1928; reprint, New York: Dover, 1986), chapter 2. Compare with Walter Benn Michaels, "Race into Culture: A Critical Genealogy of Cultural Identity," *Critical Inquiry* 18, no. 4 (1992): 683, where he writes, "The modern concept of culture is not . . . a critique of racism; it is a form of racism." See also Robert J. C. Young, "The Complicity of Culture: Arnold's Ethnographic Politics," chapter 3 in his *Colonial Desire: Hybridity in Theory, Culture, and Practice* (New York: Routledge, 1995). For Richard Fox, see his edited volume *Recapturing Anthropology*.

14. Edward W. Said, "Representing the Colonized: Anthropology's Interlocutors," *Critical Inquiry* 15, no. 2 (1989): 208.

15. Arjun Appadurai, "Global Ethnoscapes: Notes and Queries for a Transnational Anthropology," in *Recapturing Anthropology*, 193–210.

16. Virginia R. Dominguez, "Invoking Culture: The Messy Side of 'Cultural Poli-

tics,'" *South Atlantic Quarterly* 91, no. 1 (1992): 20. This passage is also quoted by Susan Hegeman in her incisive essay "Imagining Totality: Rhetorics of and Versus 'Culture,'" *Common Knowledge* 6, no. 3 (1997): 59.

17. E. B. Tylor, *Primitive Culture: Researches into the Development of Mythology, Philosophy, Religion, Language, Art and Custom*, vol. 1 (1871; reprint, Boston: Estes & Lauriat, 1874), 1. Compare to George W. Stocking, Jr., "Matthew Arnold, E. B. Tylor, and the Uses of Invention," in *Race, Culture, and Evolution: Essays in the History of Anthropology* (New York: Free Press, 1968), 69–90.

18. Clyde Kluckhohn, "Cultural Anthropology: New Uses for 'Barbarians,'" in *Frontiers of Knowledge in the Study of Man*, ed. Lynn White (New York: Harper, 1956), 37. See Hegeman, "Imagining Totality," for a discussion of how the "ineffable complexity of culture" has typically been signaled through a "trope of enumeration" or "jumble-sale model" (53). "[I]t has become fairly common in work dealing with things 'cultural,'" Hegeman writes, to provide "metonymic chains of association without offering any theorization about how the features of the analysis, the links in the chain, actually connect" (55–56). Hegeman has in mind here not only ethnographic but also New Historicist scholarship. The heavy reliance on lists in much cultural studies work offers further substantiation of her view. Compare with Alan Liu's remarks on the function of the list and of "etc." in postmodern cultural criticism, in "Local Transcendence: Cultural Criticism, Postmodernism, and the Romanticism of Detail," *Representations* 32 (1990): 75–113, especially 84–87.

19. Malinowski, *Argonauts*, 176.

20. Matthew Arnold, *Culture and Anarchy*, ed. J. Dover Wilson (Cambridge: Cambridge University Press, 1966), 81.

21. Michel de Certeau, *The Practice of Everyday Life*, trans. Steven Rendall (Berkeley: University of California Press, 1988), 24–28 and throughout.

22. John Fiske, "Cultural Studies and the Culture of Everyday Life," in *CS*, 157.

23. The phrase *"agenbite of inwit"* is borrowed from James Joyce's *Ulysses*. See Weldon Thornton, *Allusions in* Ulysses*: An Annotated List* (Chapel Hill: University of North Carolina Press, 1968), 21–22: *"Ayenbite of Inwyt* (Remorse of Conscience) is the title of a moral treatise [composed in 1279 for the use of Philip II of France] . . . translated from the French about 1340."

24. Ernst Cassirer, *An Essay on Man: An Introduction to a Philosophy of Human Culture* (New Haven: Yale University Press, 1944), 36.

25. Charlotte Brontë, *Jane Eyre* (1847; reprint, Harmondsworth: Penguin, 1966), 141.

26. The Bartons's home is "almost crammed with furniture (sure sign of good times among the mills)": this family is just as much interested in "thickening" its domestic environment as the one referred to in the cultural studies example. See Elizabeth Gaskell, *Mary Barton* (1848; reprint, Oxford: World's Classics, 1987), 13.

27. Christopher Herbert, *Culture and Anomie: Ethnographic Imagination in the Nineteenth Century* (Chicago: University of Chicago Press, 1991), 251.

28. Of course, such oppositional arguments have the problem that, as T.S. Eliot put it, "every sub-culture is dependent upon that from which it is an off-shoot," each "depends upon the survival of that against which it protests" (*Notes*, in *Christianity and Culture*, 140). Every dominant culture should be so lucky as to have opponents and subverters like the ones celebrated by cultural studies.

29. Stuart Hall, "Cultural Studies and Its Theoretical Legacies," in *CS*, 284.

30. Edward Sapir, "Culture, Genuine and Spurious," in *Culture, Language, and Personality: Selected Essays*, ed. David G. Mandelbaum (Berkeley: University of California Press, 1960), 78–199.

31. Herbert, *Culture and Anomie*, 163.

32. John Stuart Mill, *On Liberty* (1859; reprint, New York: Macmillan, 1956), 87.

33. Eliot, *Notes*, in *Christianity and Culture*, 104. I have altered Eliot's verb tense here.

34. Appadurai, "Putting Hierarchy in its Place"; Tylor, *Primitive Culture*, 1:22.

35. Gamst and Norbeck, *Ideas of Culture*, 35.

36. R. R. Marrett, quoted in George W. Stocking, Jr., "The Ethnographer's Magic: Fieldwork in British Anthropology from Tylor to Malinowski," in *Observers Observed: Essays on Ethnographic Fieldwork*, ed. George W. Stocking, Jr. (Madison: University of Wisconsin Press, 1983), 91–92.

37. Gamst and Norbeck, *Ideas of Culture*, 5.

38. Elizabeth Ermarth, *Realism and Consensus in the English Novel* (Princeton: Princeton University Press, 1983), 8, 18, 20. Because her excellent analysis is concerned primarily with aesthetic and epistemological matters, Ermarth does not explicitly pursue the connection between the "horizontal field of experience" and "culture."

39. This and the previous quotation are from Malinowski, *Argonauts*, 51.

40. Herbert, *Culture and Anomie*, 5.

41. Carlyle, "Signs of the Times," in *Selected Writings*, ed. Alan Shelstone (Harmondsworth: Penguin, 1971), 70.

42. Gamst and Norbeck, *Ideas of Culture*, 4–5.

43. Herbert, *Culture and Anomie*, 1–28.

44. John Fiske, "Cultural Studies and the Culture of Everyday Life," in *CS*, 157.

45. Sherry Ortner, "Resistance and the Problem of Ethnographic Refusal," *Comparative Studies in Society and History* 37 (1995): 173–93.

46. Charlotte Brontë, *Shirley* (1849; Harmondsworth: Penguin, 1974), 335.

47. And, as Walter Benn Michaels succinctly expressed it, "there are no anti-essentialist accounts of identity." Michaels, "Race into Culture," 683–84, note 39.

48. Marshall Sahlins, *Waiting for Foucault* (Cambridge: Prickly Pear Pamphlet no. 2, 1993), 13–14.

49. Promotional materials for the 1990 conference noted that "Cultural Studies is . . . in the process of being more widely institutionalized and commodified" and indicated that the conference was "designed not only to reflect on these events, but also to intervene in them" (quoted in *CS*, 293). And yet, one discussion-period questioner, quoting these words back at the organizers and featured speakers, lamented that "[i]n its structure, the conference most definitely privileges certain people, empowering them to speak while disempowering others," that it "duplicates the traditional structures of power which practitioners of cultural studies almost uniformly claim to be committed to subverting" (*CS*, 293). Her protest fizzled out when one of the featured speakers, bell hooks, took her to task for failing to grasp what it is to be truly disempowered.

50. Émile Durkheim, "What Is a Social Fact?" in *The Rules of Sociological Method and Selected Texts on Sociology and Its Method*, ed. Steven Lukes, trans. W. D. Halls (New York: Free Press, 1982); A. L. Kroeber, "The Superorganic," *Amer-*

ican Anthropologist, n.s., 19 (1917): 163–213; I. A. Richards, *Principles of Literary Criticism* (1925; reprint, New York: Harcourt, Brace & World, n.d.); Stanley Fish, "Anti-Professionalism," in *Doing What Comes Naturally: Change, Rhetoric, and the Practice of Theory in Literary and Legal Studies* (Oxford: Clarendon, 1989); Gerald Graff, "Co-optation," in *The New Historicism*, ed. H. Aram Veeser (New York: Routledge, 1989), 168–81.

51. The so-called "New Historicism" had preceded cultural studies in this. Leading off a critical anthology of the movement, one of its founders specifically disavowed any idea of a New Historicist "doctrine," adding, rather swaggeringly, "and I ought to be the one to know." See Stephen Greenblatt, "Towards a Poetics of Culture," in *The New Historicism*, 1.

52. Quotations in this paragraph are from *CS*, 2, 11, 3, 617.

53. Lawrence Rothfield, "Allegories of Policing," *Critical Texts* 5, no. 3 (1988): 33.

54. Karl Marx and Friedrich Engels, *The Communist Manifesto*, in *The Marx-Engels Reader*, ed. Robert C. Tucker, 2nd ed. (New York: Norton, 1978), 476.

55. *CS*, 13, 10.

56. Arnold, *Culture and Anarchy*, 48.

Notes on Contributors

AMANDA ANDERSON is Professor of English at Johns Hopkins University. She is the author of *Tainted Souls and Painted Faces: The Rhetoric of Fallenness in Victorian Culture* (Cornell University Press, 1993) and *The Powers of Distance: Cosmopolitanism and the Cultivation of Detachment* (Princeton University Press, 2001). She has published numerous articles on Victorian studies, critical theory, and feminist theory, in journals such as *diacritics, Victorian Studies, Cultural Critique, Social Text*, and the *Yale Journal of Criticism*. She is currently completing a book on forms of debate in contemporary intellectual culture, titled *The Way We Argue Now*.

JAMES BUZARD is Associate Professor of Literature at the Massachusetts Institute of Technology and the author of *The Beaten Track: European Tourism, Literature, and the Ways to "Culture," 1800–1918* (Oxford University Press, 1993). He has recently coedited *Victorian Ethnographies*, a special issue of *Victorian Studies*, and is writing the book *Anywhere's Nowhere: Fictions of Autoethnography in the United Kingdom* (forthcoming, Princeton University Press). His essays have appeared in the *Yale Journal of Criticism, Victorian Studies, Raritan, Modernism/Modernity, PMLA*, and other journals and books.

LAUREN M. E. GOODLAD is Assistant Professor of English at the University of Washington, Seattle, where she works on Victorian studies, gothic literature and cultural studies. Her publications have appeared in journals including *ELH, Genre, Social Text*, and *Victorian Literature and Culture*. She has completed a manuscript, tentatively entitled *Victorian Literature and the Victorian State: Character and Discipline in a Liberal Society, 1832–1911* and is currently coediting a volume of essays on contemporary gothic culture.

LIAH GREENFELD is University Professor and Professor of Political Science and Sociology at Boston University. Her books include *Center: Ideas and Institutions* (University of Chicago Press, 1988), co-edited with Michael Martin, *Different Worlds: A Study in the Sociology of Taste, Choice, and Success in Art* (Cambridge University Press, 1989), *Nationalism: Five Roads to Modernity* (Harvard University Press, 1993), *Nacionalisme I Modernitat*, a volume of essays, prepared for Catalan audiences (University of Valencia Press, 1999), and *The Spirit of Capitalism: Nationalism and Economic Growth* (Harvard University Press, 2001).

JOHN GUILLORY is Professor of English at New York University. He is the author of *Poetic Authority: Spenser, Milton, and Literary History* (Columbia University Press, 1983), *Cultural Capital: The Problem of Literary Canon Formation* (University of Chicago, 1993), and essays on various topics in Renaissance literature and in the history of criticism. He is currently completing a book on the sociology of literary study in the U.S. university, titled *Literary Study in the Age of the New Class*.

SIMON JOYCE is Assistant Professor of English at Texas Christian University, where he teaches nineteenth- and twentieth-century British literature and culture. He has written a number of articles on cultural studies, crime fiction, and late-Victorian social policy, and recently completed a book-length manuscript titled *Capital Offenses: Geographies of Class and Crime in Victorian London*. He is currently at work on a new project, *Victorians in the Rear View Mirror*, which considers how the past has been envisioned, represented, used, and abused in the twentieth century.

HENRIKA KUKLICK is Professor in and Chair of the Department of History and Sociology of Science at the University of Pennsylvania. Her articles have appeared in various journals, including the *American Ethnologist*, *Annual Review of Sociology*, *Sociological Quarterly*, and *Theory and Society*. Her works include *The Savage Within: The Social History of British Anthropology, 1885–1945* (Cambridge University Press, 1991), and her most recent edited volume, with Robert Kohler, *Science in the Field* (University of Chicago Press, 1996).

CHRISTOPHER LANE is Professor of English at Northwestern University. He is the author of *The Burdens of Intimacy* (University of Chicago Press, 1999) and *The Ruling Passion* (Duke University Press, 1995), as well as the editor of *The Psychoanalysis of Race* (Columbia University Press, 1998) and coeditor of *Homosexuality and Psychoanalysis* (University of Chicago Press, 2001). He is currently finishing a book on Victorian misanthropy, provisionally titled *Civilized Hatred: The Antisocial Life in Victorian Fiction.*

JEFF NUNOKAWA is Associate Professor of English at Princeton University. He has published *The Afterlife of Property: Domestic Security and the Victorian Novel* (Princeton University Press, 1994), and is currently completing a book about the fantasy of managing desire and desirability in the work of Oscar Wilde. He has published essays on Victorian literature that have appeared in various journals and collections, including "The Importance of Being Bored: The Dividends of Ennui in *The Picture of Dorian Gray*," in *Novel Gazing: Queer Readings in Fiction*, ed. Eve Kosofsky Sedgwick (Duke University Press, 1996); "Sexuality in the Victorian Novel," in *The Cambridge Companion to the Victorian Novel* (2001); and "*In Memoriam* and the Extinction of the Homosexual" (*ELH*).

ARKADY PLOTNITSKY is Professor of English and a Director of the Theory and Cultural Studies Program at Purdue University. His books include *Reconfigurations: Critical Theory and General Economy* (University of Florida Press, 1993); *In the Shadow of Hegel: Complementarity, History, and the Unconscious* (University of Florida Press, 1993); *Complementarity: Anti-Epistemology After Bohr and Derrida* (Duke University Press, 1994); and *The Knowable and the Unknowable: Modern Science and Nonclassical Thought* (University of Michigan Press, 2001). He is currently at work on two books: *Minute Particulars: Romanticism and Epistemology* and *Niels Bohr: Physics, Philosophy, and the Practice of Reading*.

IVAN STRENSKI is the Holstein Family and Community Professor of Religious Studies and the Chair of the Department of Religious Studies at the University of California, Riverside. He is the author of six books and approximately forty articles.

His published work deals with a variety of subjects, including racial and political myth, Waco and public policy, sacrifice, and the concept of religion and its relation to power. His most recent books deal with the interrelations of Durkheimian thought (especially about sacrifice) with the major religious traditions of France. These are *Durkheim and the Jews of France* (University of Chicago Press, 1997) and *Contesting Sacrifice: Religion, Nationalism and Social Thought in France* (forthcoming, University of Chicago Press, 2002) and *"Theology" and the First Theory of Sacrifice* (forthcoming). He is North American editor of *Religion*.

JOSEPH VALENTE is Associate Professor of English, Critical Theory, and Women's Studies at the University of Illinois. He is the author of *James Joyce and the Problem of Justice: Negotiating Sexual and Colonial Difference* (Cambridge University Press, 1995) and the editor of *Quare Joyce* (University of Michigan Press, 1998). His new book is titled *Dracula's Crypt: Bram Stoker, Irishness, and the Question of Blood* (University of Illinois Press, 2001). He was awarded a Mellon Fellowship for his current project, "Contested Territory: Race and Manhood in Modern Irish Literature."

GAURI VISWANATHAN is Class of 1933 Professor of English and Comparative Literature at Columbia University. She is the author of *Masks of Conquest: Literary Study and British Rule in India* (Columbia University Press, 1989) and *Outside the Fold: Conversion, Modernity, and Belief* (Princeton University Press, 1998), which won, among other awards, the 1999 Harry Levin Prize given by the American Comparative Literature Association and the 1999 James Russell Lowell Prize by the Modern Language Association.

ATHENA VRETTOS is Associate Professor of English and Director of Graduate Studies at Case Western Reserve University. She is the author of *Somatic Fictions: Imagining Illness in Victorian Culture* (Stanford University Press, 1995). Recently she has published articles on Victorian psychology and theories of habit, and she is working on a book on nineteenth-century conceptualizations of mental space titled *Mental Economies: Victorian Fiction, Psychology, and Spaces of Mind*. She has been awarded fellowships from the John Simon Guggenheim Foundation and the National Endowment for the Humanities for this project.

Index